TUNDRA COMIC STRIP PRE

TRUE NORTH

by

Chad Carpenter...

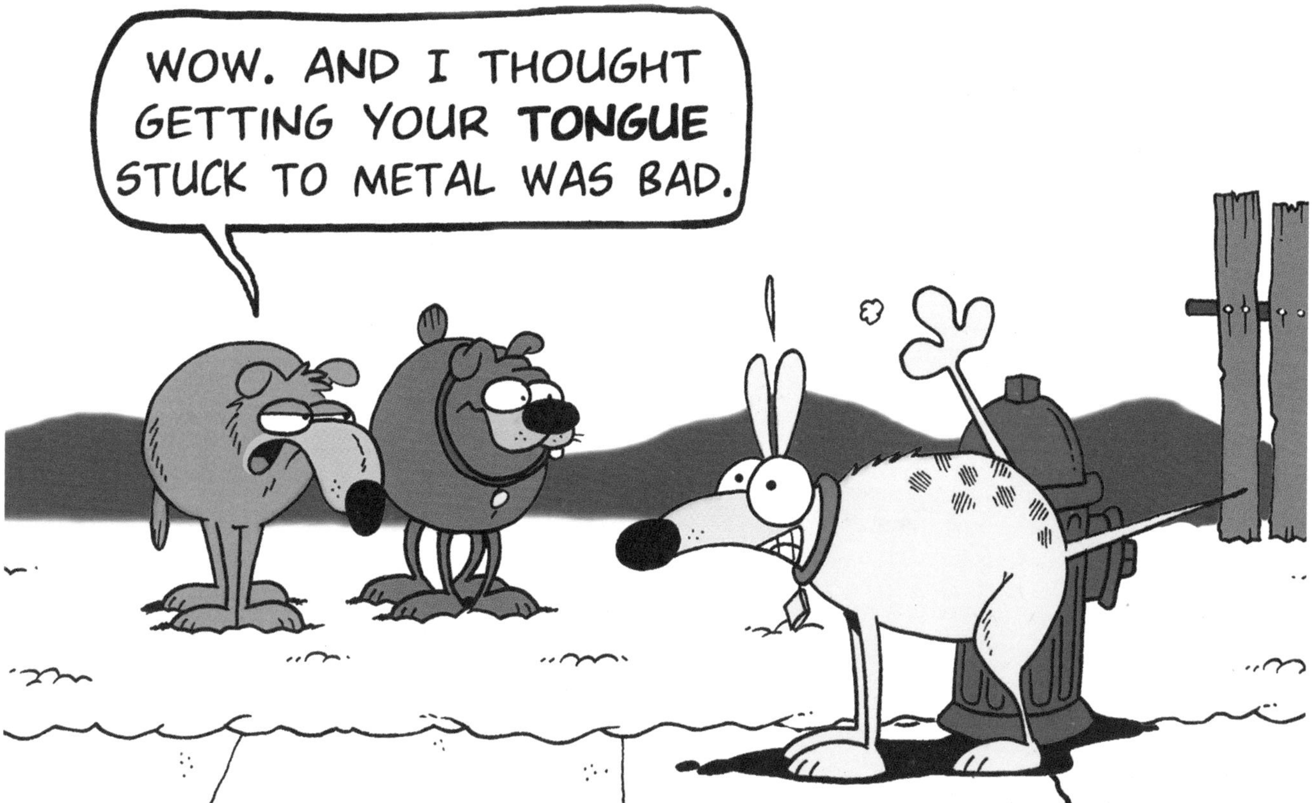
WOW. AND I THOUGHT GETTING YOUR **TONGUE** STUCK TO METAL WAS BAD.

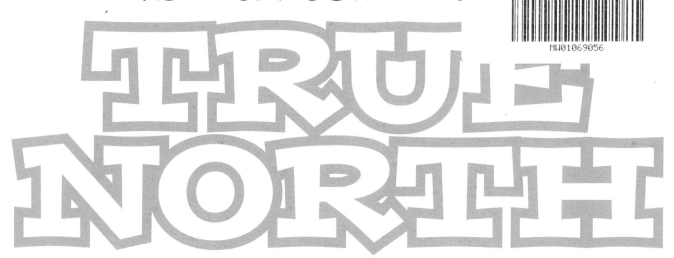

Altitude Publishing Canada Ltd.

PUBLISHED BY ALTITUDE PUBLISHING CANADA LTD.
1500 Railway Avenue, Canmore, Alberta T1W 1P6
www.altitudepublishing.com
1-800-957-6888

First published 2003 in newspapers; first compiled 2004 in *Tundra: Freeze Dried Comics*.

Publisher	Stephen Hutchings
Associate Publisher	Kara Turner
Proofreader	Michelle Lomberg

*We acknowledge the financial support of the Government
of Canada through the Book Publishing Industry Development
Program (BPIDP) for our publishing activities.*

Altitude GreenTree Program
*Altitude Publishing will plant twice as many trees as were used
in the manufacturing of this product.*

Library and Archives Canada Cataloguing in Publication

Carpenter, Chad, 1967-
    True north / Chad Carpenter.

ISBN 1-55153-754-0

    I. Title.

PN6727.C384T78 2006   741.5973   C2006-904971-8

Printed and bound in Canada by Friesens
2 4 6 8 9 7 5 3 1

For my moose, Evangeline,
and the squirrels
whom I dare not name

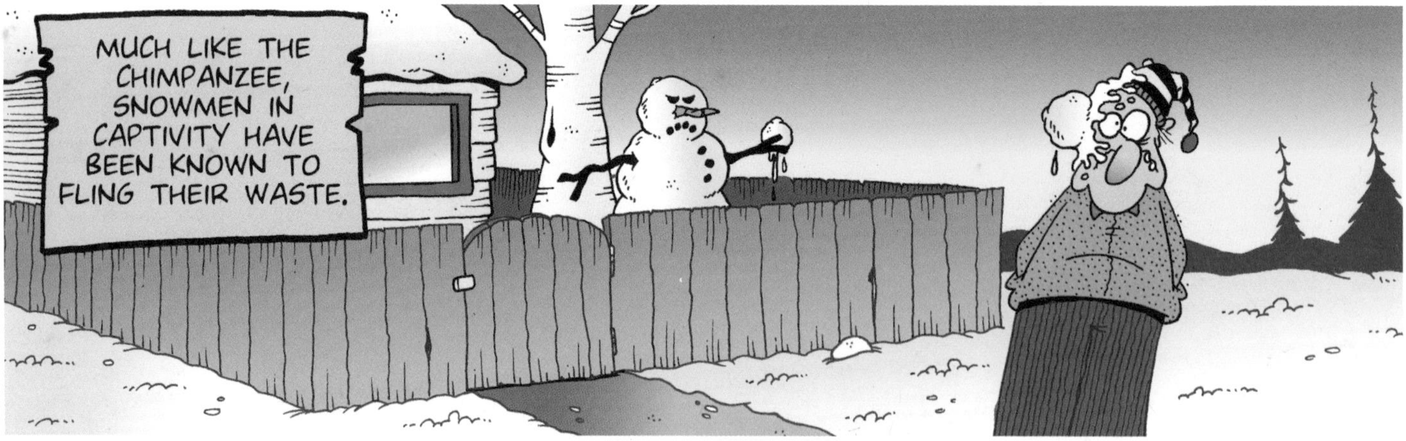
MUCH LIKE THE CHIMPANZEE, SNOWMEN IN CAPTIVITY HAVE BEEN KNOWN TO FLING THEIR WASTE.

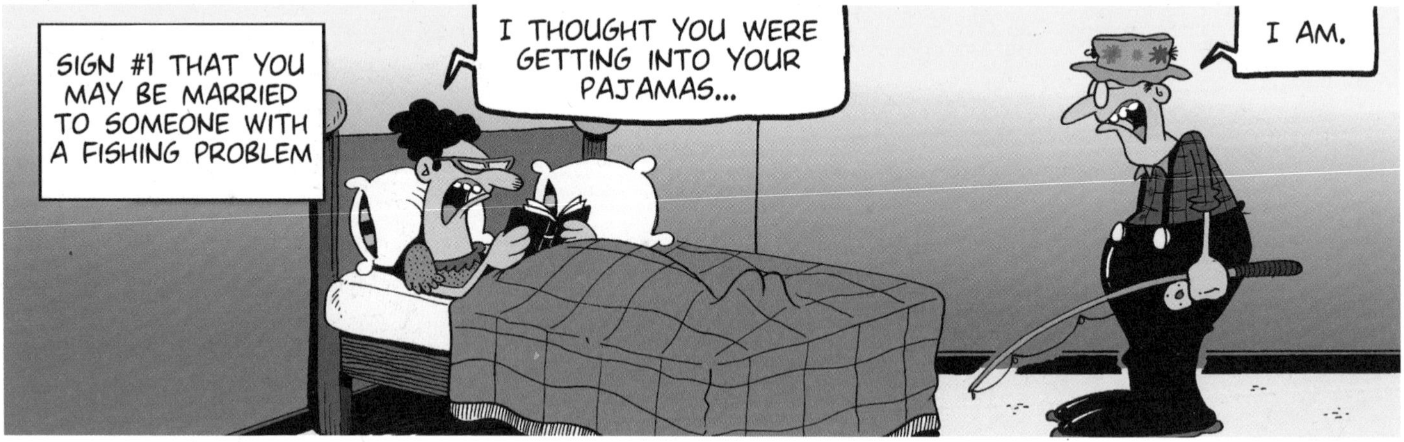
SIGN #1 THAT YOU MAY BE MARRIED TO SOMEONE WITH A FISHING PROBLEM
I THOUGHT YOU WERE GETTING INTO YOUR PAJAMAS...
I AM.

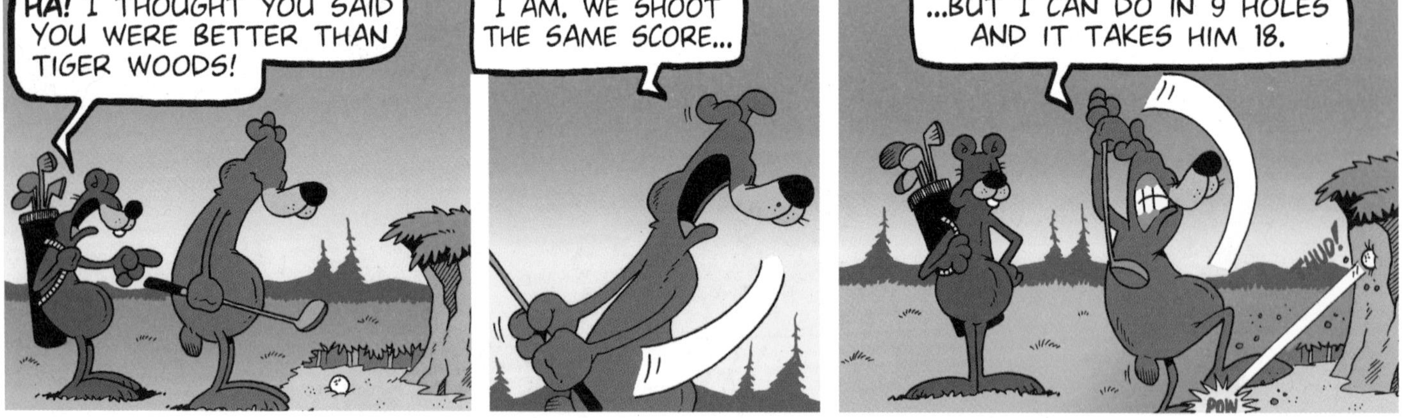
HA! I THOUGHT YOU SAID YOU WERE BETTER THAN TIGER WOODS!
I AM. WE SHOOT THE SAME SCORE...
...BUT I CAN DO IN 9 HOLES AND IT TAKES HIM 18.
THUD!
POW

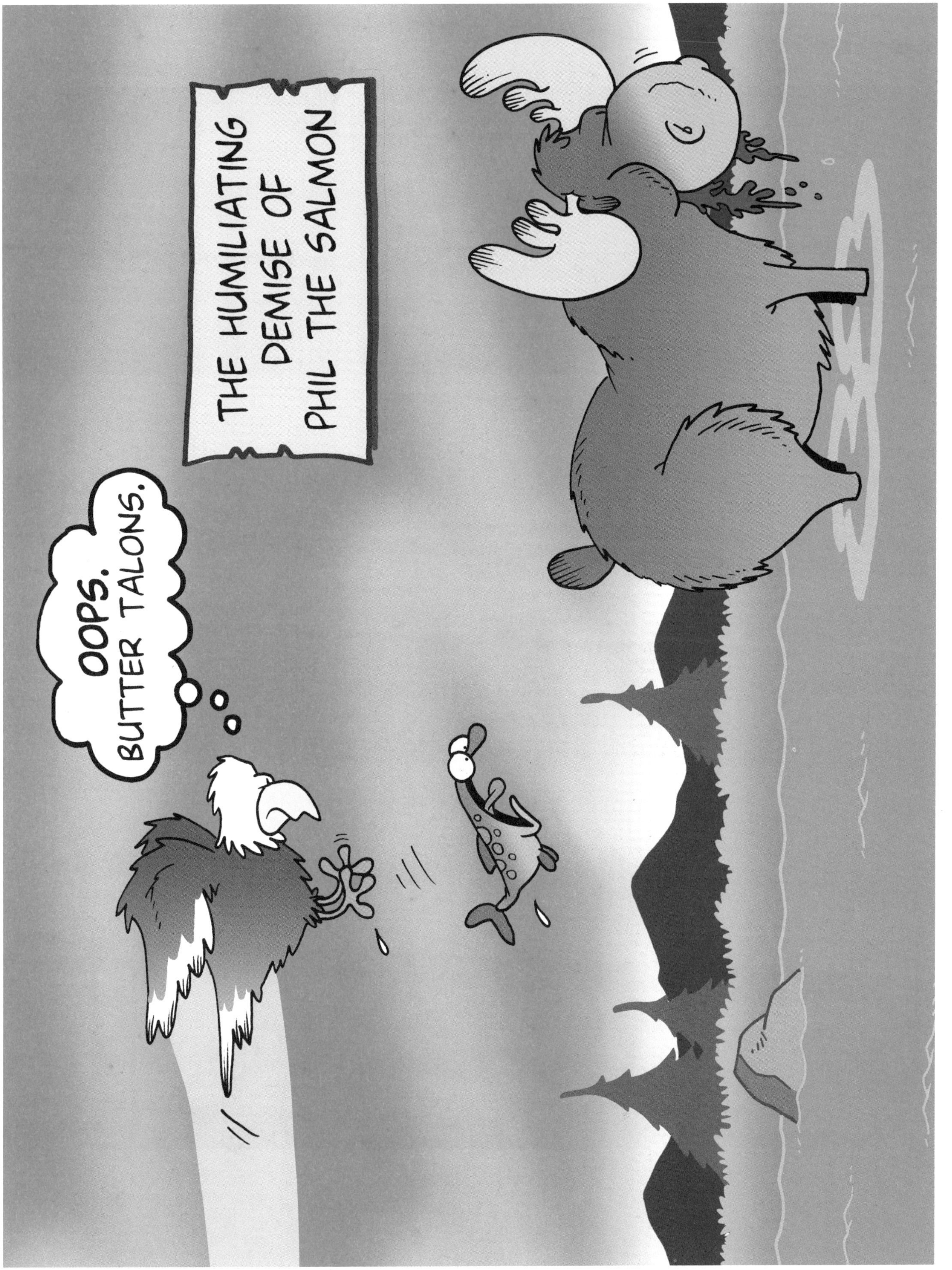
THE HUMILIATING DEMISE OF PHIL THE SALMON
OOPS. BUTTER TALONS.

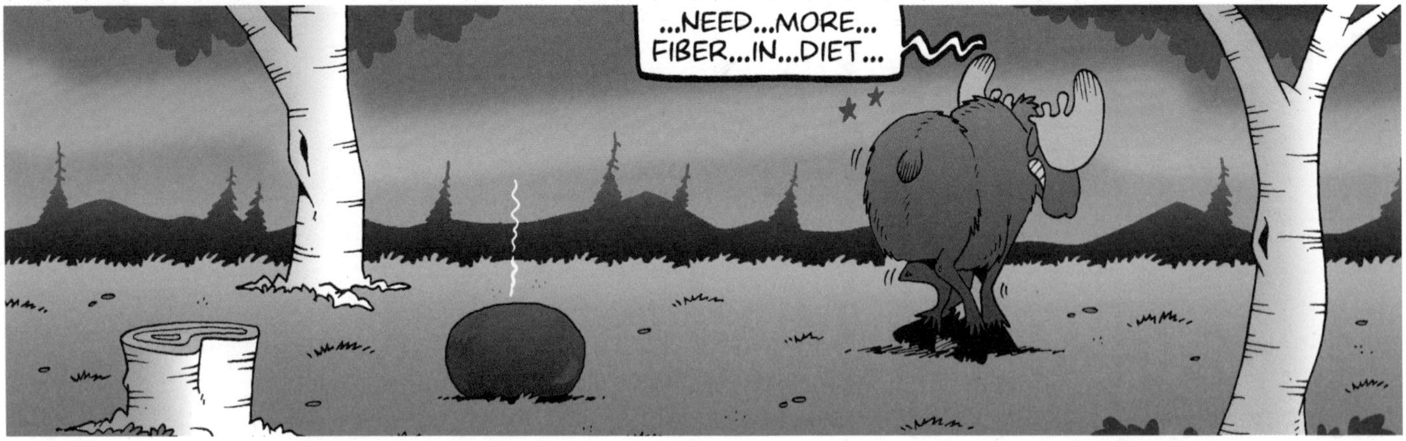
...NEED...MORE...
FIBER...IN...DIET...

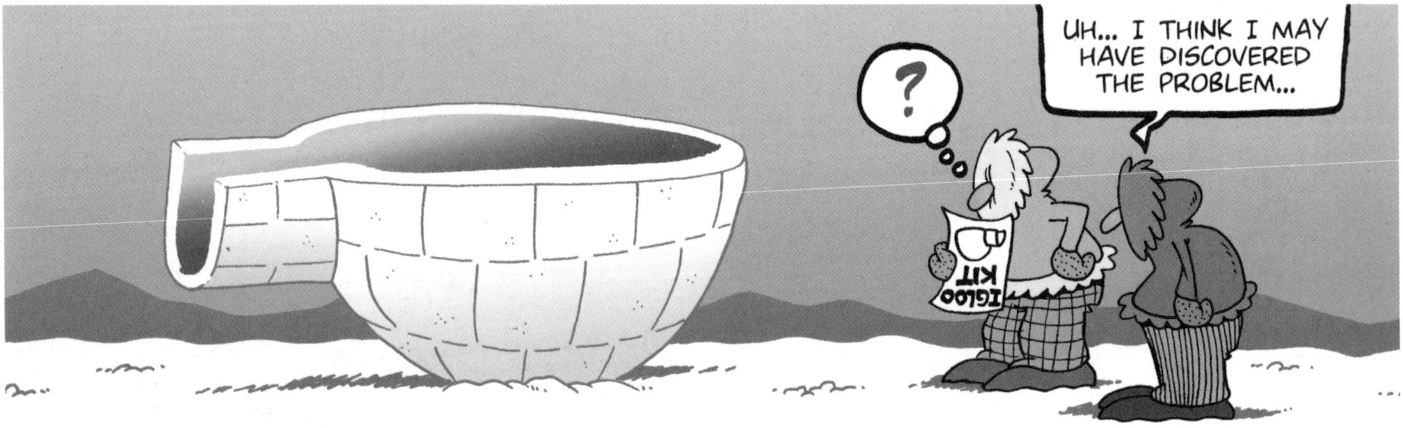
UH... I THINK I MAY
HAVE DISCOVERED
THE PROBLEM...
?
IGLOO
KIT

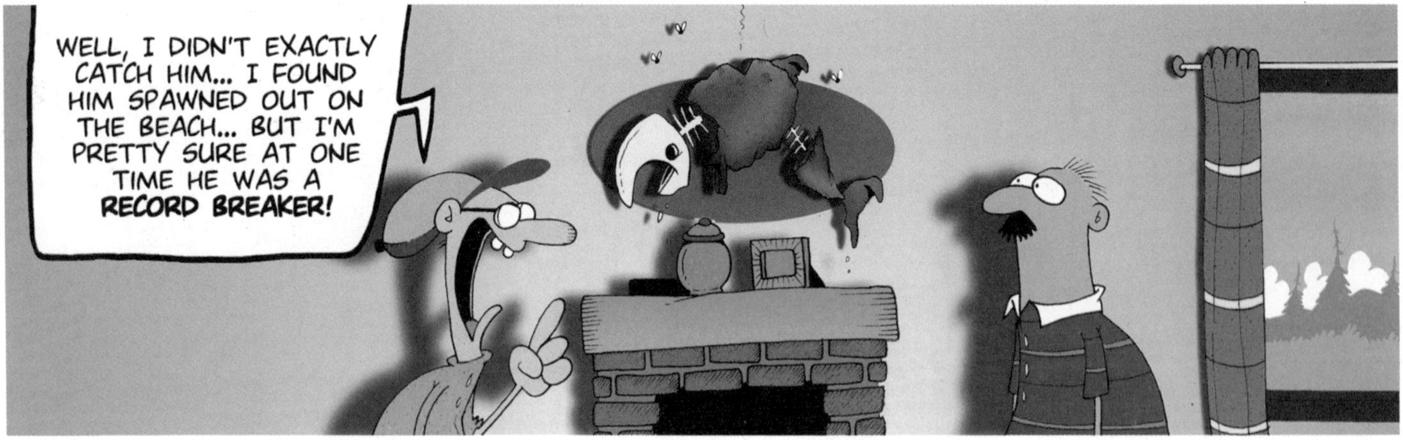
WELL, I DIDN'T EXACTLY
CATCH HIM... I FOUND
HIM SPAWNED OUT ON
THE BEACH... BUT I'M
PRETTY SURE AT ONE
TIME HE WAS A
RECORD BREAKER!

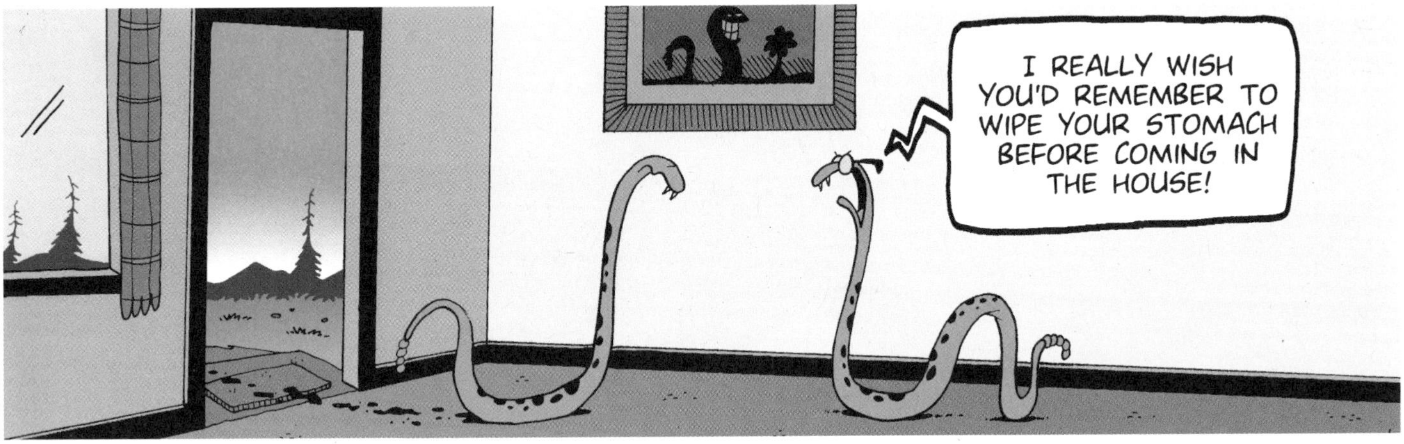
I REALLY WISH YOU'D REMEMBER TO WIPE YOUR STOMACH BEFORE COMING IN THE HOUSE!

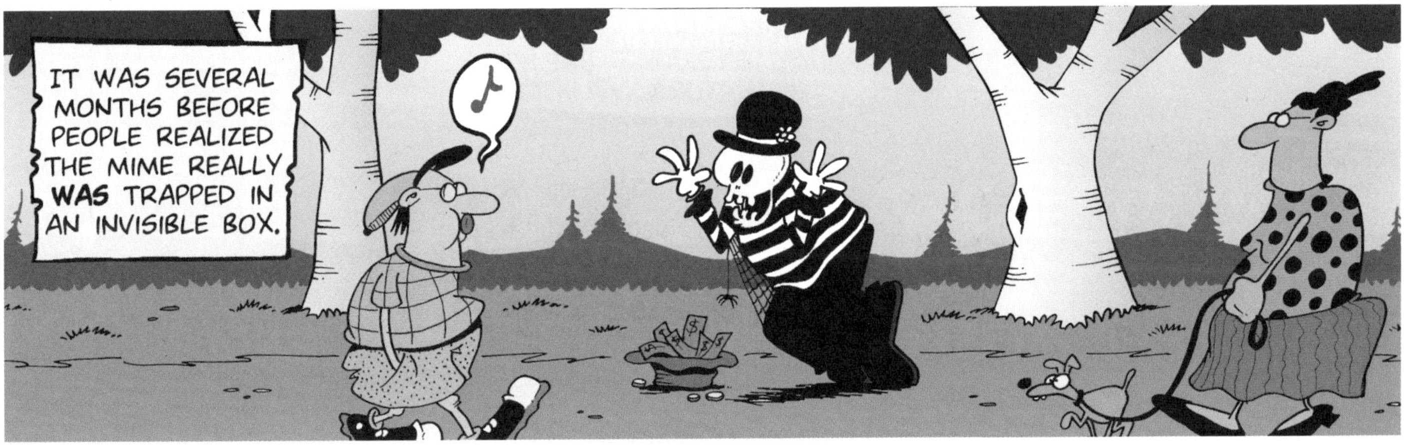
IT WAS SEVERAL MONTHS BEFORE PEOPLE REALIZED THE MIME REALLY **WAS** TRAPPED IN AN INVISIBLE BOX.

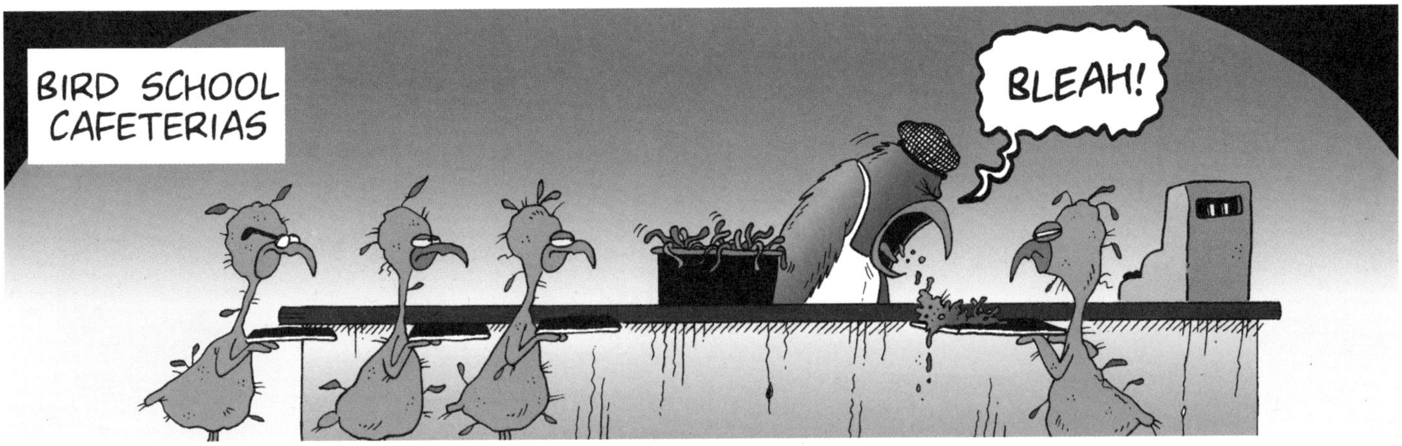
BIRD SCHOOL CAFETERIAS
BLEAH!

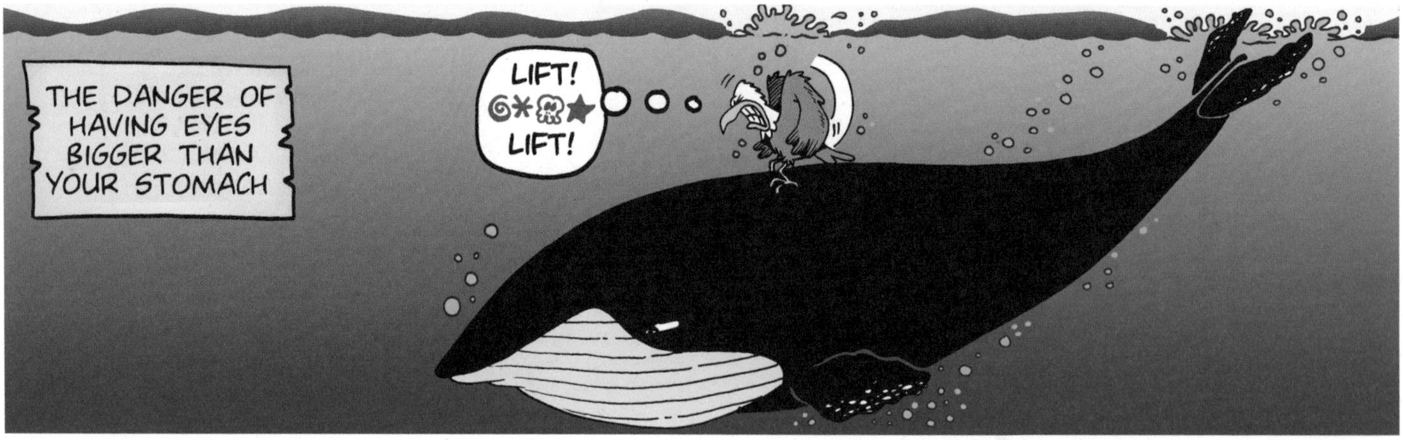
THE DANGER OF HAVING EYES BIGGER THAN YOUR STOMACH
LIFT! LIFT!

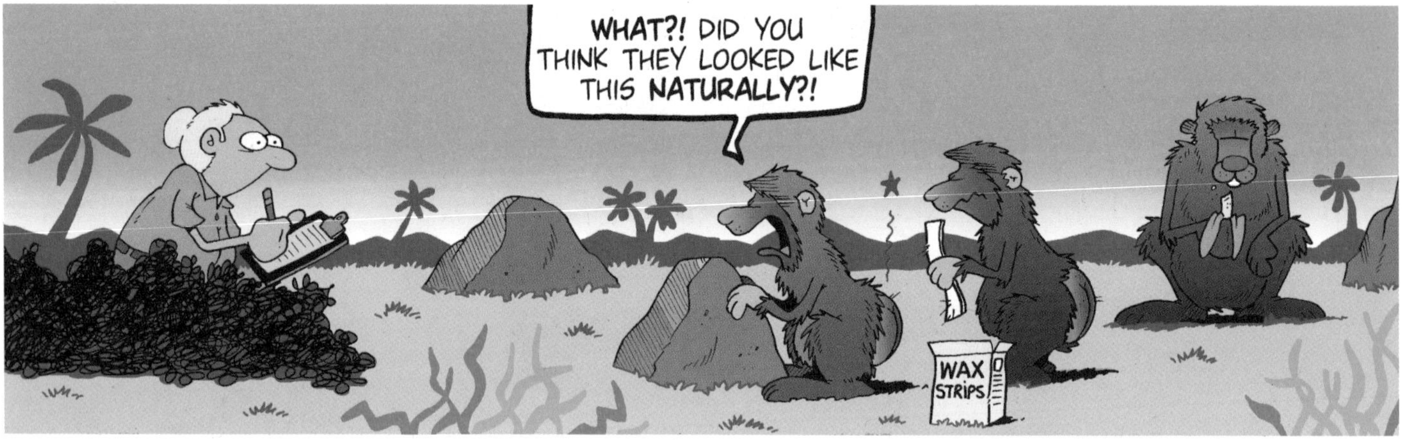
WHAT?! DID YOU THINK THEY LOOKED LIKE THIS NATURALLY?!
WAX STRIPS

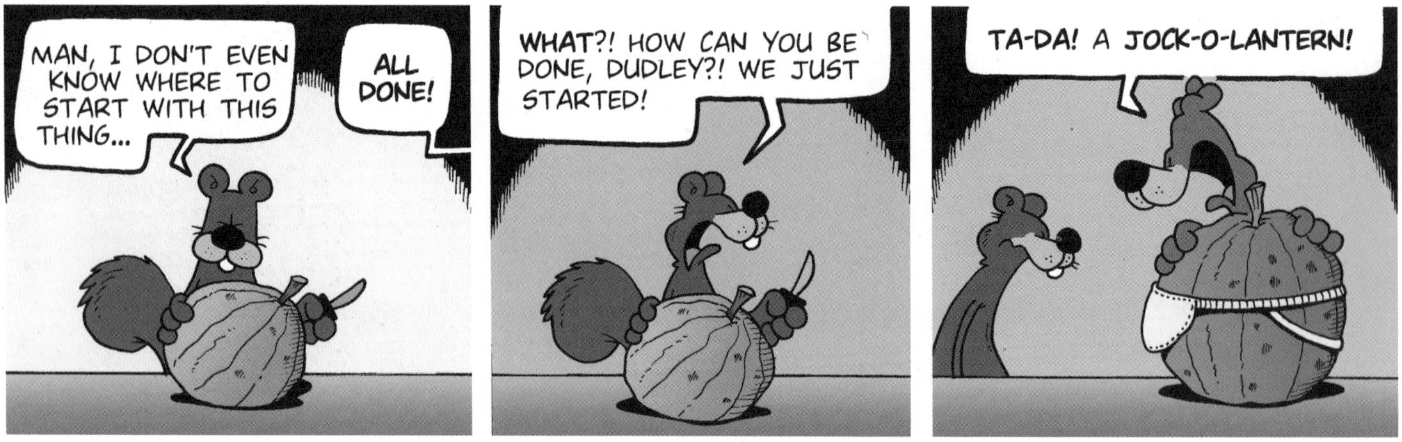
MAN, I DON'T EVEN KNOW WHERE TO START WITH THIS THING...
ALL DONE!
WHAT?! HOW CAN YOU BE DONE, DUDLEY?! WE JUST STARTED!
TA-DA! A JOCK-O-LANTERN!

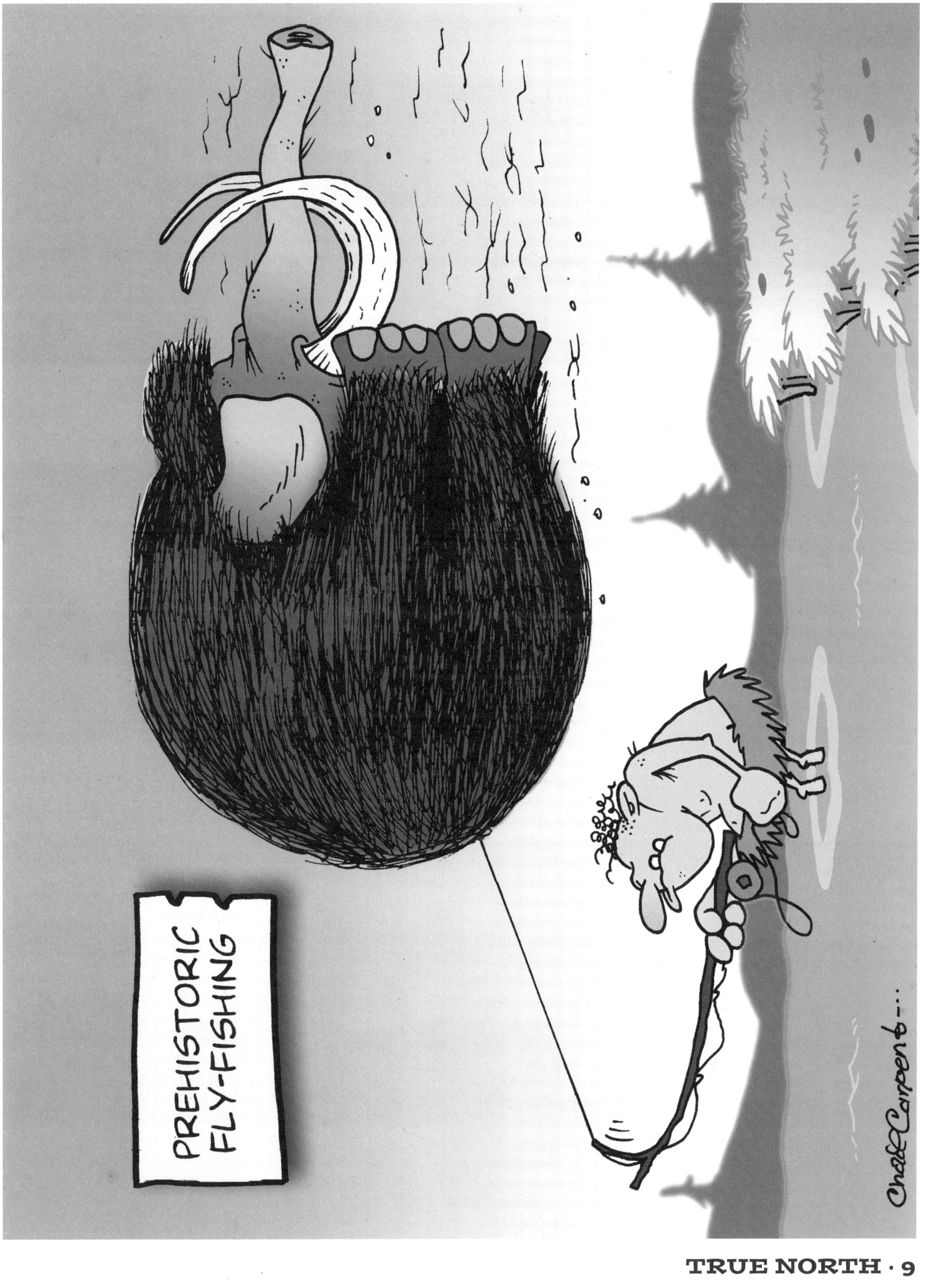
PREHISTORIC
FLY-FISHING

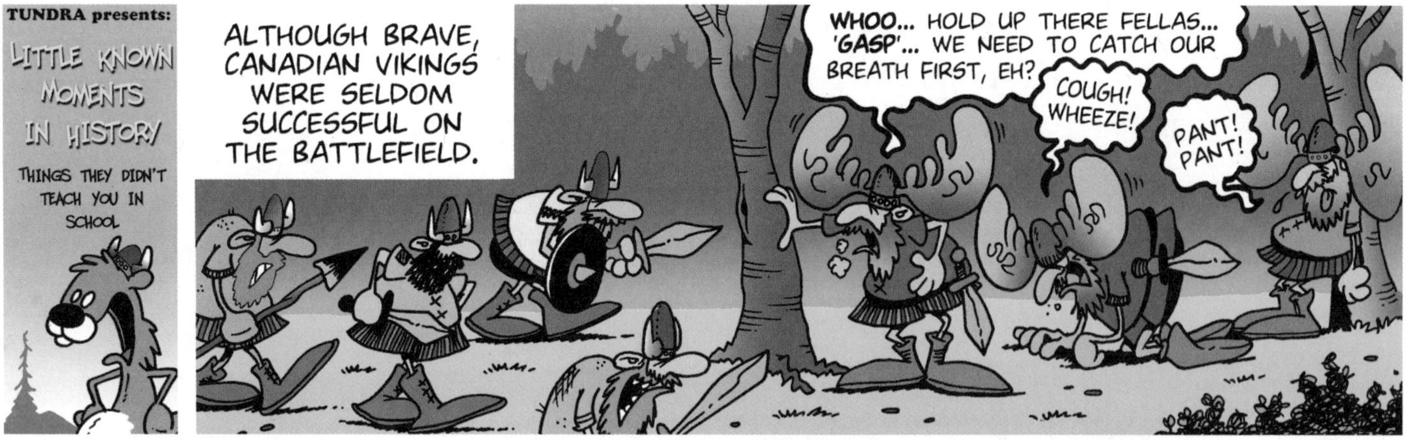
TUNDRA presents:
LITTLE KNOWN MOMENTS IN HISTORY
THINGS THEY DIDN'T TEACH YOU IN SCHOOL
ALTHOUGH BRAVE, CANADIAN VIKINGS WERE SELDOM SUCCESSFUL ON THE BATTLEFIELD.
WHOO... HOLD UP THERE FELLAS... 'GASP'... WE NEED TO CATCH OUR BREATH FIRST, EH?
COUGH! WHEEZE!
PANT! PANT!

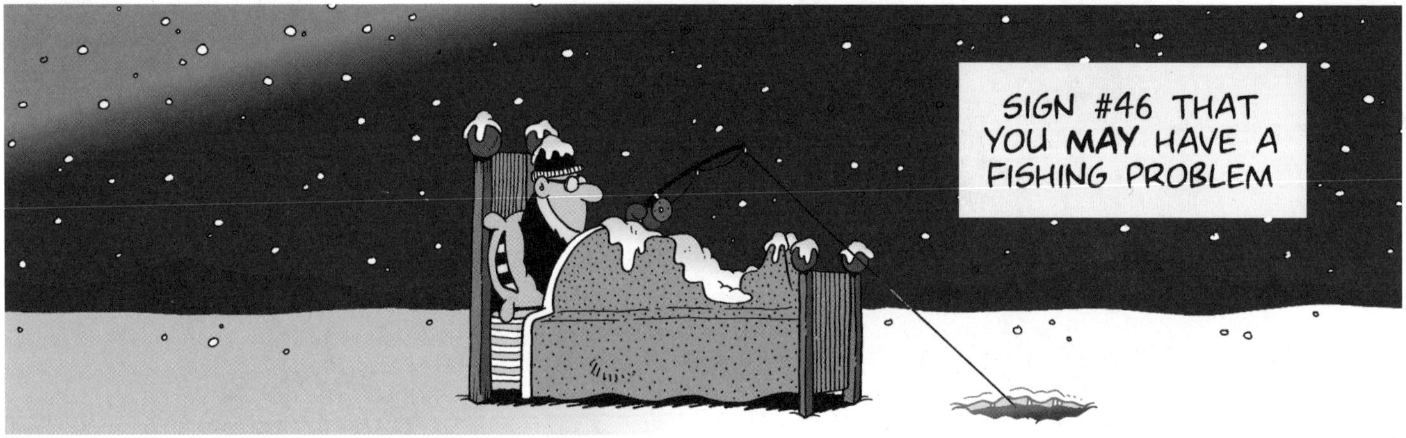
SIGN #46 THAT YOU MAY HAVE A FISHING PROBLEM

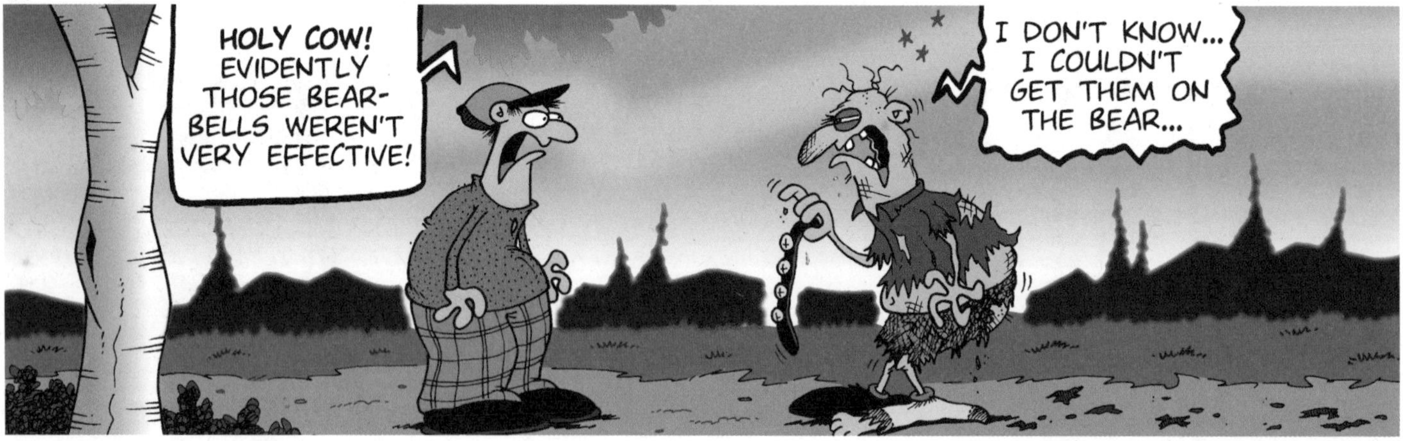
HOLY COW! EVIDENTLY THOSE BEAR-BELLS WEREN'T VERY EFFECTIVE!
I DON'T KNOW... I COULDN'T GET THEM ON THE BEAR...

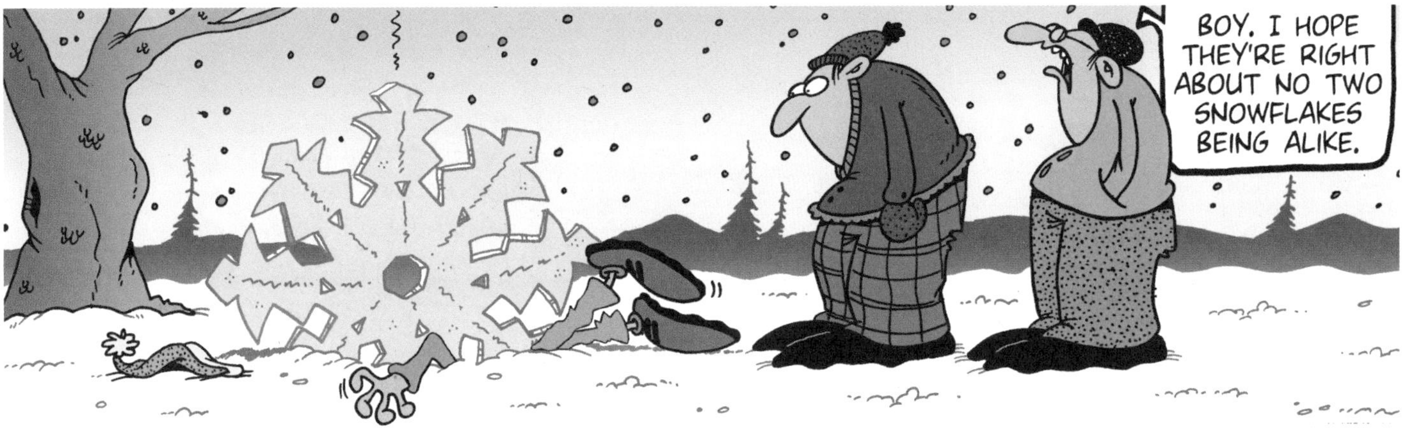
BOY. I HOPE THEY'RE RIGHT ABOUT NO TWO SNOWFLAKES BEING ALIKE.

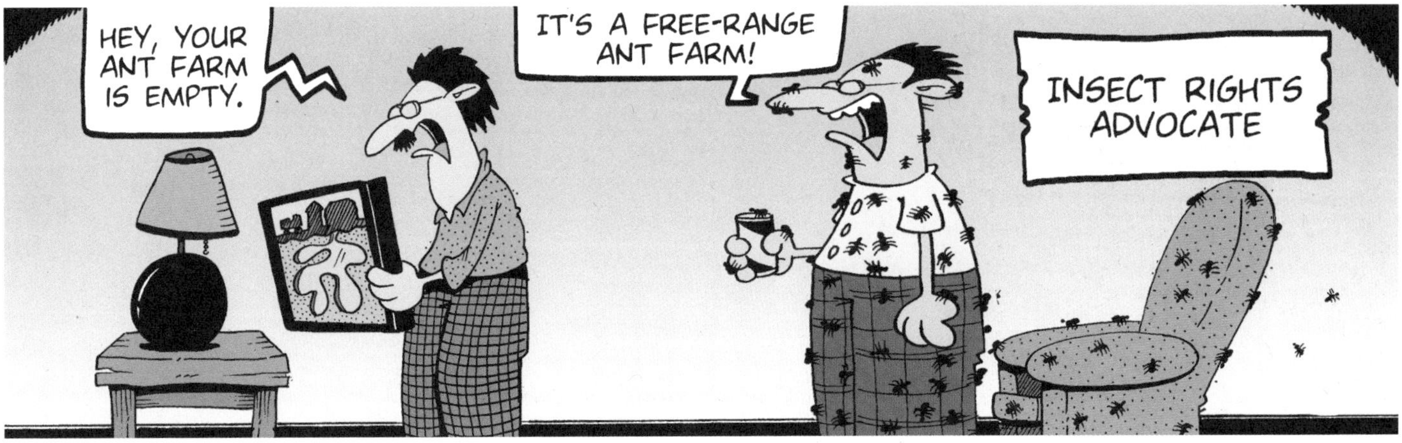
HEY, YOUR ANT FARM IS EMPTY.
IT'S A FREE-RANGE ANT FARM!
INSECT RIGHTS ADVOCATE

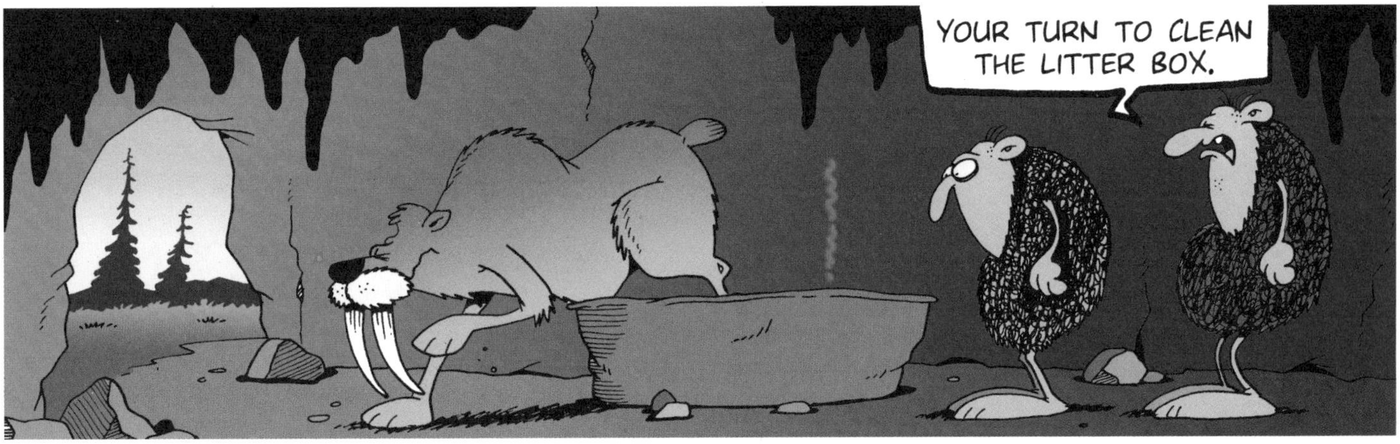
YOUR TURN TO CLEAN THE LITTER BOX.

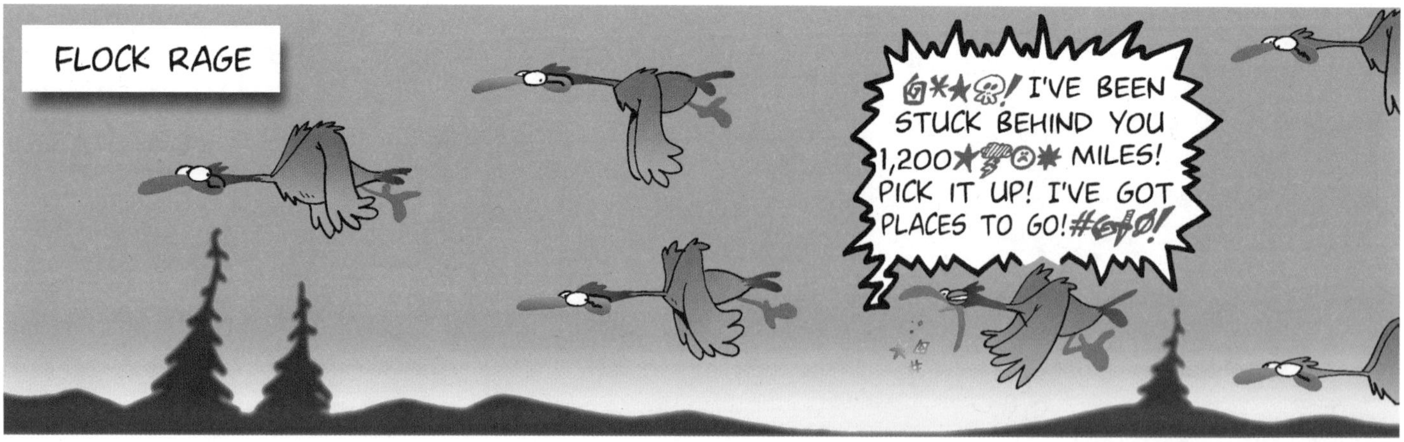
FLOCK RAGE
@*★☠! I'VE BEEN STUCK BEHIND YOU 1,200★☂☹✱ MILES! PICK IT UP! I'VE GOT PLACES TO GO!#6/Ø!

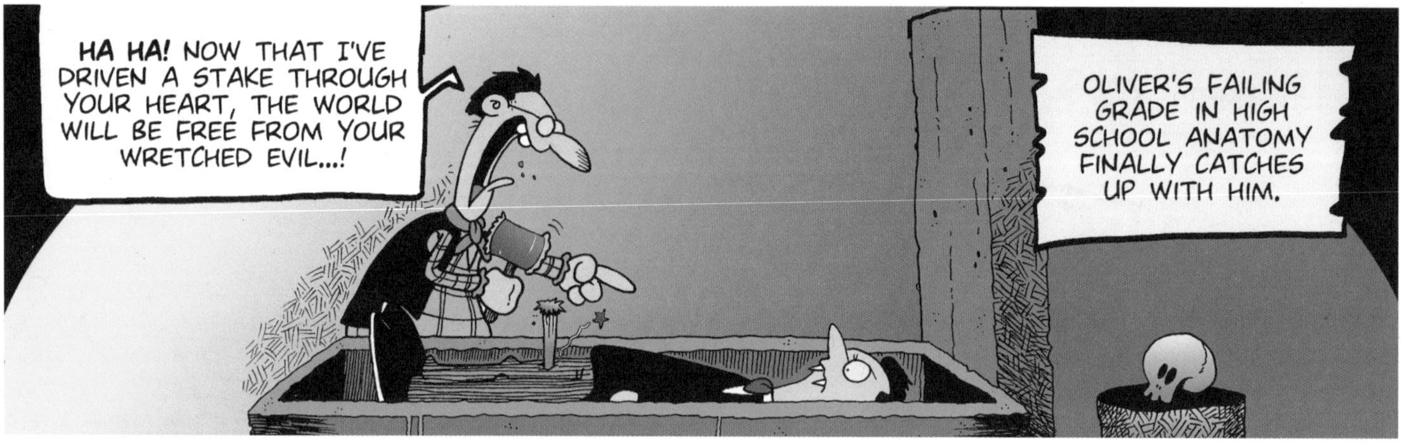
HA HA! NOW THAT I'VE DRIVEN A STAKE THROUGH YOUR HEART, THE WORLD WILL BE FREE FROM YOUR WRETCHED EVIL...!
OLIVER'S FAILING GRADE IN HIGH SCHOOL ANATOMY FINALLY CATCHES UP WITH HIM.

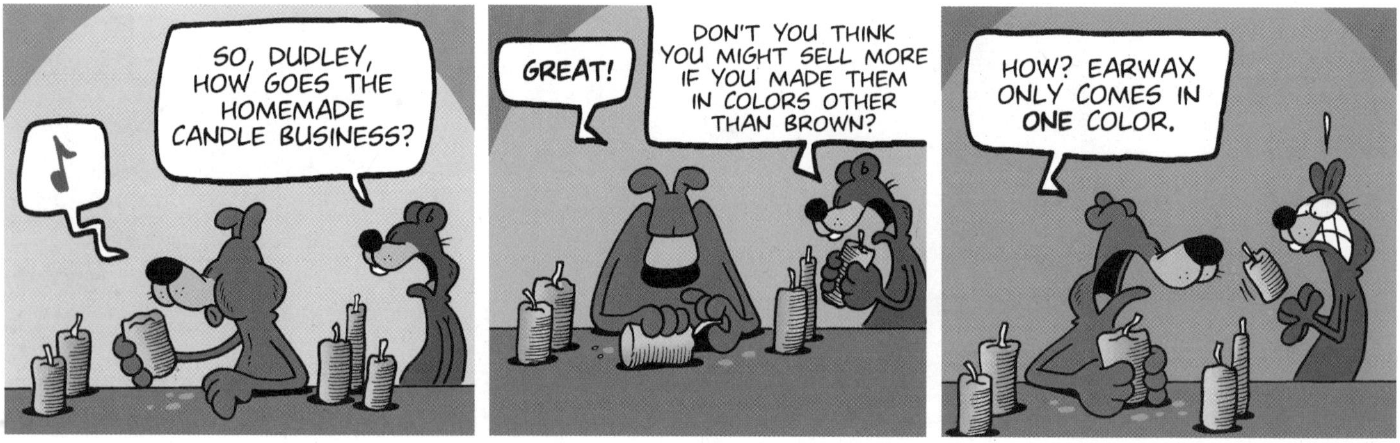
♪
SO, DUDLEY, HOW GOES THE HOMEMADE CANDLE BUSINESS?
GREAT!
DON'T YOU THINK YOU MIGHT SELL MORE IF YOU MADE THEM IN COLORS OTHER THAN BROWN?
HOW? EARWAX ONLY COMES IN ONE COLOR.
!

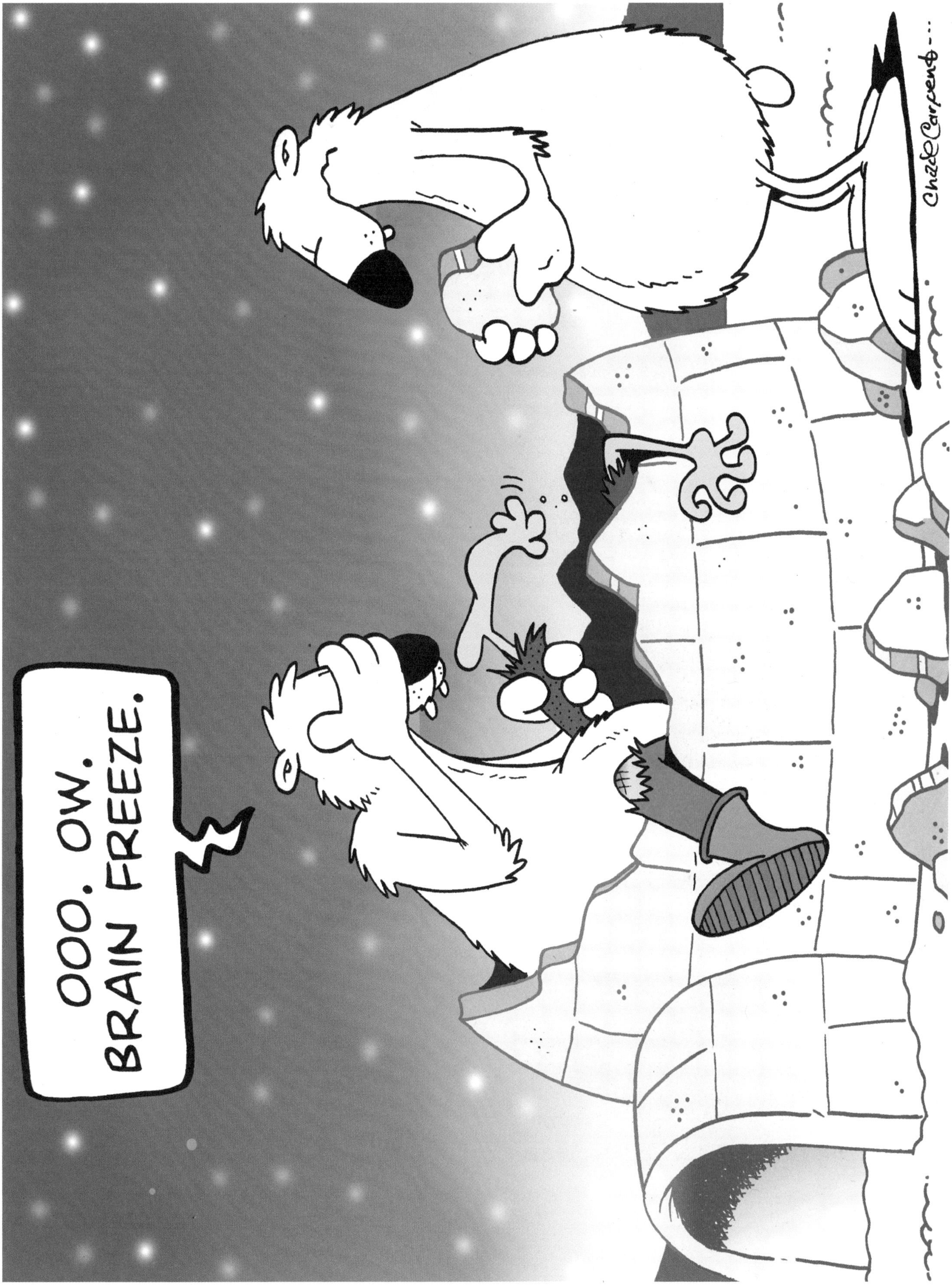
OOO. OW. BRAIN FREEZE.
Chad Carpenter

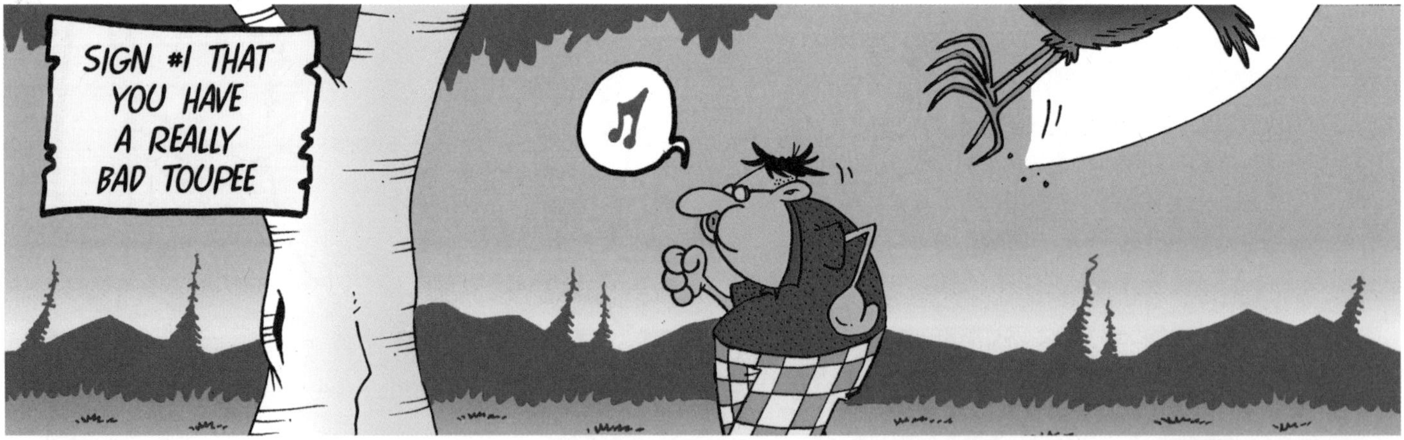
SIGN #1 THAT YOU HAVE A REALLY BAD TOUPEE

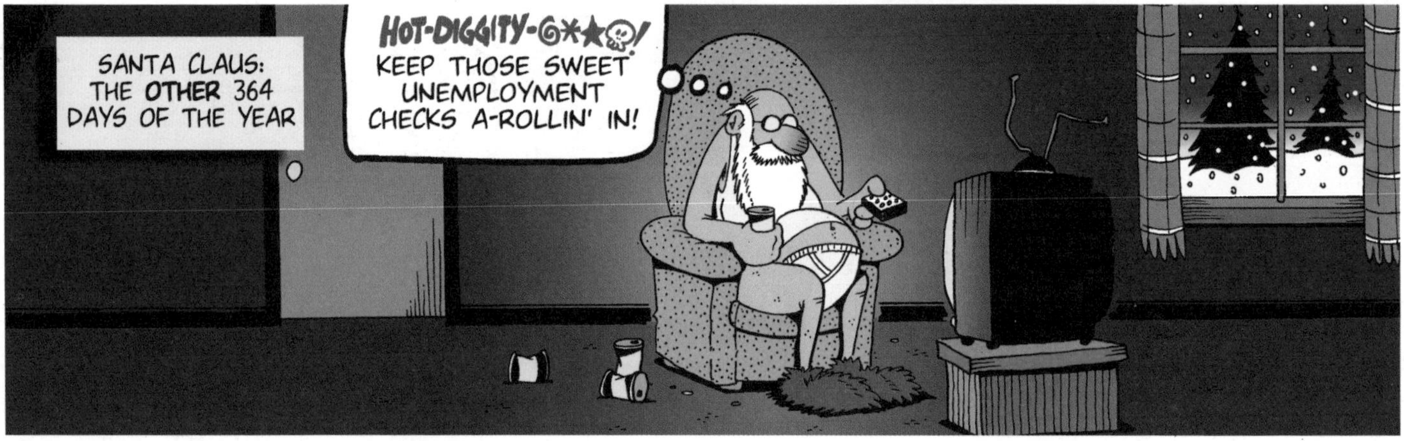
SANTA CLAUS: THE OTHER 364 DAYS OF THE YEAR
HOT-DIGGITY-
KEEP THOSE SWEET UNEMPLOYMENT CHECKS A-ROLLIN' IN!

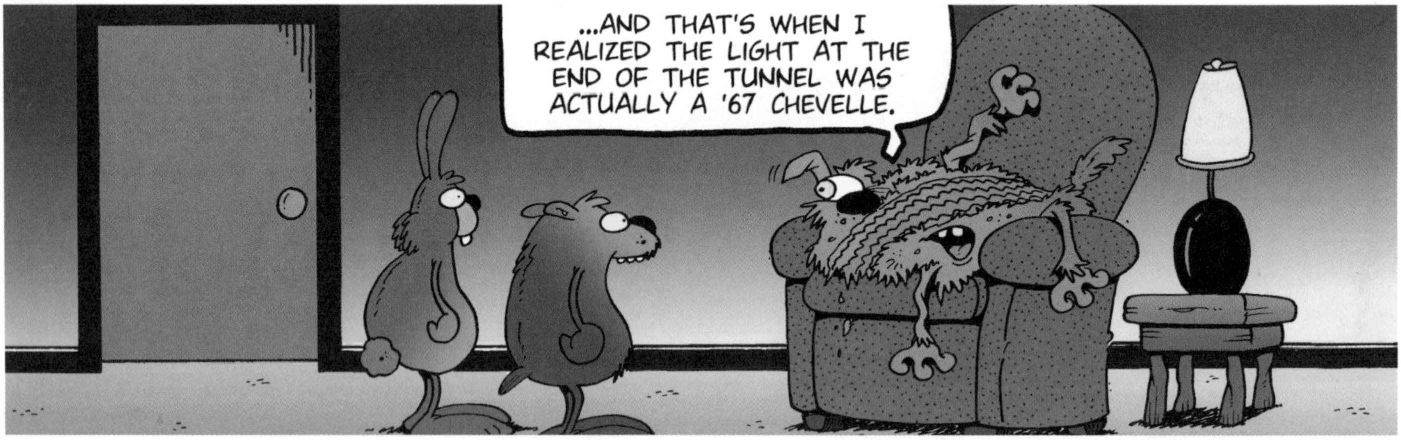
...AND THAT'S WHEN I REALIZED THE LIGHT AT THE END OF THE TUNNEL WAS ACTUALLY A '67 CHEVELLE.

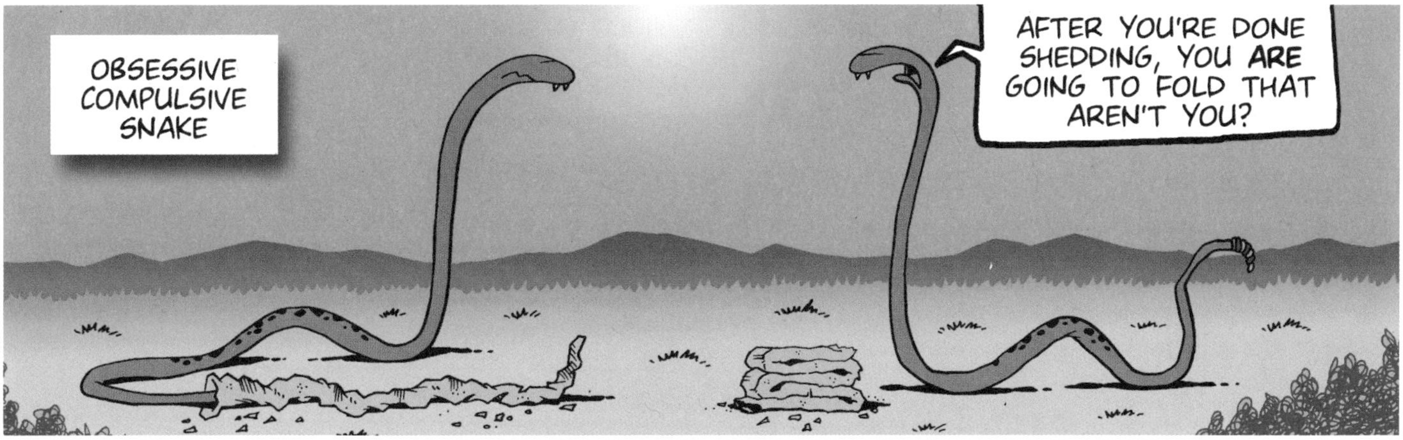
OBSESSIVE COMPULSIVE SNAKE
AFTER YOU'RE DONE SHEDDING, YOU **ARE** GOING TO FOLD THAT AREN'T YOU?

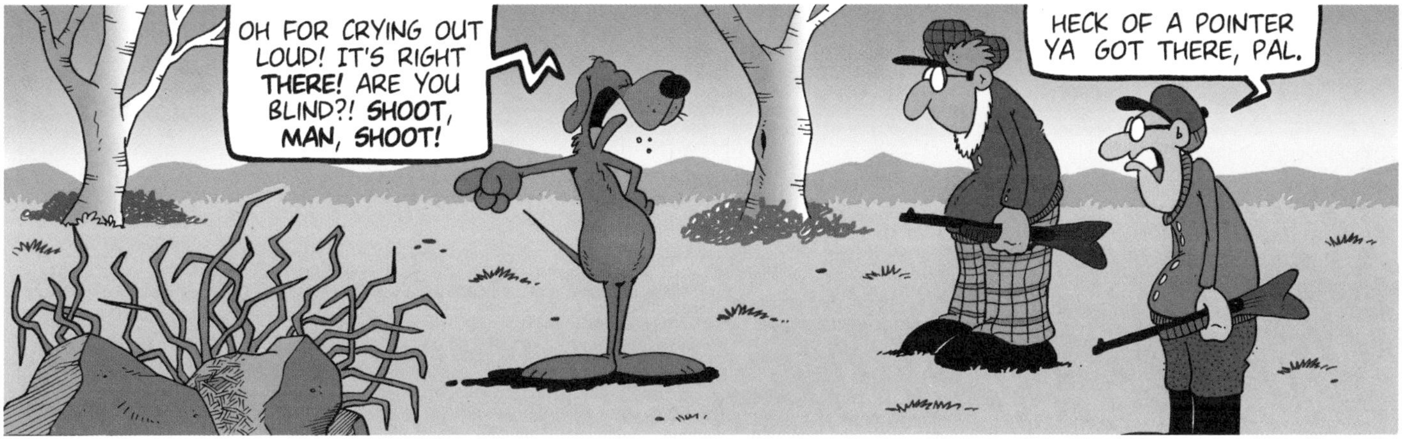
OH FOR CRYING OUT LOUD! IT'S RIGHT **THERE!** ARE YOU BLIND?! **SHOOT, MAN, SHOOT!**
HECK OF A POINTER YA GOT THERE, PAL.

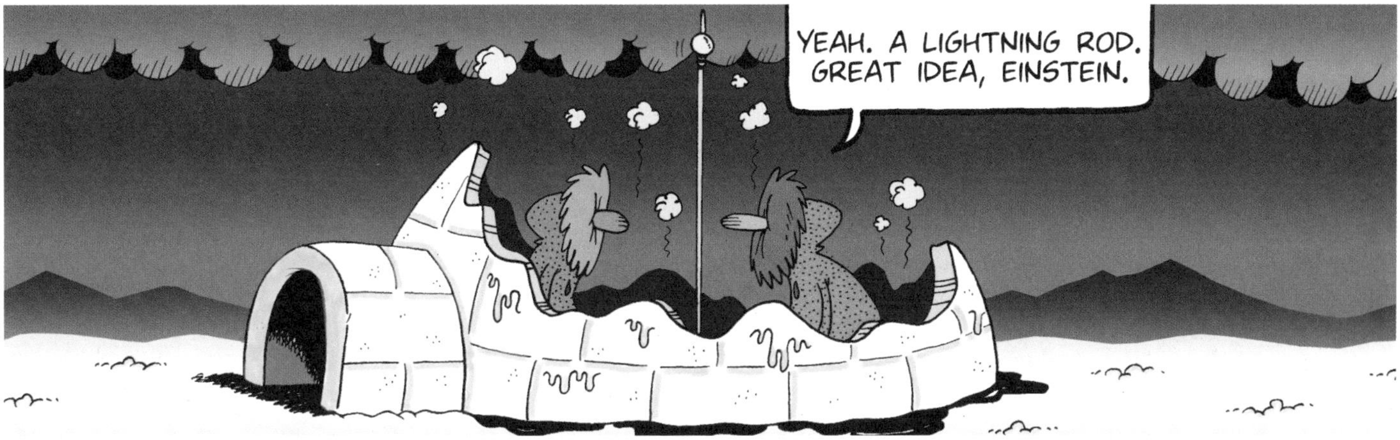
YEAH. A LIGHTNING ROD. GREAT IDEA, EINSTEIN.

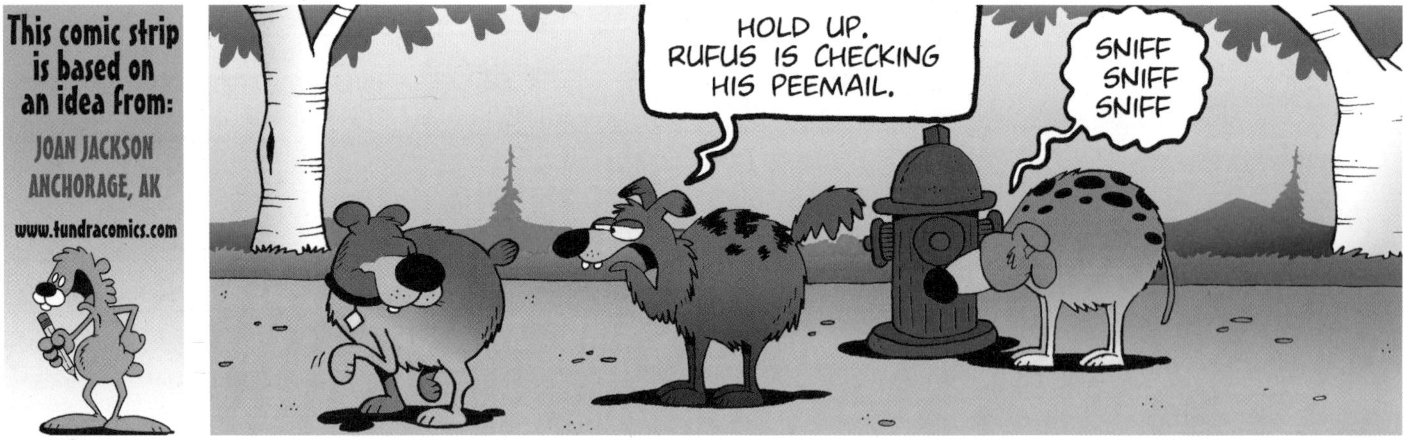
This comic strip is based on an idea from:
JOAN JACKSON
ANCHORAGE, AK
www.tundracomics.com
HOLD UP. RUFUS IS CHECKING HIS PEEMAIL.
SNIFF SNIFF SNIFF

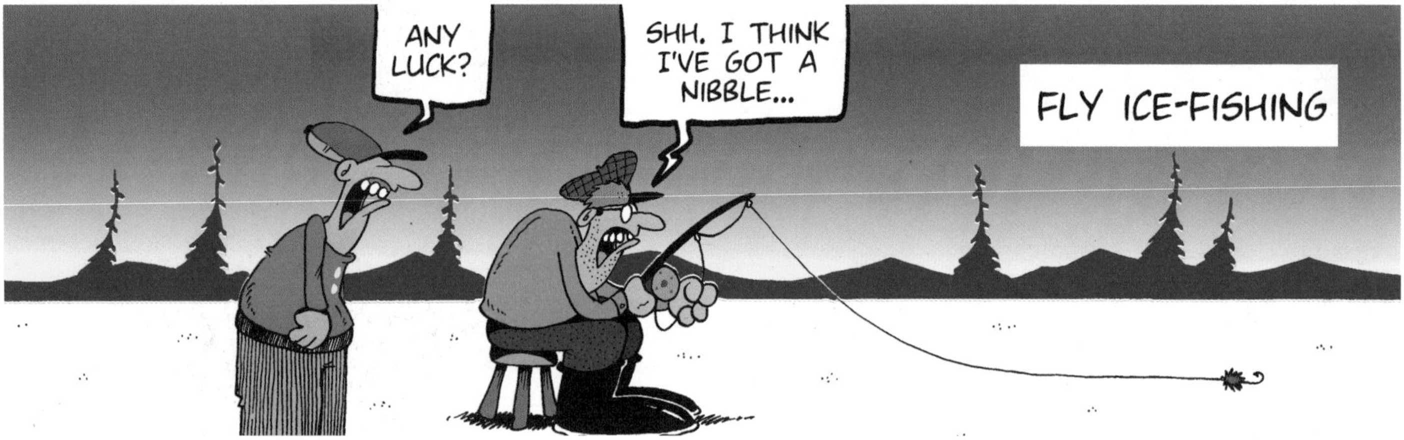
ANY LUCK?
SHH. I THINK I'VE GOT A NIBBLE...
FLY ICE-FISHING

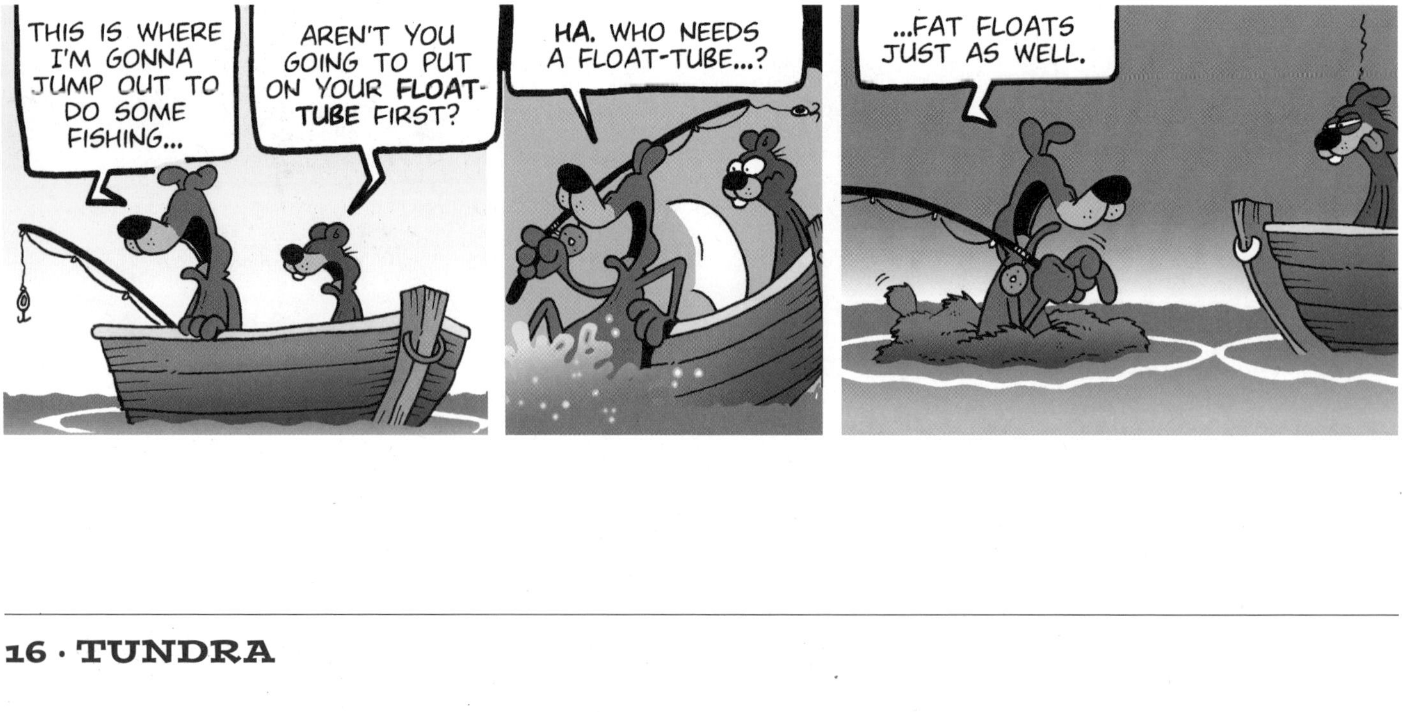
THIS IS WHERE I'M GONNA JUMP OUT TO DO SOME FISHING...
AREN'T YOU GOING TO PUT ON YOUR FLOAT-TUBE FIRST?
HA. WHO NEEDS A FLOAT-TUBE...?
...FAT FLOATS JUST AS WELL.

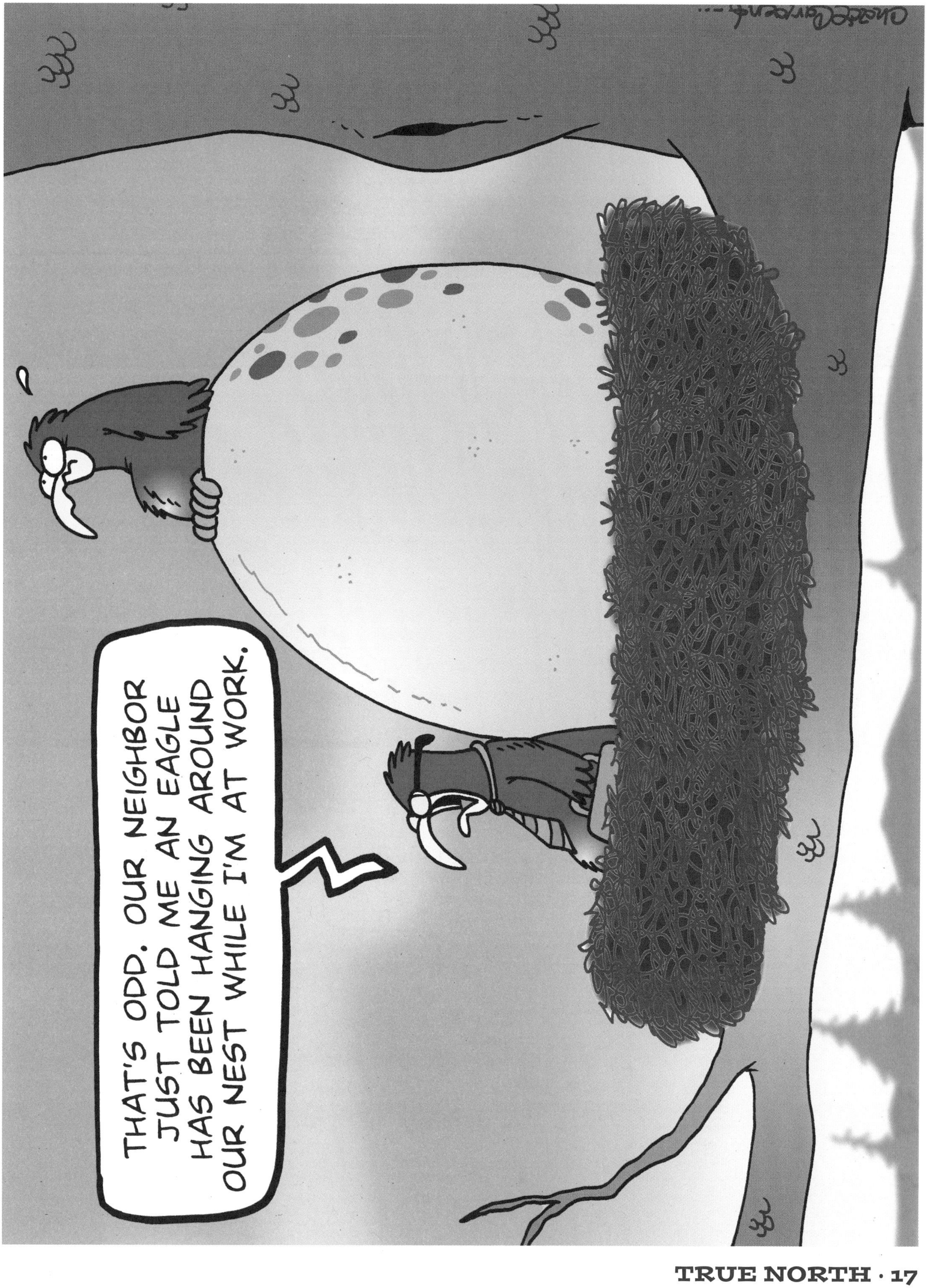
THAT'S ODD. OUR NEIGHBOR JUST TOLD ME AN EAGLE HAS BEEN HANGING AROUND OUR NEST WHILE I'M AT WORK.

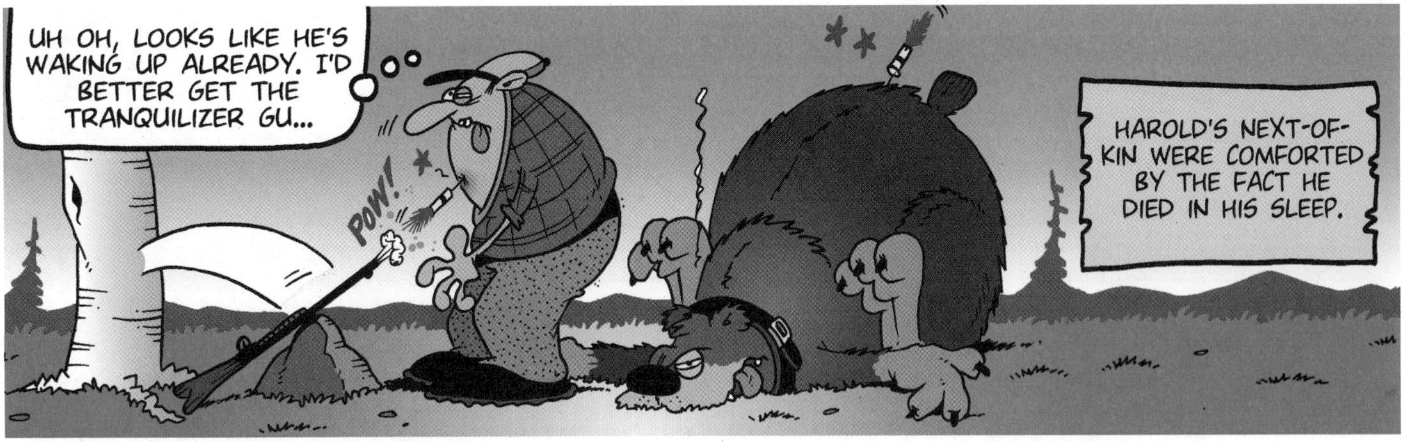
UH OH, LOOKS LIKE HE'S WAKING UP ALREADY. I'D BETTER GET THE TRANQUILIZER GU...
POW!
HAROLD'S NEXT-OF-KIN WERE COMFORTED BY THE FACT HE DIED IN HIS SLEEP.

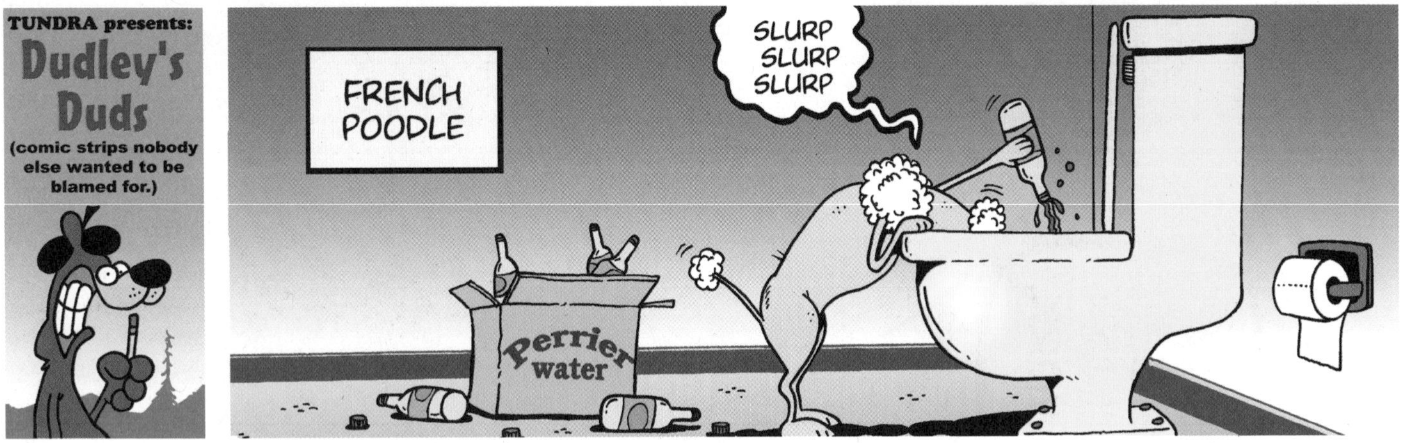
TUNDRA presents:
Dudley's Duds
(comic strips nobody else wanted to be blamed for.)
FRENCH POODLE
SLURP SLURP SLURP
Perrier water

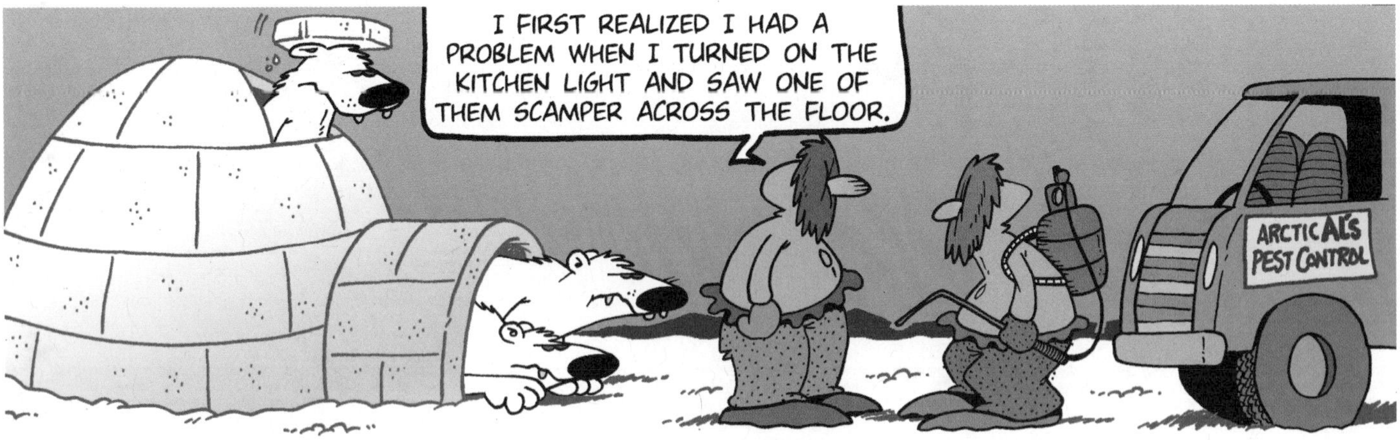
I FIRST REALIZED I HAD A PROBLEM WHEN I TURNED ON THE KITCHEN LIGHT AND SAW ONE OF THEM SCAMPER ACROSS THE FLOOR.
ARCTIC AL'S PEST CONTROL

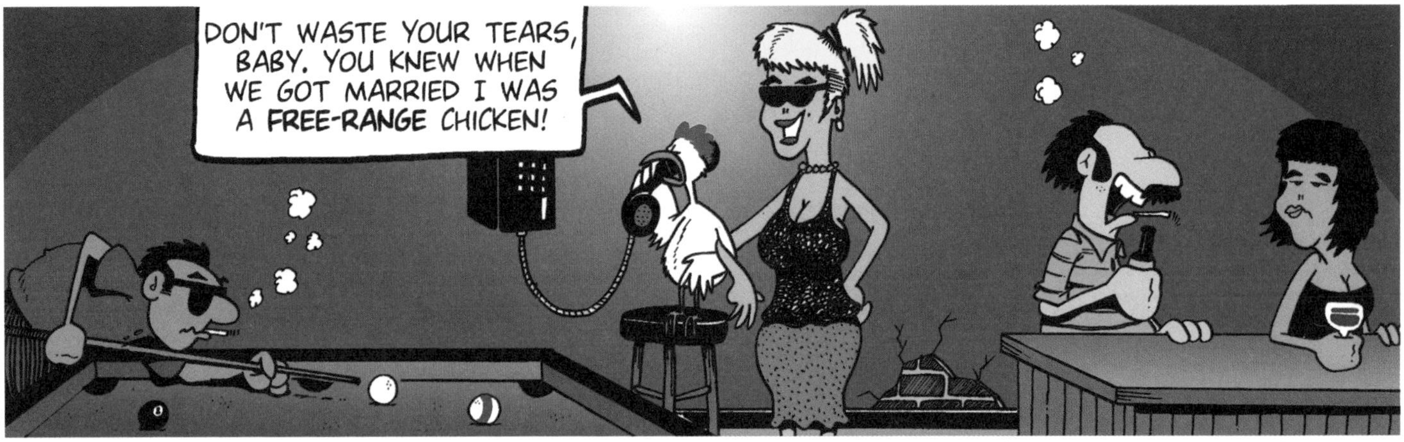
DON'T WASTE YOUR TEARS, BABY. YOU KNEW WHEN WE GOT MARRIED I WAS A **FREE-RANGE** CHICKEN!

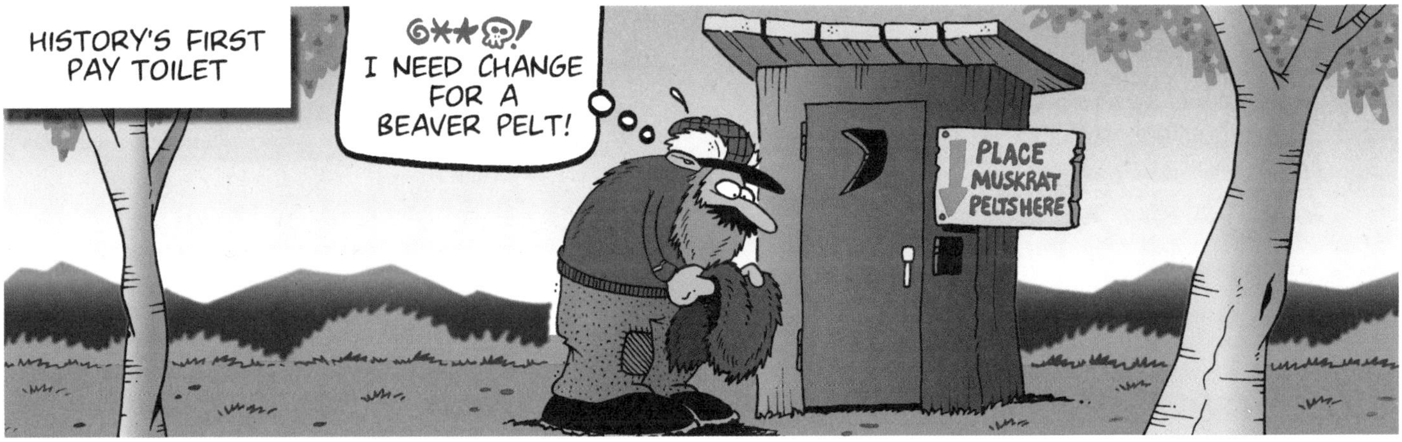
HISTORY'S FIRST PAY TOILET
I NEED CHANGE FOR A BEAVER PELT!
PLACE MUSKRAT PELTS HERE

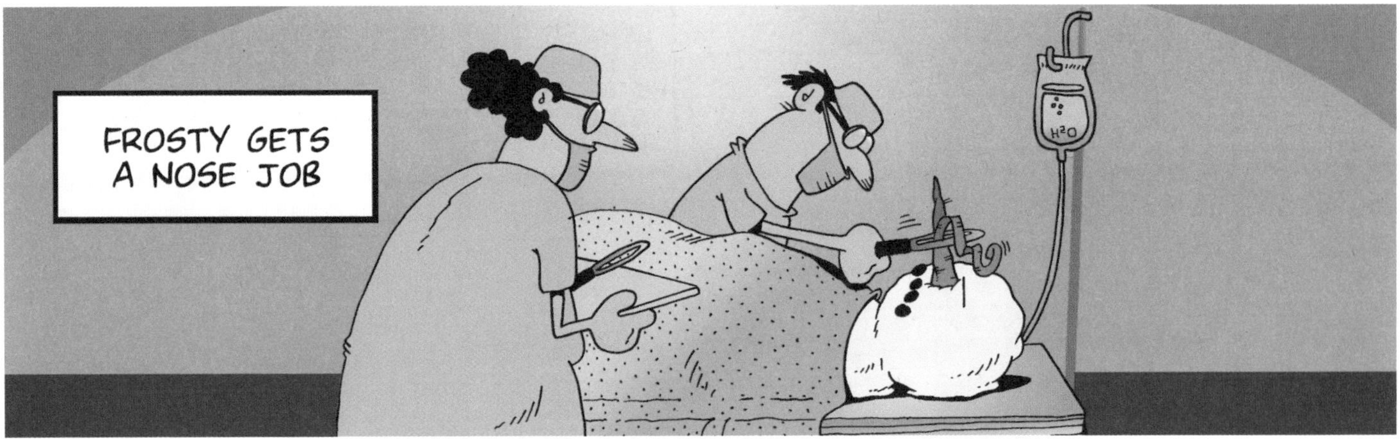
FROSTY GETS A NOSE JOB

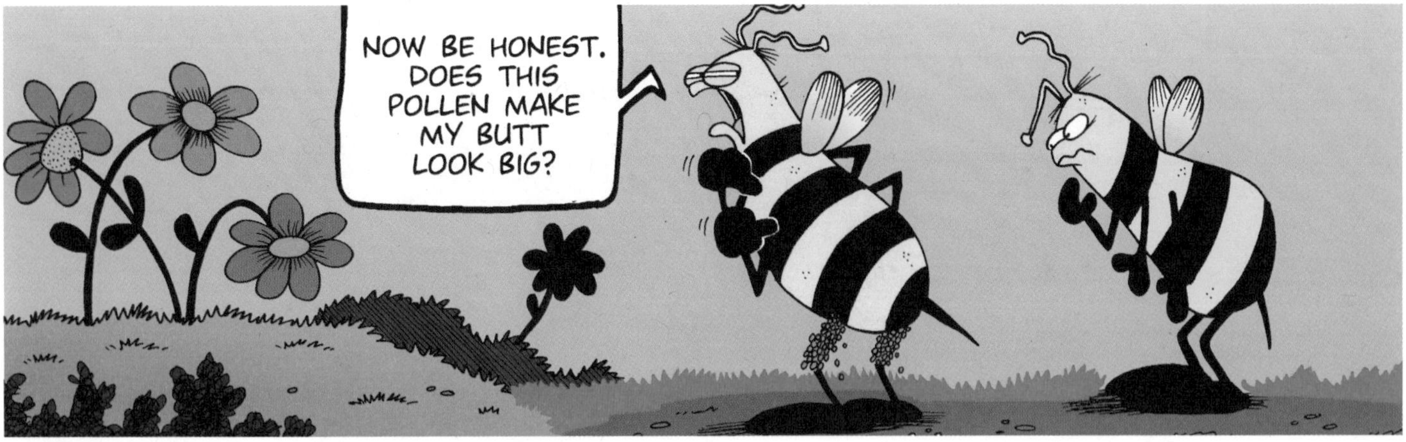
NOW BE HONEST. DOES THIS POLLEN MAKE MY BUTT LOOK BIG?

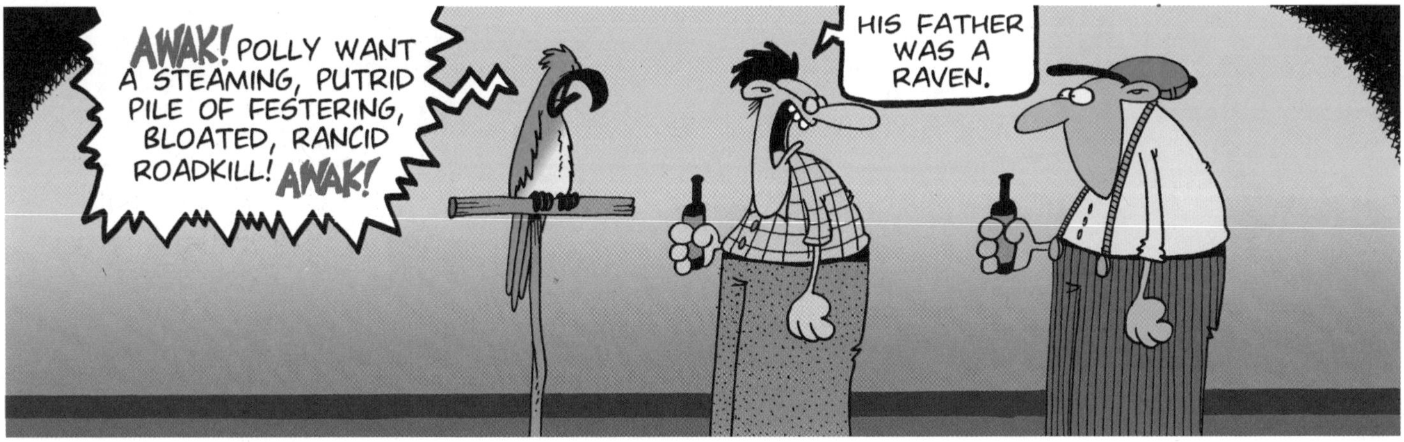
AWAK! POLLY WANT A STEAMING, PUTRID PILE OF FESTERING, BLOATED, RANCID ROADKILL! AWAK!
HIS FATHER WAS A RAVEN.

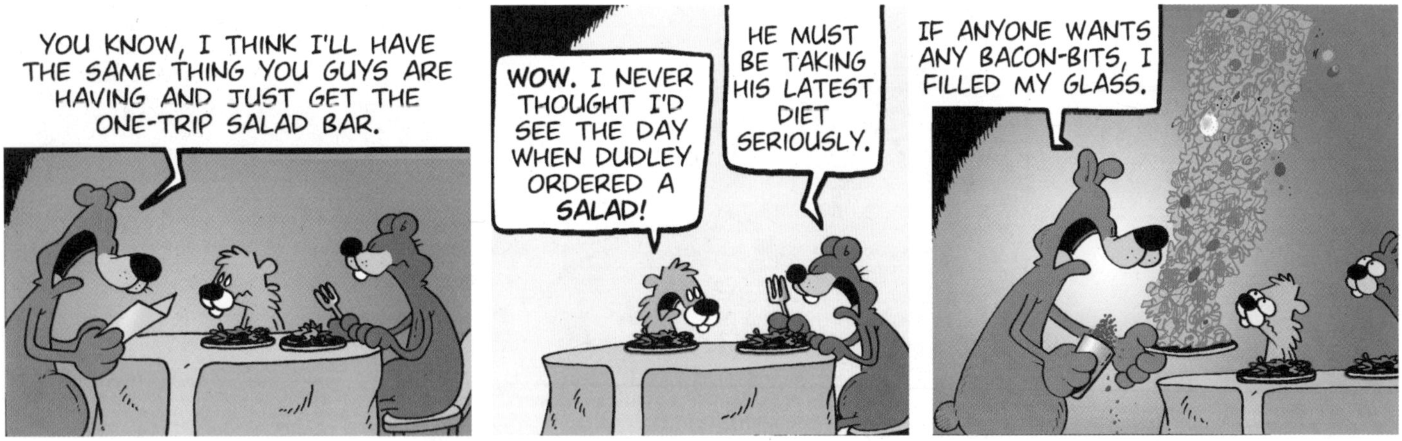
YOU KNOW, I THINK I'LL HAVE THE SAME THING YOU GUYS ARE HAVING AND JUST GET THE ONE-TRIP SALAD BAR.
WOW. I NEVER THOUGHT I'D SEE THE DAY WHEN DUDLEY ORDERED A SALAD!
HE MUST BE TAKING HIS LATEST DIET SERIOUSLY.
IF ANYONE WANTS ANY BACON-BITS, I FILLED MY GLASS.

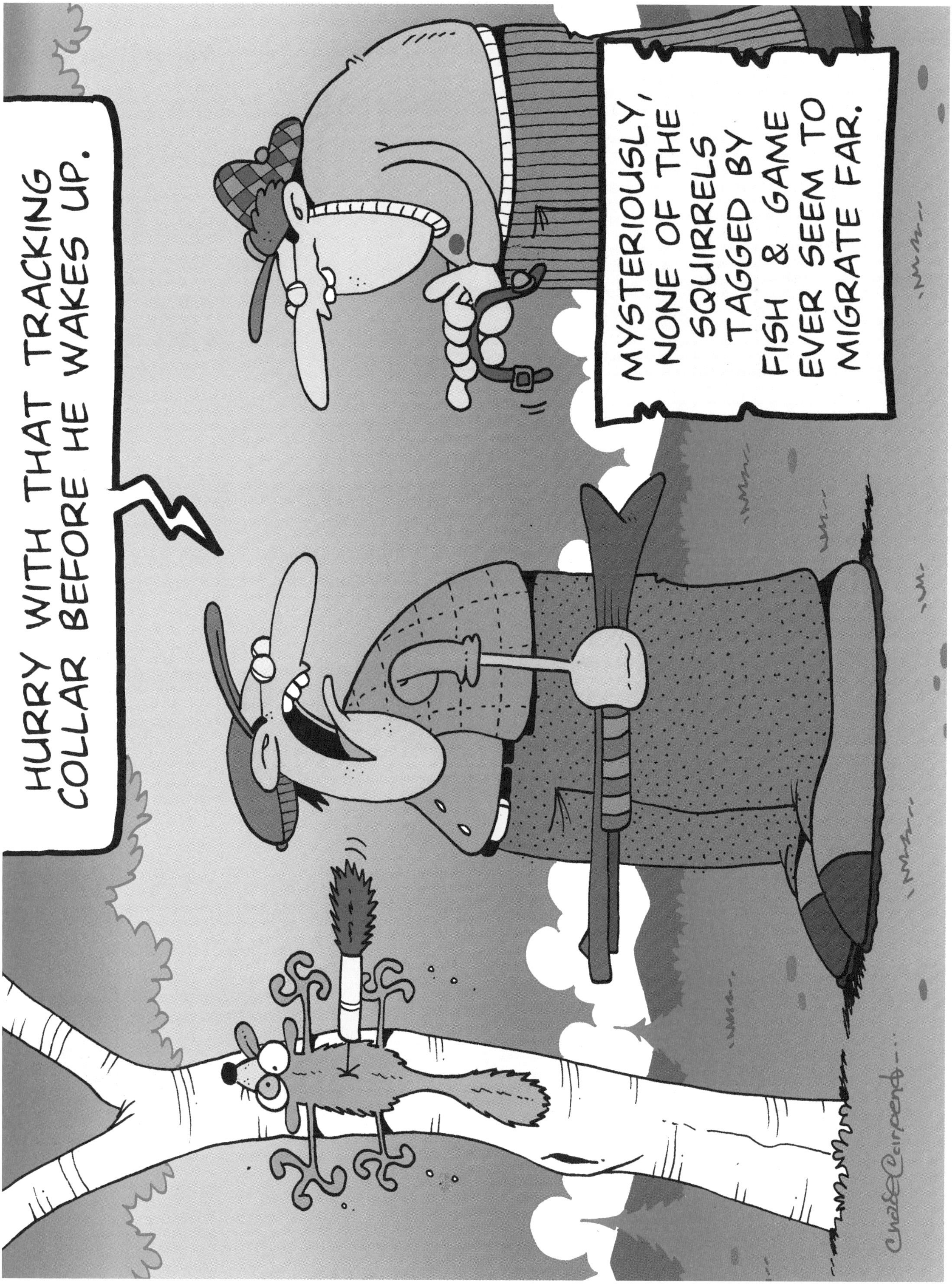
HURRY WITH THAT TRACKING COLLAR BEFORE HE WAKES UP.
MYSTERIOUSLY, NONE OF THE SQUIRRELS TAGGED BY FISH & GAME EVER SEEM TO MIGRATE FAR.

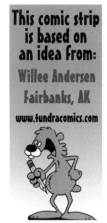

This comic strip is based on an idea from:

Willee Andersen
Fairbanks, AK

www.tundracomics.com

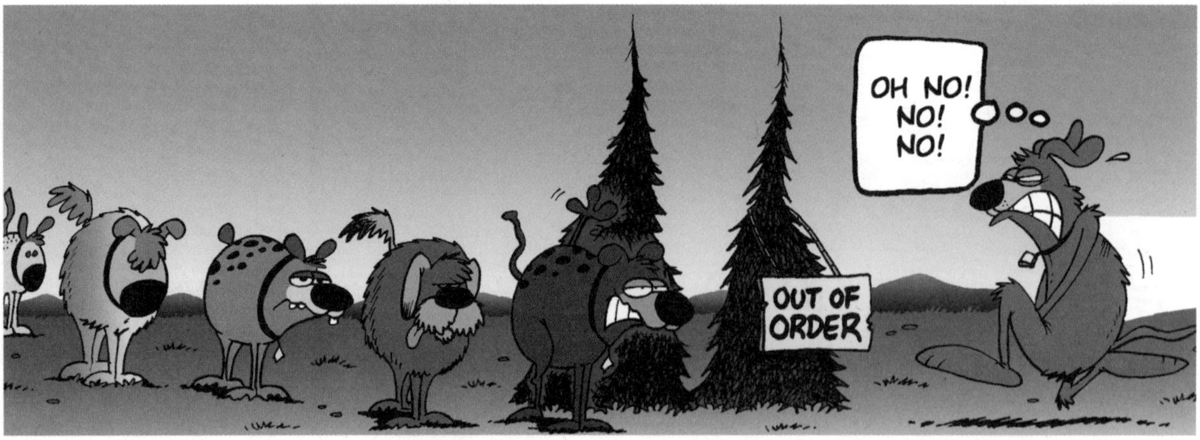
OH NO! NO! NO!
OUT OF ORDER

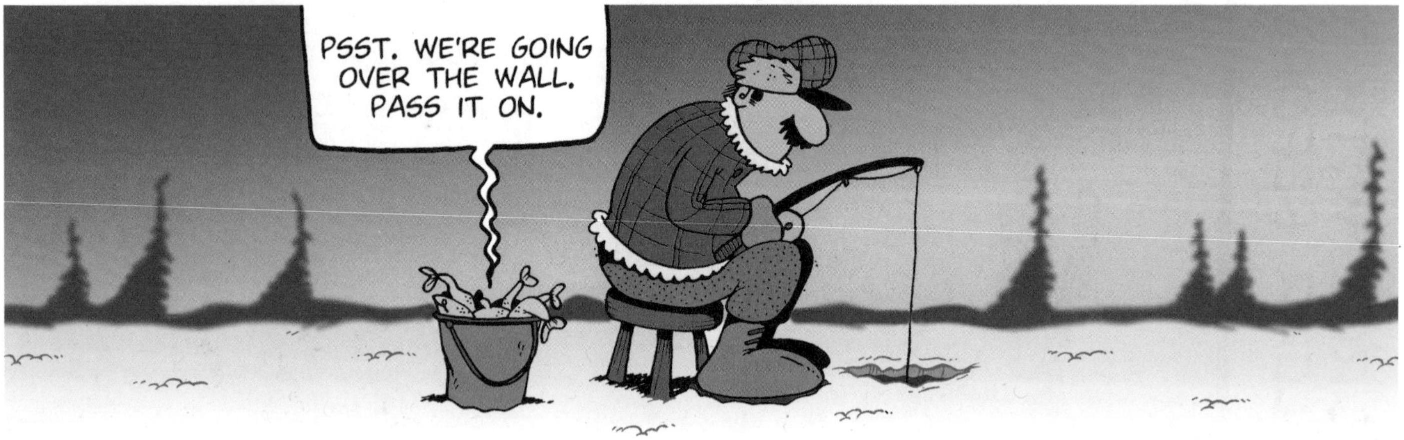
PSST. WE'RE GOING OVER THE WALL. PASS IT ON.

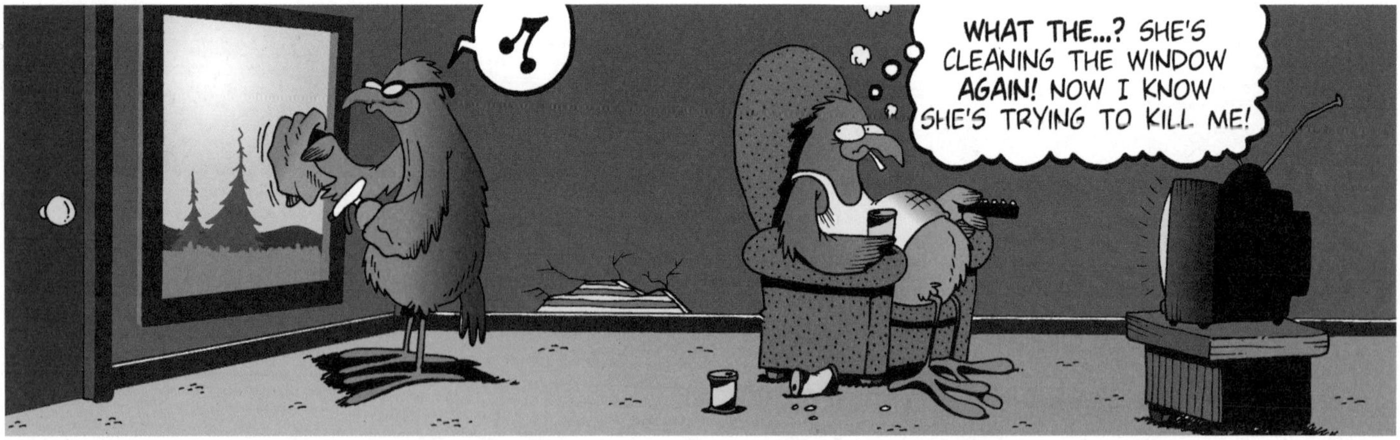
WHAT THE...? SHE'S CLEANING THE WINDOW AGAIN! NOW I KNOW SHE'S TRYING TO KILL ME!

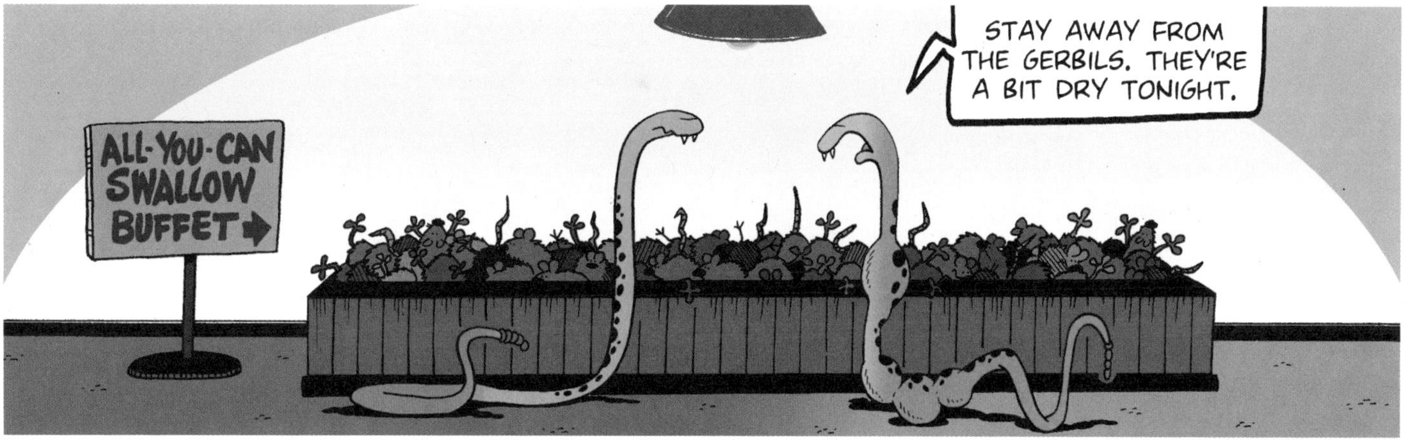
STAY AWAY FROM THE GERBILS. THEY'RE A BIT DRY TONIGHT.
ALL-YOU-CAN SWALLOW BUFFET

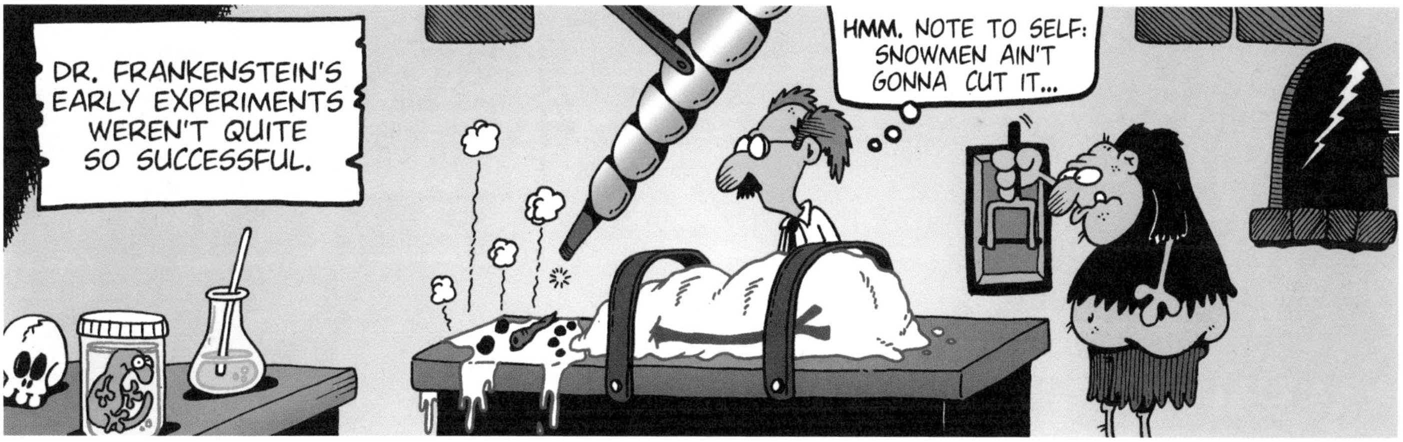
DR. FRANKENSTEIN'S EARLY EXPERIMENTS WEREN'T QUITE SO SUCCESSFUL.
HMM. NOTE TO SELF: SNOWMEN AIN'T GONNA CUT IT...

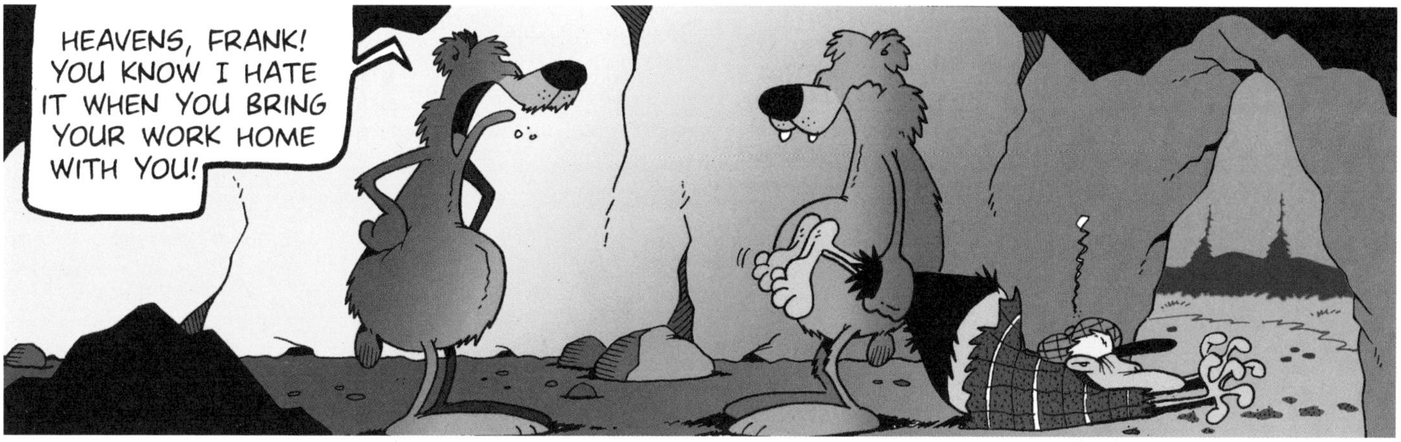
HEAVENS, FRANK! YOU KNOW I HATE IT WHEN YOU BRING YOUR WORK HOME WITH YOU!

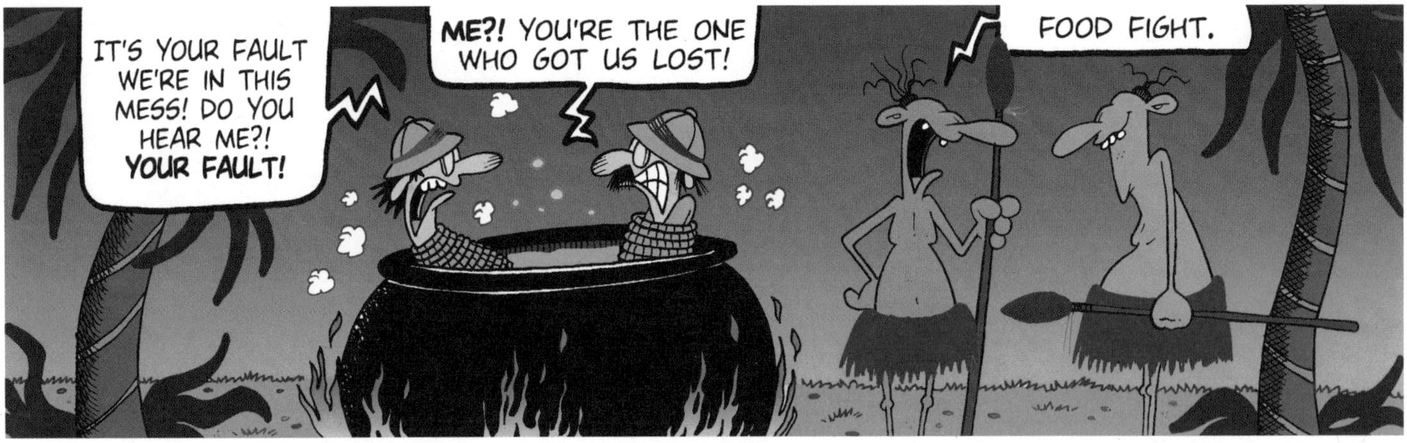
IT'S YOUR FAULT WE'RE IN THIS MESS! DO YOU HEAR ME?! YOUR FAULT!
ME?! YOU'RE THE ONE WHO GOT US LOST!
FOOD FIGHT.

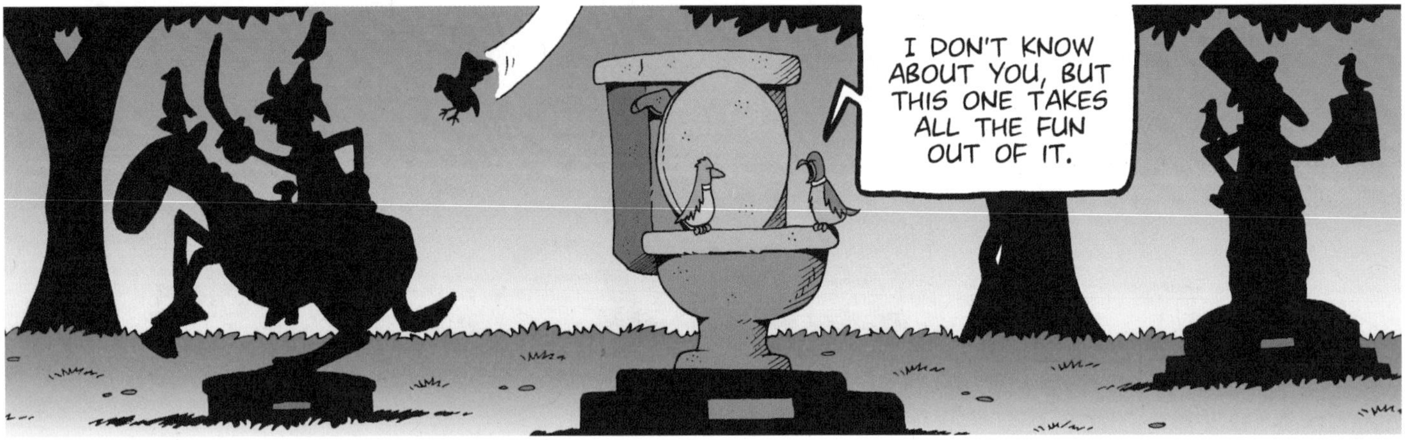
I DON'T KNOW ABOUT YOU, BUT THIS ONE TAKES ALL THE FUN OUT OF IT.

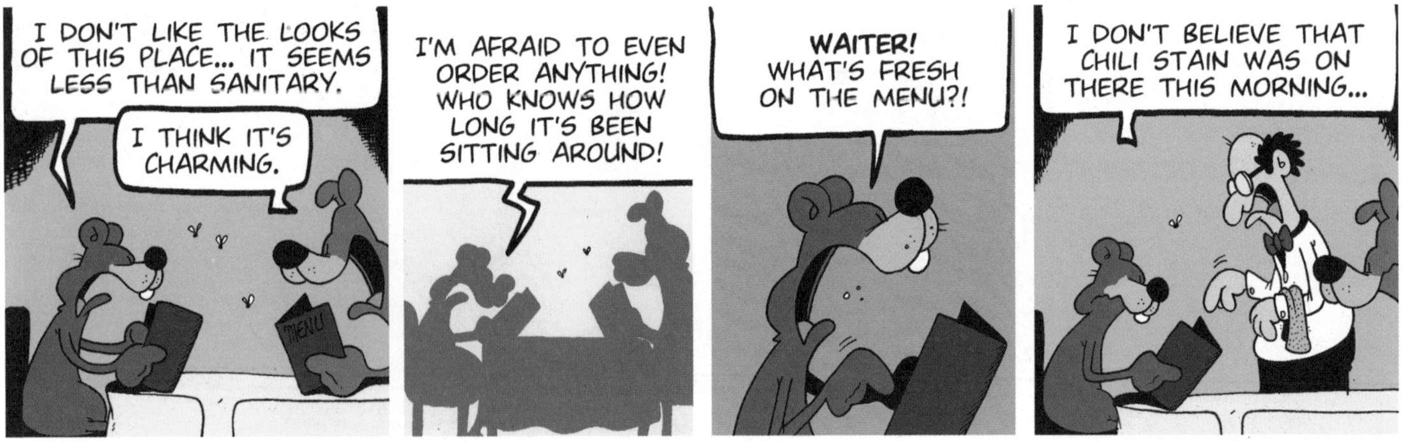
I DON'T LIKE THE LOOKS OF THIS PLACE... IT SEEMS LESS THAN SANITARY.
I THINK IT'S CHARMING.
MENU
I'M AFRAID TO EVEN ORDER ANYTHING! WHO KNOWS HOW LONG IT'S BEEN SITTING AROUND!
WAITER! WHAT'S FRESH ON THE MENU?!
I DON'T BELIEVE THAT CHILI STAIN WAS ON THERE THIS MORNING...

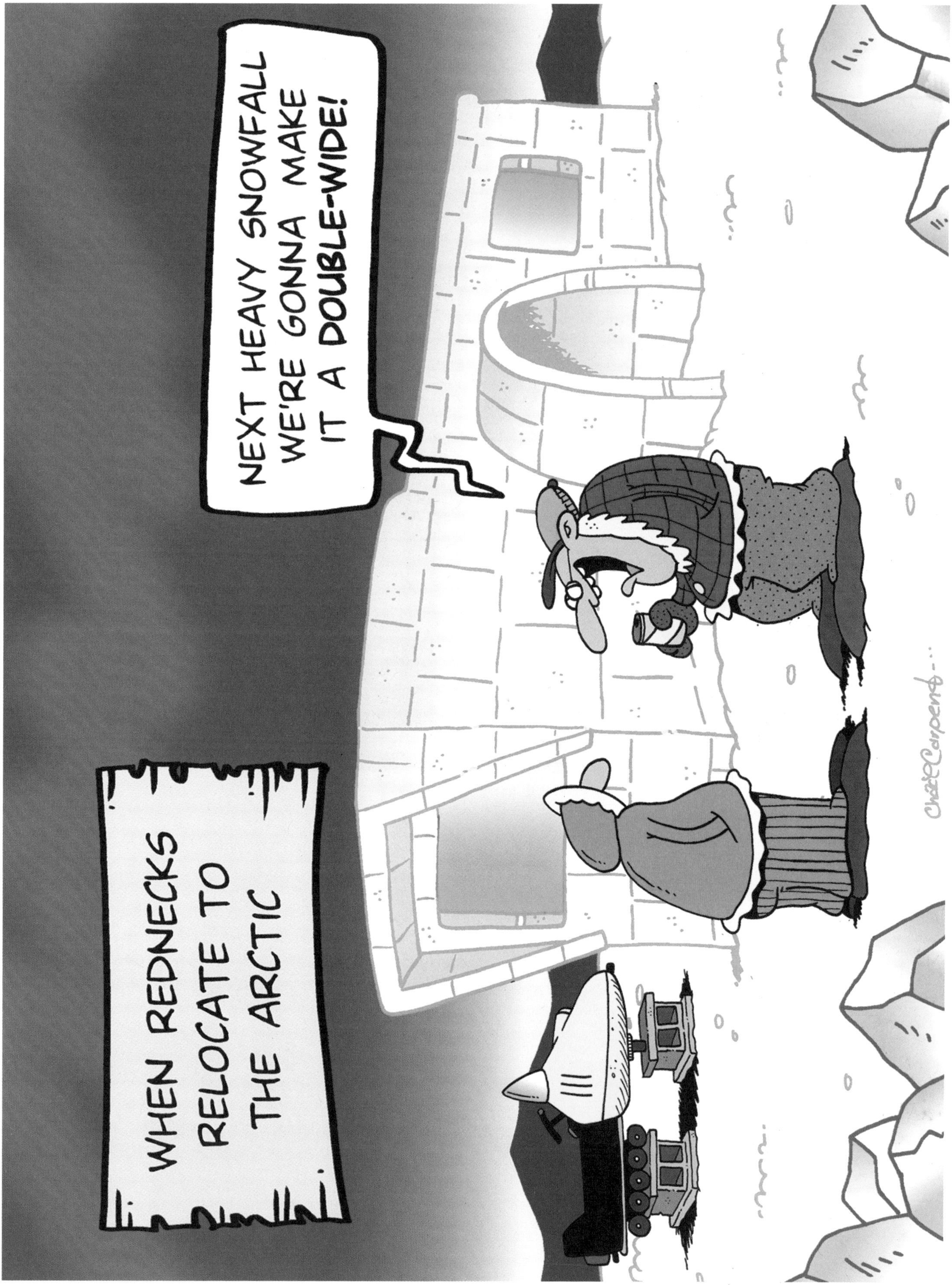
WHEN REDNECKS RELOCATE TO THE ARCTIC
NEXT HEAVY SNOWFALL WE'RE GONNA MAKE IT A DOUBLE-WIDE!

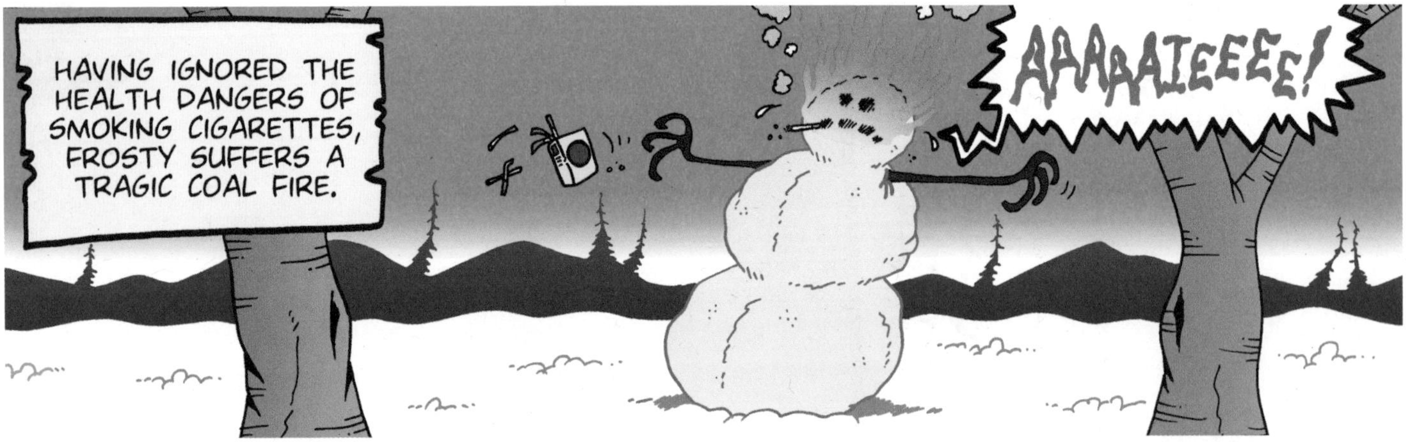
HAVING IGNORED THE HEALTH DANGERS OF SMOKING CIGARETTES, FROSTY SUFFERS A TRAGIC COAL FIRE.
AAAAAAIEEEEE!

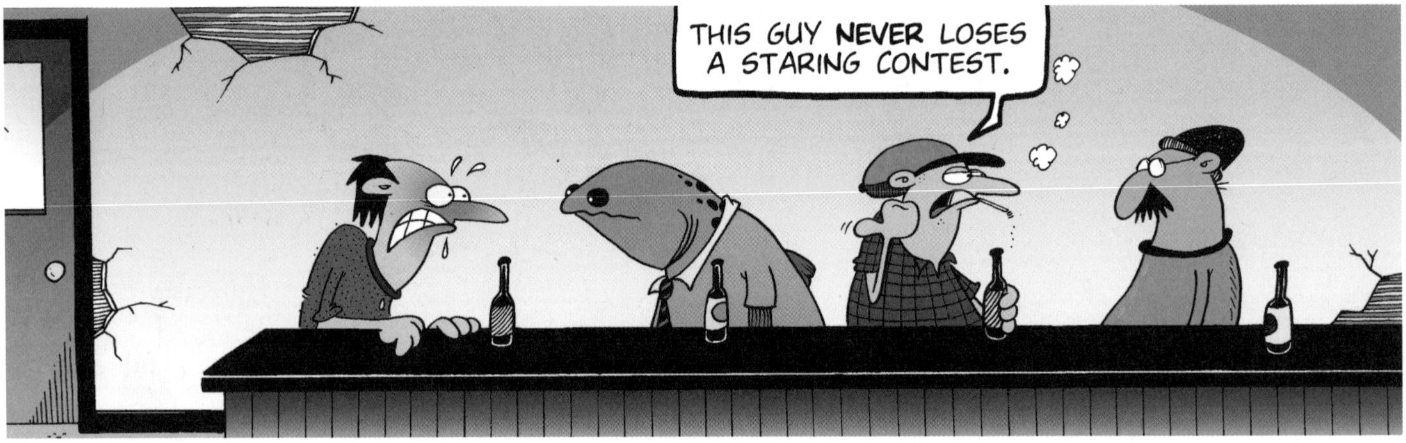
THIS GUY **NEVER** LOSES A STARING CONTEST.

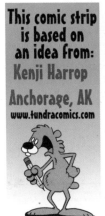

This comic strip is based on an idea from:
Kenji Harrop
Anchorage, AK
www.tundracomics.com

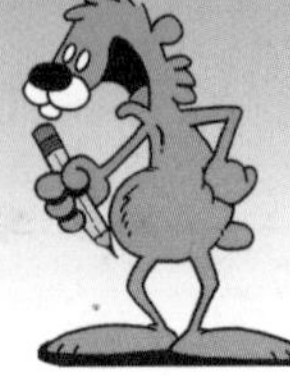

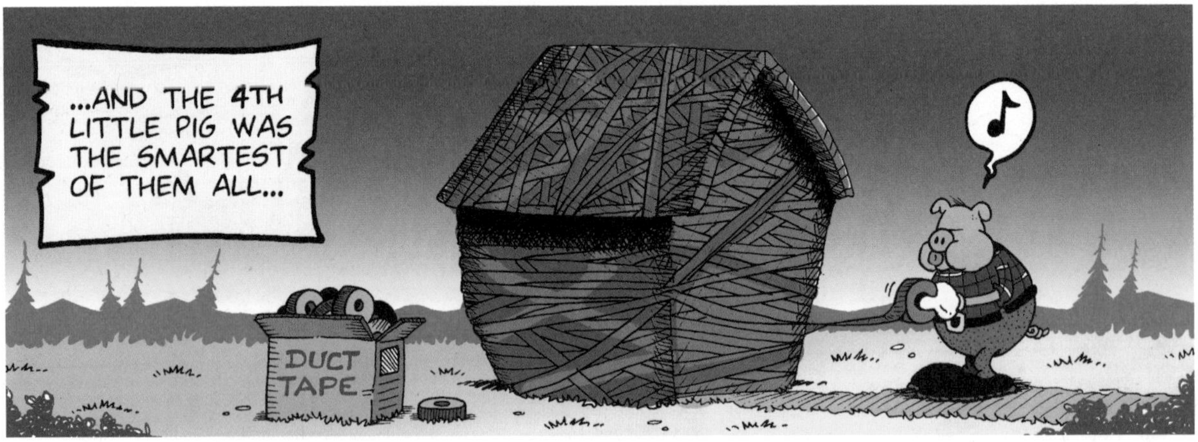
...AND THE 4TH LITTLE PIG WAS THE SMARTEST OF THEM ALL...
DUCT TAPE

This comic strip is based on an idea from:

Teddy Larranaga
Fairbanks, AK
www.tundracomics.com

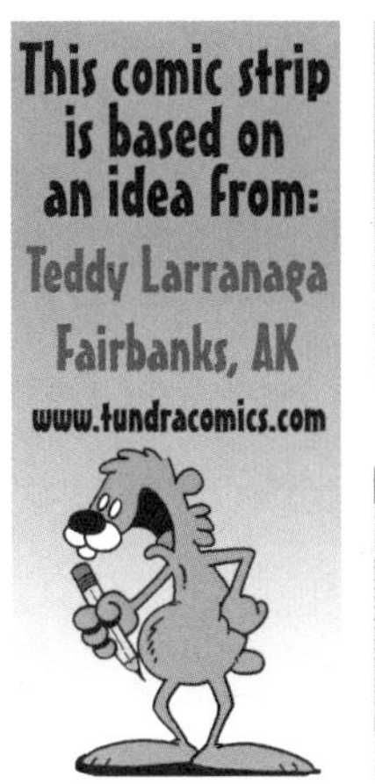

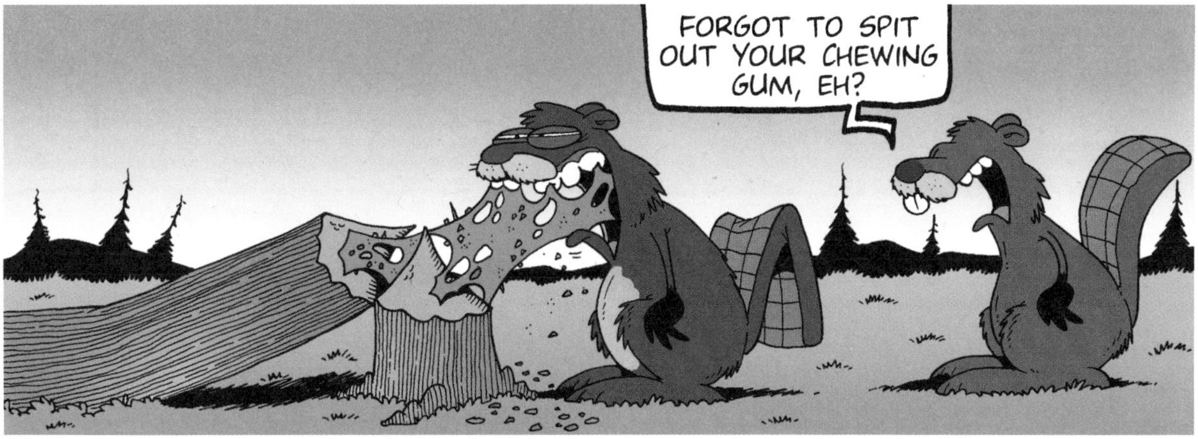
FORGOT TO SPIT OUT YOUR CHEWING GUM, EH?

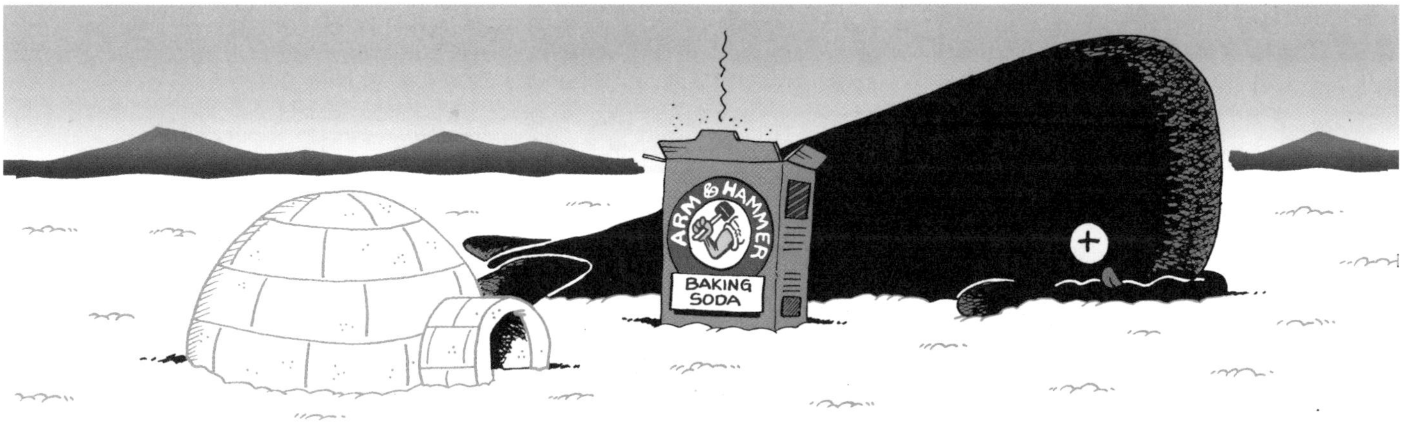
ARM & HAMMER
BAKING SODA

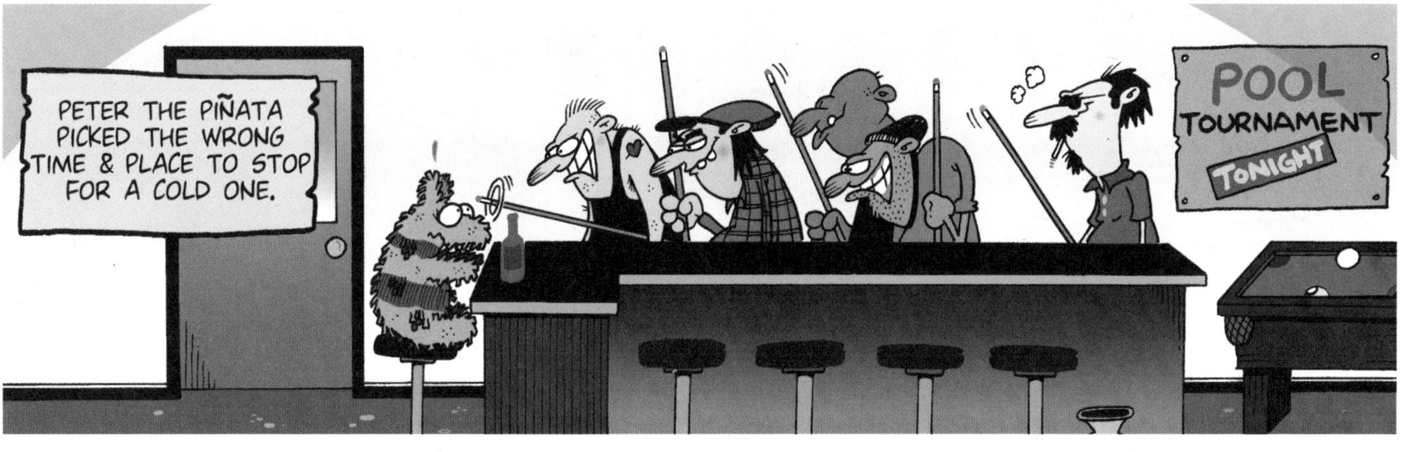
PETER THE PIÑATA PICKED THE WRONG TIME & PLACE TO STOP FOR A COLD ONE.
POOL TOURNAMENT
TONIGHT

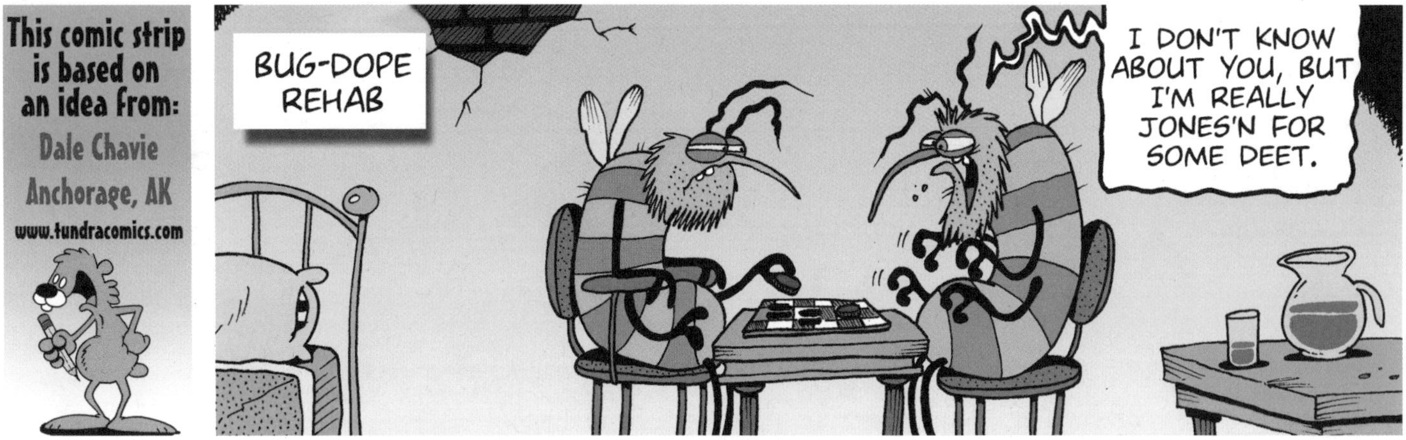
This comic strip is based on an idea from:
Dale Chavie
Anchorage, AK
www.tundracomics.com
BUG-DOPE REHAB
I DON'T KNOW ABOUT YOU, BUT I'M REALLY JONES'N FOR SOME DEET.

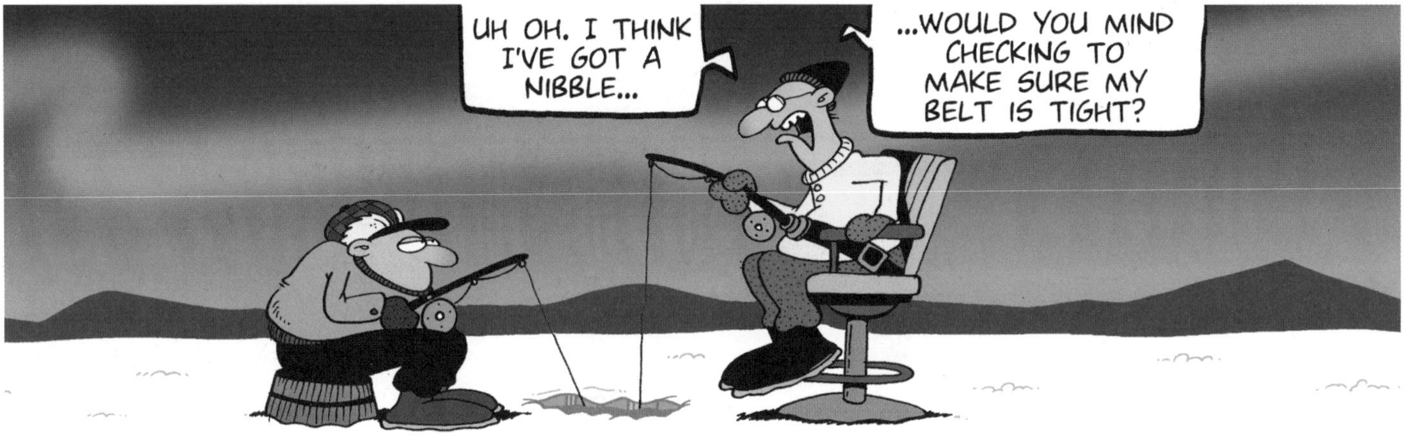
UH OH. I THINK I'VE GOT A NIBBLE...
...WOULD YOU MIND CHECKING TO MAKE SURE MY BELT IS TIGHT?

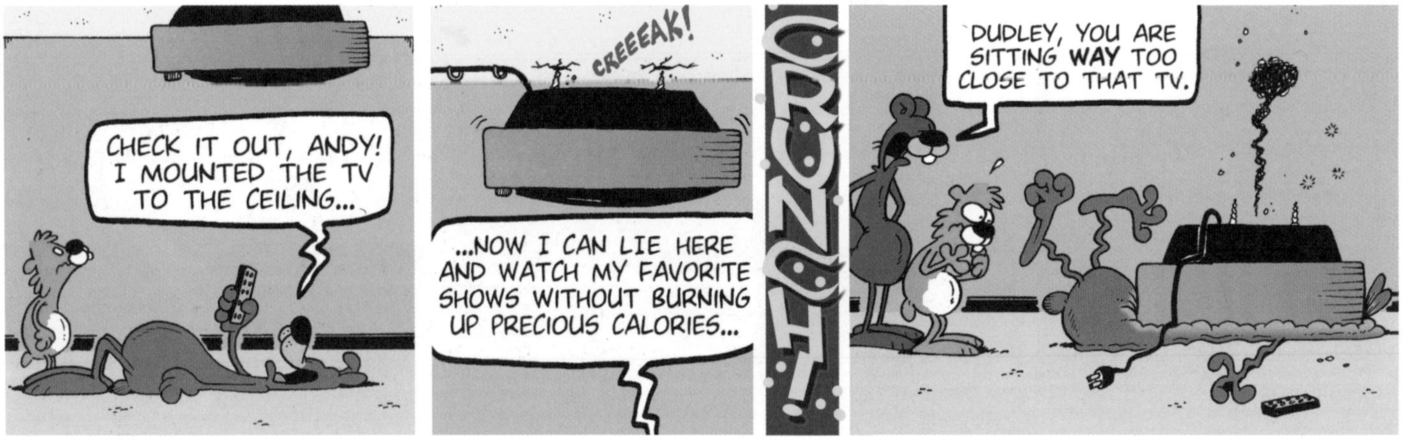
CHECK IT OUT, ANDY! I MOUNTED THE TV TO THE CEILING...
CREEEAK!
...NOW I CAN LIE HERE AND WATCH MY FAVORITE SHOWS WITHOUT BURNING UP PRECIOUS CALORIES...
CRUNCH!
DUDLEY, YOU ARE SITTING WAY TOO CLOSE TO THAT TV.

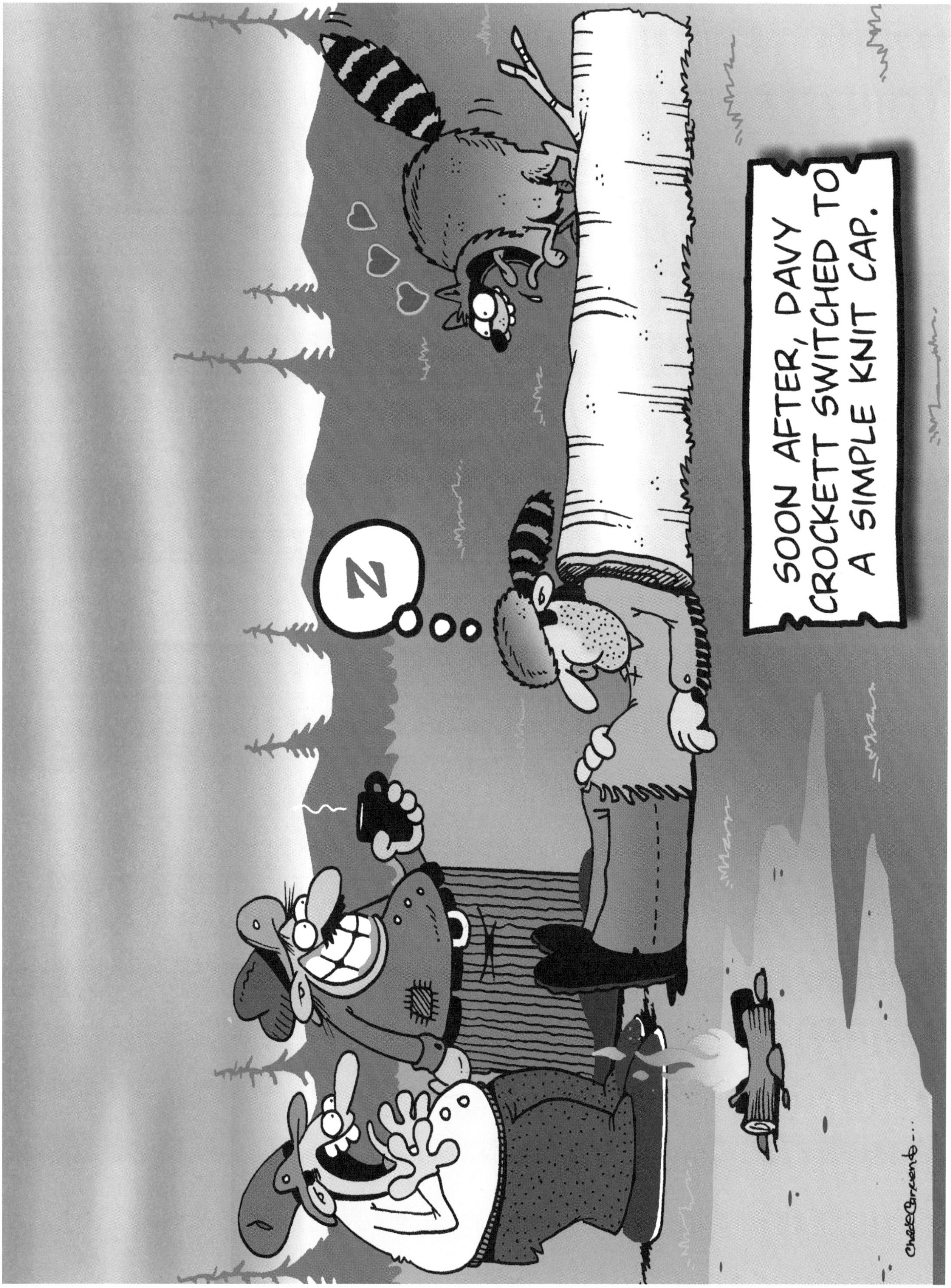
SOON AFTER, DAVY CROCKETT SWITCHED TO A SIMPLE KNIT CAP.
Z

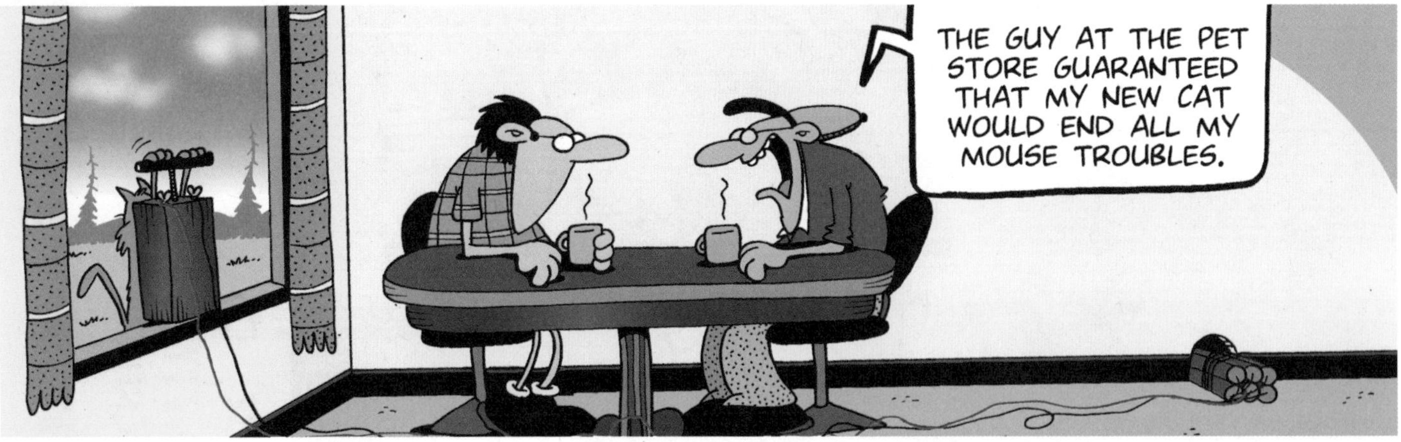
THE GUY AT THE PET STORE GUARANTEED THAT MY NEW CAT WOULD END ALL MY MOUSE TROUBLES.

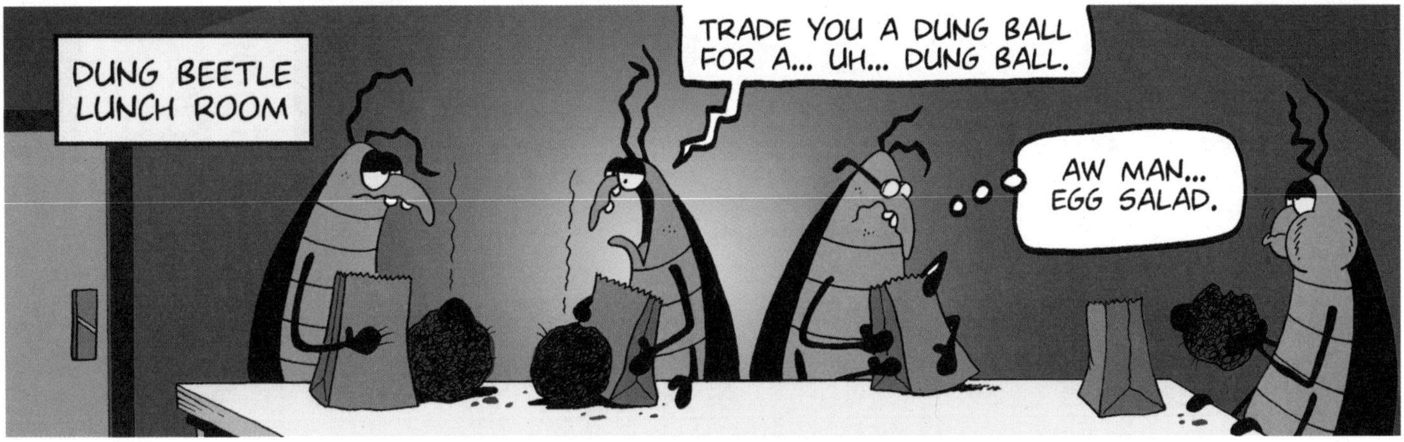
DUNG BEETLE LUNCH ROOM
TRADE YOU A DUNG BALL FOR A... UH... DUNG BALL.
AW MAN... EGG SALAD.

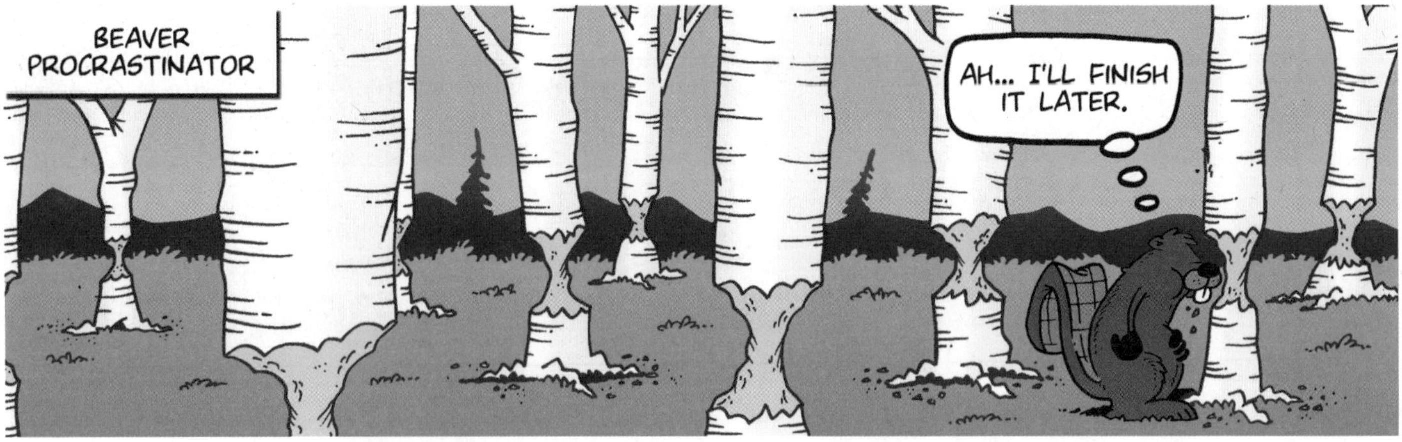
BEAVER PROCRASTINATOR
AH... I'LL FINISH IT LATER.

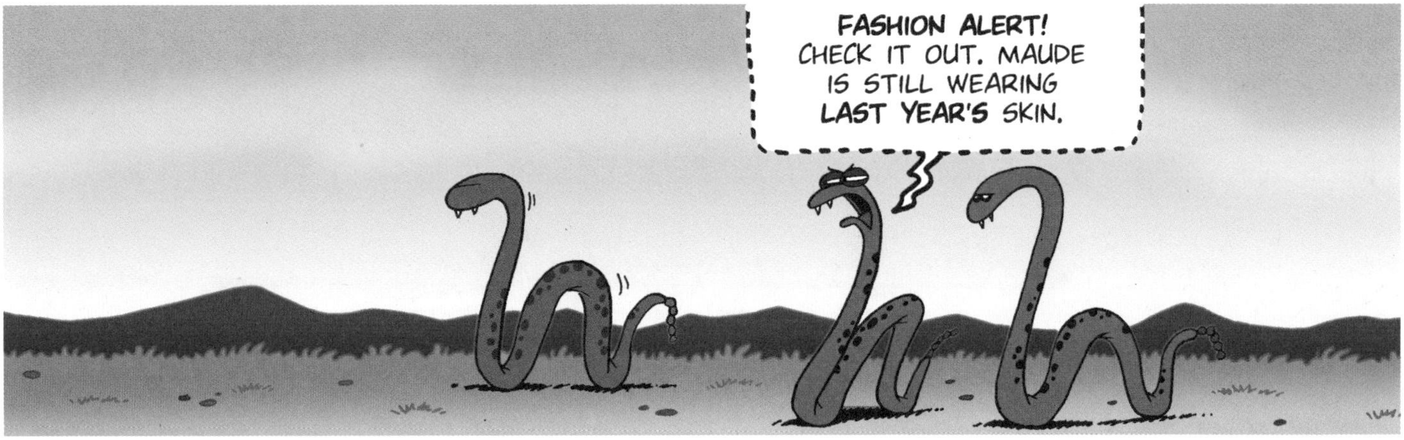
FASHION ALERT! CHECK IT OUT. MAUDE IS STILL WEARING LAST YEAR'S SKIN.

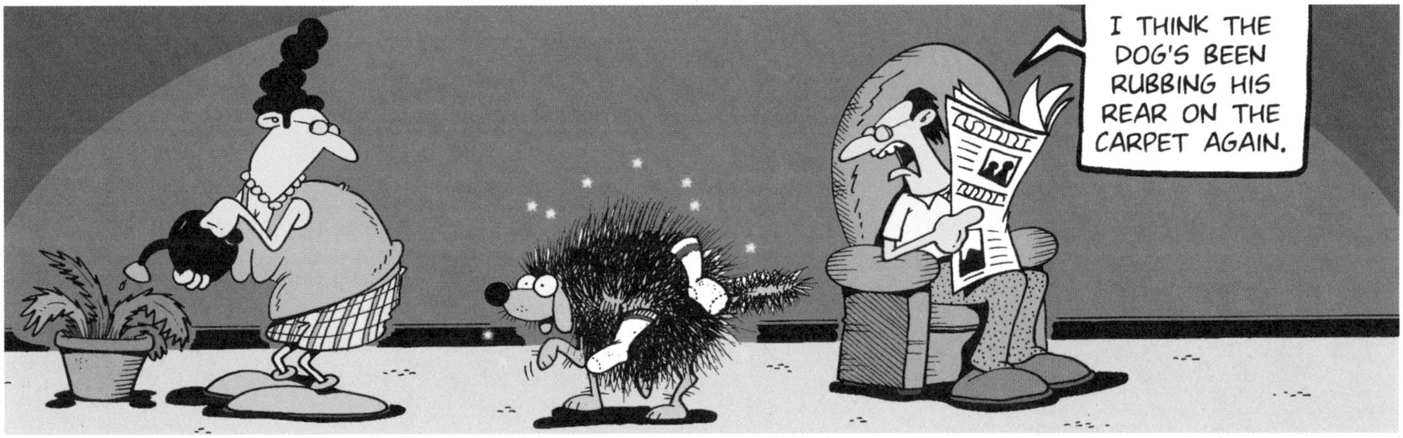
I THINK THE DOG'S BEEN RUBBING HIS REAR ON THE CARPET AGAIN.

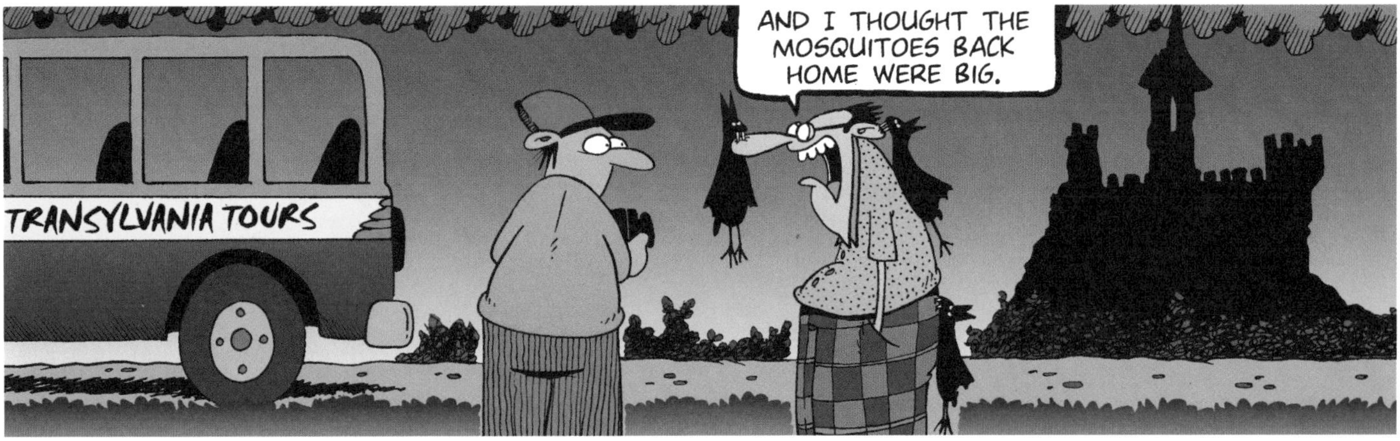
TRANSYLVANIA TOURS
AND I THOUGHT THE MOSQUITOES BACK HOME WERE BIG.

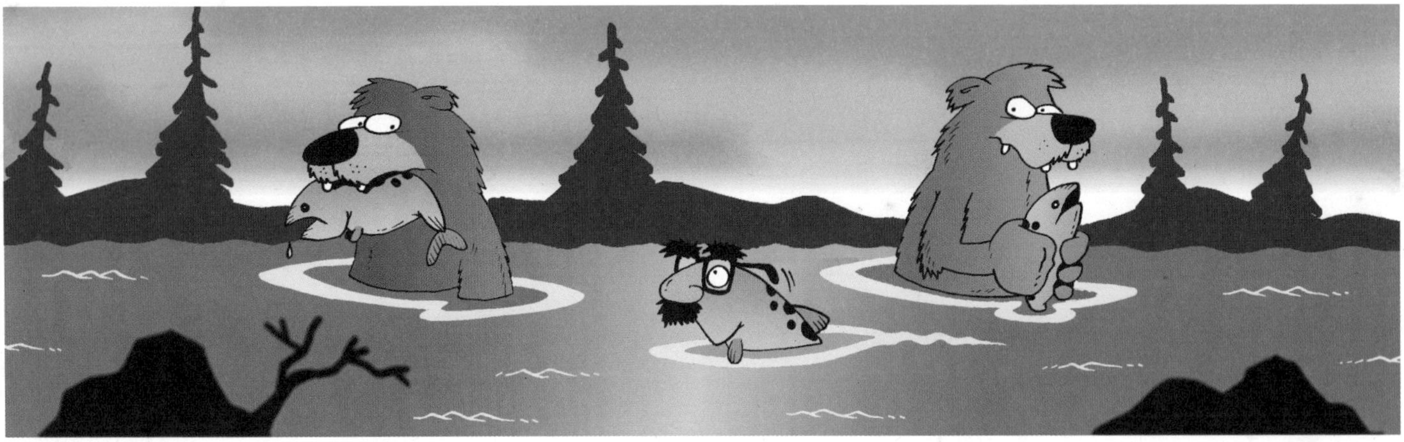

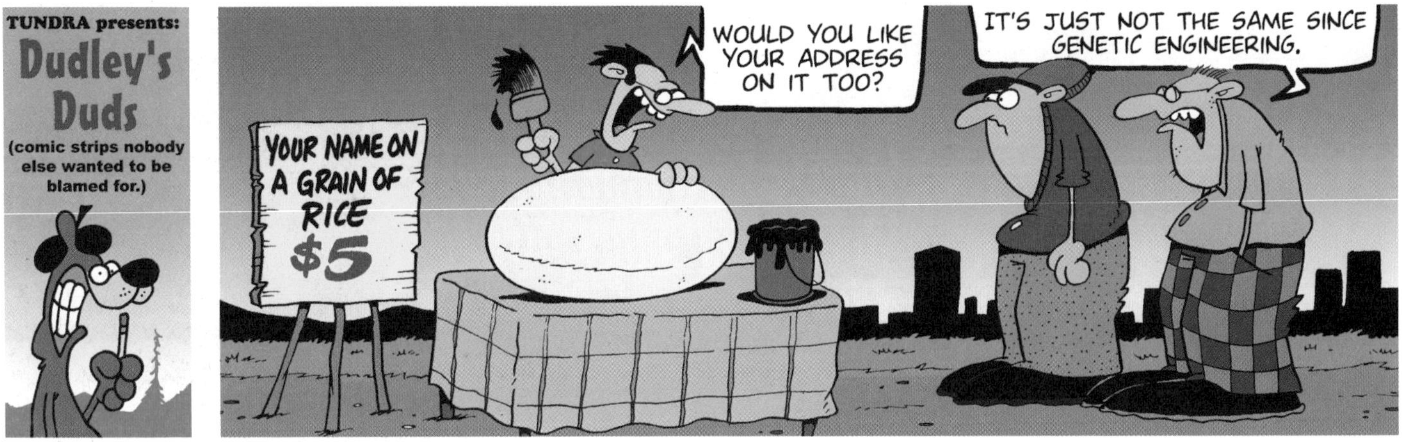
TUNDRA presents:
Dudley's Duds
(comic strips nobody else wanted to be blamed for.)
YOUR NAME ON A GRAIN OF RICE $5
WOULD YOU LIKE YOUR ADDRESS ON IT TOO?
IT'S JUST NOT THE SAME SINCE GENETIC ENGINEERING.

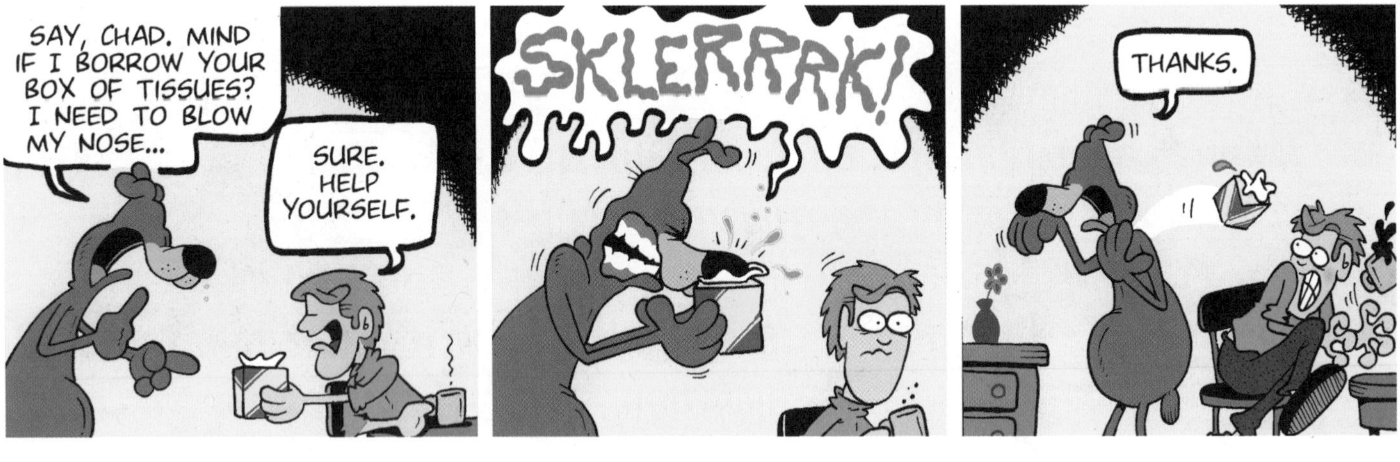
SAY, CHAD. MIND IF I BORROW YOUR BOX OF TISSUES? I NEED TO BLOW MY NOSE...
SURE. HELP YOURSELF.
SKLERRRK!
THANKS.

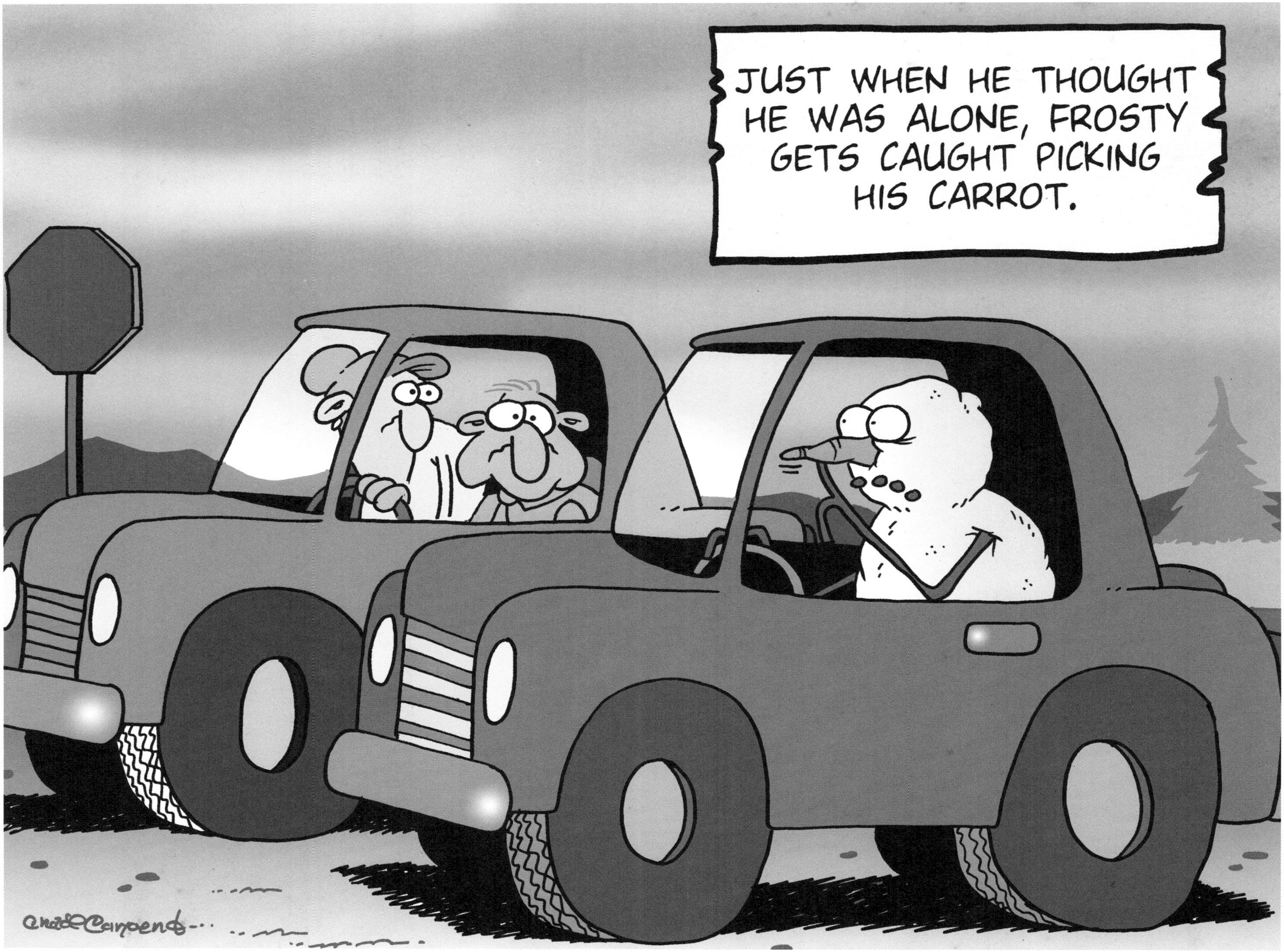
JUST WHEN HE THOUGHT HE WAS ALONE, FROSTY GETS CAUGHT PICKING HIS CARROT.

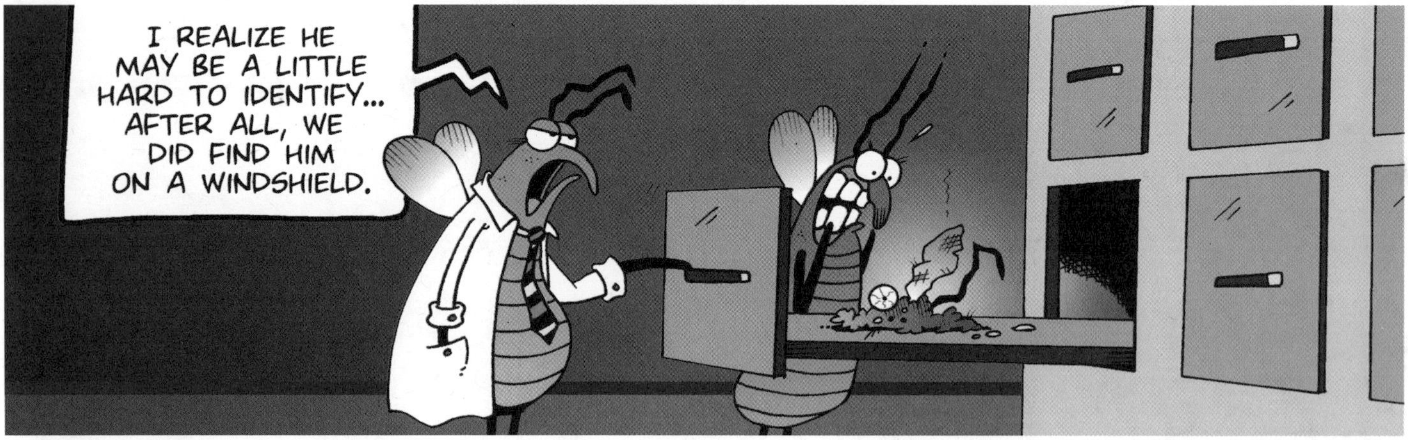
I REALIZE HE MAY BE A LITTLE HARD TO IDENTIFY... AFTER ALL, WE DID FIND HIM ON A WINDSHIELD.

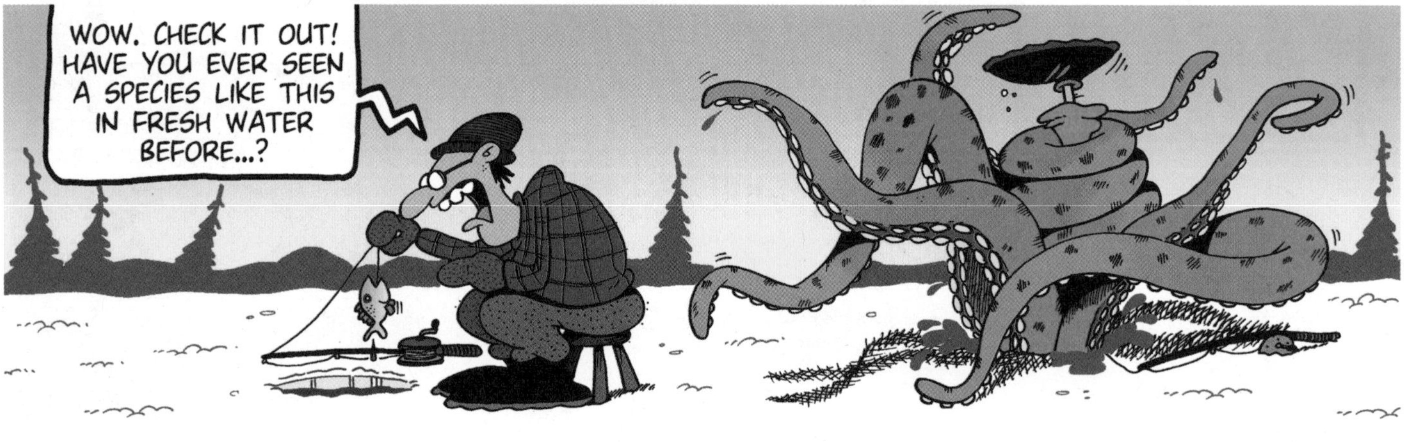
WOW. CHECK IT OUT! HAVE YOU EVER SEEN A SPECIES LIKE THIS IN FRESH WATER BEFORE...?

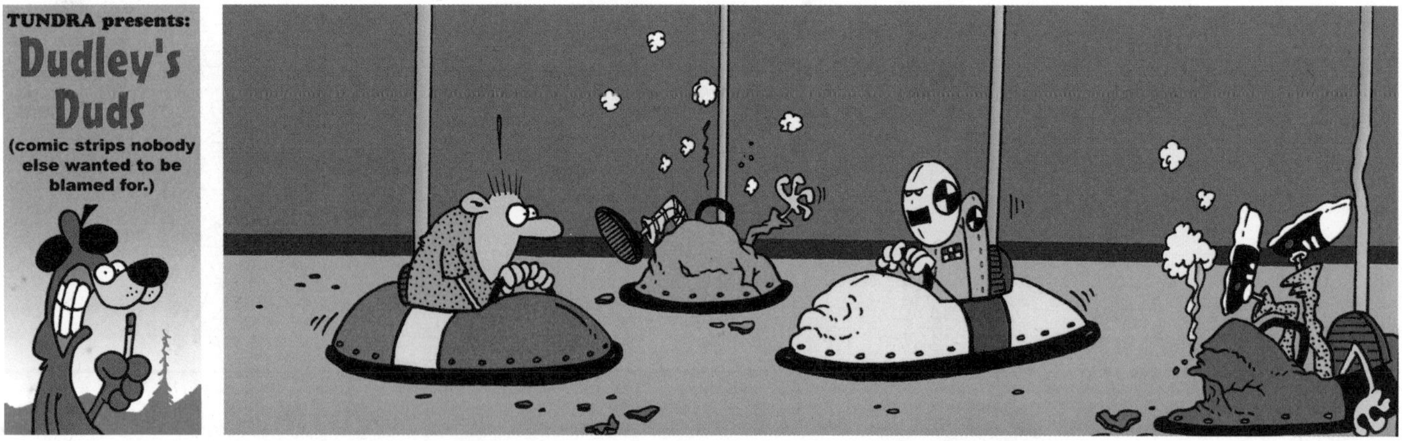
TUNDRA presents:
Dudley's Duds
(comic strips nobody else wanted to be blamed for.)

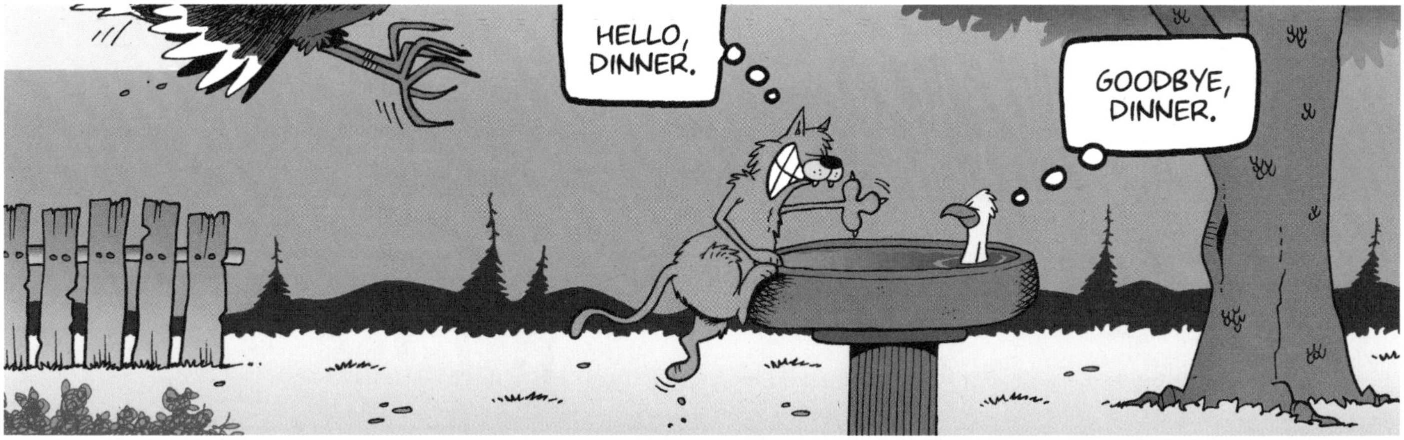
HELLO, DINNER.
GOODBYE, DINNER.

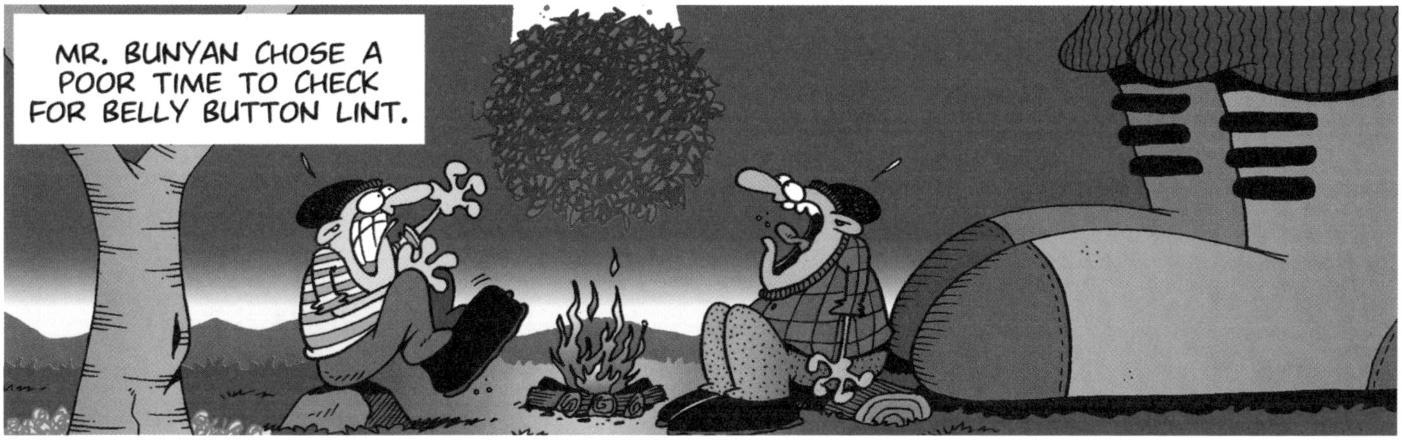
MR. BUNYAN CHOSE A POOR TIME TO CHECK FOR BELLY BUTTON LINT.

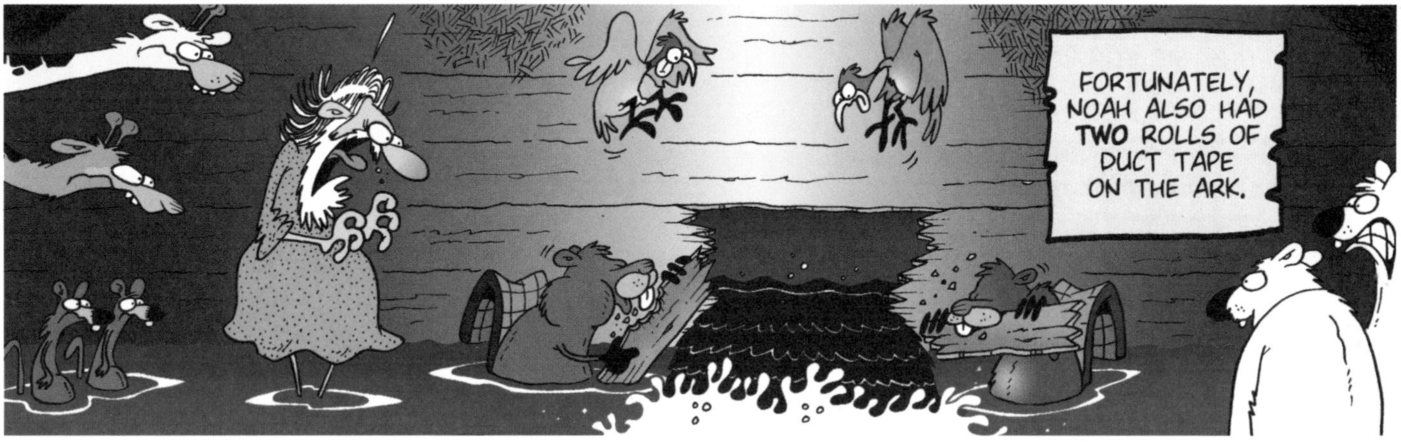
FORTUNATELY, NOAH ALSO HAD **TWO** ROLLS OF DUCT TAPE ON THE ARK.

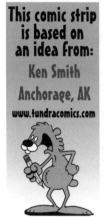

This comic strip is based on an idea from:
Ken Smith
Anchorage, AK
www.tundracomics.com

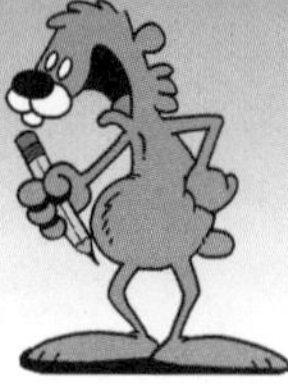

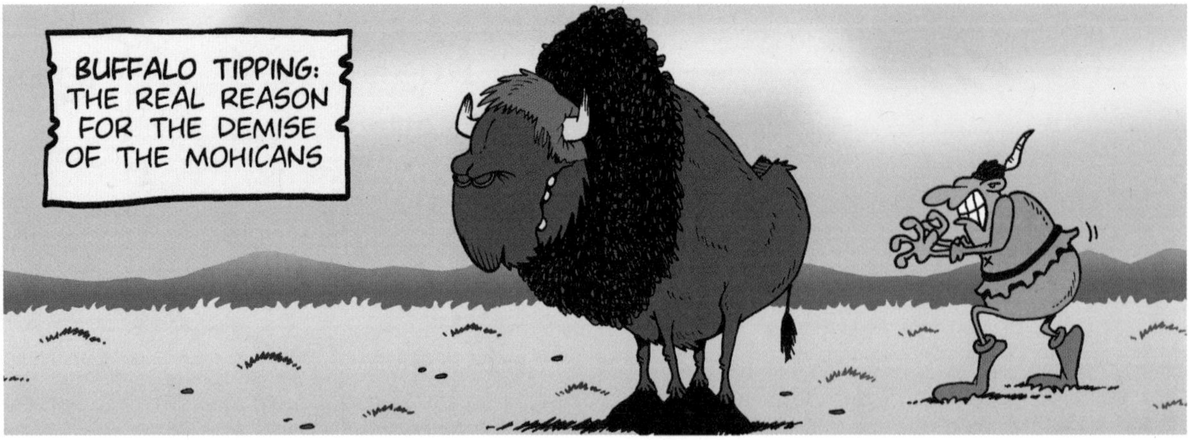
BUFFALO TIPPING: THE REAL REASON FOR THE DEMISE OF THE MOHICANS

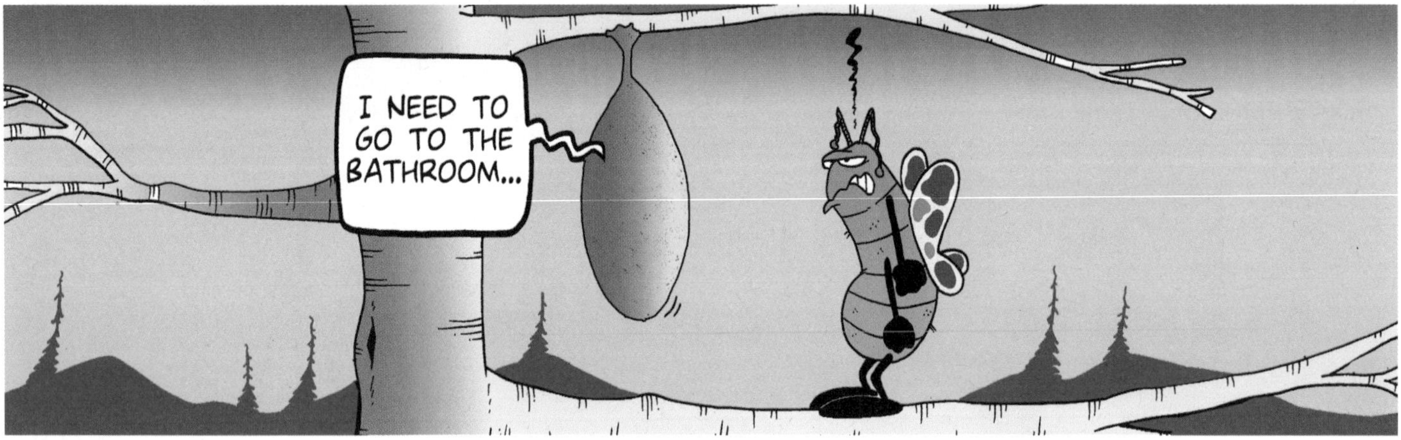
I NEED TO GO TO THE BATHROOM...

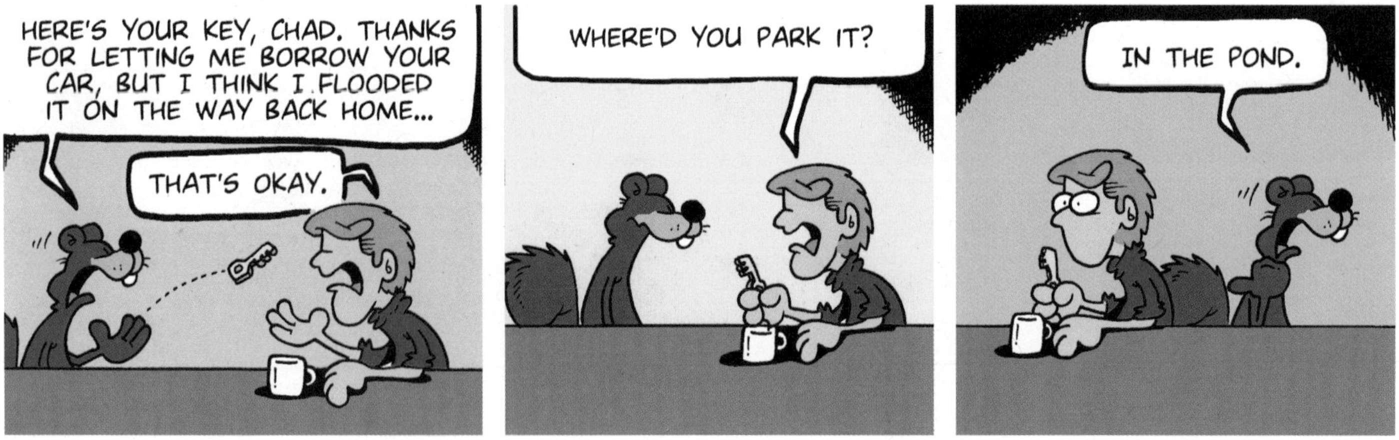
HERE'S YOUR KEY, CHAD. THANKS FOR LETTING ME BORROW YOUR CAR, BUT I THINK I FLOODED IT ON THE WAY BACK HOME...
THAT'S OKAY.
WHERE'D YOU PARK IT?
IN THE POND.

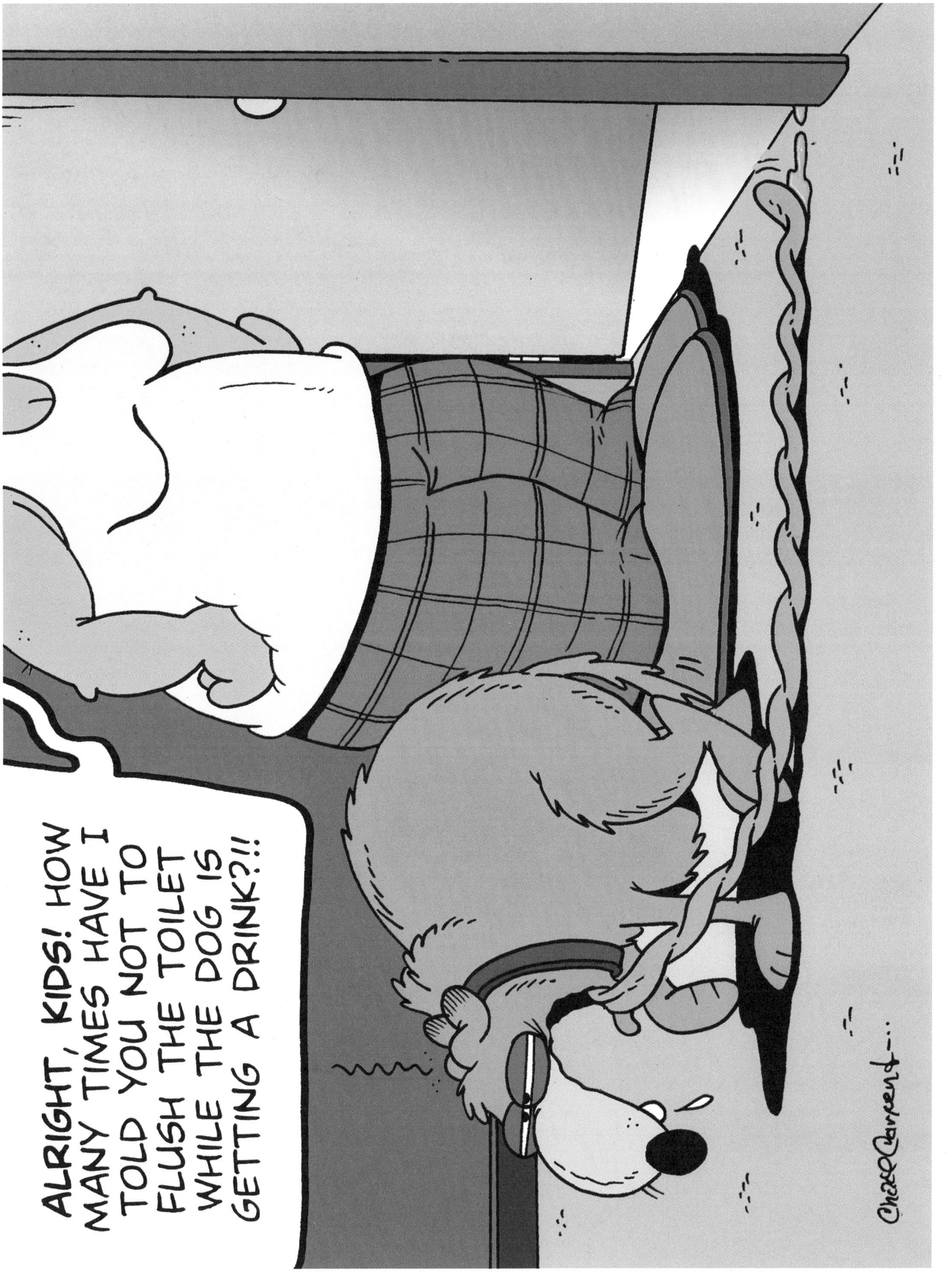
ALRIGHT, KIDS! HOW MANY TIMES HAVE I TOLD YOU NOT TO FLUSH THE TOILET WHILE THE DOG IS GETTING A DRINK?!!
Chad Carpenter

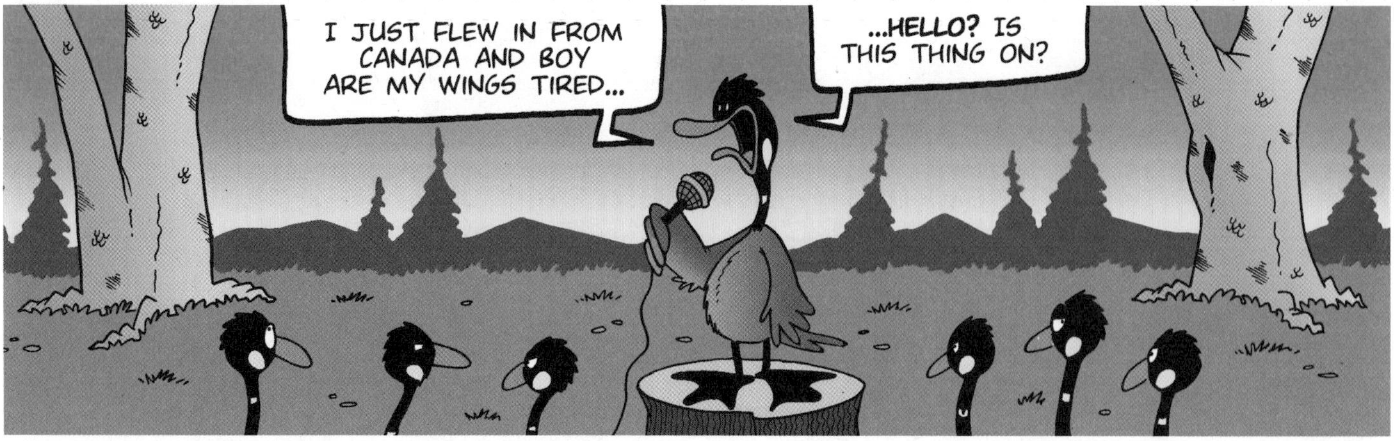
I JUST FLEW IN FROM CANADA AND BOY ARE MY WINGS TIRED...
...HELLO? IS THIS THING ON?

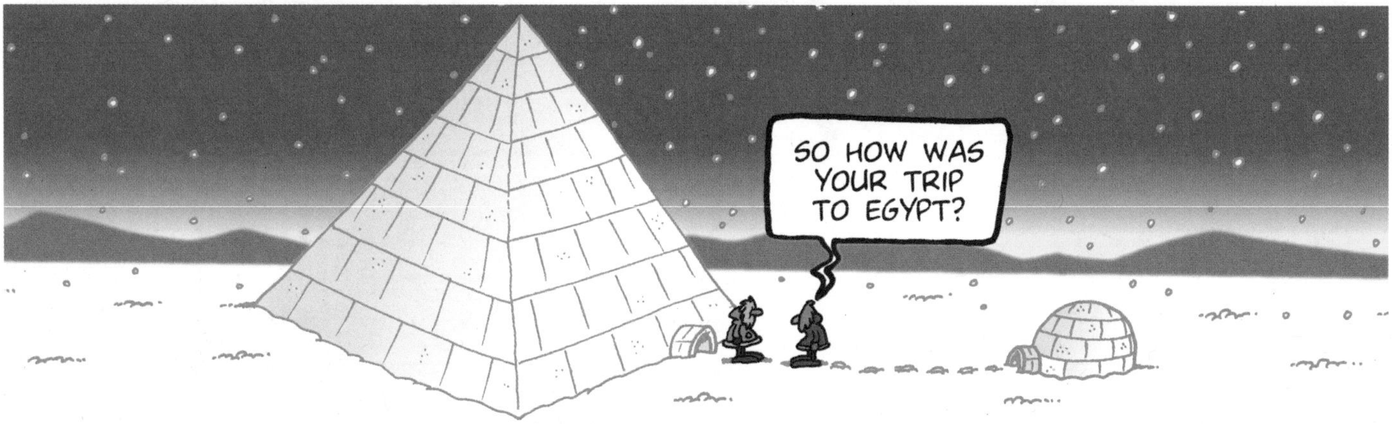
SO HOW WAS YOUR TRIP TO EGYPT?

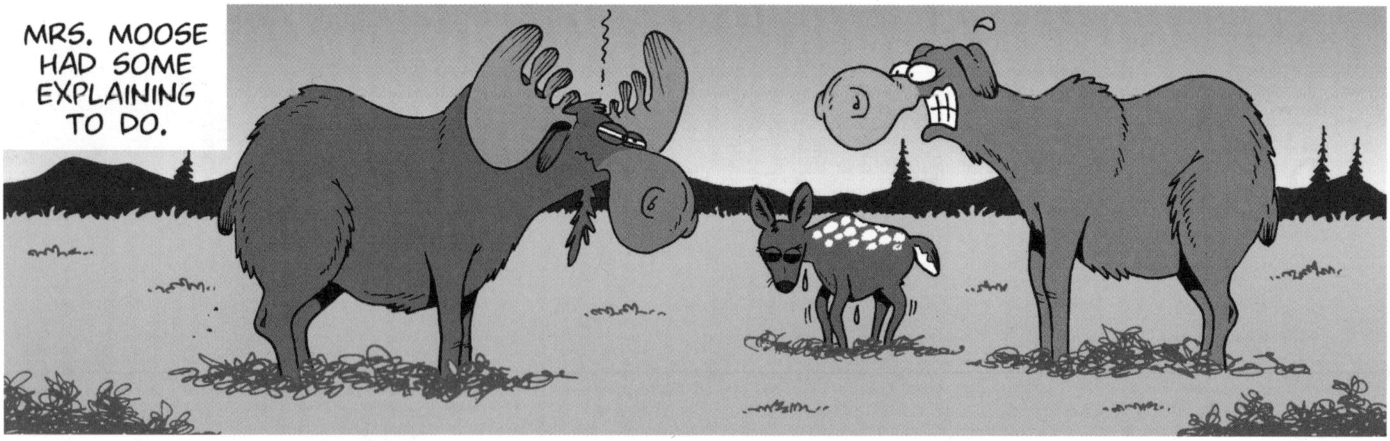
MRS. MOOSE HAD SOME EXPLAINING TO DO.

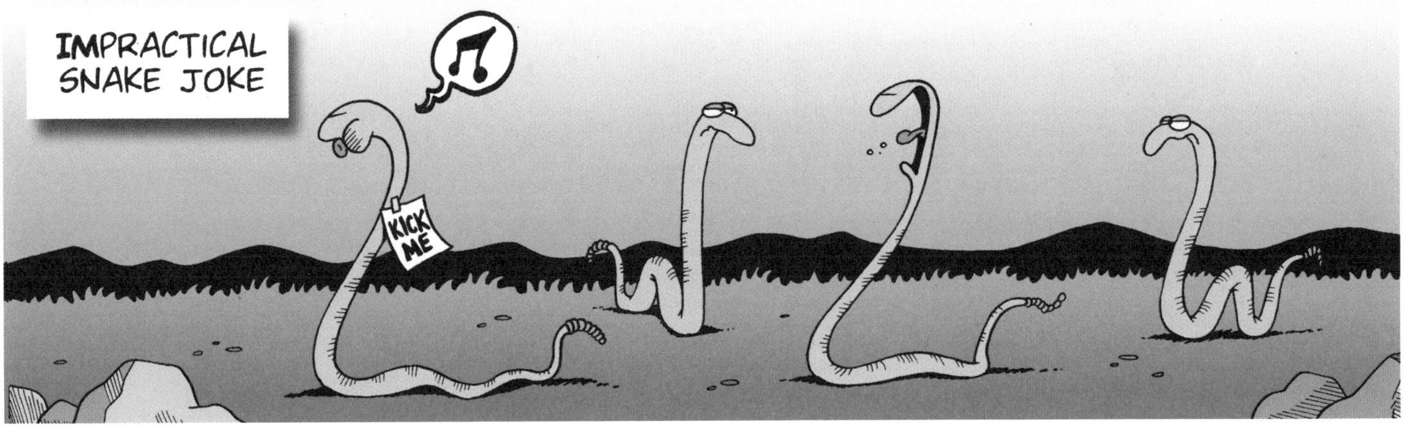
IMPRACTICAL SNAKE JOKE
KICK ME

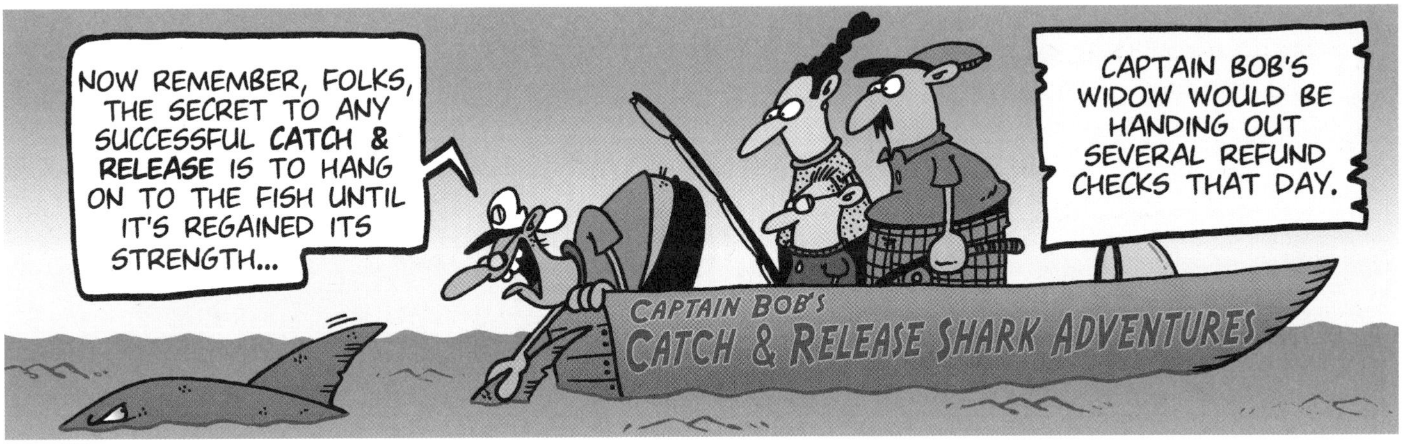
NOW REMEMBER, FOLKS, THE SECRET TO ANY SUCCESSFUL CATCH & RELEASE IS TO HANG ON TO THE FISH UNTIL IT'S REGAINED ITS STRENGTH...
CAPTAIN BOB'S WIDOW WOULD BE HANDING OUT SEVERAL REFUND CHECKS THAT DAY.
CAPTAIN BOB'S CATCH & RELEASE SHARK ADVENTURES

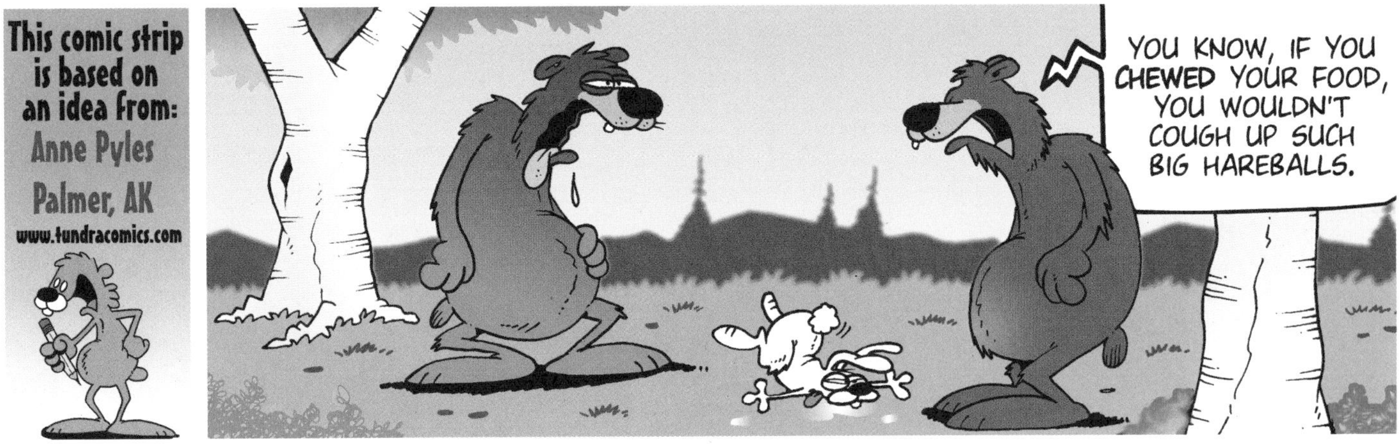
This comic strip is based on an idea from: Anne Pyles Palmer, AK
www.tundracomics.com
YOU KNOW, IF YOU CHEWED YOUR FOOD, YOU WOULDN'T COUGH UP SUCH BIG HAREBALLS.

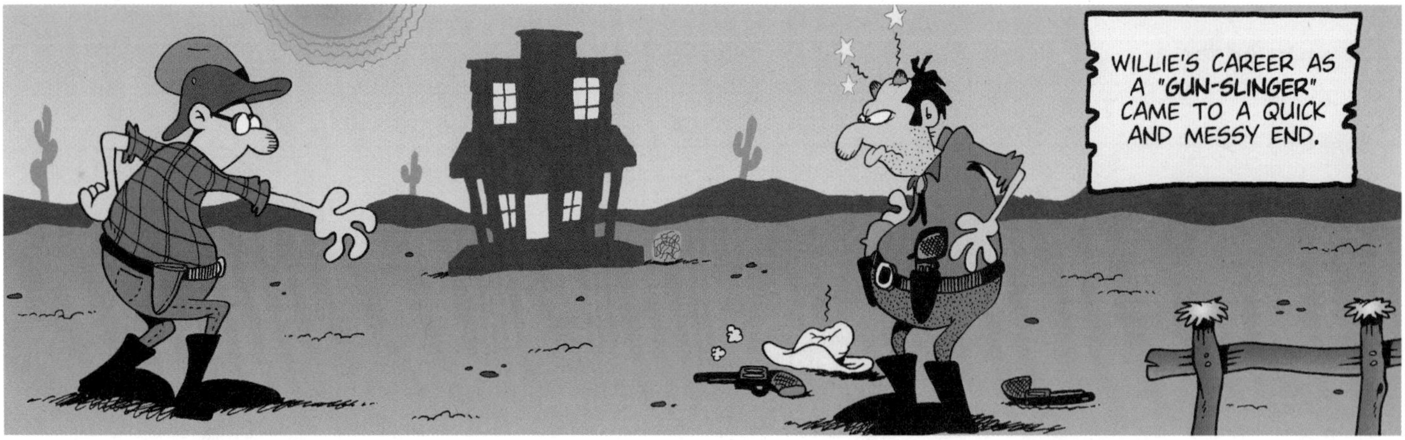
WILLIE'S CAREER AS A "GUN-SLINGER" CAME TO A QUICK AND MESSY END.

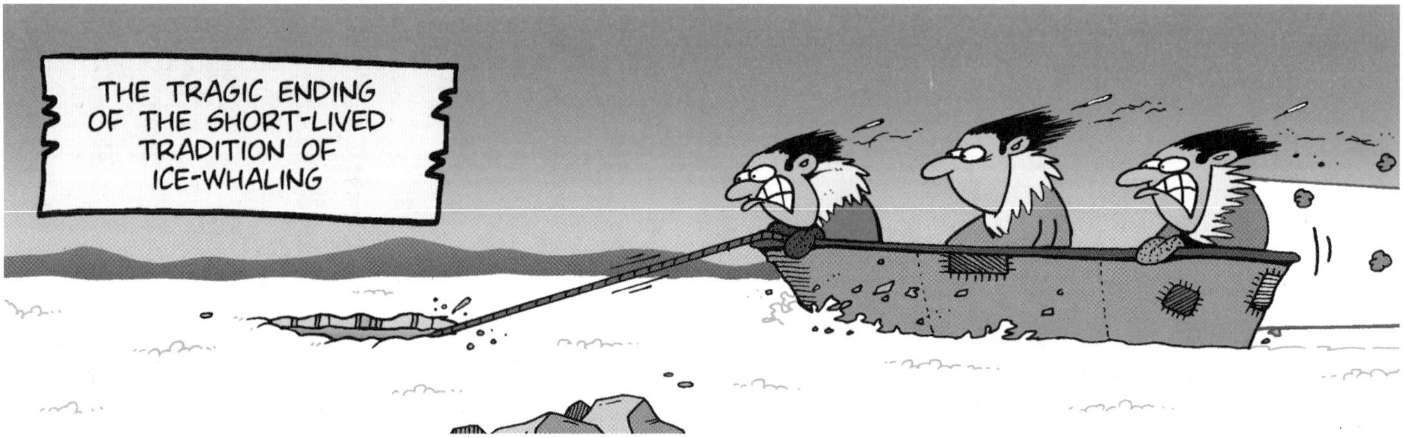
THE TRAGIC ENDING OF THE SHORT-LIVED TRADITION OF ICE-WHALING

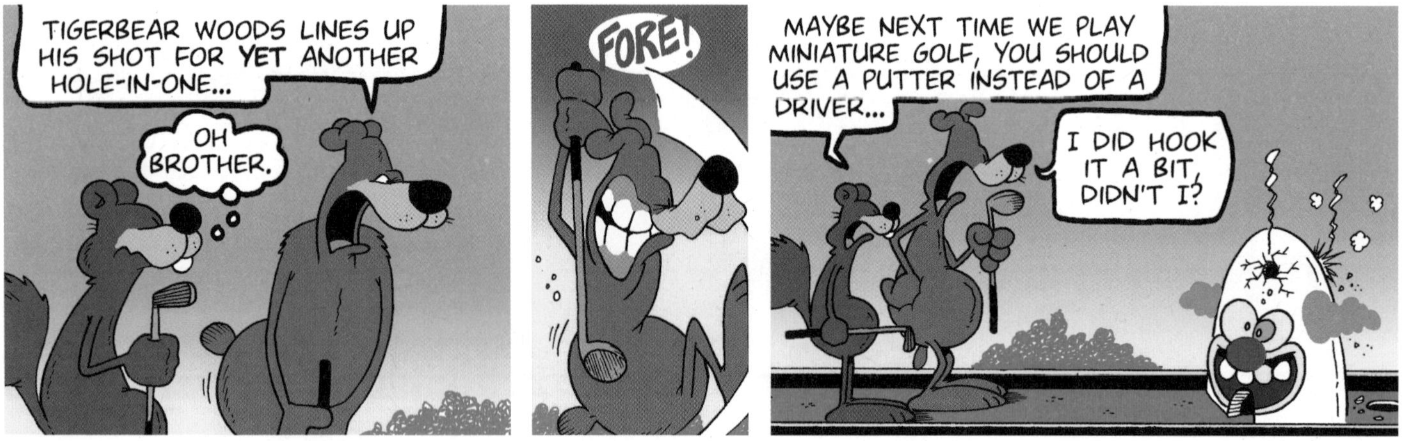
TIGERBEAR WOODS LINES UP HIS SHOT FOR YET ANOTHER HOLE-IN-ONE...
OH BROTHER.
FORE!
MAYBE NEXT TIME WE PLAY MINIATURE GOLF, YOU SHOULD USE A PUTTER INSTEAD OF A DRIVER...
I DID HOOK IT A BIT, DIDN'T I?

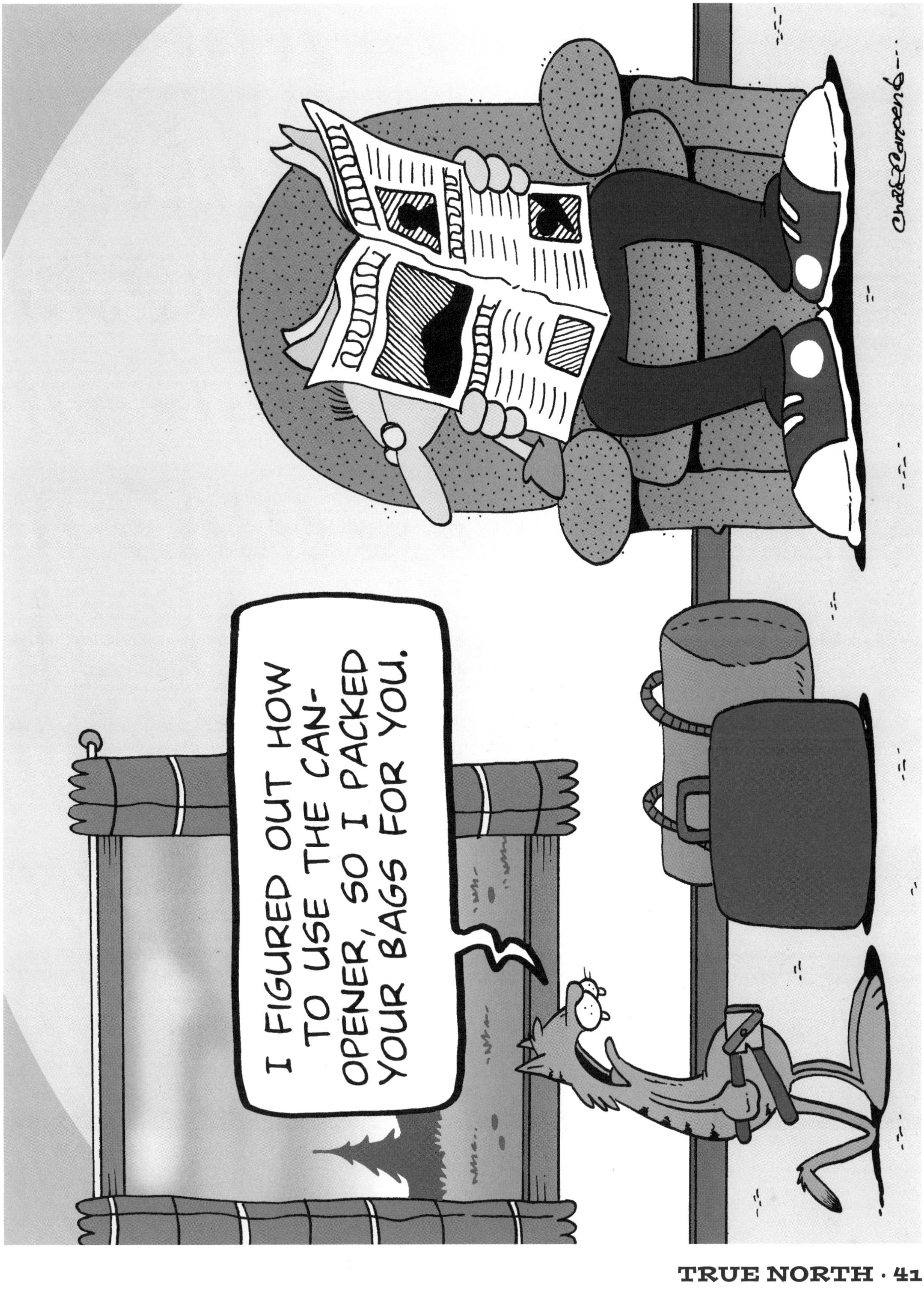
I FIGURED OUT HOW TO USE THE CAN-OPENER, SO I PACKED YOUR BAGS FOR YOU.

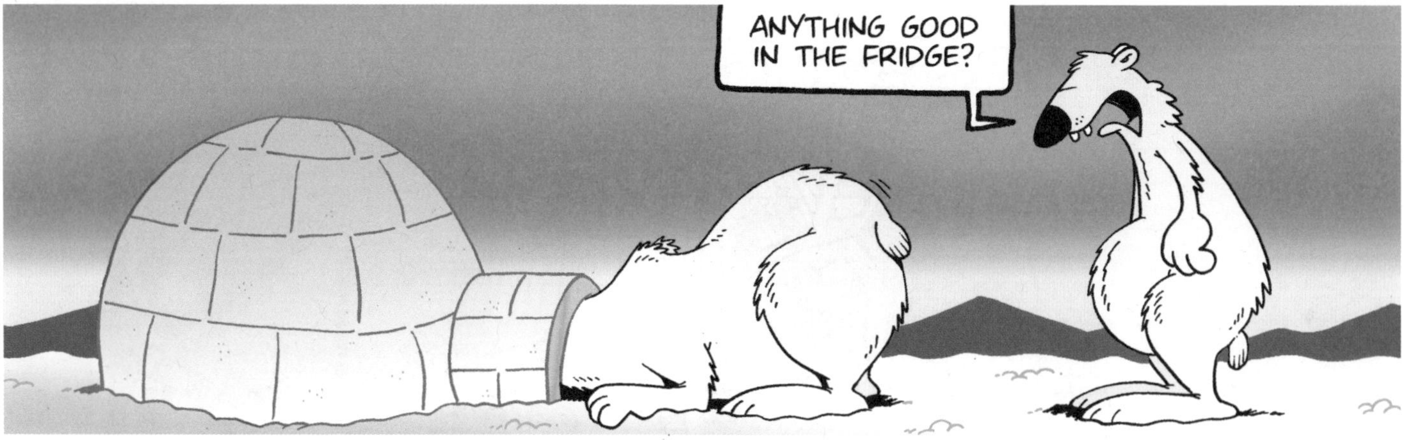
ANYTHING GOOD IN THE FRIDGE?

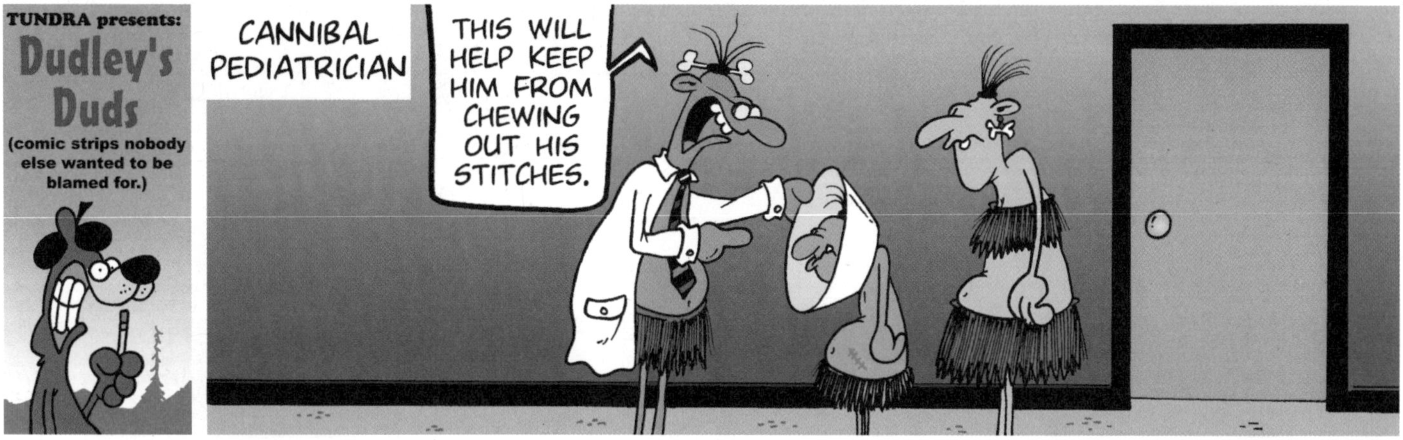
TUNDRA presents:
Dudley's Duds
(comic strips nobody else wanted to be blamed for.)
CANNIBAL PEDIATRICIAN
THIS WILL HELP KEEP HIM FROM CHEWING OUT HIS STITCHES.

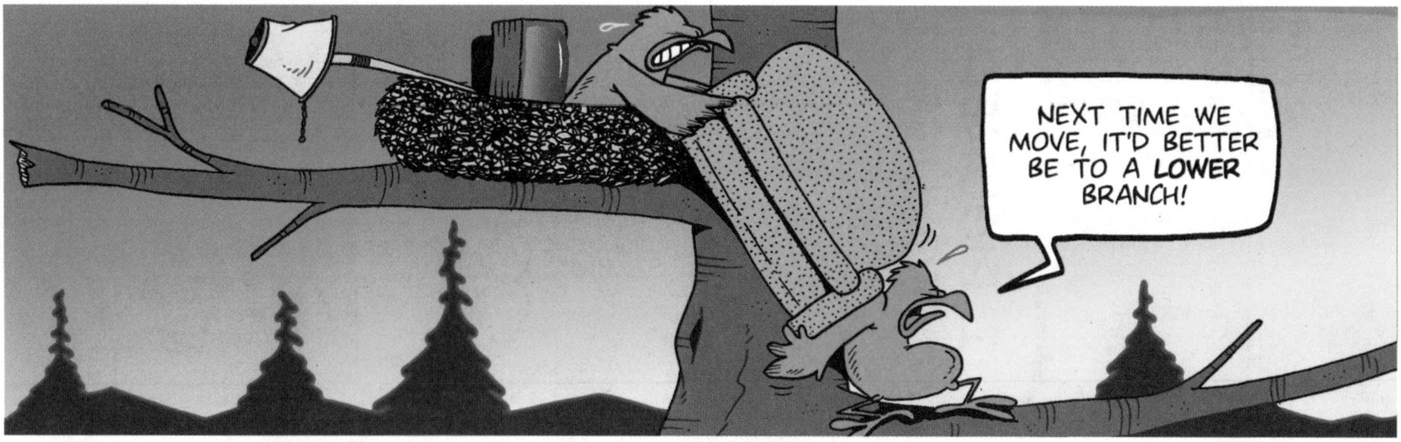
NEXT TIME WE MOVE, IT'D BETTER BE TO A LOWER BRANCH!

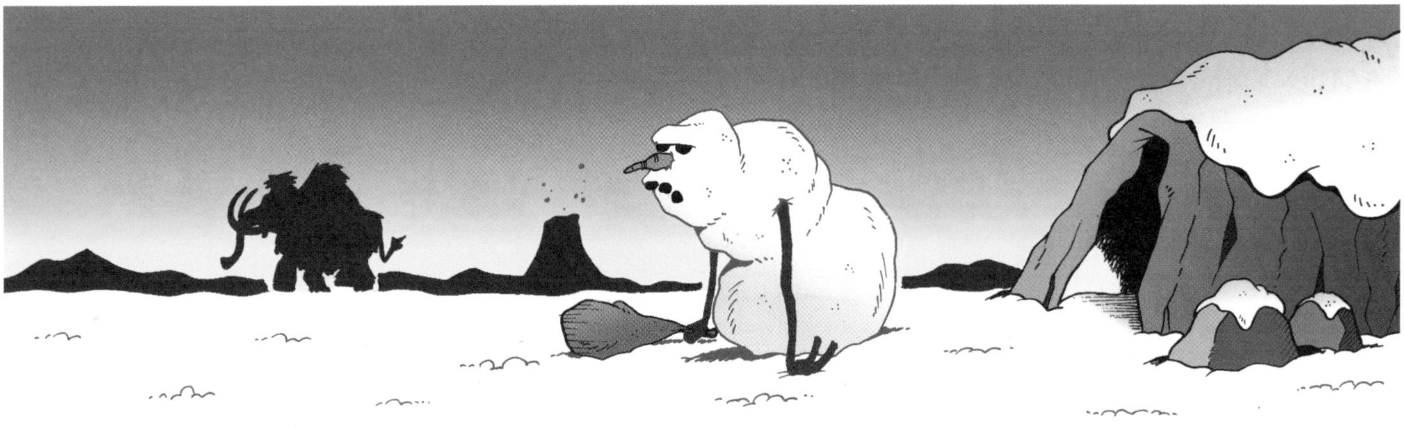

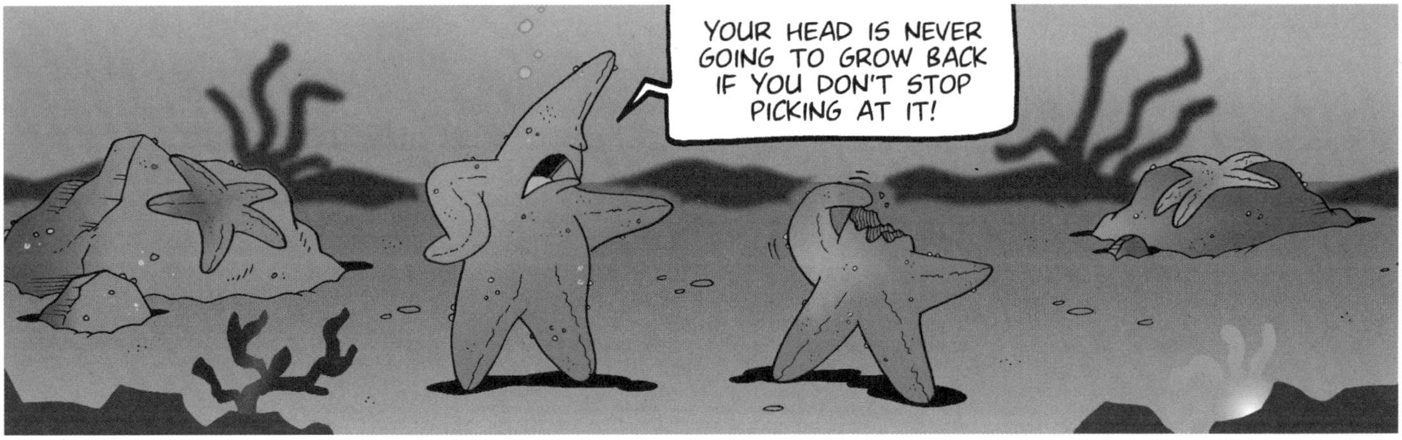
YOUR HEAD IS NEVER GOING TO GROW BACK IF YOU DON'T STOP PICKING AT IT!

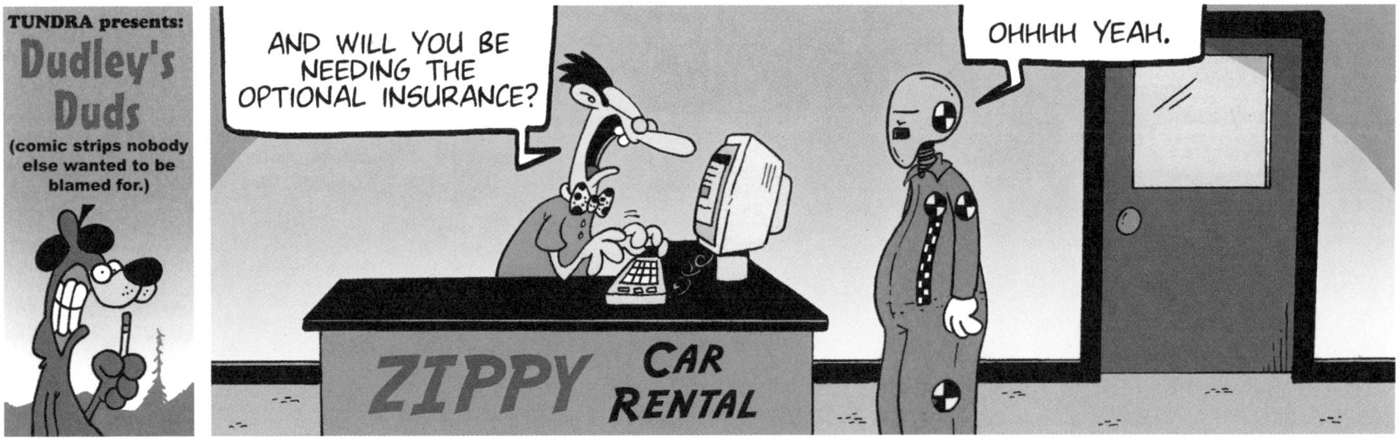
TUNDRA presents:
Dudley's Duds
(comic strips nobody else wanted to be blamed for.)
AND WILL YOU BE NEEDING THE OPTIONAL INSURANCE?
OHHHH YEAH.
ZIPPY CAR RENTAL

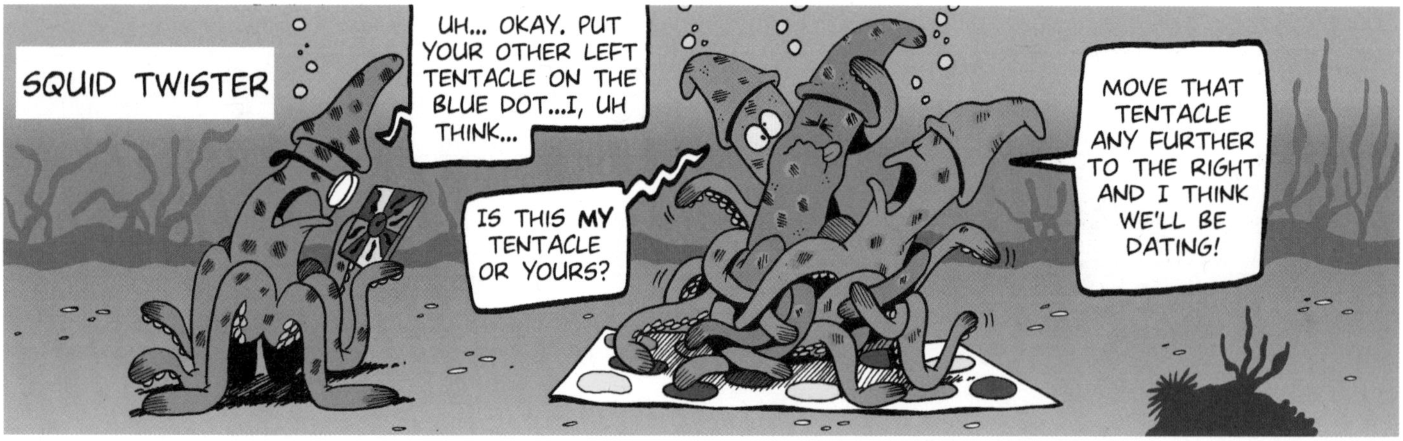
SQUID TWISTER
UH... OKAY. PUT YOUR OTHER LEFT TENTACLE ON THE BLUE DOT...I, UH THINK...
IS THIS MY TENTACLE OR YOURS?
MOVE THAT TENTACLE ANY FURTHER TO THE RIGHT AND I THINK WE'LL BE DATING!

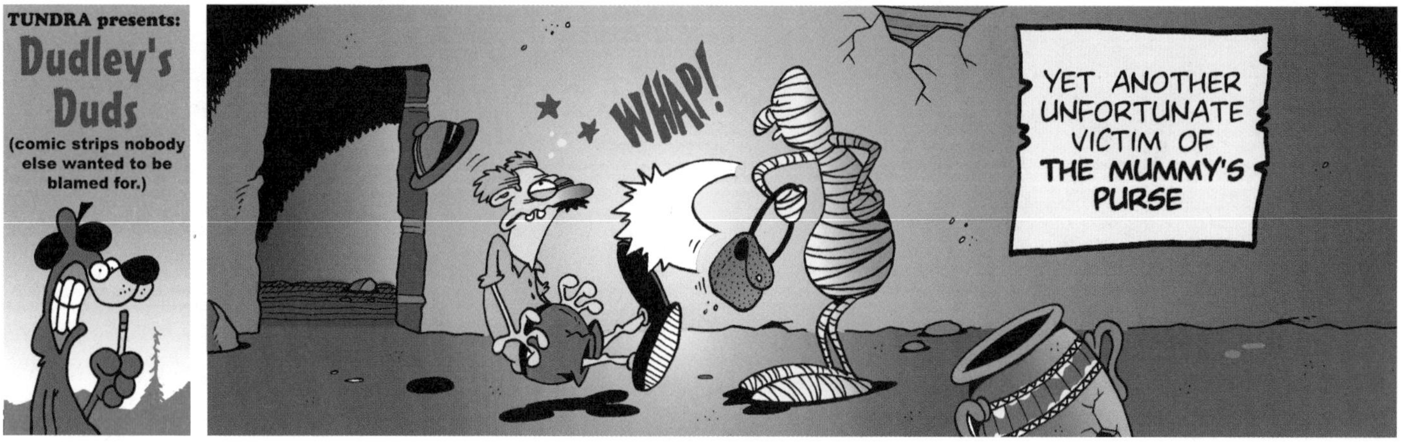
TUNDRA presents:
Dudley's Duds
(comic strips nobody else wanted to be blamed for.)
WHAP!
YET ANOTHER UNFORTUNATE VICTIM OF THE MUMMY'S PURSE

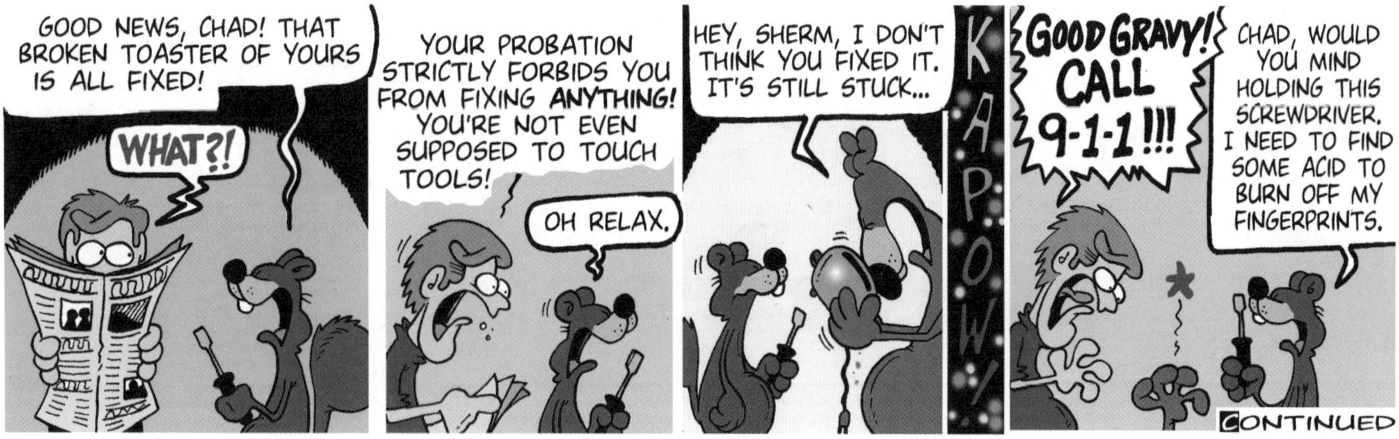
GOOD NEWS, CHAD! THAT BROKEN TOASTER OF YOURS IS ALL FIXED!
WHAT?!
YOUR PROBATION STRICTLY FORBIDS YOU FROM FIXING ANYTHING! YOU'RE NOT EVEN SUPPOSED TO TOUCH TOOLS!
OH RELAX.
HEY, SHERM, I DON'T THINK YOU FIXED IT. IT'S STILL STUCK...
KAPOW!
GOOD GRAVY! CALL 9-1-1!!!
CHAD, WOULD YOU MIND HOLDING THIS SCREWDRIVER. I NEED TO FIND SOME ACID TO BURN OFF MY FINGERPRINTS.
CONTINUED

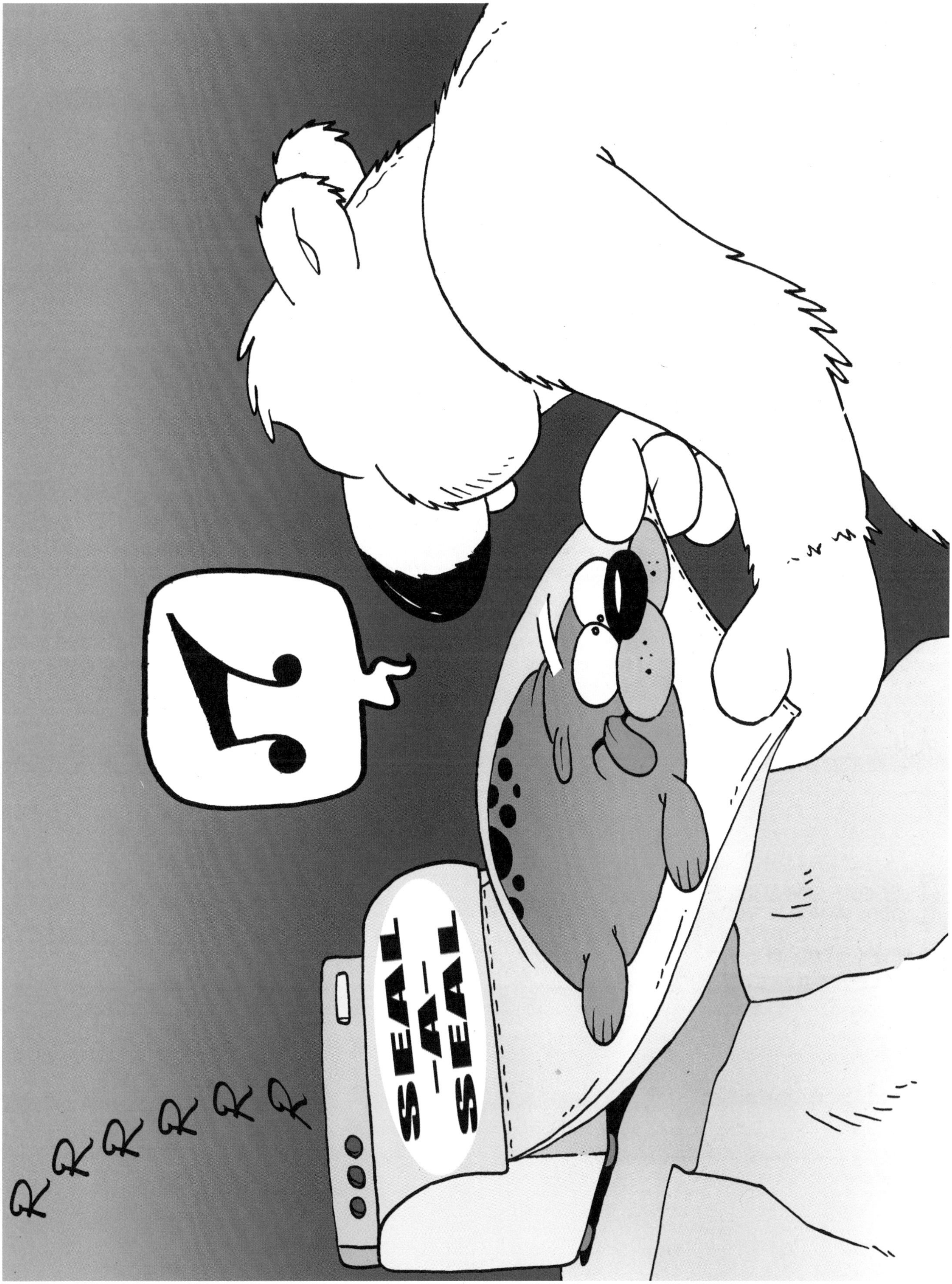
SEAL
-A-
SEAL

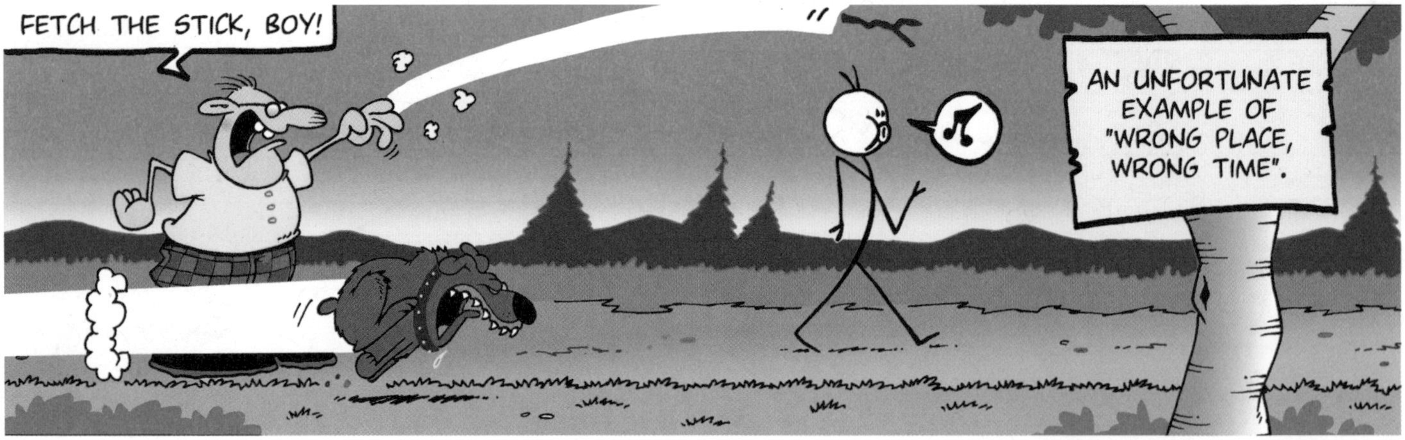
FETCH THE STICK, BOY!
AN UNFORTUNATE EXAMPLE OF "WRONG PLACE, WRONG TIME".

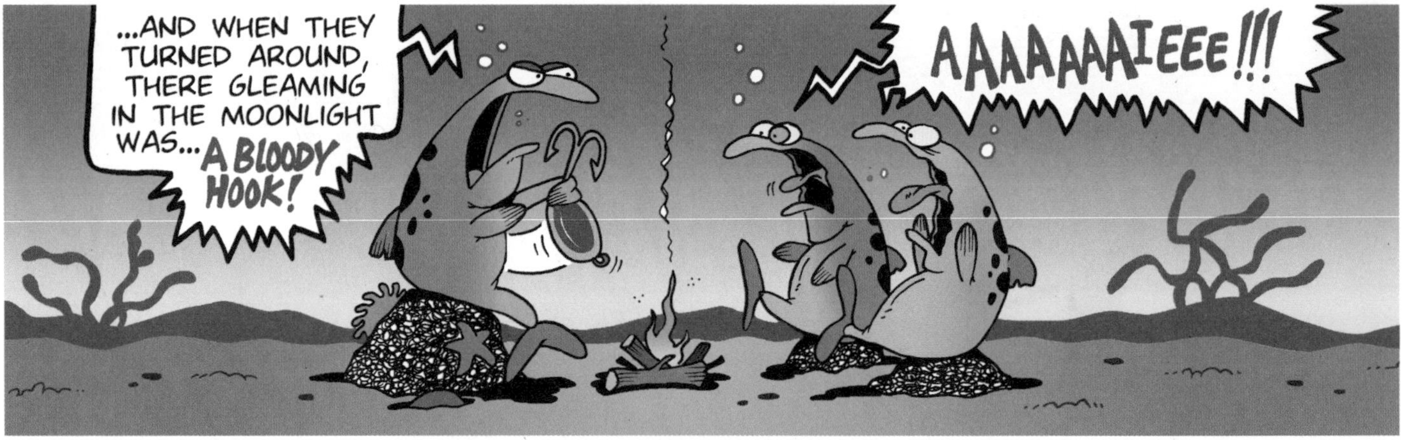
...AND WHEN THEY TURNED AROUND, THERE GLEAMING IN THE MOONLIGHT WAS... A BLOODY HOOK!
AAAAAAAIEEE!!!

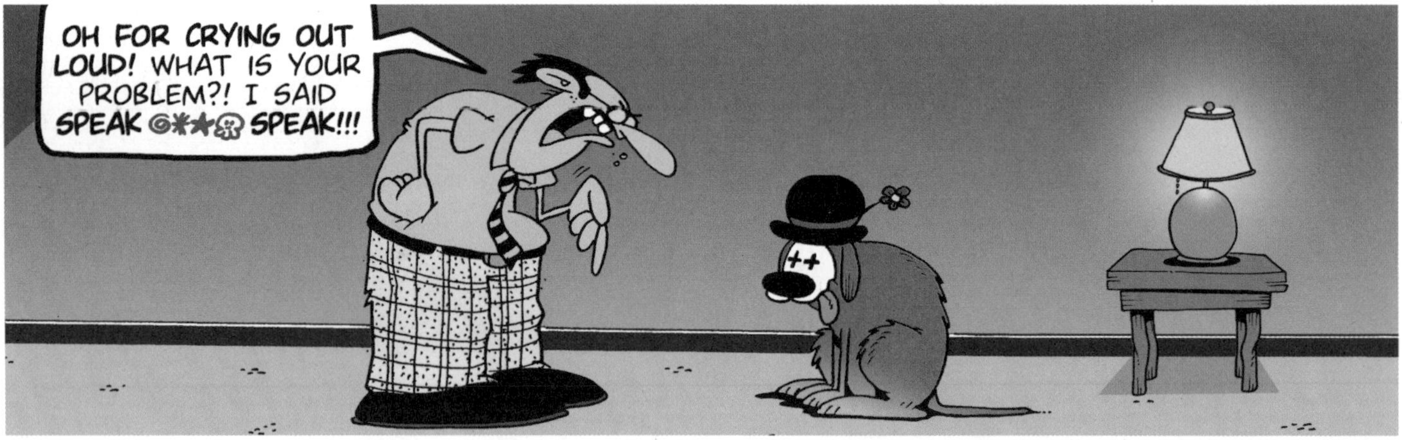
OH FOR CRYING OUT LOUD! WHAT IS YOUR PROBLEM?! I SAID SPEAK @*★* SPEAK!!!

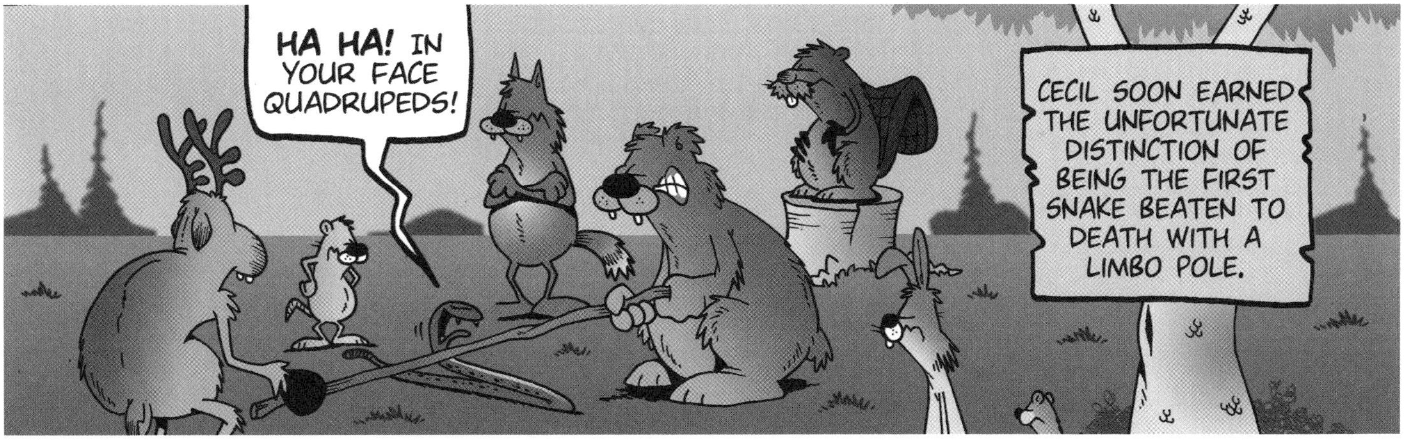
HA HA! IN YOUR FACE QUADRUPEDS!
CECIL SOON EARNED THE UNFORTUNATE DISTINCTION OF BEING THE FIRST SNAKE BEATEN TO DEATH WITH A LIMBO POLE.

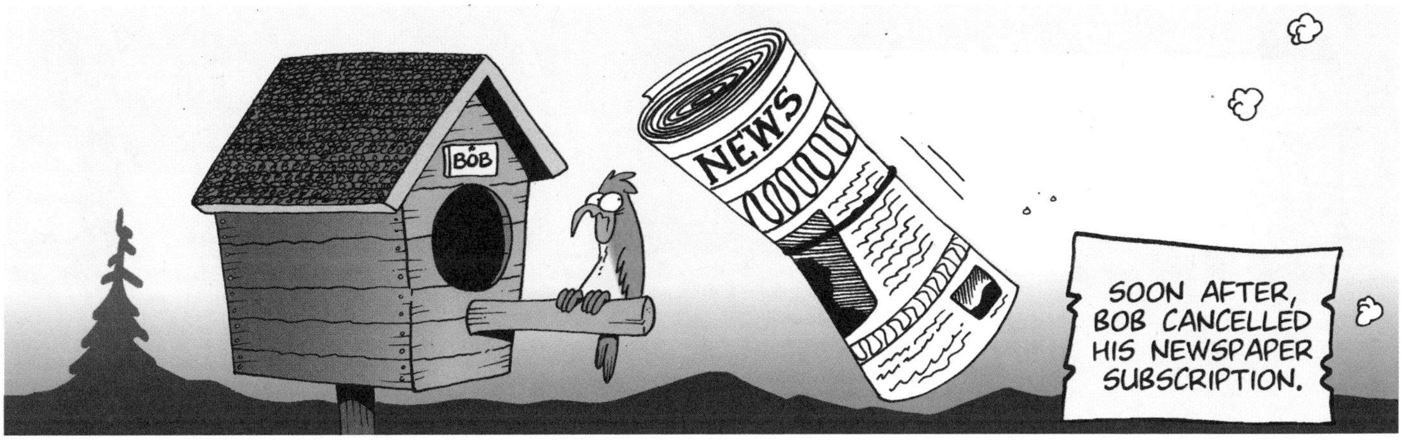
BOB
NEWS
SOON AFTER, BOB CANCELLED HIS NEWSPAPER SUBSCRIPTION.

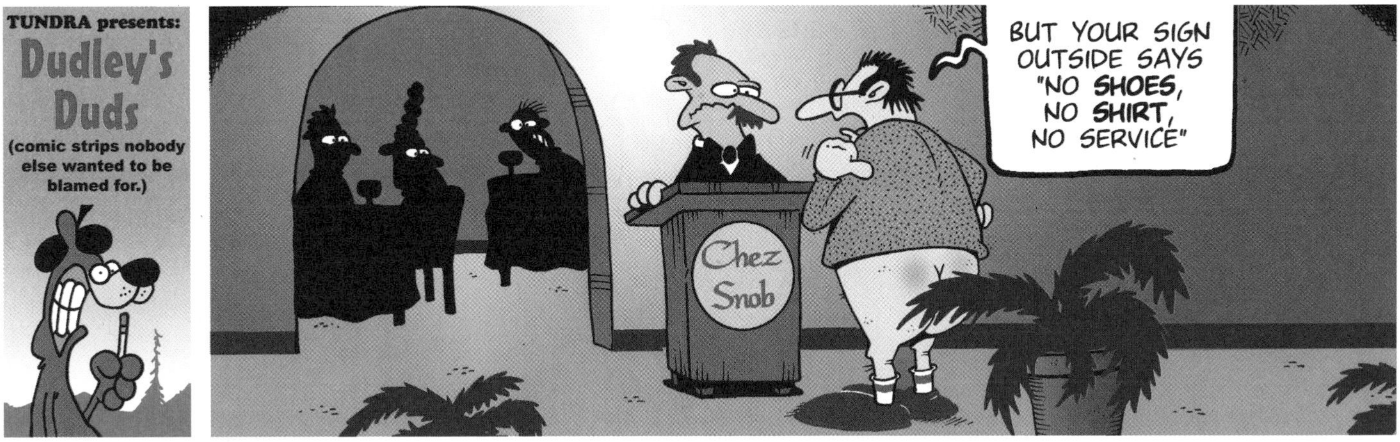
TUNDRA presents:
Dudley's Duds
(comic strips nobody else wanted to be blamed for.)
Chez Snob
BUT YOUR SIGN OUTSIDE SAYS "NO SHOES, NO SHIRT, NO SERVICE"

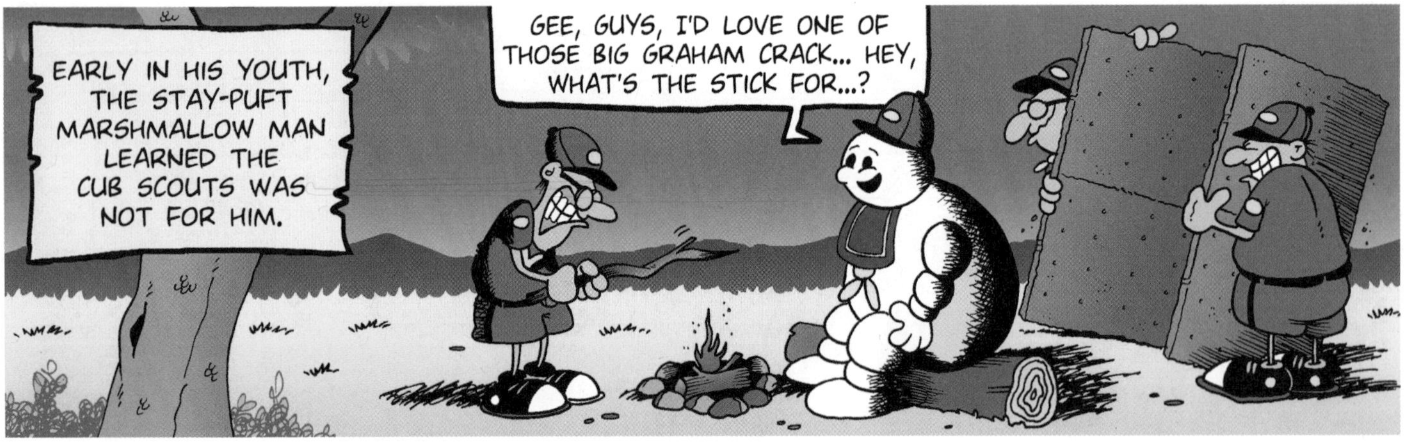
EARLY IN HIS YOUTH, THE STAY-PUFT MARSHMALLOW MAN LEARNED THE CUB SCOUTS WAS NOT FOR HIM.
GEE, GUYS, I'D LOVE ONE OF THOSE BIG GRAHAM CRACK... HEY, WHAT'S THE STICK FOR...?

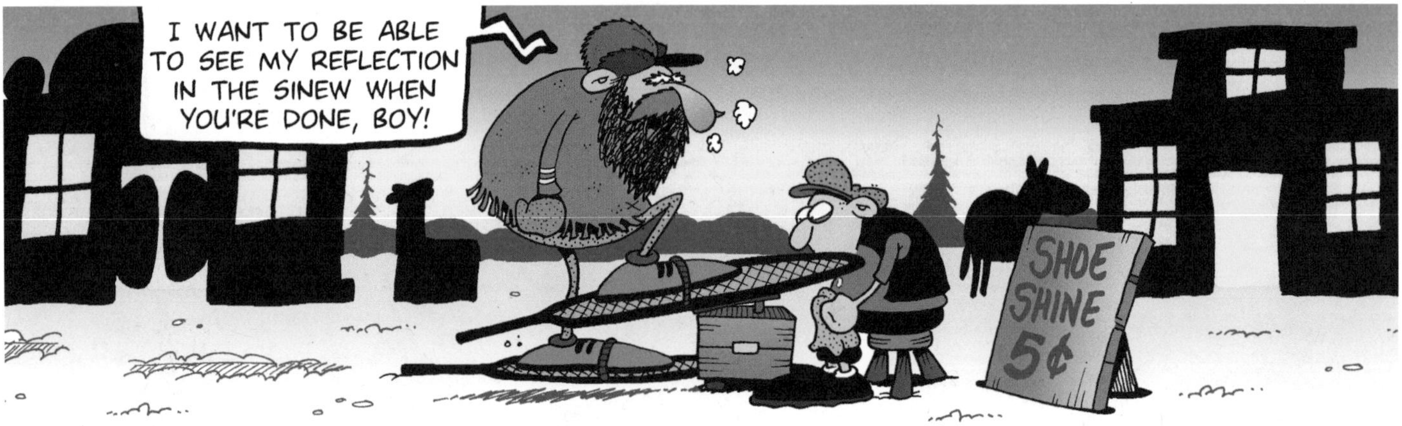
I WANT TO BE ABLE TO SEE MY REFLECTION IN THE SINEW WHEN YOU'RE DONE, BOY!
SHOE SHINE 5¢

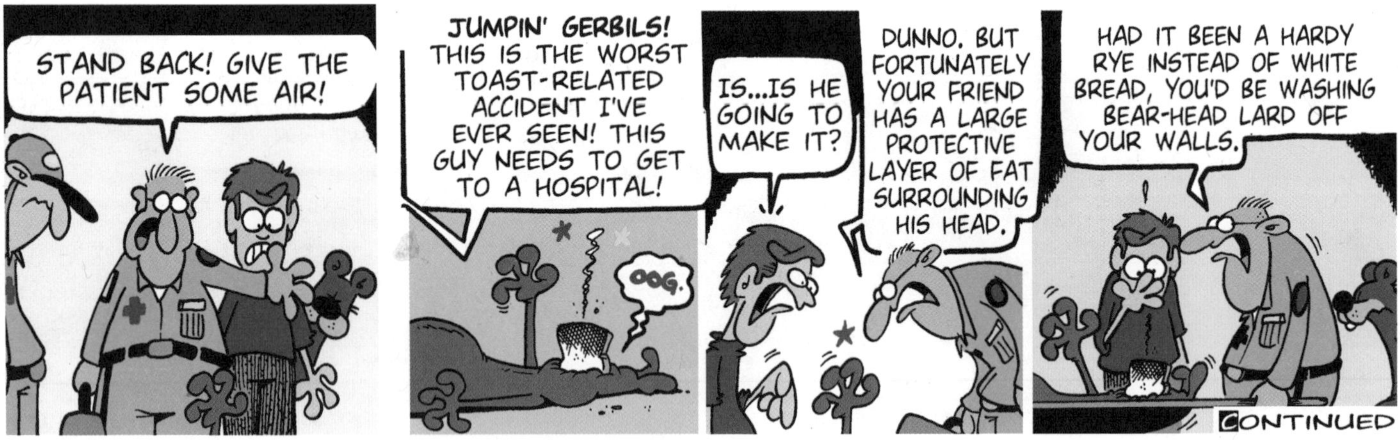
STAND BACK! GIVE THE PATIENT SOME AIR!
JUMPIN' GERBILS! THIS IS THE WORST TOAST-RELATED ACCIDENT I'VE EVER SEEN! THIS GUY NEEDS TO GET TO A HOSPITAL!
OOG.
IS...IS HE GOING TO MAKE IT?
DUNNO. BUT FORTUNATELY YOUR FRIEND HAS A LARGE PROTECTIVE LAYER OF FAT SURROUNDING HIS HEAD.
HAD IT BEEN A HARDY RYE INSTEAD OF WHITE BREAD, YOU'D BE WASHING BEAR-HEAD LARD OFF YOUR WALLS.
CONTINUED

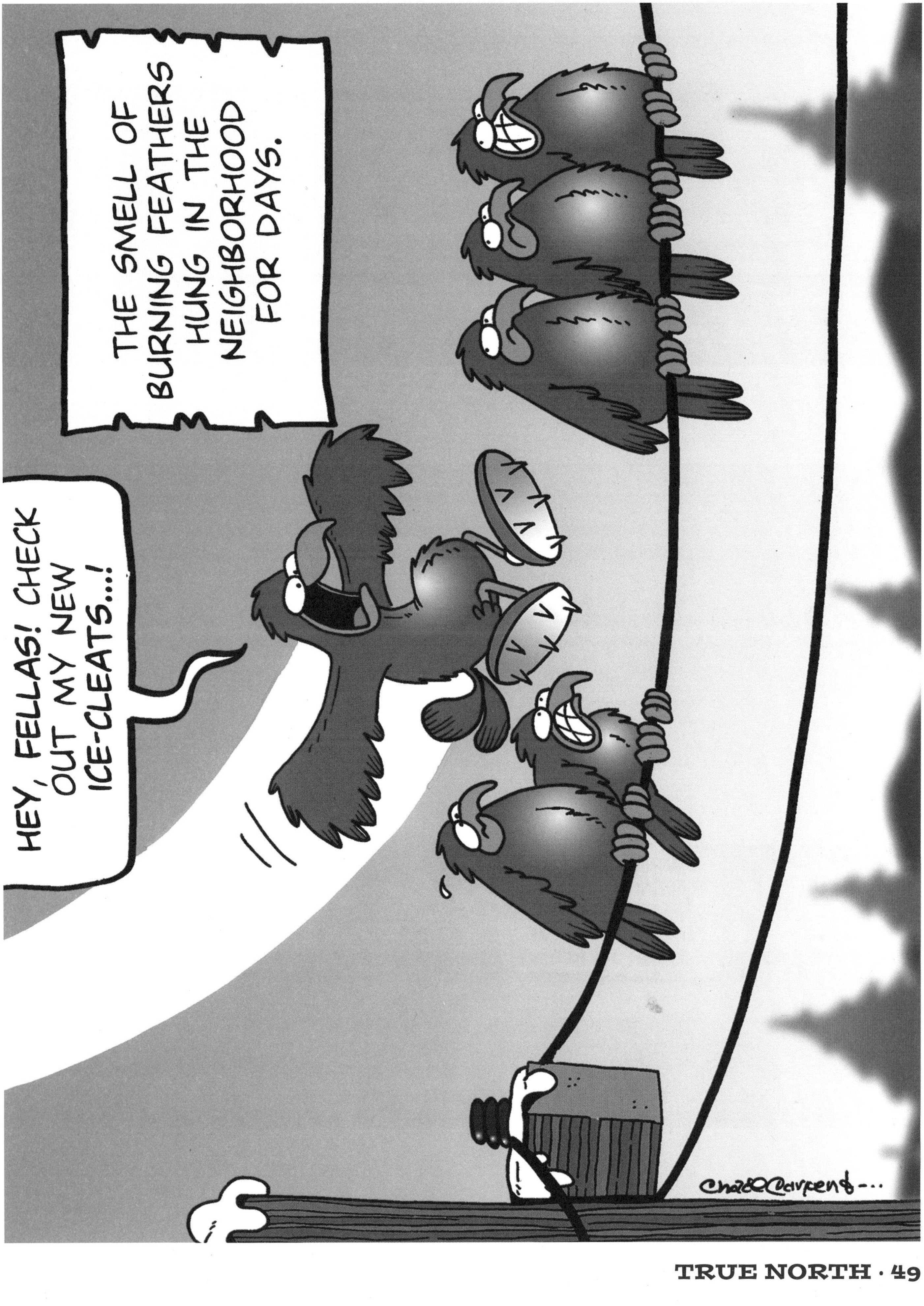

HEY, FELLAS! CHECK OUT MY NEW ICE-CLEATS...!
THE SMELL OF BURNING FEATHERS HUNG IN THE NEIGHBORHOOD FOR DAYS.

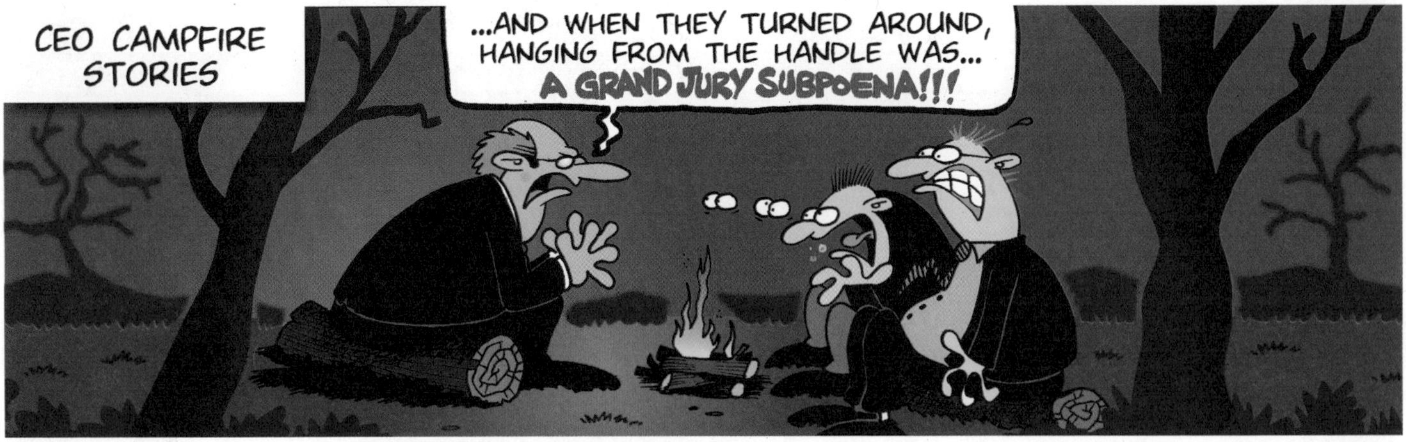
CEO CAMPFIRE STORIES
...AND WHEN THEY TURNED AROUND, HANGING FROM THE HANDLE WAS... A GRAND JURY SUBPOENA!!!

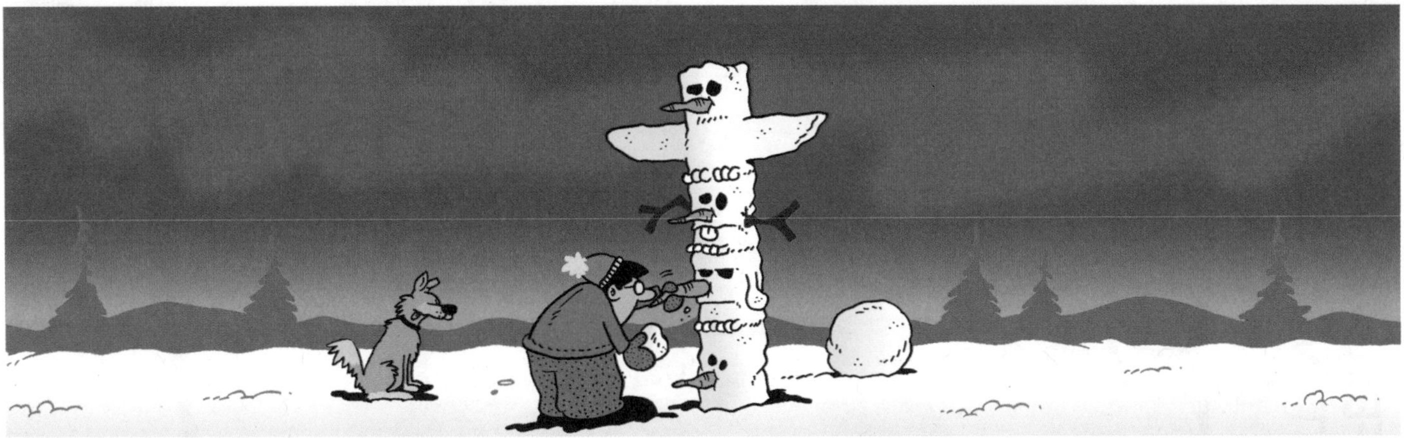

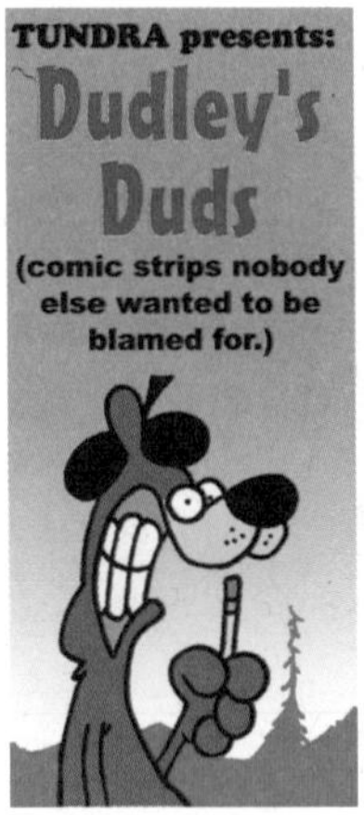
TUNDRA presents:
Dudley's Duds
(comic strips nobody else wanted to be blamed for.)

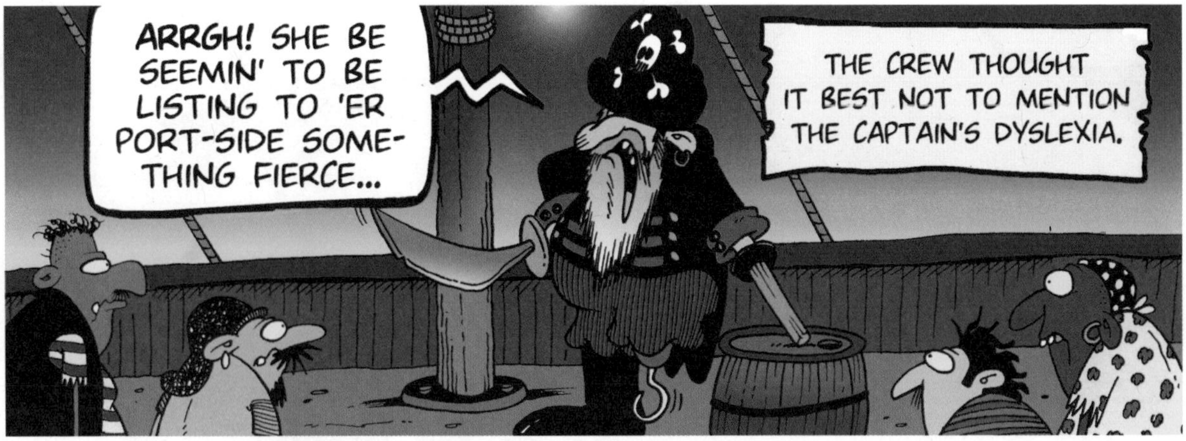
ARRGH! SHE BE SEEMIN' TO BE LISTING TO 'ER PORT-SIDE SOMETHING FIERCE...
THE CREW THOUGHT IT BEST NOT TO MENTION THE CAPTAIN'S DYSLEXIA.

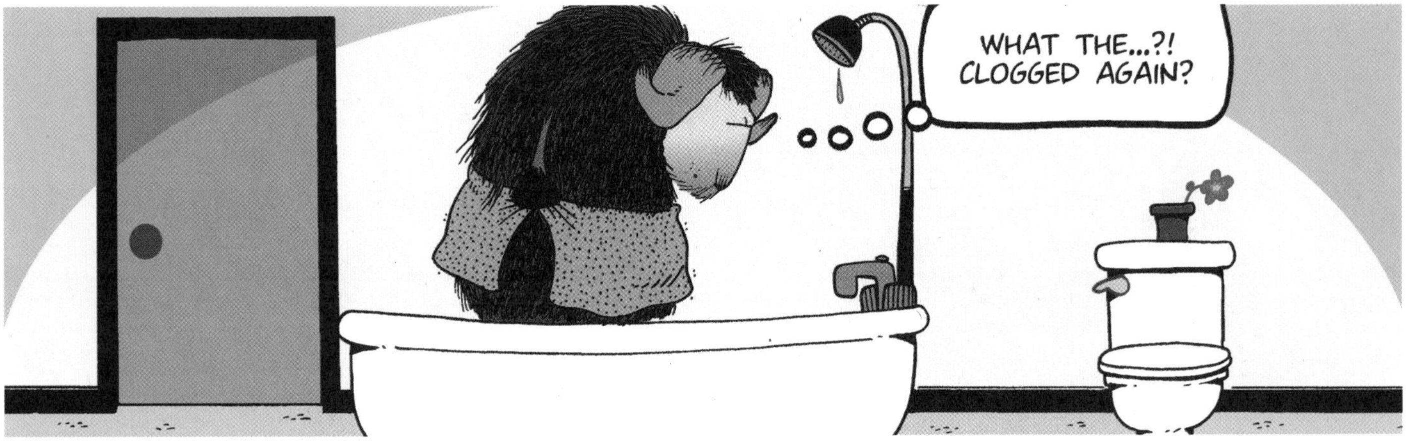
WHAT THE...?! CLOGGED AGAIN?

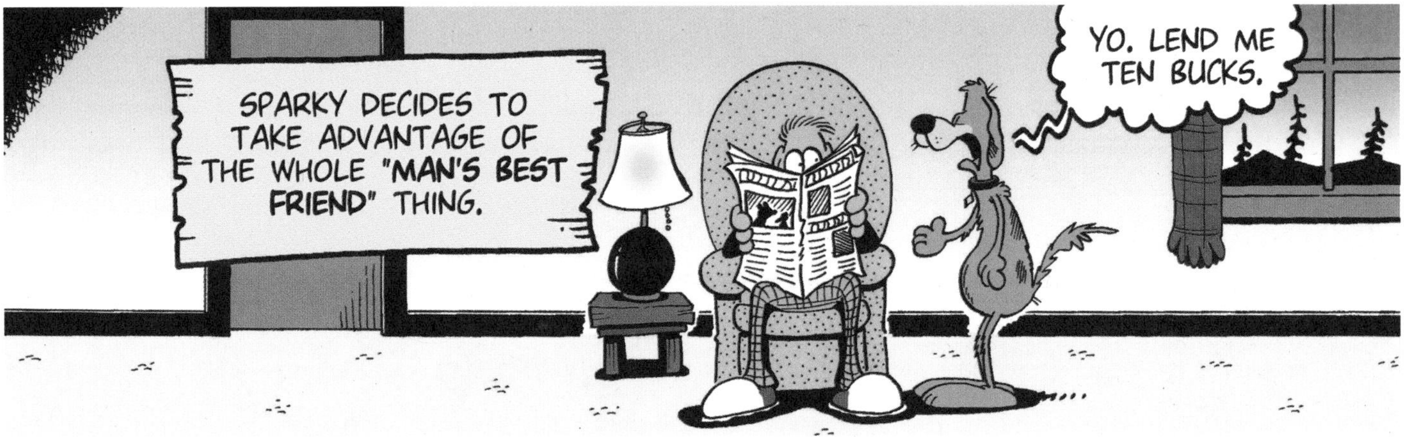
SPARKY DECIDES TO TAKE ADVANTAGE OF THE WHOLE "MAN'S BEST FRIEND" THING.
YO. LEND ME TEN BUCKS.

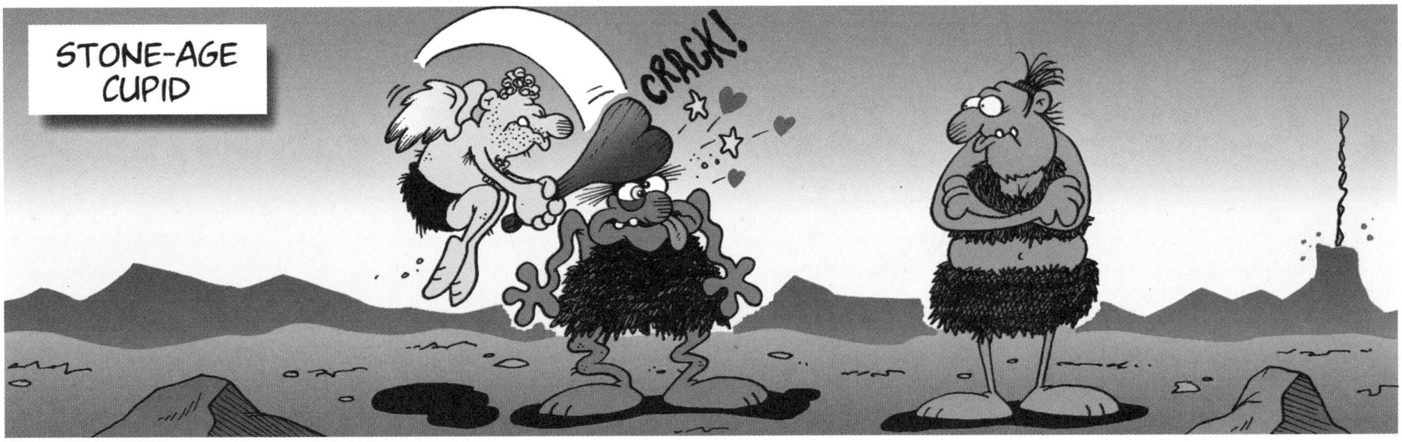
STONE-AGE CUPID
CRACK!

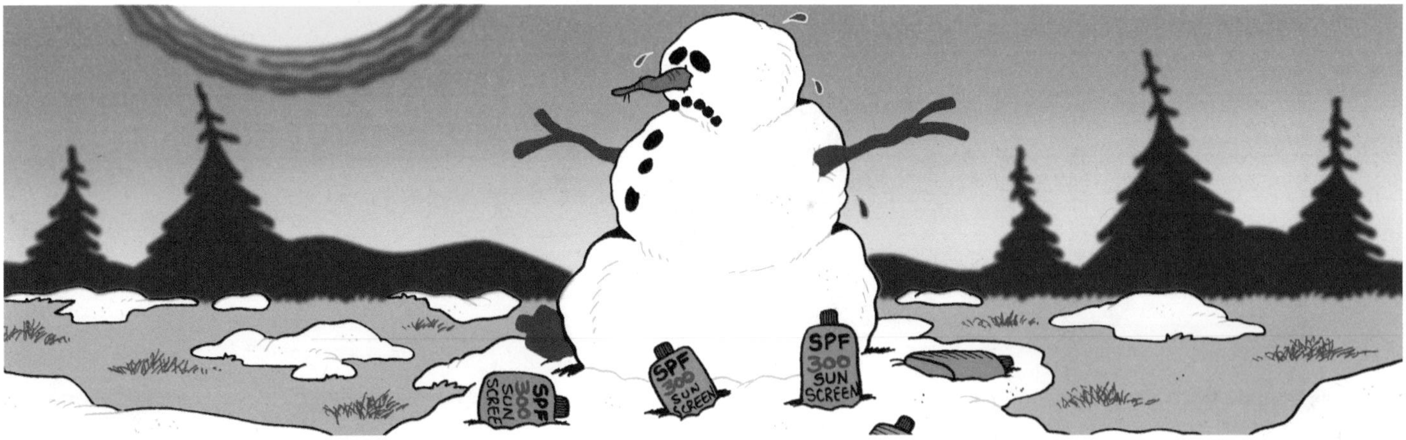
SPF 300 SUN SCREE
SPF 300 SUN SCREEN
SPF 300 SUN SCREEN

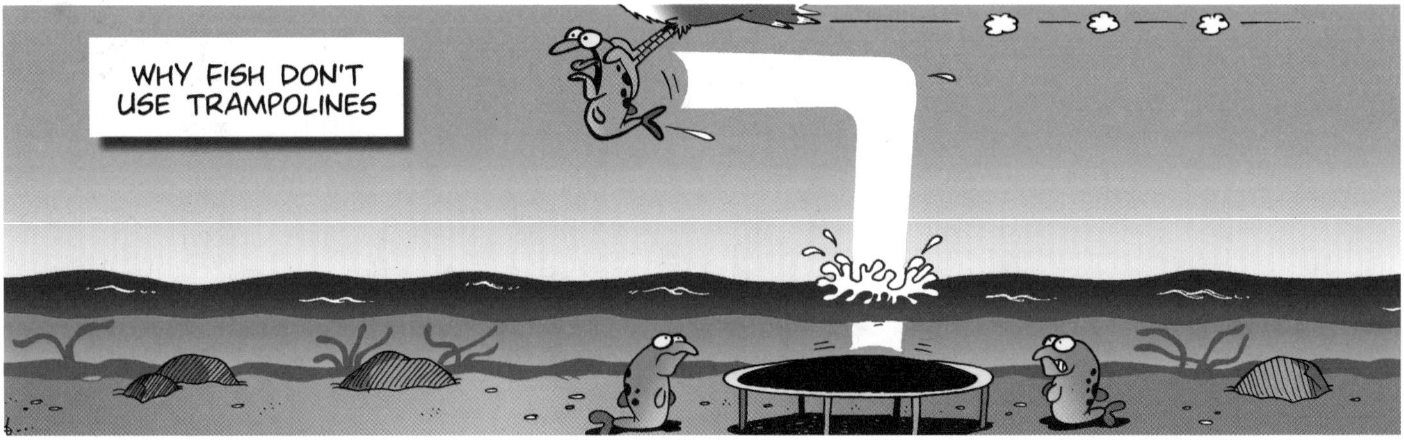
WHY FISH DON'T USE TRAMPOLINES

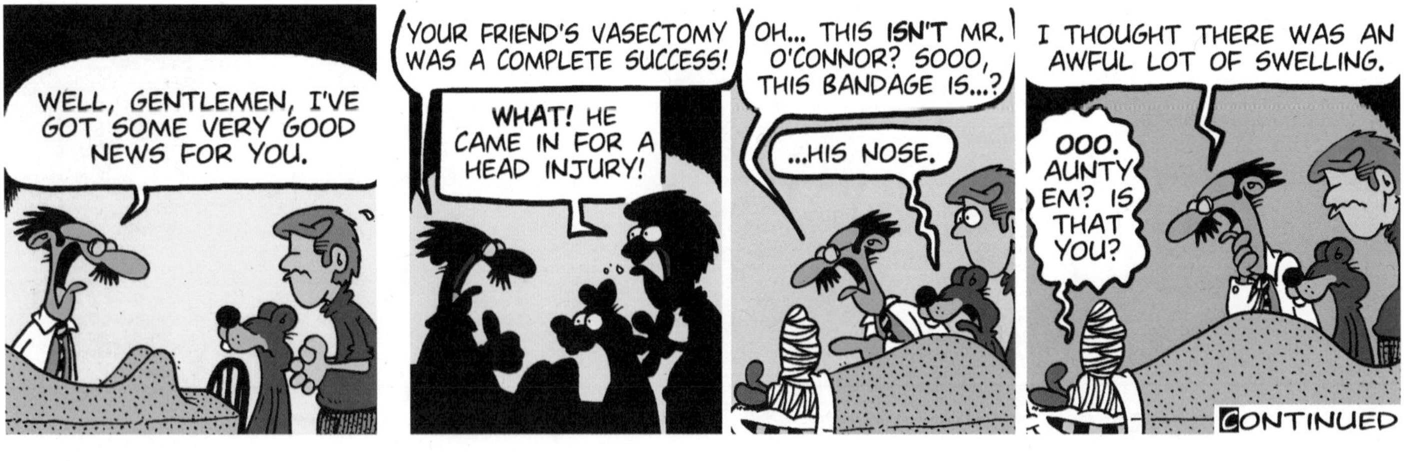
WELL, GENTLEMEN, I'VE GOT SOME VERY GOOD NEWS FOR YOU.
YOUR FRIEND'S VASECTOMY WAS A COMPLETE SUCCESS!
WHAT! HE CAME IN FOR A HEAD INJURY!
OH... THIS ISN'T MR. O'CONNOR? SOOO, THIS BANDAGE IS...?
...HIS NOSE.
I THOUGHT THERE WAS AN AWFUL LOT OF SWELLING.
OOO. AUNTY EM? IS THAT YOU?
CONTINUED

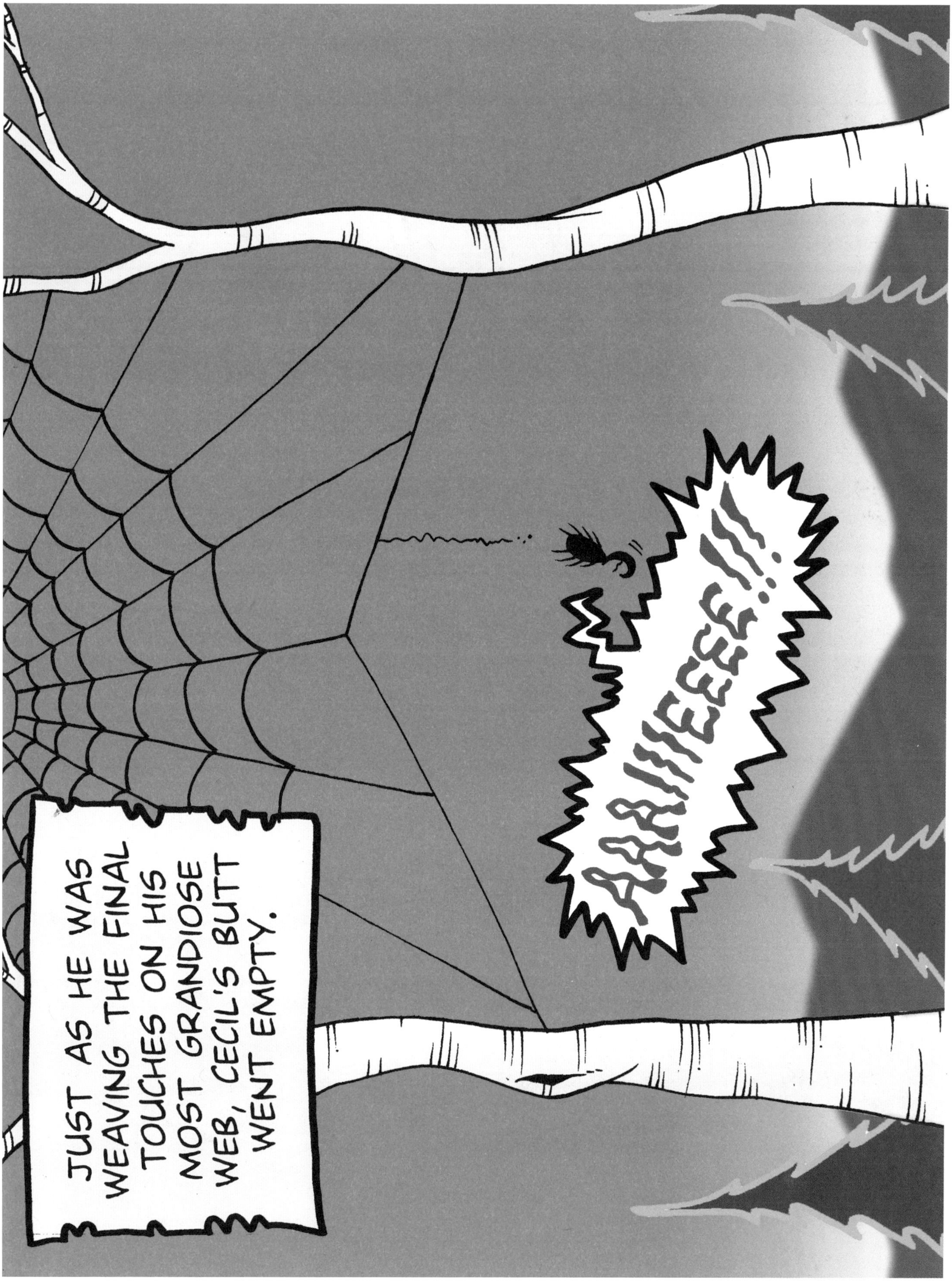
JUST AS HE WAS WEAVING THE FINAL TOUCHES ON HIS MOST GRANDIOSE WEB, CECIL'S BUTT WENT EMPTY.
AAAIIIEEEEE!!!

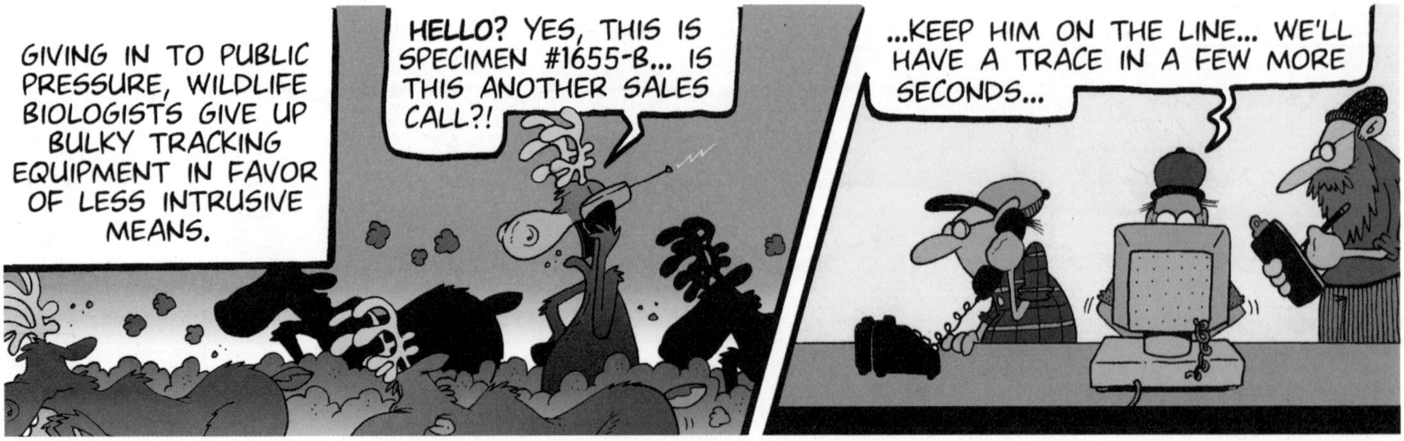
GIVING IN TO PUBLIC PRESSURE, WILDLIFE BIOLOGISTS GIVE UP BULKY TRACKING EQUIPMENT IN FAVOR OF LESS INTRUSIVE MEANS.
HELLO? YES, THIS IS SPECIMEN #1655-B... IS THIS ANOTHER SALES CALL?!
...KEEP HIM ON THE LINE... WE'LL HAVE A TRACE IN A FEW MORE SECONDS...

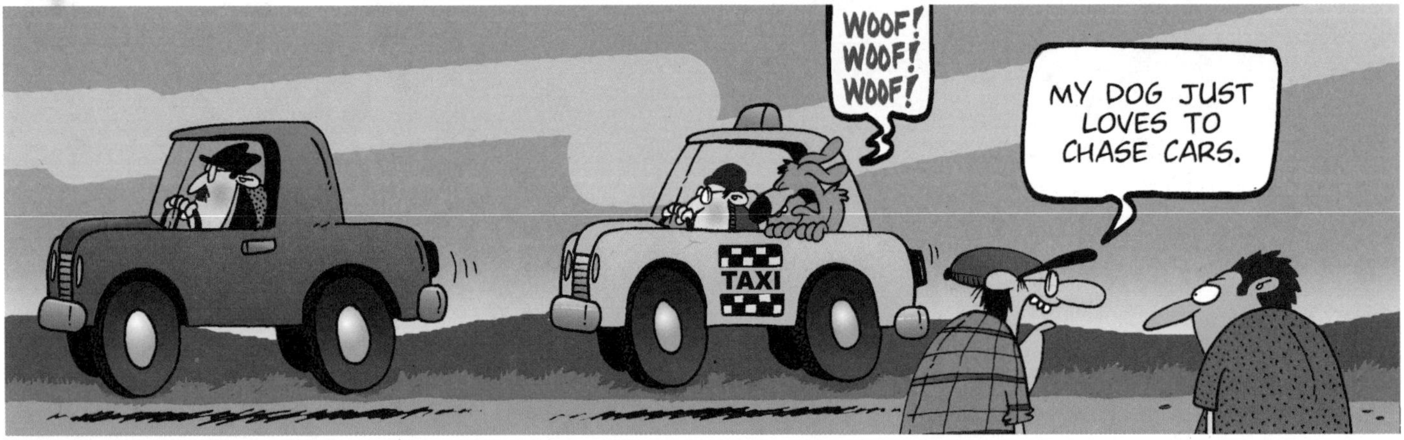
WOOF! WOOF! WOOF!
TAXI
MY DOG JUST LOVES TO CHASE CARS.

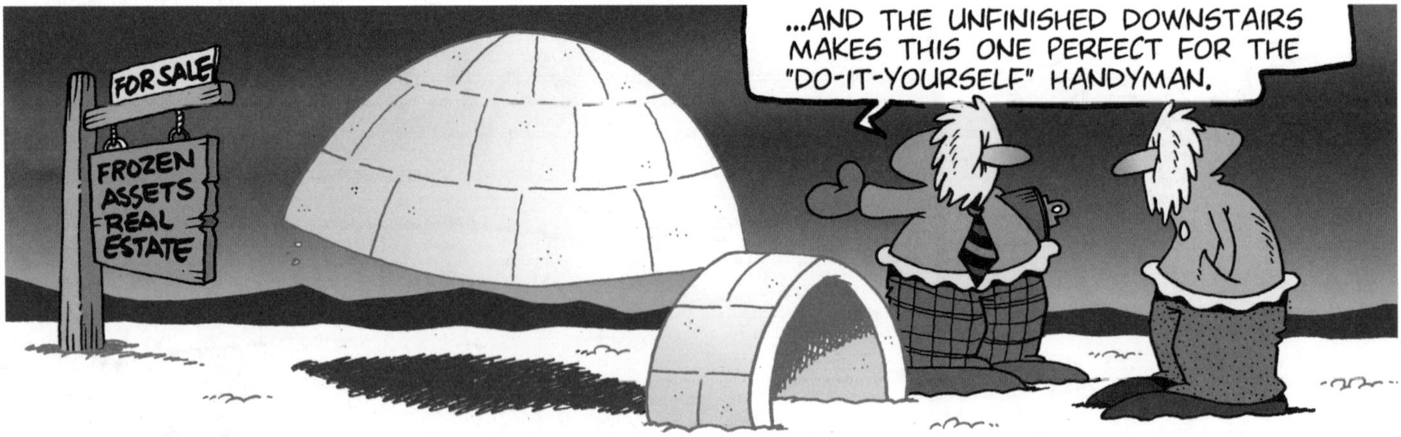
FOR SALE
FROZEN ASSETS REAL ESTATE
...AND THE UNFINISHED DOWNSTAIRS MAKES THIS ONE PERFECT FOR THE "DO-IT-YOURSELF" HANDYMAN.

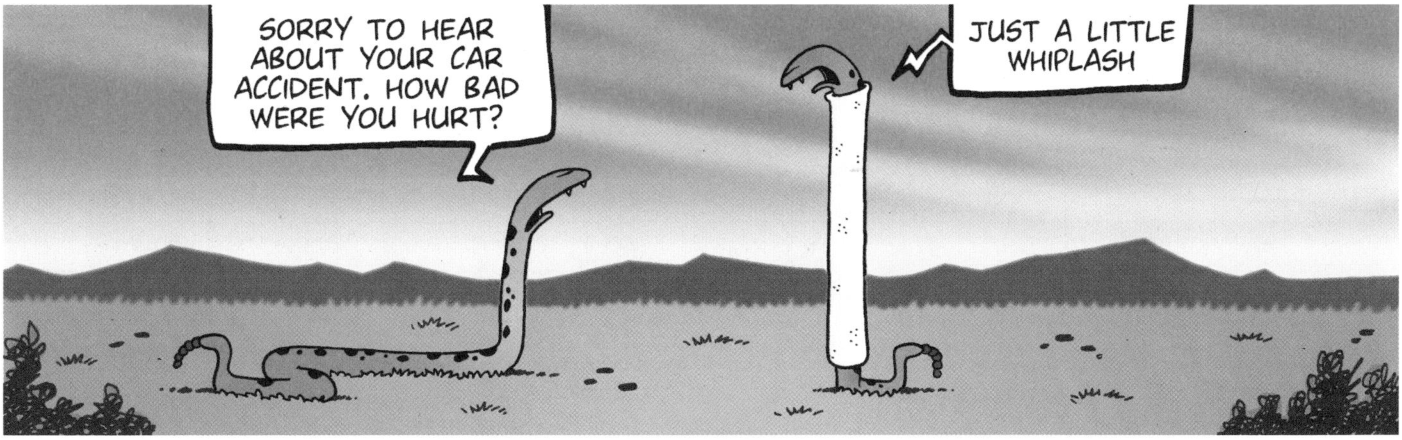
SORRY TO HEAR ABOUT YOUR CAR ACCIDENT. HOW BAD WERE YOU HURT?
JUST A LITTLE WHIPLASH

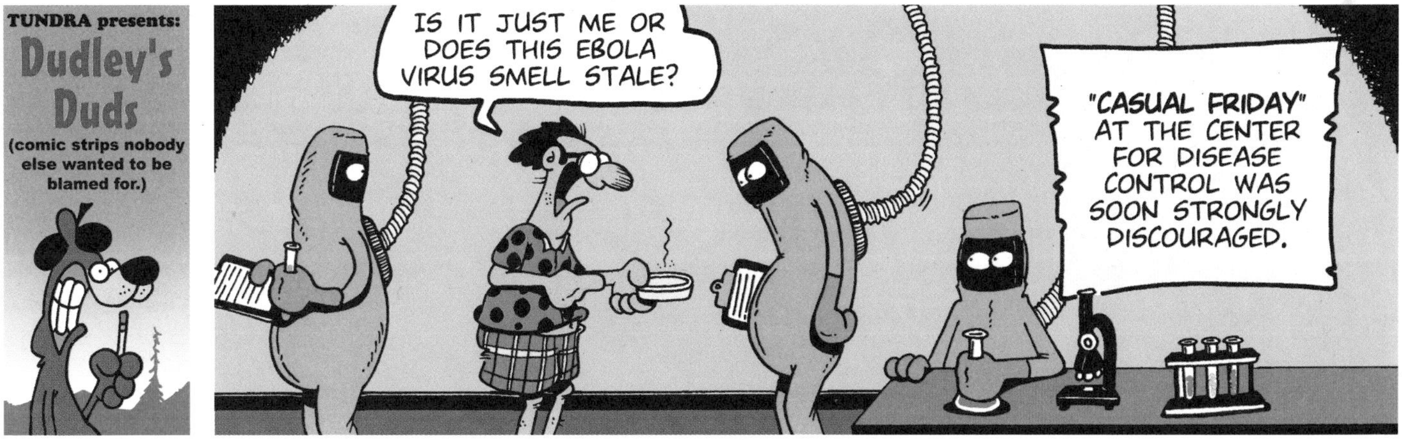
TUNDRA presents:
Dudley's Duds
(comic strips nobody else wanted to be blamed for.)
IS IT JUST ME OR DOES THIS EBOLA VIRUS SMELL STALE?
"CASUAL FRIDAY" AT THE CENTER FOR DISEASE CONTROL WAS SOON STRONGLY DISCOURAGED.

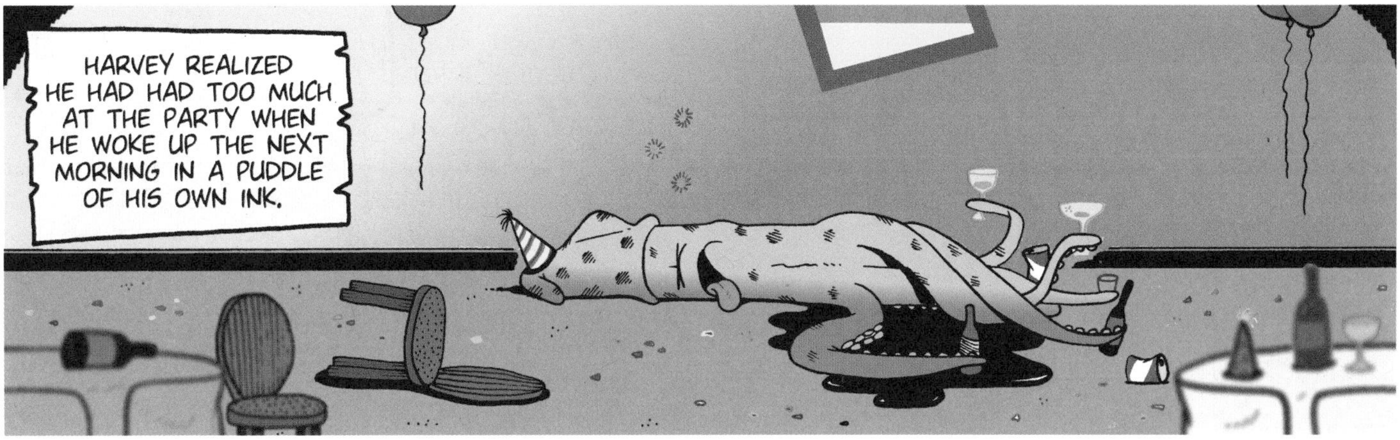
HARVEY REALIZED HE HAD HAD TOO MUCH AT THE PARTY WHEN HE WOKE UP THE NEXT MORNING IN A PUDDLE OF HIS OWN INK.

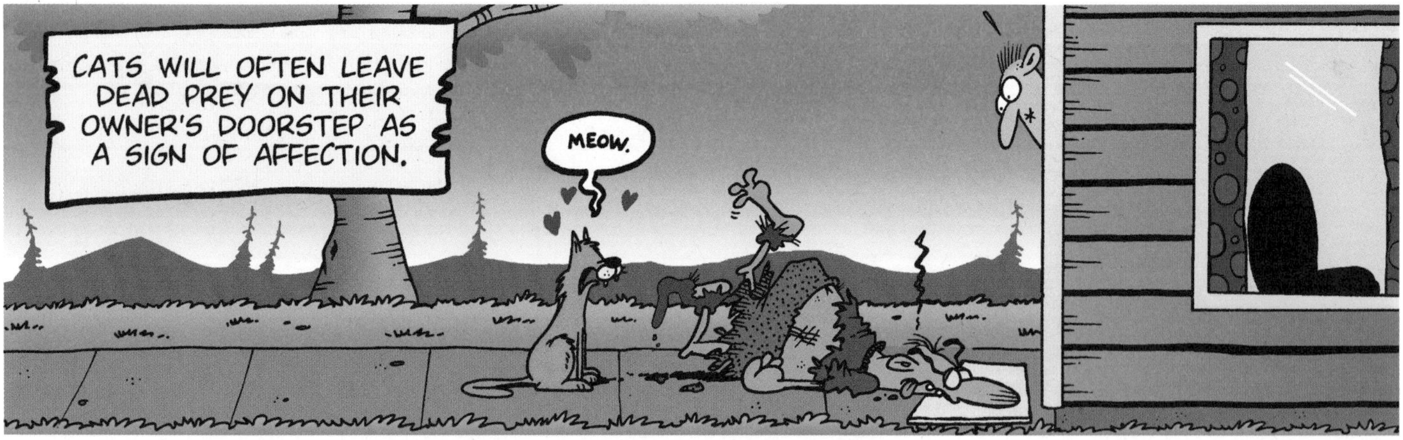
CATS WILL OFTEN LEAVE DEAD PREY ON THEIR OWNER'S DOORSTEP AS A SIGN OF AFFECTION.
MEOW.

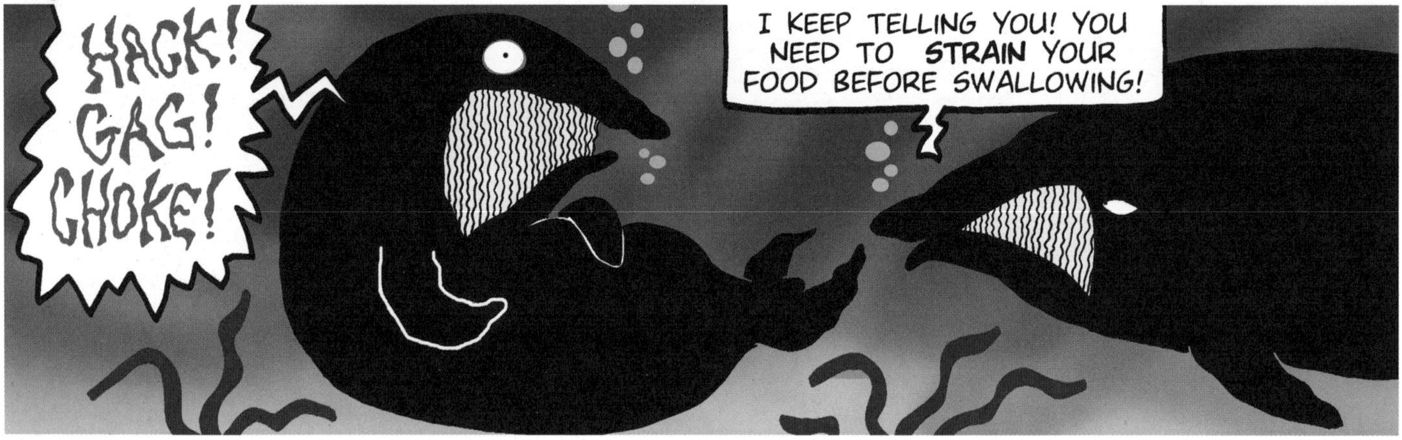
HACK! GAG! CHOKE!
I KEEP TELLING YOU! YOU NEED TO **STRAIN** YOUR FOOD BEFORE SWALLOWING!

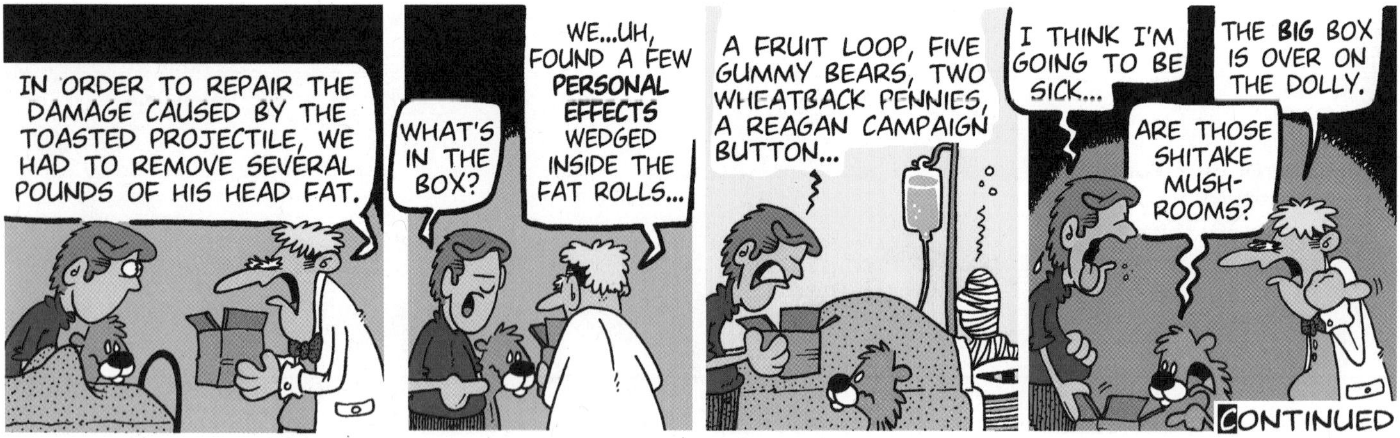
IN ORDER TO REPAIR THE DAMAGE CAUSED BY THE TOASTED PROJECTILE, WE HAD TO REMOVE SEVERAL POUNDS OF HIS HEAD FAT.
WHAT'S IN THE BOX?
WE...UH, FOUND A FEW **PERSONAL EFFECTS** WEDGED INSIDE THE FAT ROLLS...
A FRUIT LOOP, FIVE GUMMY BEARS, TWO WHEATBACK PENNIES, A REAGAN CAMPAIGN BUTTON...
I THINK I'M GOING TO BE SICK...
THE **BIG** BOX IS OVER ON THE DOLLY.
ARE THOSE SHITAKE MUSH-ROOMS?
CONTINUED

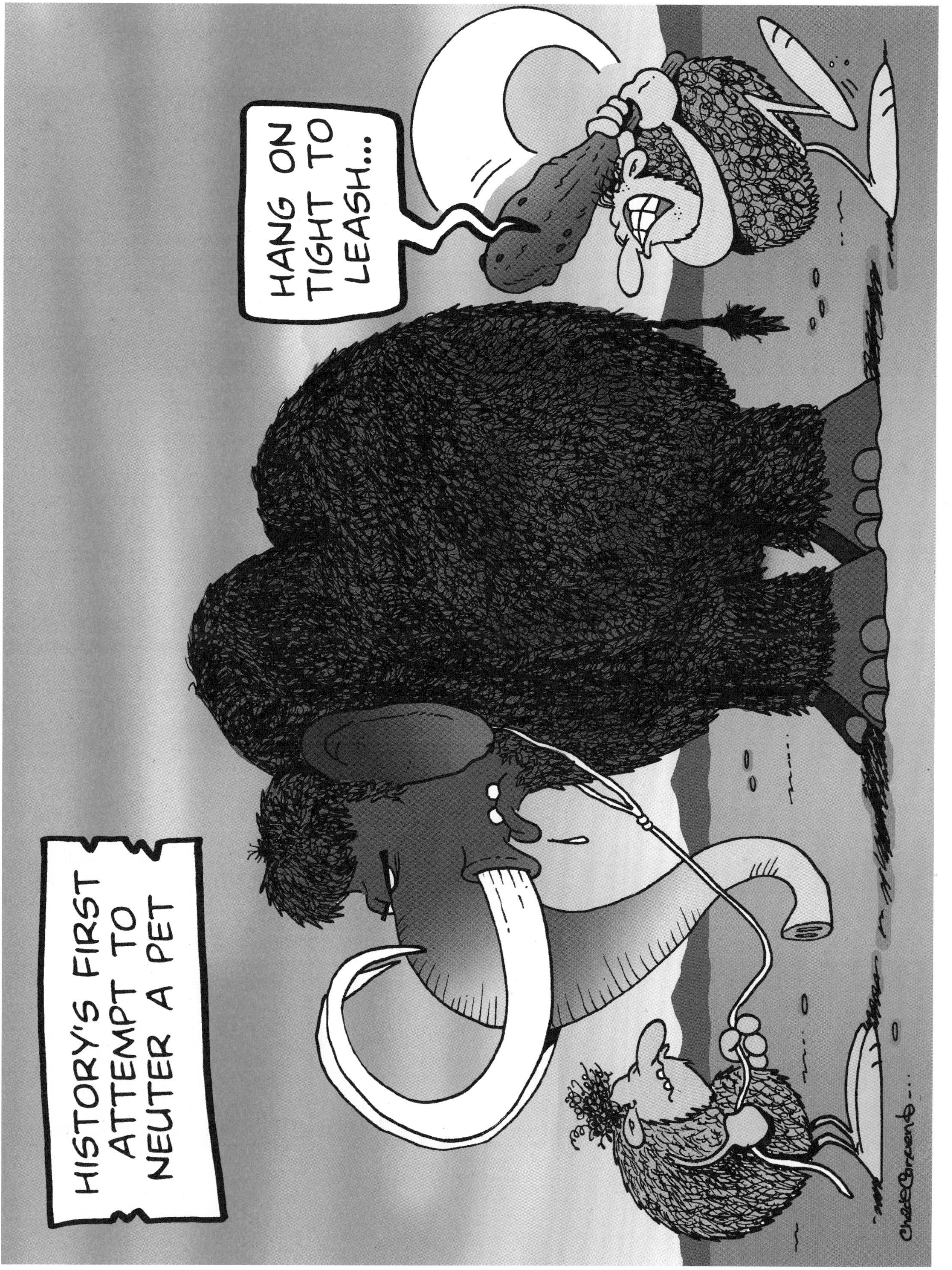
HISTORY'S FIRST ATTEMPT TO NEUTER A PET
HANG ON TIGHT TO LEASH...

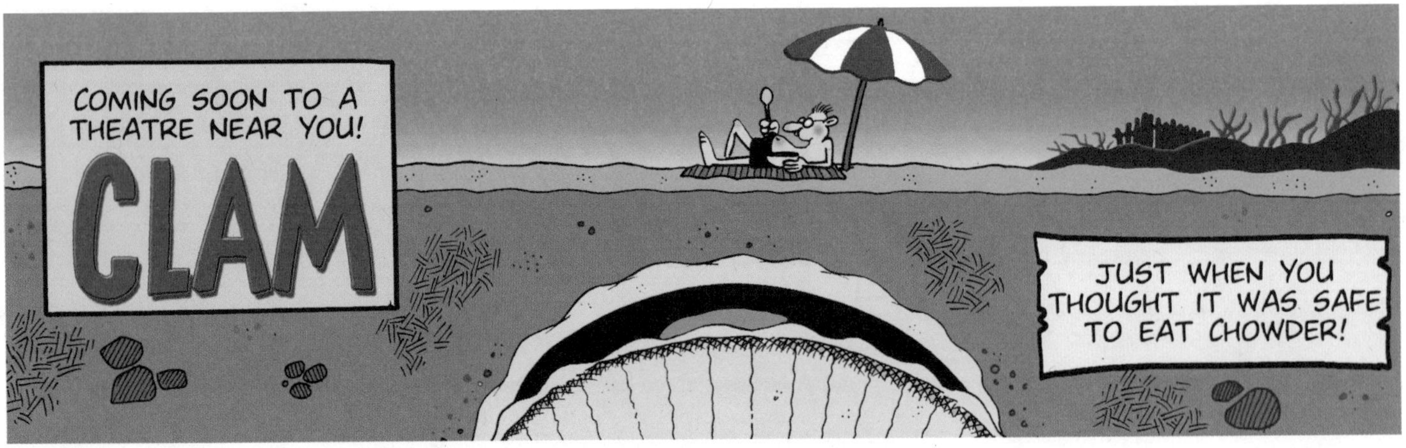
COMING SOON TO A THEATRE NEAR YOU!
CLAM
JUST WHEN YOU THOUGHT IT WAS SAFE TO EAT CHOWDER!

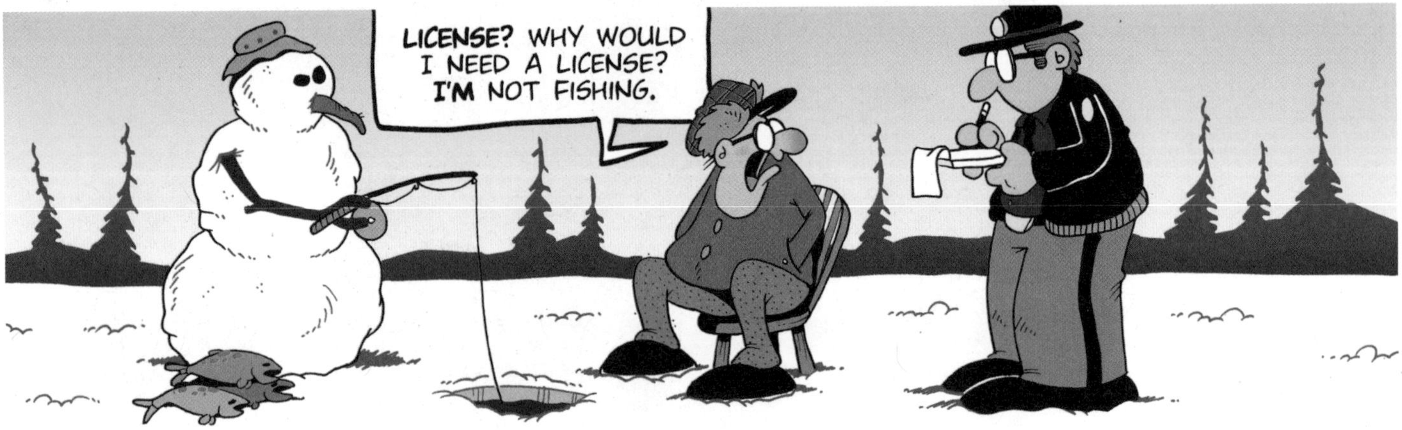
LICENSE? WHY WOULD I NEED A LICENSE? I'M NOT FISHING.

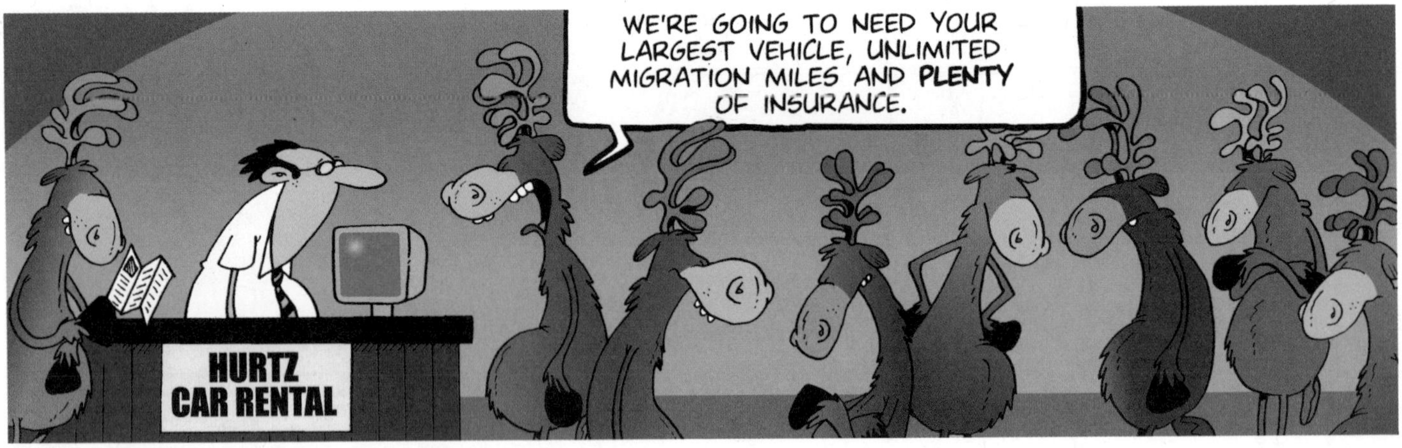
WE'RE GOING TO NEED YOUR LARGEST VEHICLE, UNLIMITED MIGRATION MILES AND PLENTY OF INSURANCE.
HURTZ CAR RENTAL

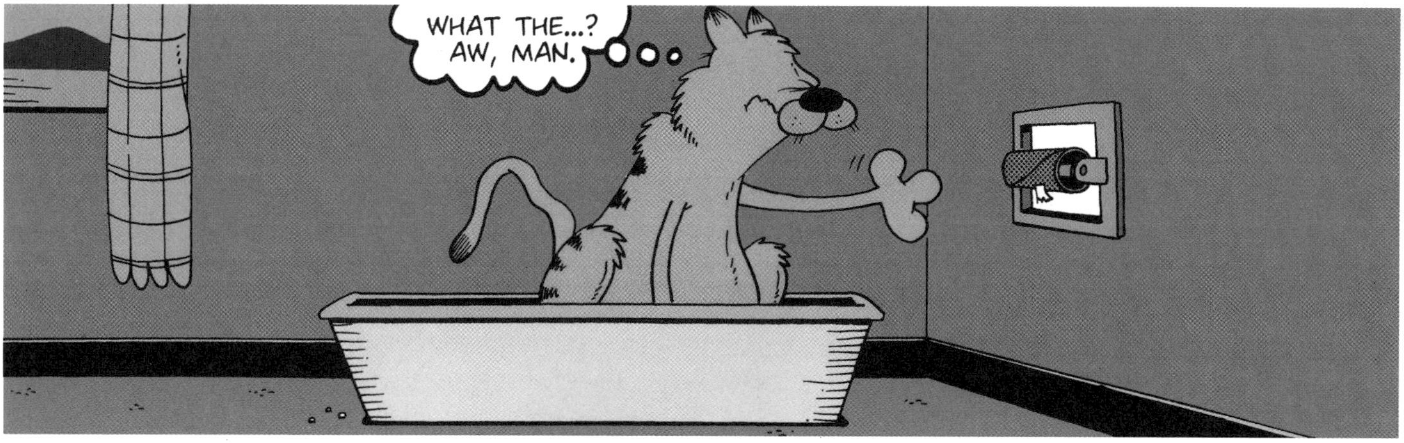
WHAT THE...? AW, MAN.

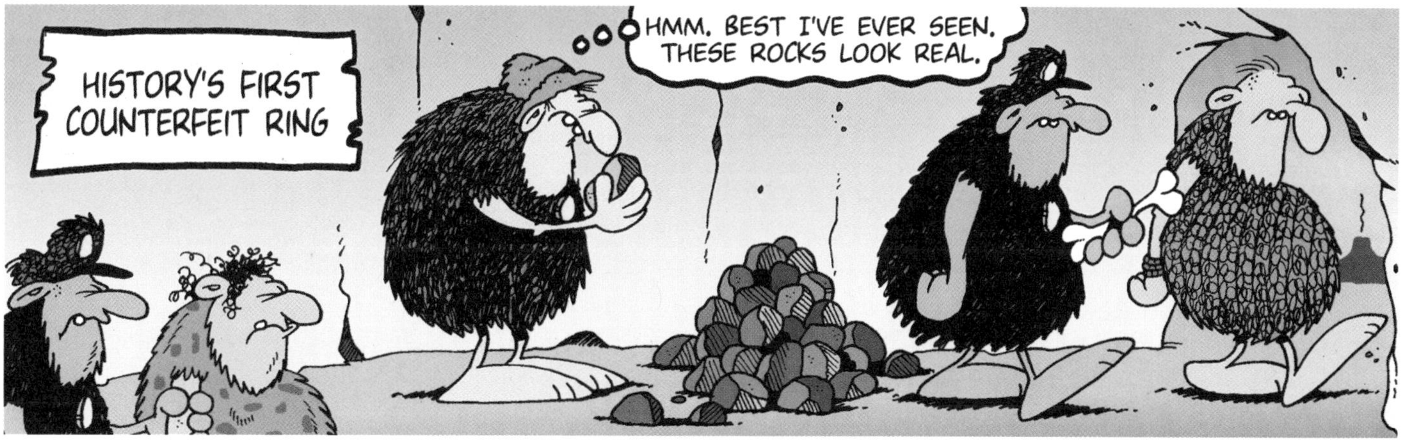
HISTORY'S FIRST COUNTERFEIT RING
HMM. BEST I'VE EVER SEEN. THESE ROCKS LOOK REAL.

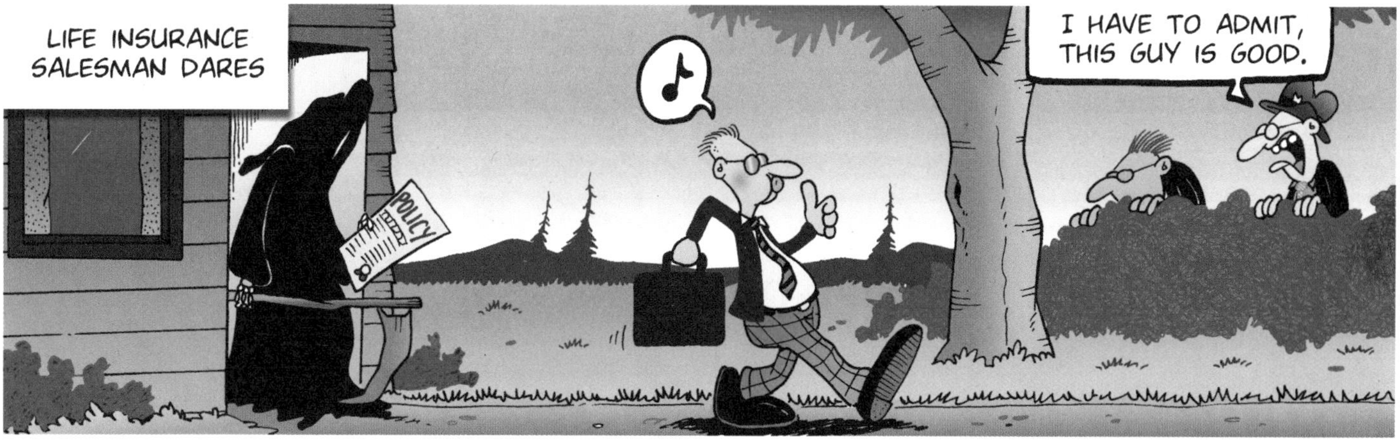
LIFE INSURANCE SALESMAN DARES
POLICY
I HAVE TO ADMIT, THIS GUY IS GOOD.

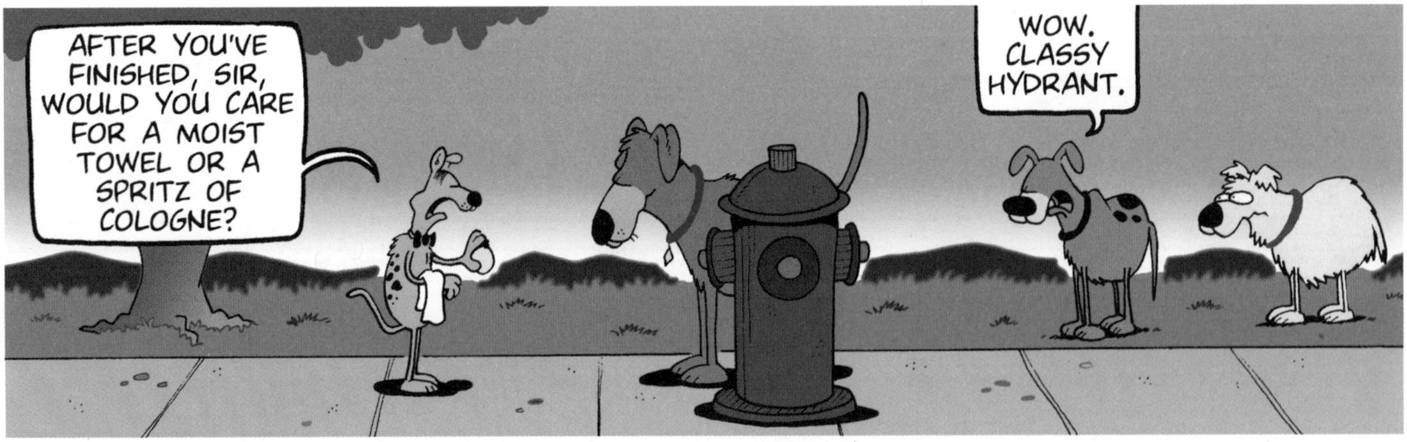
AFTER YOU'VE FINISHED, SIR, WOULD YOU CARE FOR A MOIST TOWEL OR A SPRITZ OF COLOGNE?
WOW. CLASSY HYDRANT.

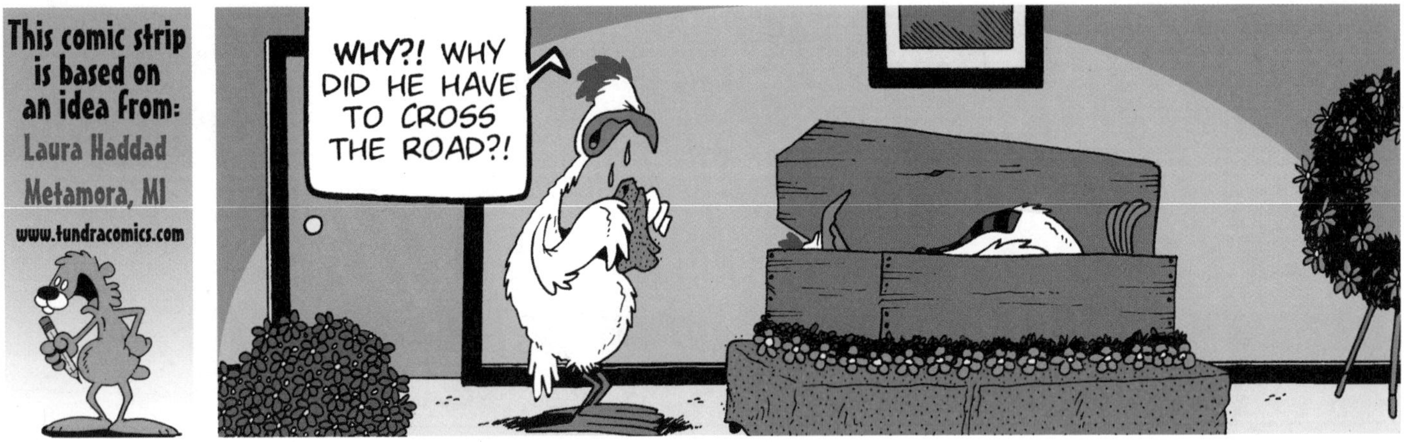
This comic strip is based on an idea from:
Laura Haddad
Metamora, MI
www.tundracomics.com
WHY?! WHY DID HE HAVE TO CROSS THE ROAD?!

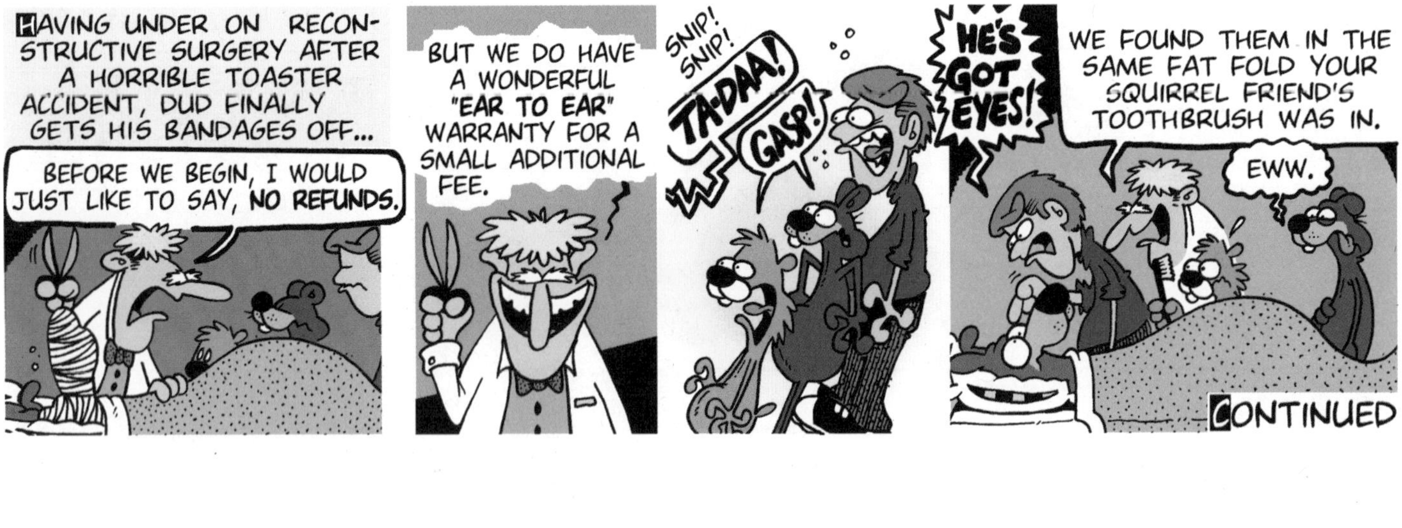
HAVING UNDER ON RECON-STRUCTIVE SURGERY AFTER A HORRIBLE TOASTER ACCIDENT, DUD FINALLY GETS HIS BANDAGES OFF...
BEFORE WE BEGIN, I WOULD JUST LIKE TO SAY, NO REFUNDS.
BUT WE DO HAVE A WONDERFUL "EAR TO EAR" WARRANTY FOR A SMALL ADDITIONAL FEE.
SNIP! SNIP!
TA-DAA!
GASP!
HE'S GOT EYES!
WE FOUND THEM IN THE SAME FAT FOLD YOUR SQUIRREL FRIEND'S TOOTHBRUSH WAS IN.
EWW.
CONTINUED

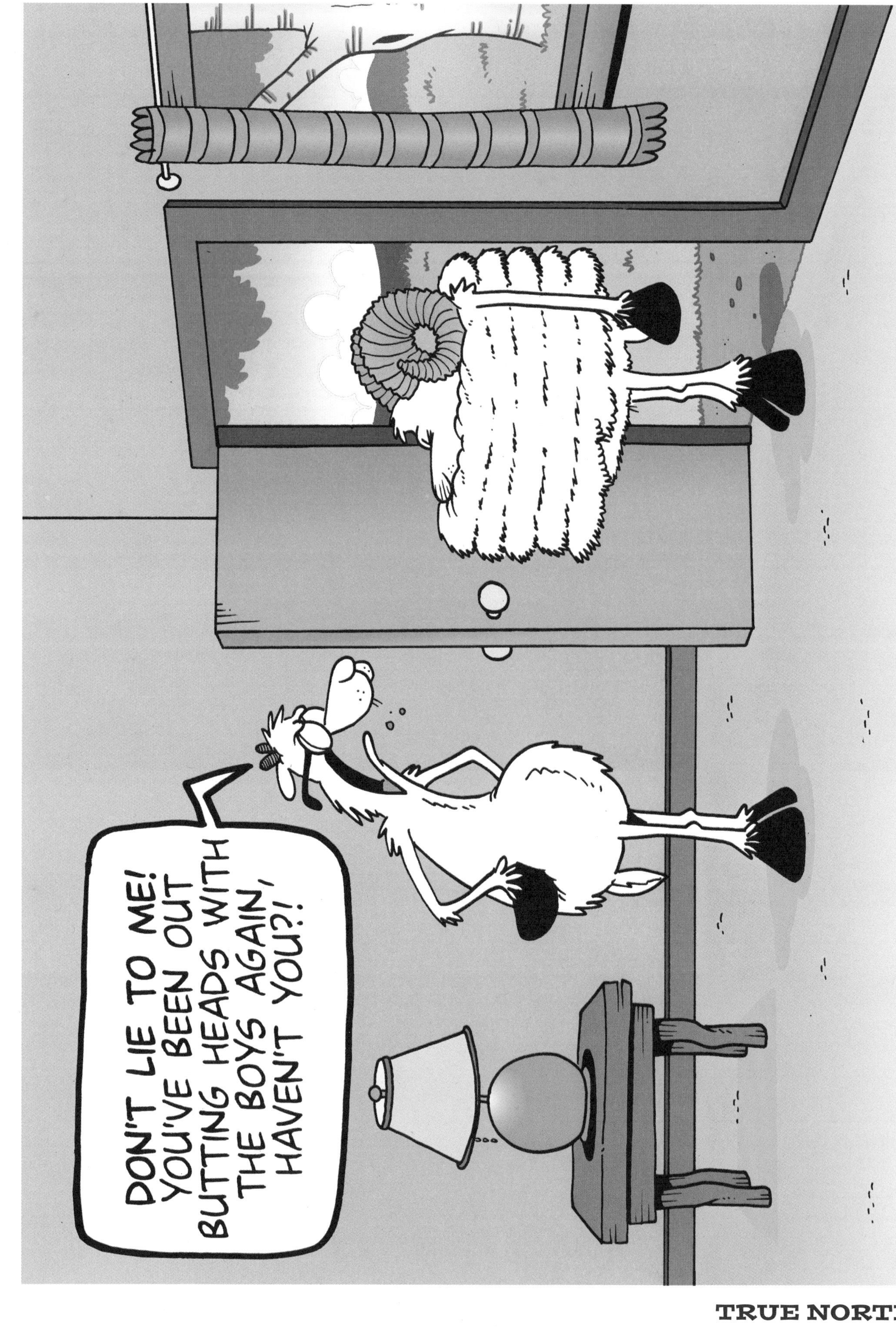
DON'T LIE TO ME! YOU'VE BEEN OUT BUTTING HEADS WITH THE BOYS AGAIN, HAVEN'T YOU?!

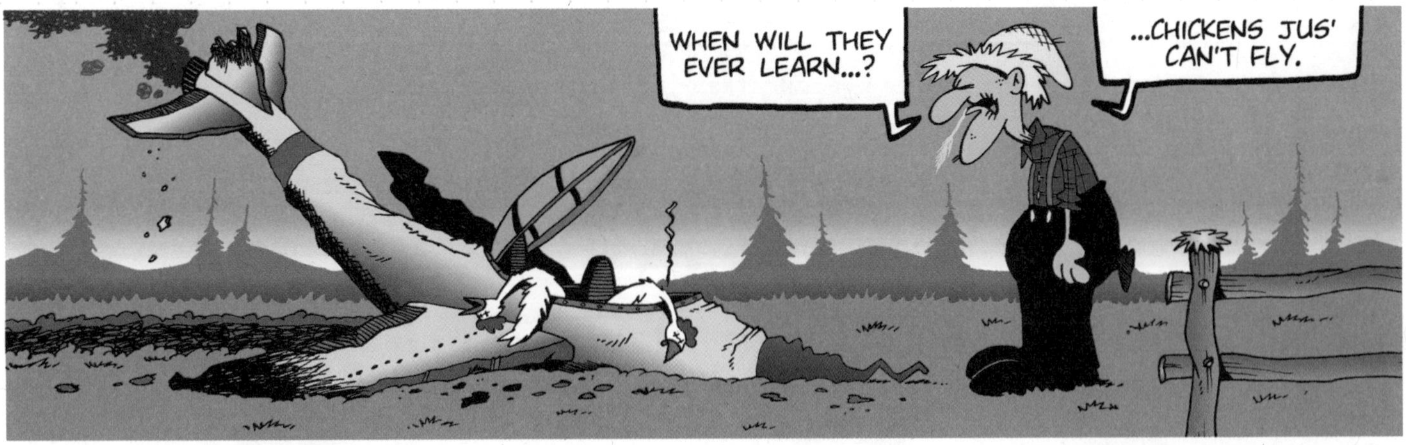
WHEN WILL THEY EVER LEARN...?
...CHICKENS JUS' CAN'T FLY.

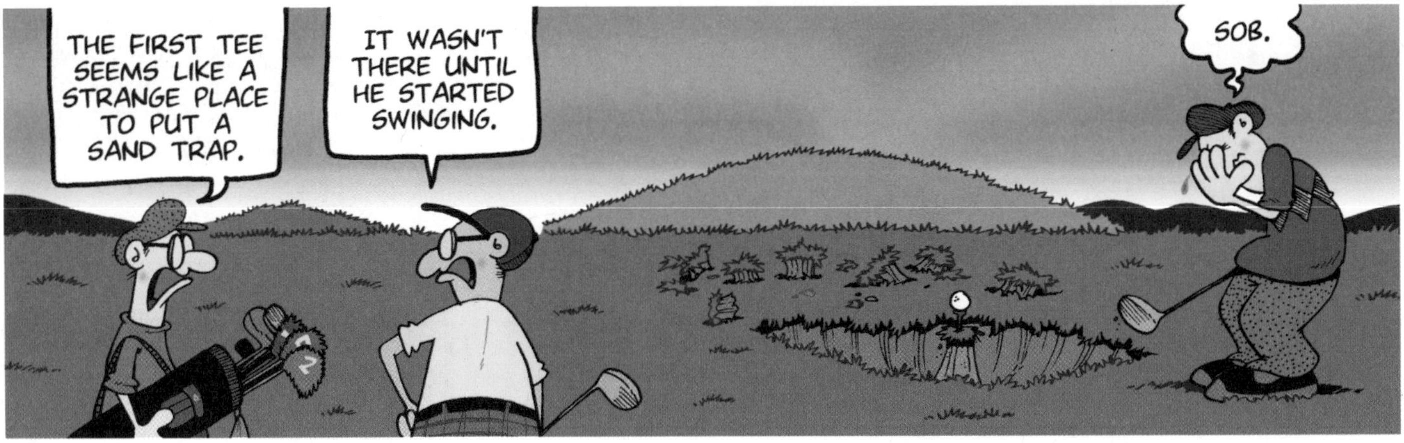
THE FIRST TEE SEEMS LIKE A STRANGE PLACE TO PUT A SAND TRAP.
IT WASN'T THERE UNTIL HE STARTED SWINGING.
SOB.

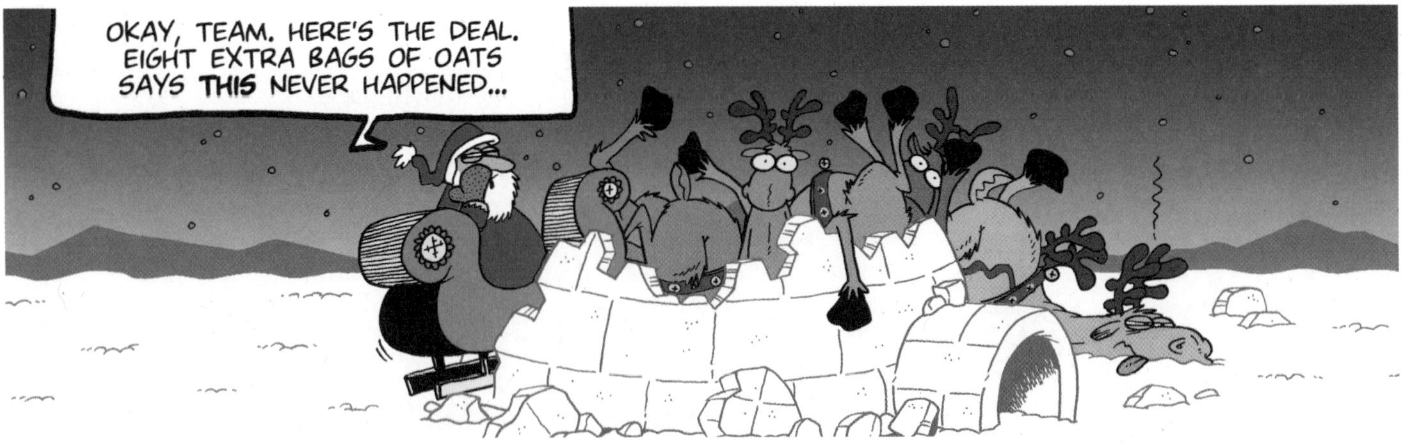
OKAY, TEAM. HERE'S THE DEAL. EIGHT EXTRA BAGS OF OATS SAYS **THIS** NEVER HAPPENED...

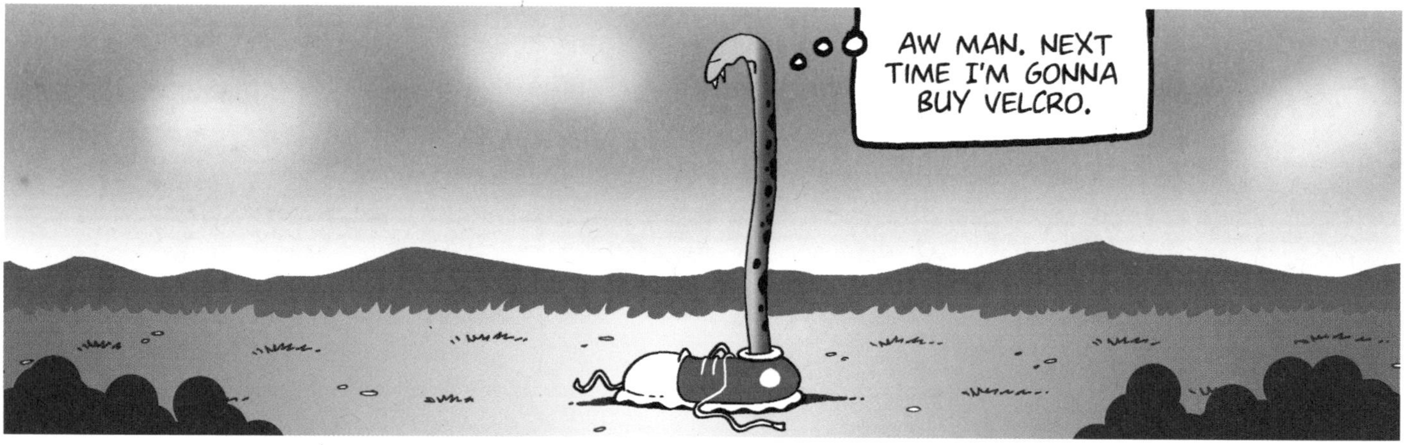
AW MAN. NEXT TIME I'M GONNA BUY VELCRO.

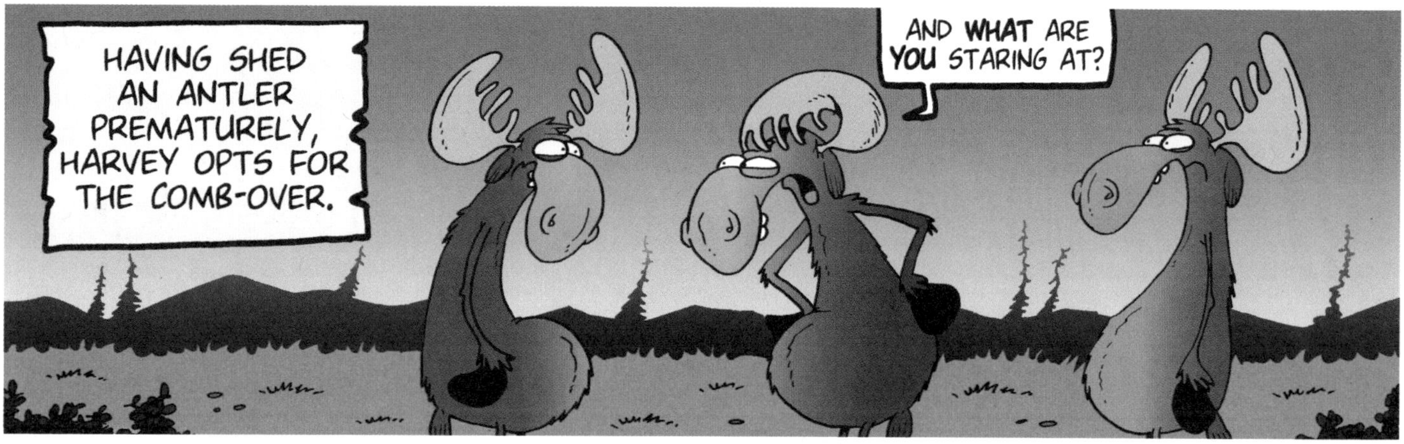
HAVING SHED AN ANTLER PREMATURELY, HARVEY OPTS FOR THE COMB-OVER.
AND WHAT ARE YOU STARING AT?

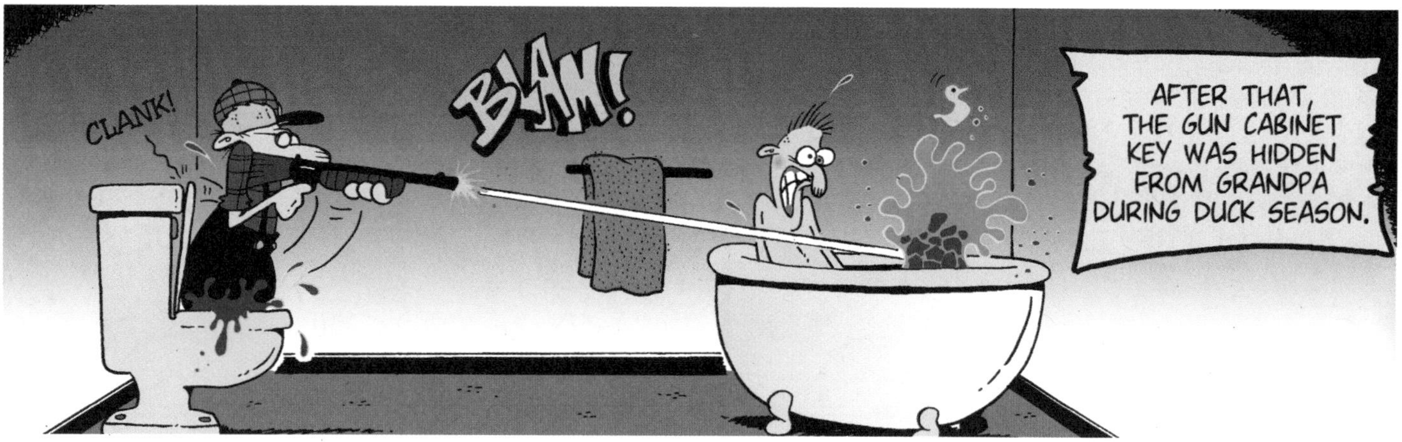
CLANK!
BLAM!
AFTER THAT, THE GUN CABINET KEY WAS HIDDEN FROM GRANDPA DURING DUCK SEASON.

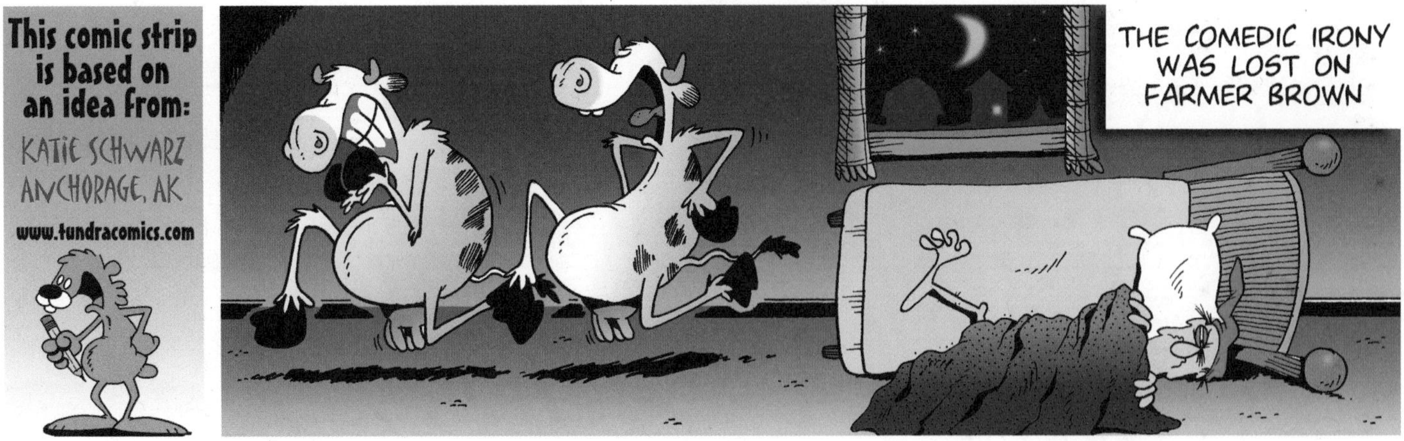
This comic strip is based on an idea from:
KATIE SCHWARZ ANCHORAGE, AK
www.tundracomics.com
THE COMEDIC IRONY WAS LOST ON FARMER BROWN

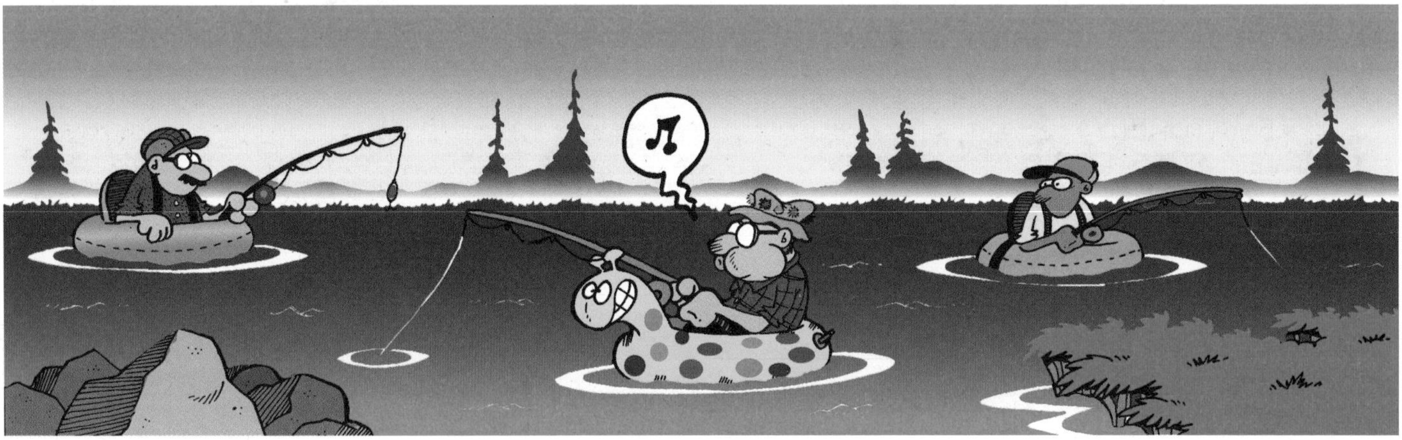

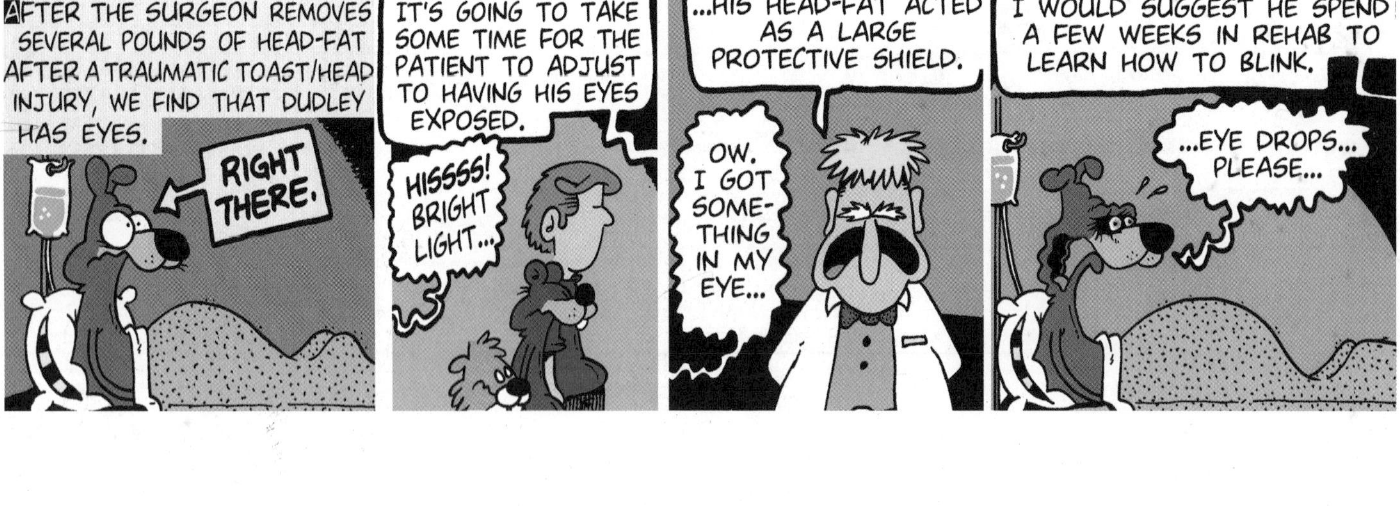
AFTER THE SURGEON REMOVES SEVERAL POUNDS OF HEAD-FAT AFTER A TRAUMATIC TOAST/HEAD INJURY, WE FIND THAT DUDLEY HAS EYES.
RIGHT THERE.
IT'S GOING TO TAKE SOME TIME FOR THE PATIENT TO ADJUST TO HAVING HIS EYES EXPOSED.
HISSSS! BRIGHT LIGHT...
...HIS HEAD-FAT ACTED AS A LARGE PROTECTIVE SHIELD.
OW. I GOT SOME-THING IN MY EYE...
I WOULD SUGGEST HE SPEND A FEW WEEKS IN REHAB TO LEARN HOW TO BLINK.
...EYE DROPS... PLEASE...

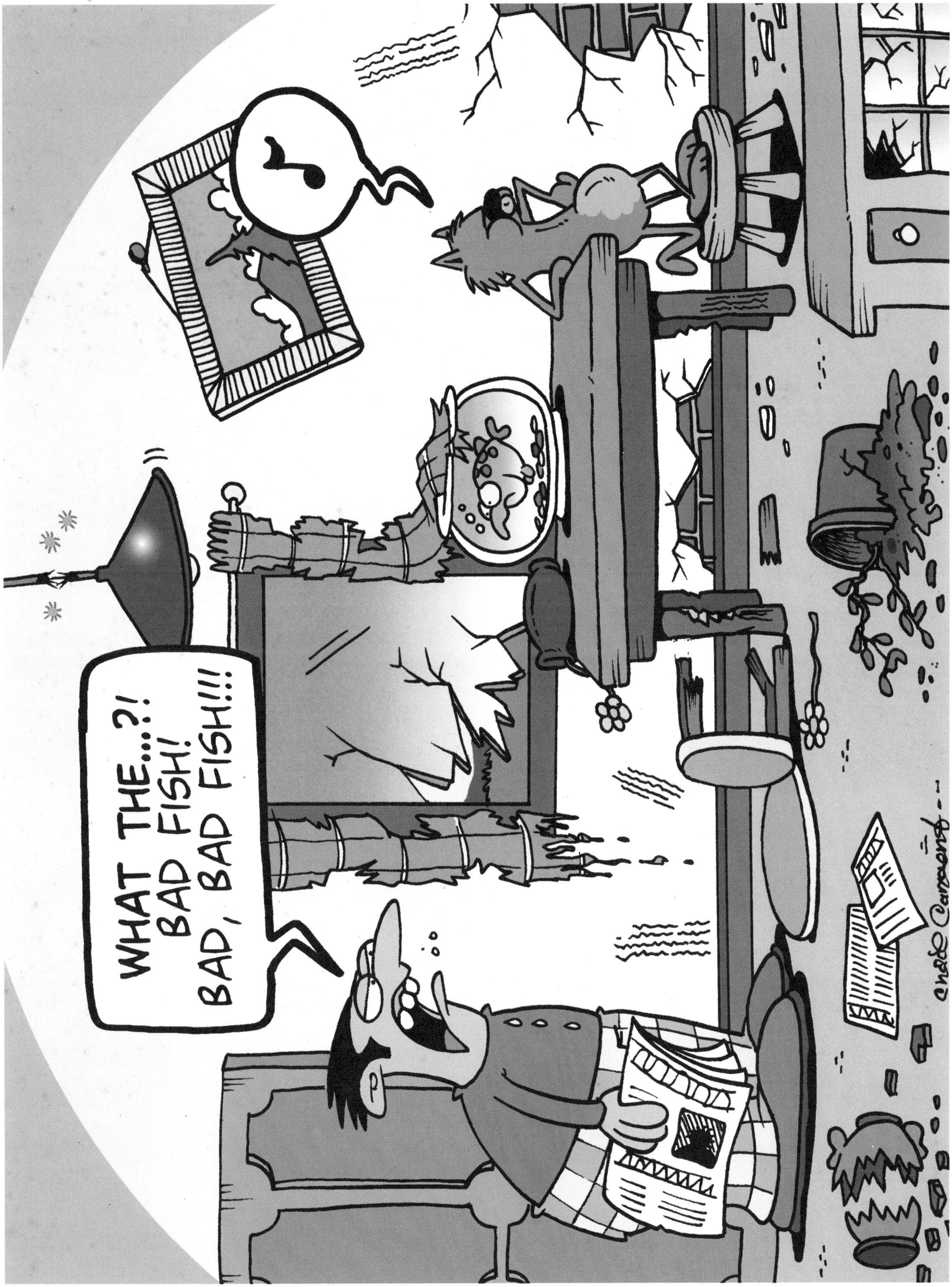
WHAT THE...?! BAD FISH! BAD, BAD FISH!!!

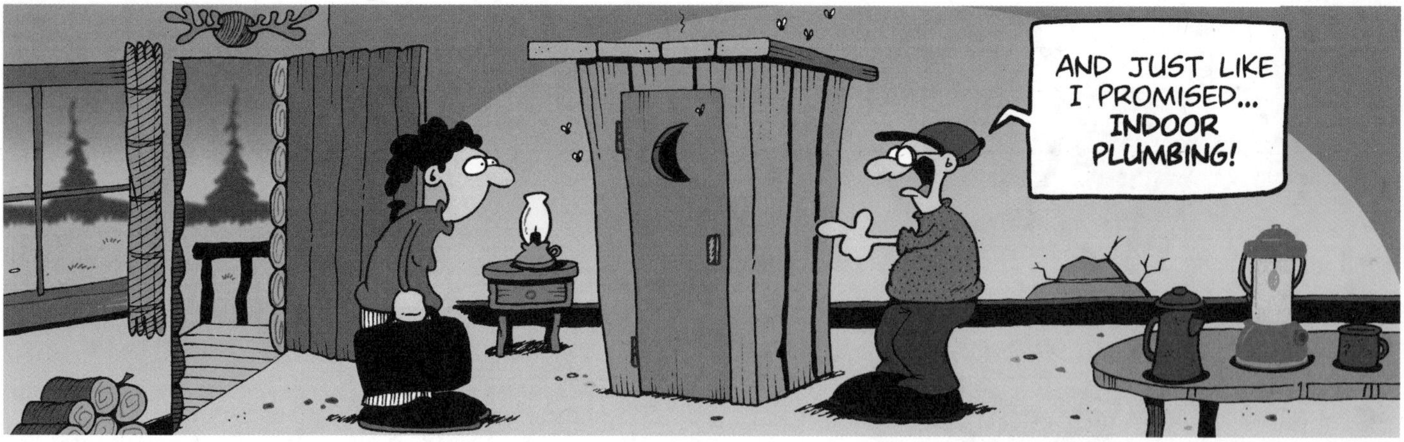
AND JUST LIKE I PROMISED... INDOOR PLUMBING!

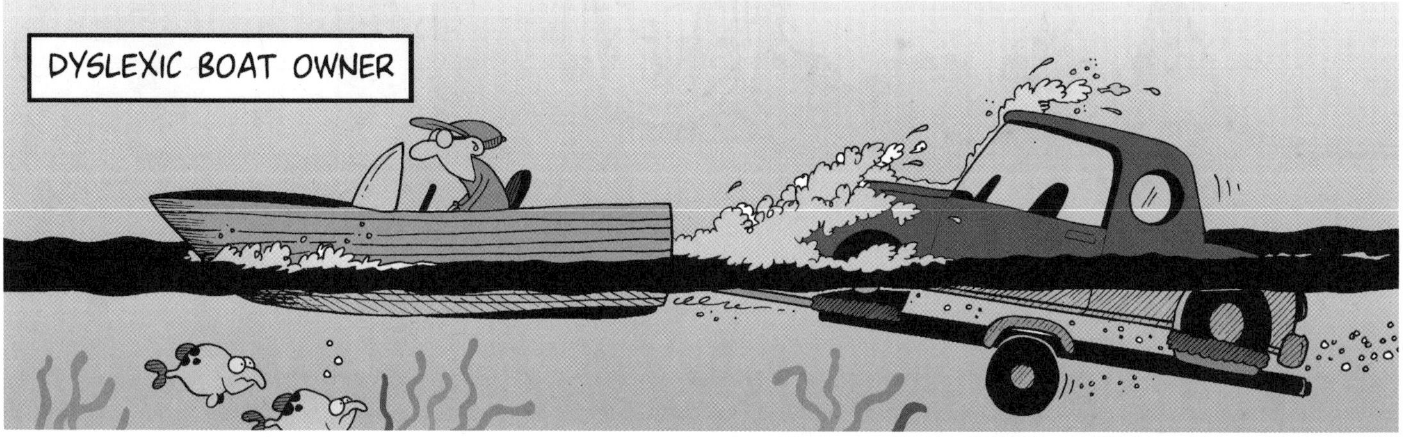
DYSLEXIC BOAT OWNER

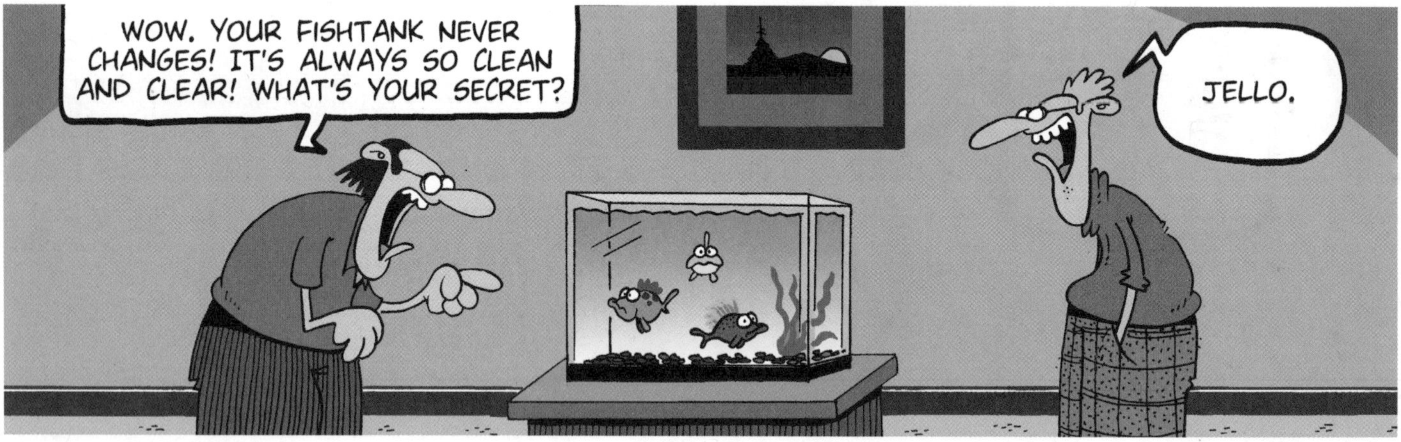
WOW. YOUR FISHTANK NEVER CHANGES! IT'S ALWAYS SO CLEAN AND CLEAR! WHAT'S YOUR SECRET?
JELLO.

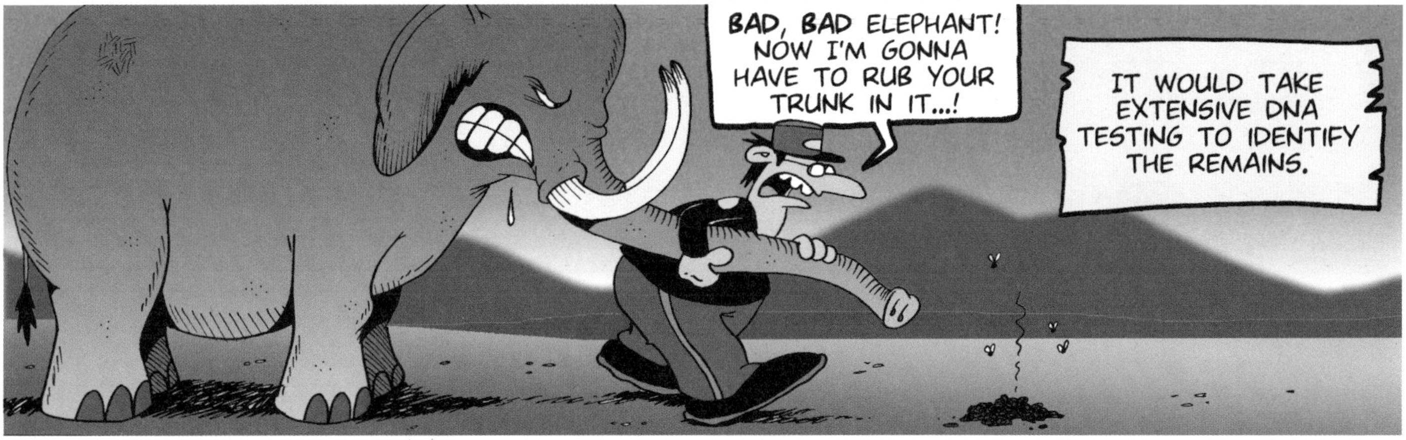
BAD, BAD ELEPHANT! NOW I'M GONNA HAVE TO RUB YOUR TRUNK IN IT...!
IT WOULD TAKE EXTENSIVE DNA TESTING TO IDENTIFY THE REMAINS.

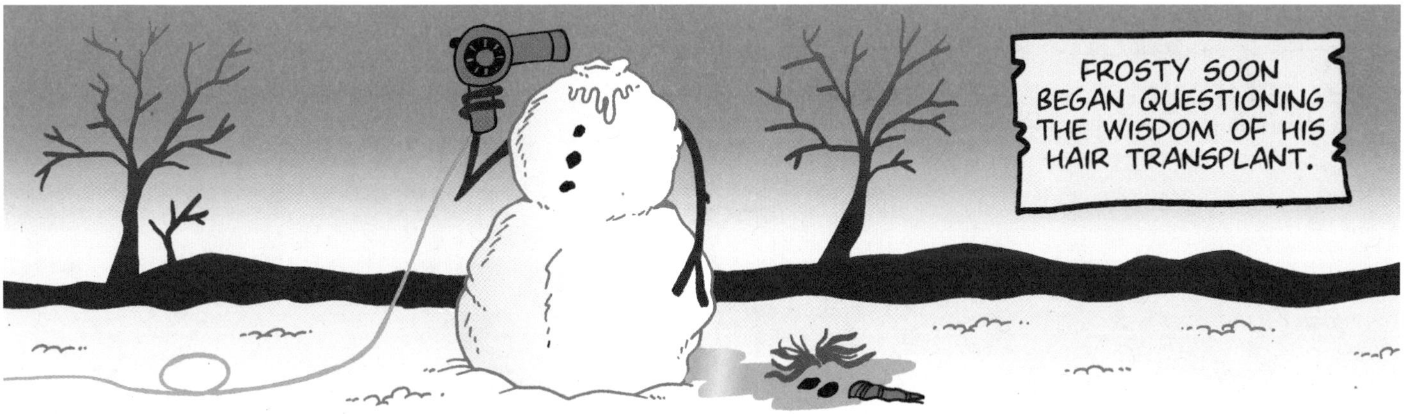
FROSTY SOON BEGAN QUESTIONING THE WISDOM OF HIS HAIR TRANSPLANT.

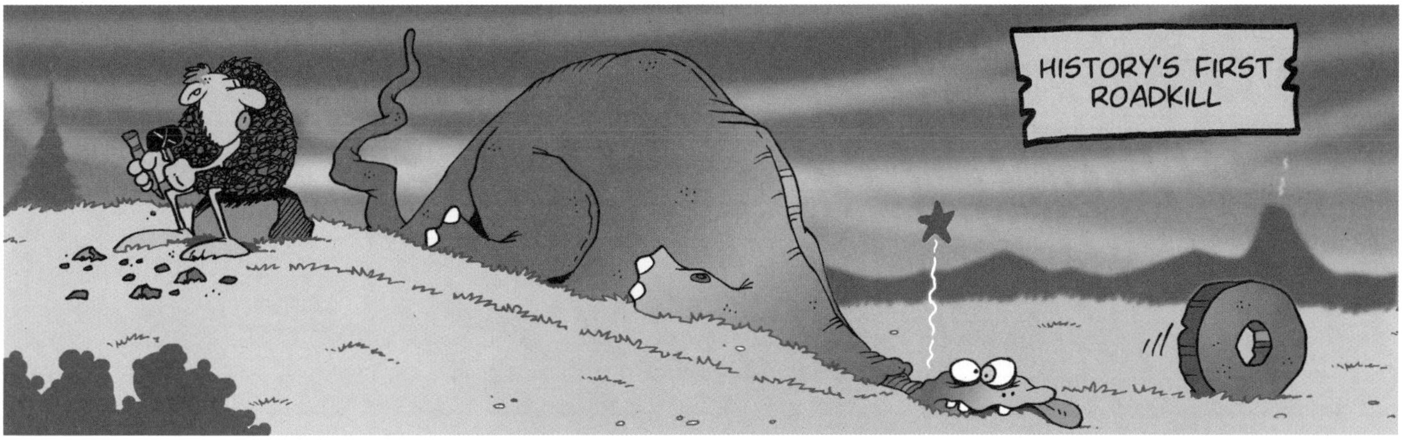
HISTORY'S FIRST ROADKILL

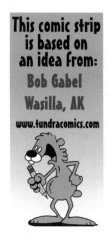

This comic strip is based on an idea from:

Bob Gabel

Wasilla, AK

www.tundracomics.com

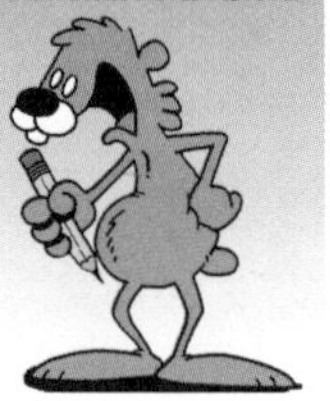

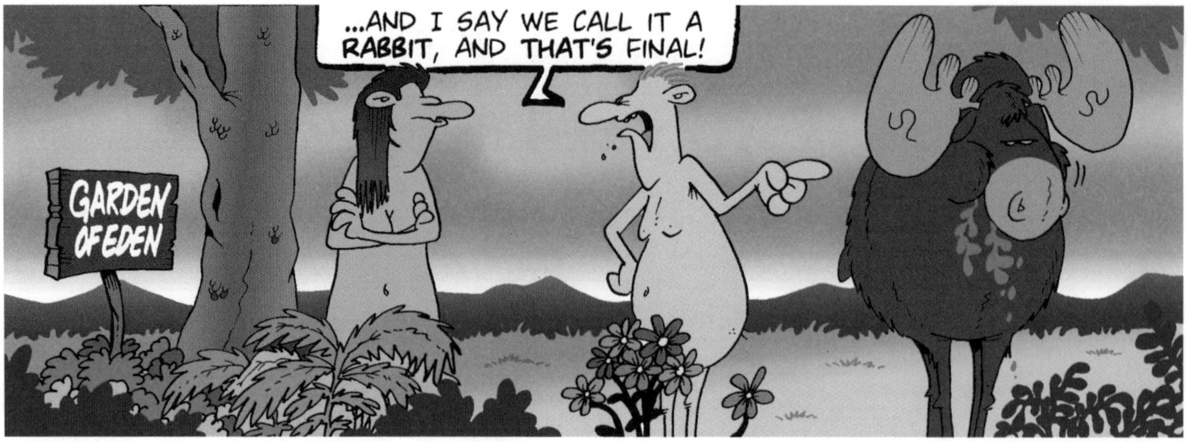
GARDEN OF EDEN
...AND I SAY WE CALL IT A RABBIT, AND THAT'S FINAL!

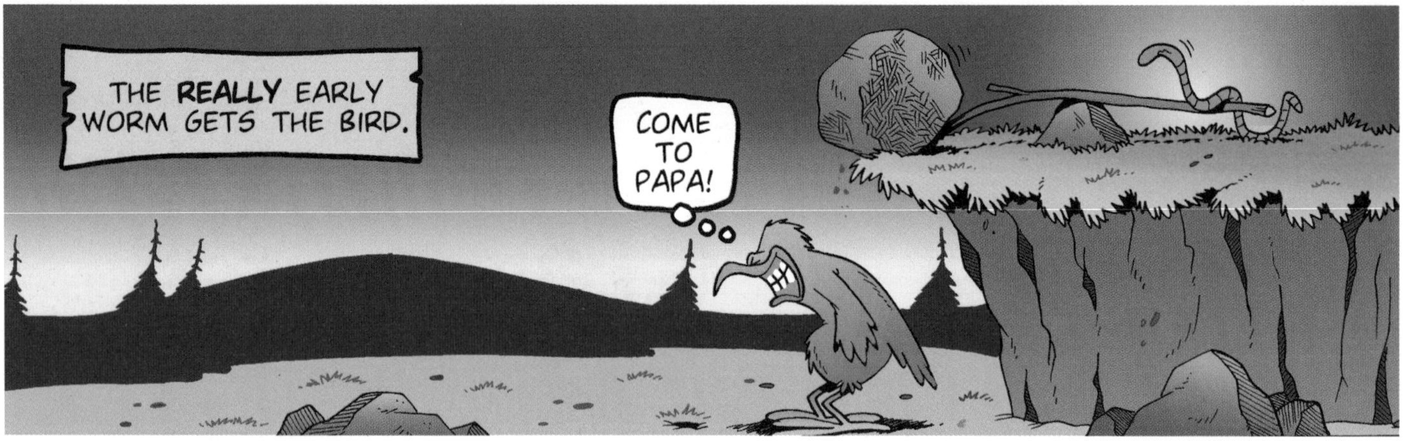
THE REALLY EARLY WORM GETS THE BIRD.
COME TO PAPA!

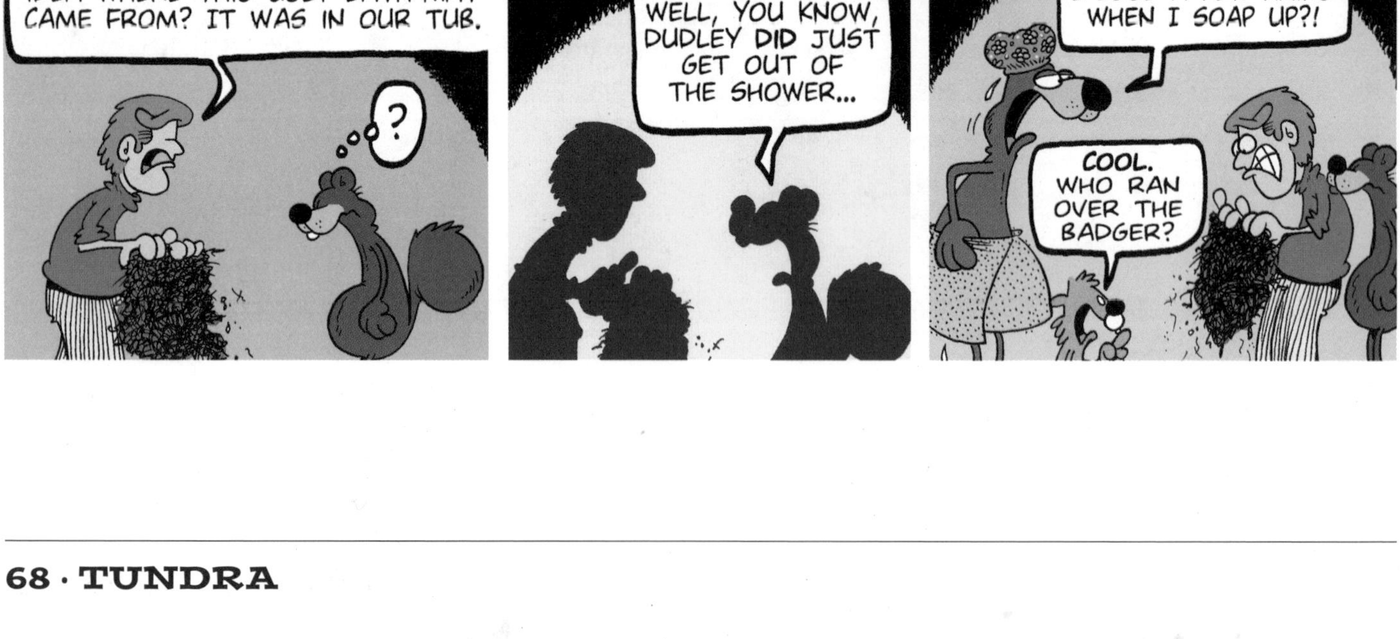
HEY, SHERM. DO YOU HAVE ANY IDEA WHERE THIS UGLY BATH-MAT CAME FROM? IT WAS IN OUR TUB.
?
WELL, YOU KNOW, DUDLEY DID JUST GET OUT OF THE SHOWER...
HEY, IS IT MY FAULT I LOSE A FEW HAIRS WHEN I SOAP UP?!
COOL. WHO RAN OVER THE BADGER?

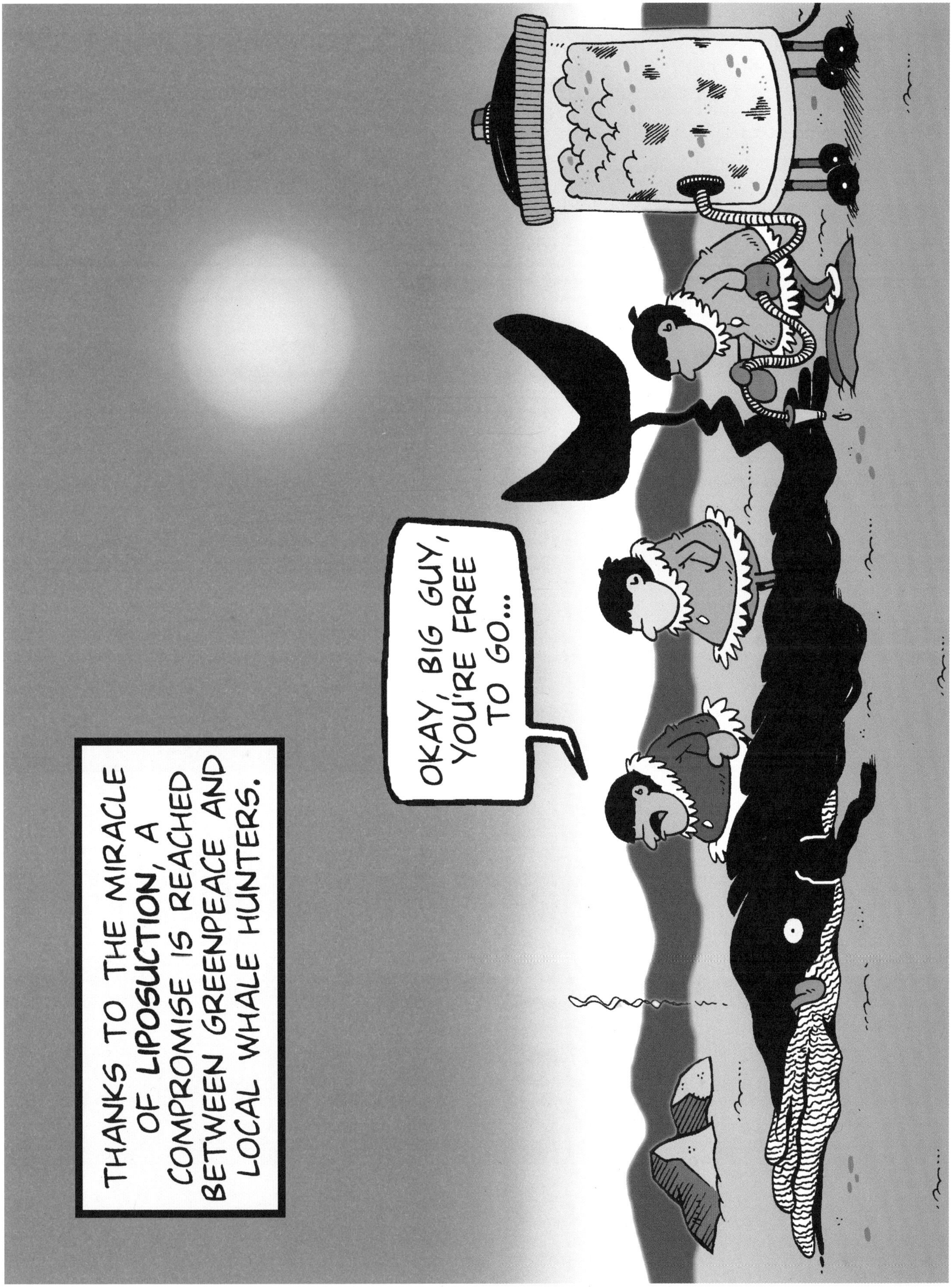
THANKS TO THE MIRACLE OF LIPOSUCTION, A COMPROMISE IS REACHED BETWEEN GREENPEACE AND LOCAL WHALE HUNTERS.
OKAY, BIG GUY, YOU'RE FREE TO GO...

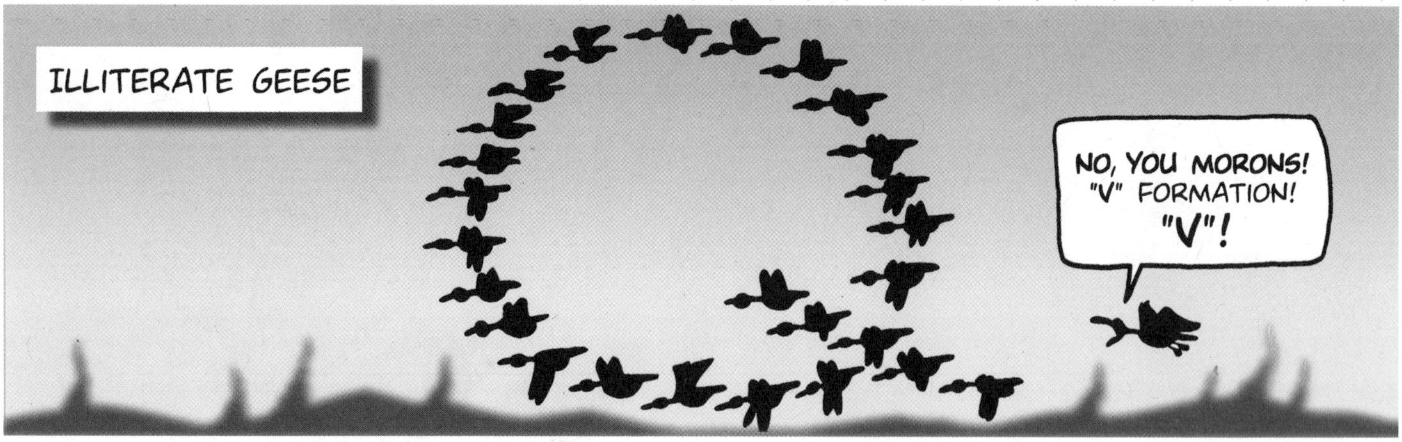
ILLITERATE GEESE
NO, YOU MORONS! "V" FORMATION! "V"!

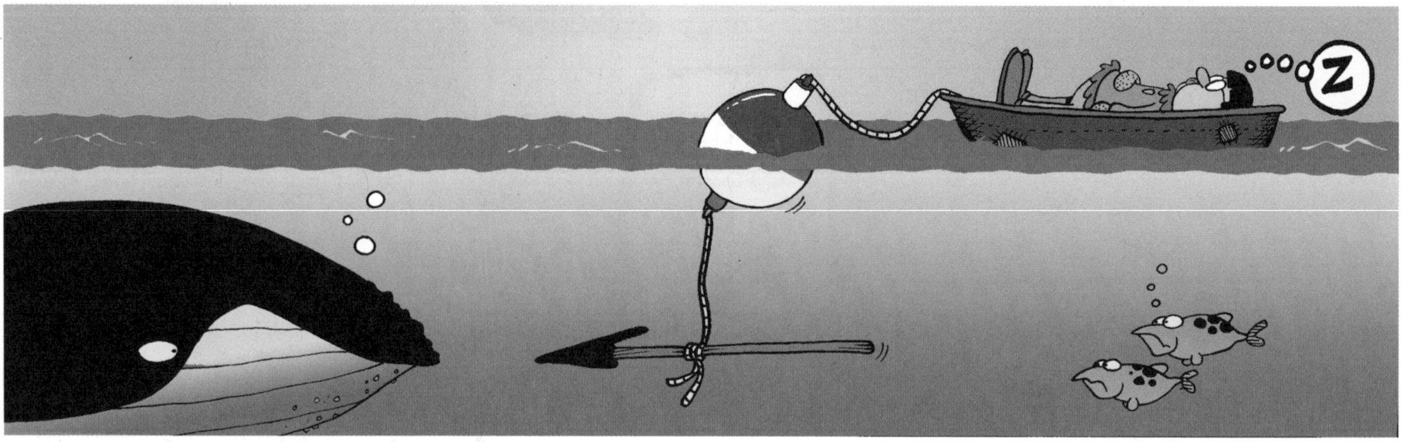
Z

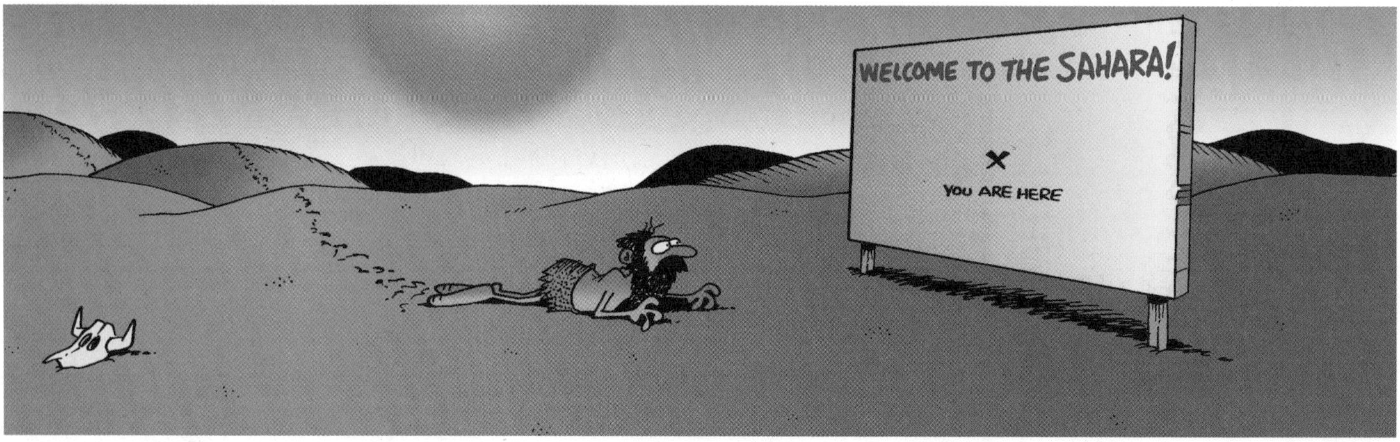
WELCOME TO THE SAHARA!
X
YOU ARE HERE

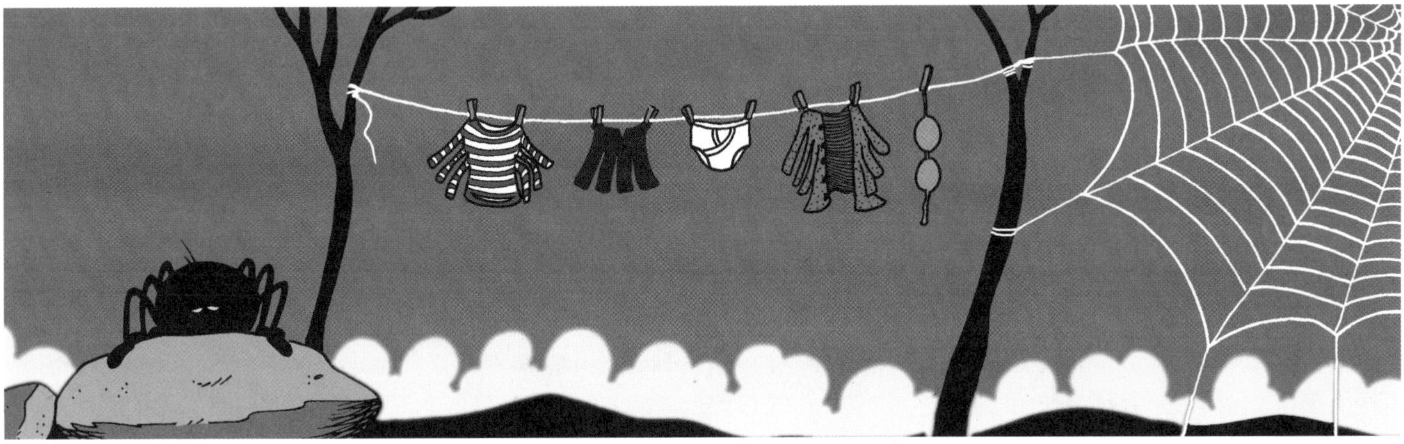

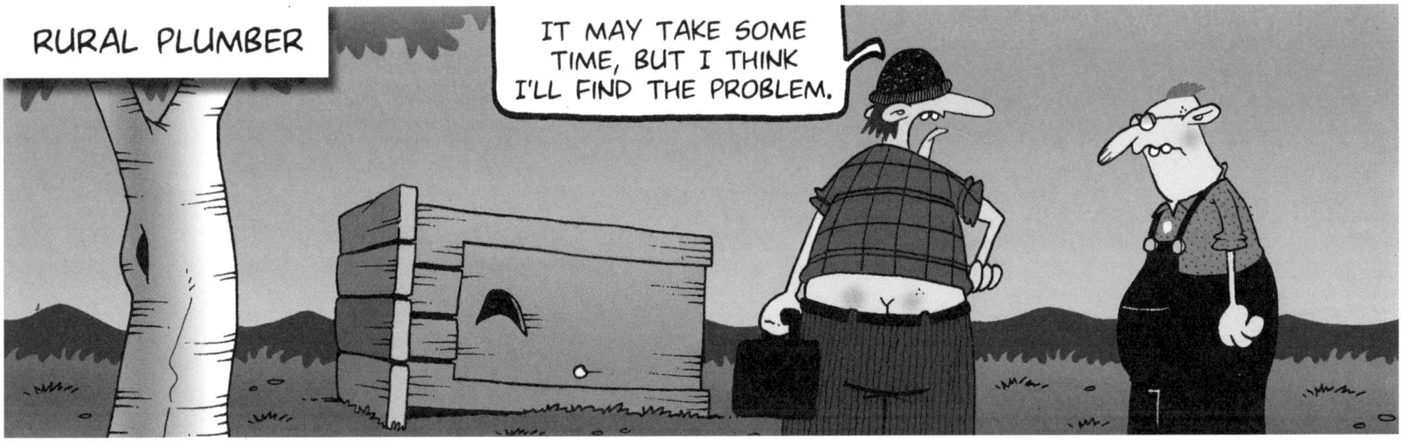
RURAL PLUMBER
IT MAY TAKE SOME TIME, BUT I THINK I'LL FIND THE PROBLEM.

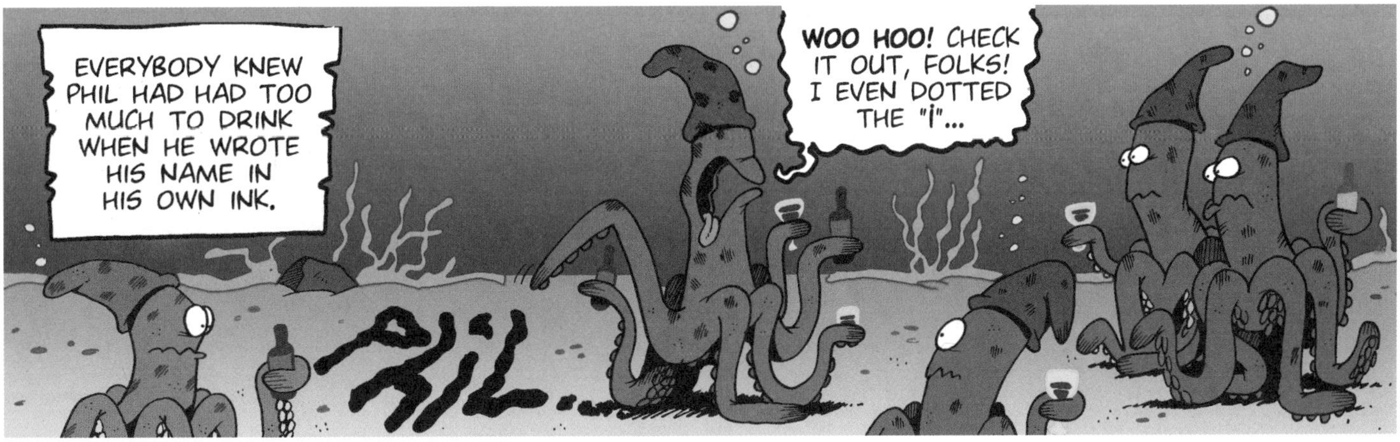
EVERYBODY KNEW PHIL HAD HAD TOO MUCH TO DRINK WHEN HE WROTE HIS NAME IN HIS OWN INK.
WOO HOO! CHECK IT OUT, FOLKS! I EVEN DOTTED THE "I"...
PHIL

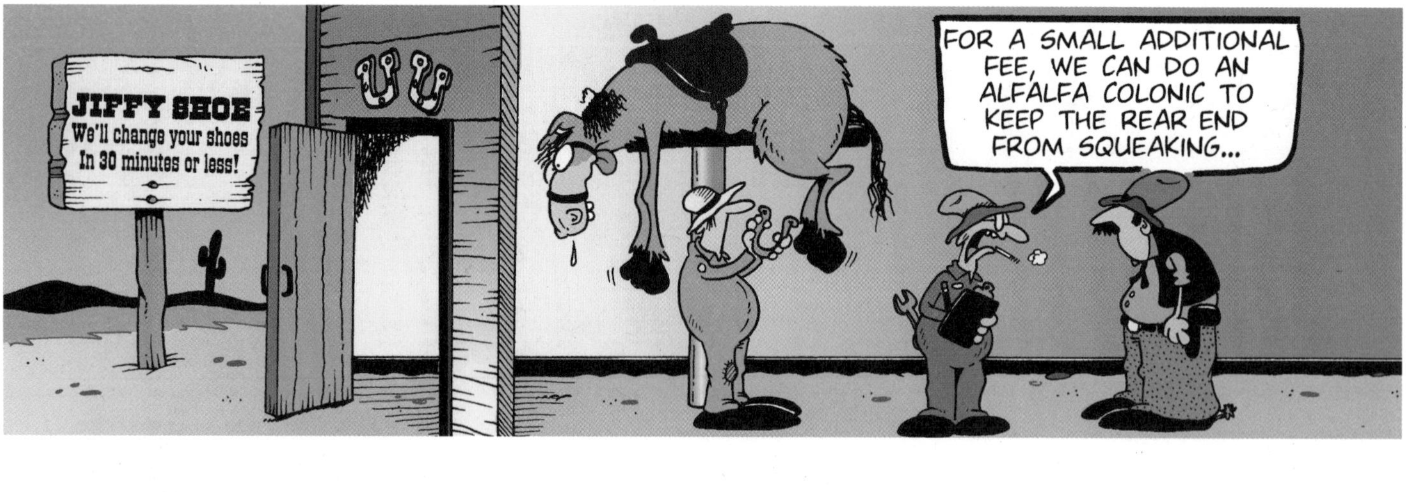
JIFFY SHOE
We'll change your shoes In 30 minutes or less!
FOR A SMALL ADDITIONAL FEE, WE CAN DO AN ALFALFA COLONIC TO KEEP THE REAR END FROM SQUEAKING...

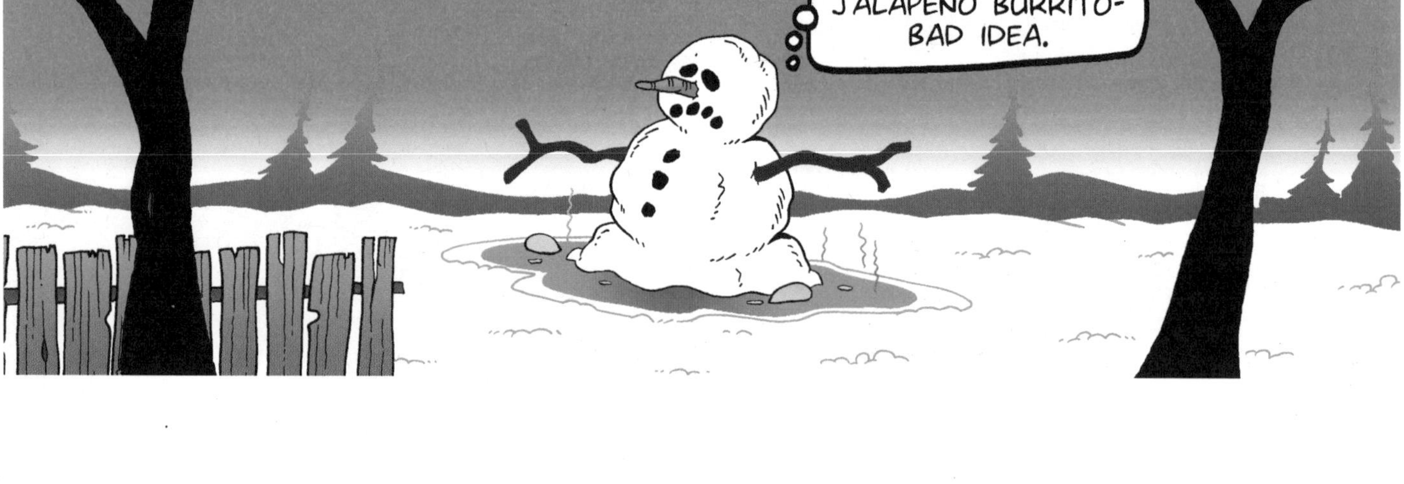
NOTE TO SELF: JALAPEÑO BURRITO-BAD IDEA.

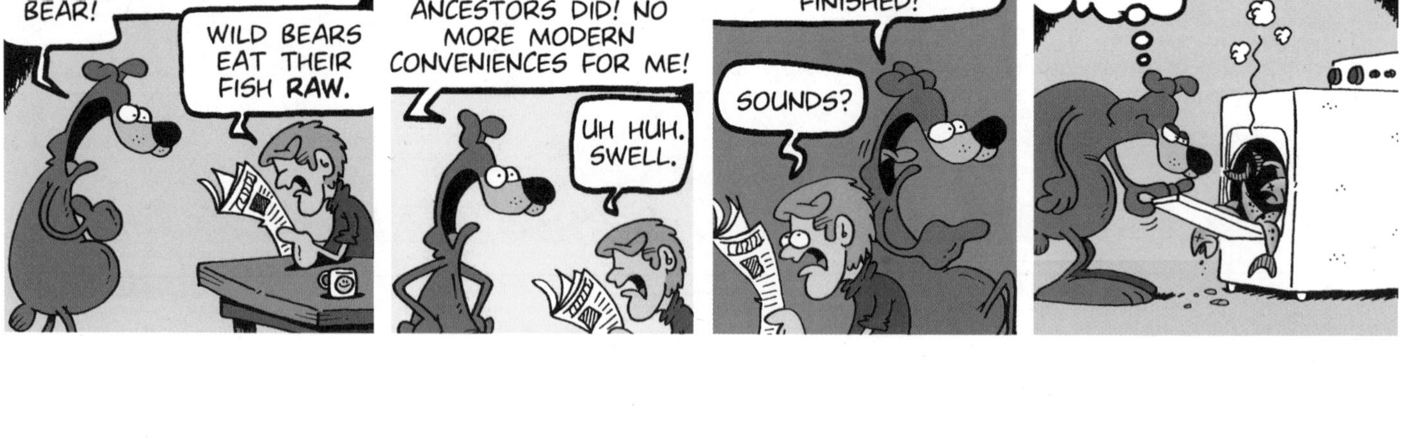
GUESS WHAT, CHAD! I'VE DECIDED TO DRY MY OWN FISH! JUST LIKE A WILD BEAR!
WILD BEARS EAT THEIR FISH RAW.
YEP. LIVING OFF THE LAND JUST LIKE MY ANCESTORS DID! NO MORE MODERN CONVENIENCES FOR ME!
UH HUH. SWELL.
IT SOUNDS LIKE MY FIRST BATCH IS JUST ABOUT FINISHED!
SOUNDS?
HMM. MAYBE I SHOULDA USED MORE STATIC-CLING SHEETS...

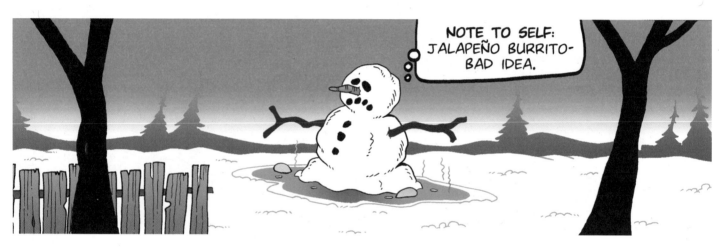

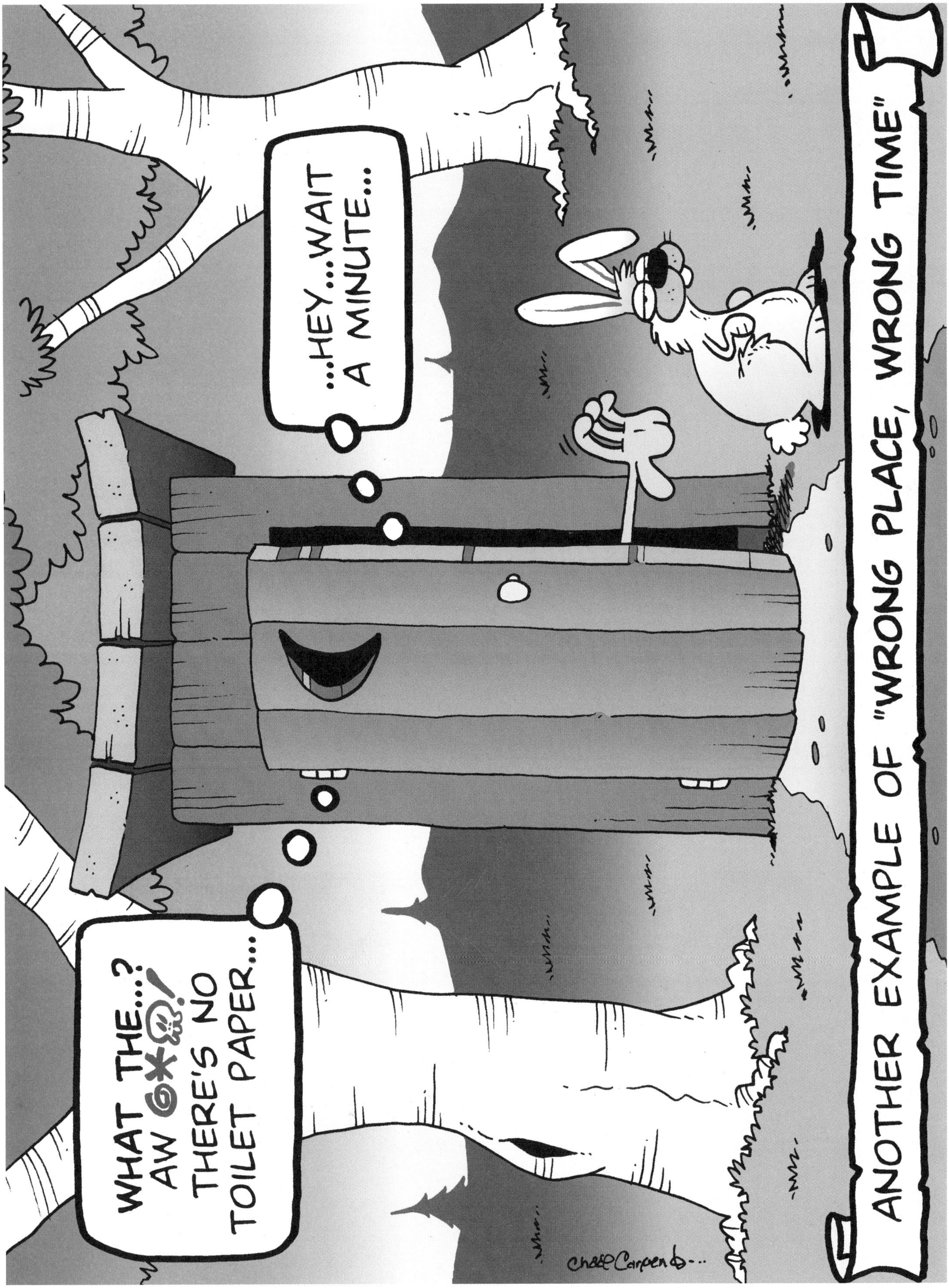
WHAT THE...? AW
THERE'S NO TOILET PAPER...
...HEY...WAIT A MINUTE...
ANOTHER EXAMPLE OF "WRONG PLACE, WRONG TIME"

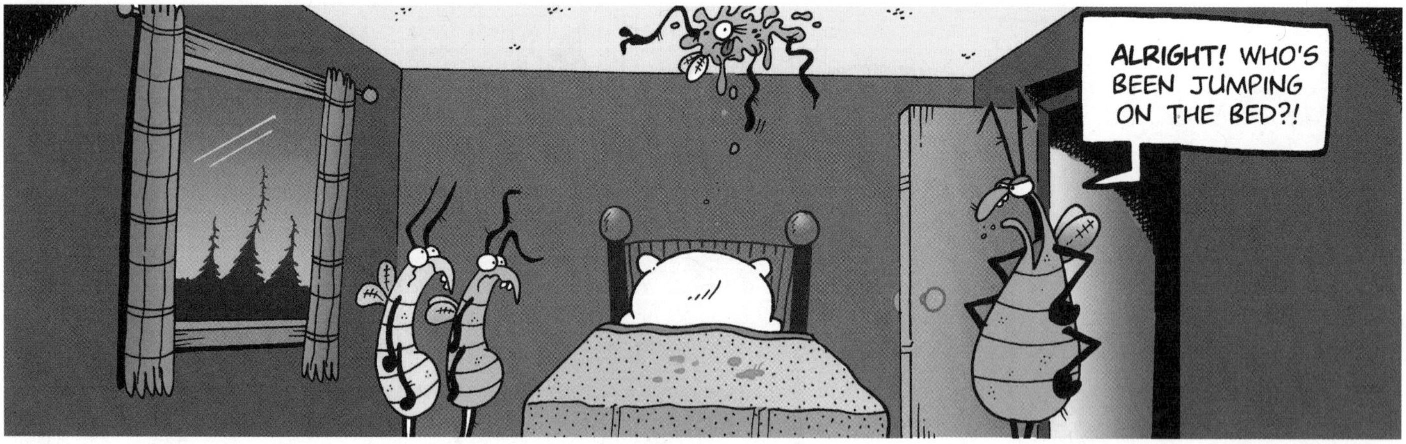
ALRIGHT! WHO'S BEEN JUMPING ON THE BED?!

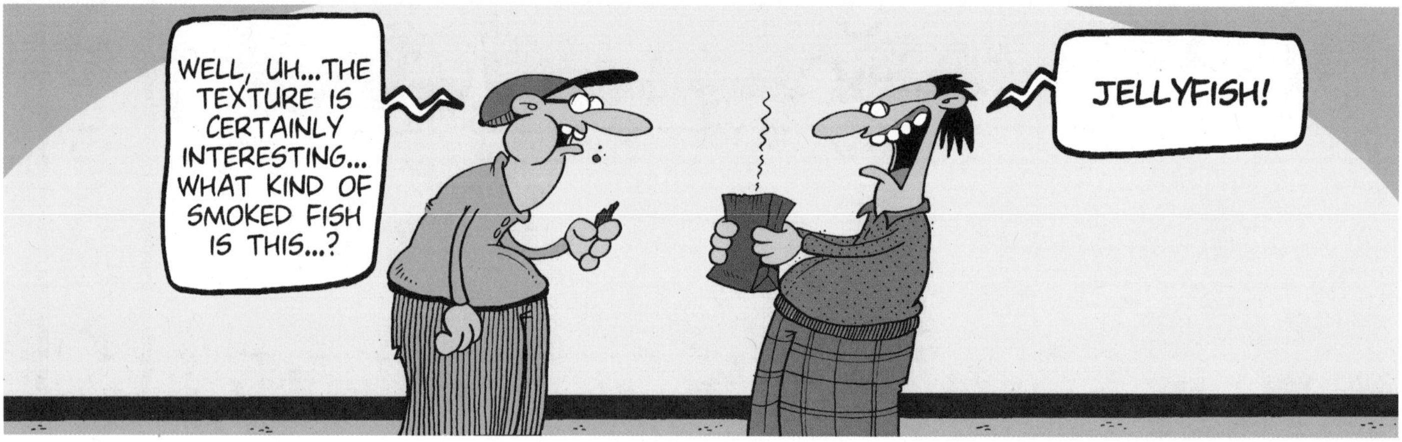
WELL, UH...THE TEXTURE IS CERTAINLY INTERESTING... WHAT KIND OF SMOKED FISH IS THIS...?
JELLYFISH!

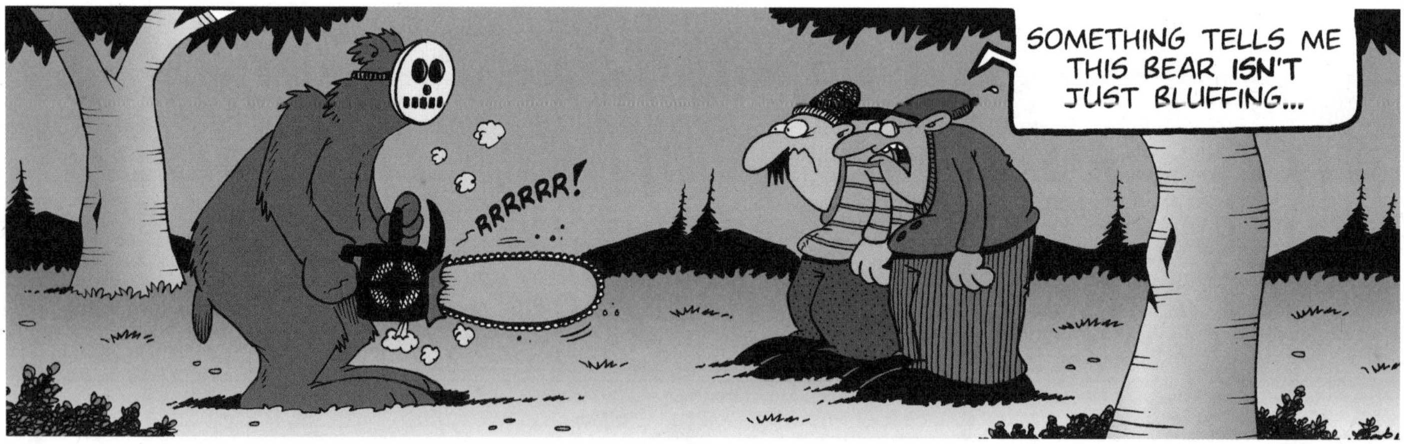
RRRRRR!
SOMETHING TELLS ME THIS BEAR ISN'T JUST BLUFFING...

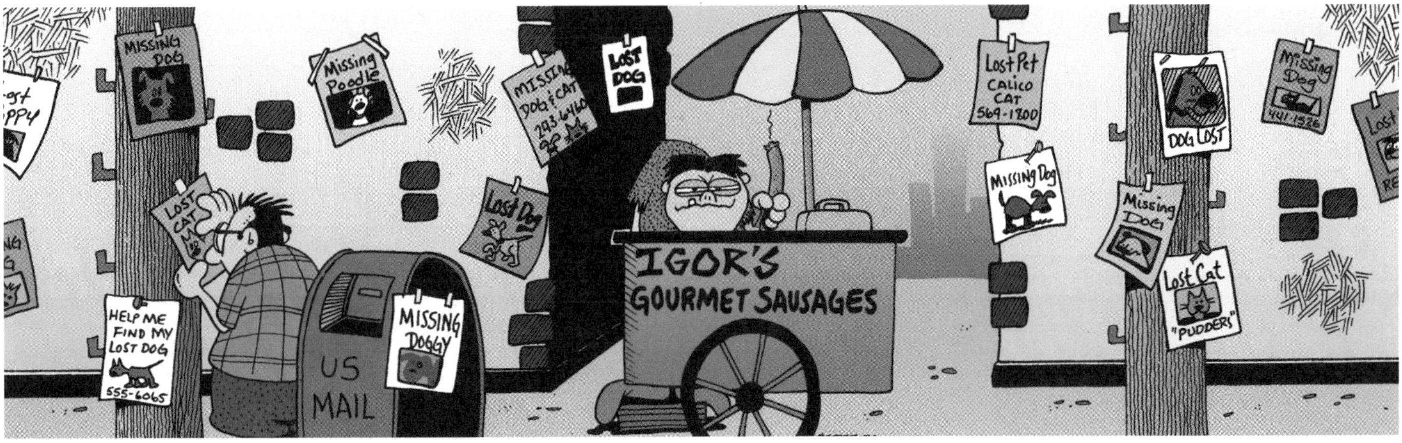
MISSING DOG
Missing Poodle
MISSING Dog & CAT 293-6460
LOST DOG
LOST CAT
HELP ME FIND MY LOST DOG 555-6065
Lost Dog
US MAIL
MISSING DOGGY
IGOR'S GOURMET SAUSAGES
Lost Pet CALICO CAT 569-1800
Missing Dog
DOG LOST
Missing Dog
Lost Cat "PUDDERS"
Missing Dog 441-1526

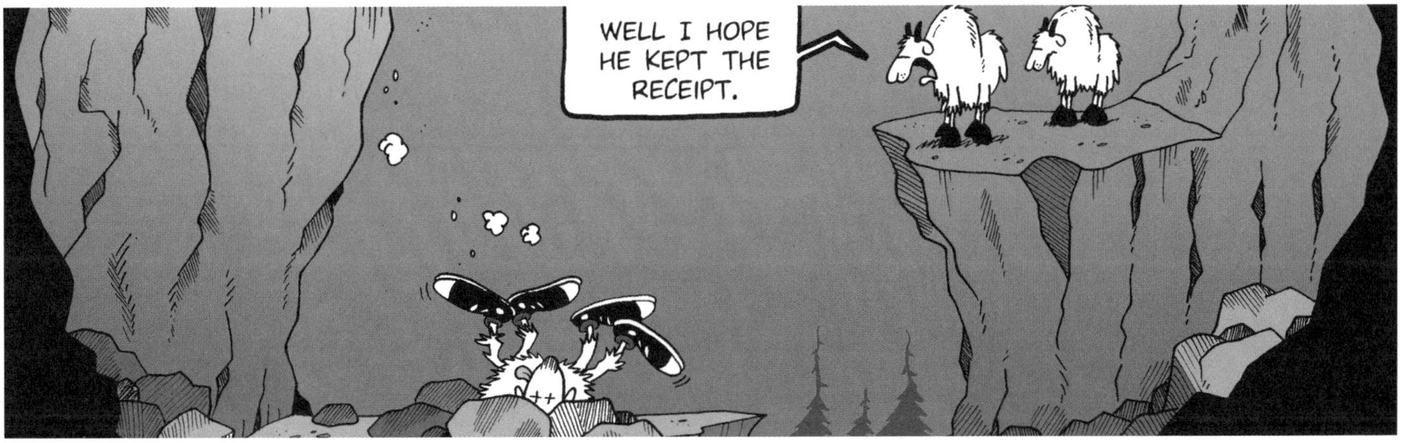
WELL I HOPE HE KEPT THE RECEIPT.

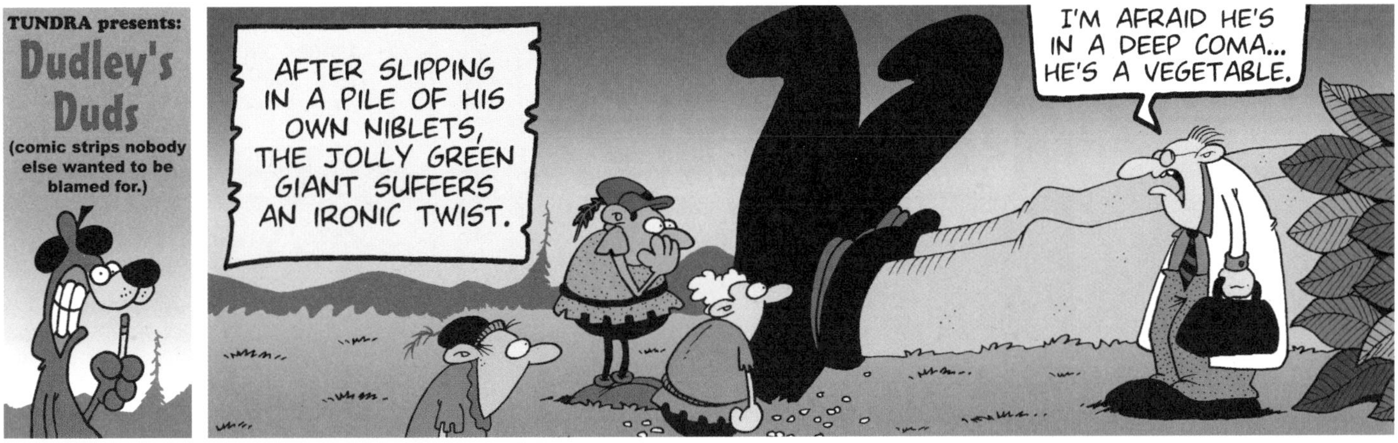
TUNDRA presents:
Dudley's Duds
(comic strips nobody else wanted to be blamed for.)
AFTER SLIPPING IN A PILE OF HIS OWN NIBLETS, THE JOLLY GREEN GIANT SUFFERS AN IRONIC TWIST.
I'M AFRAID HE'S IN A DEEP COMA... HE'S A VEGETABLE.

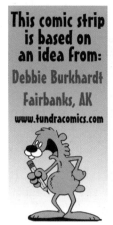

This comic strip is based on an idea from:
Debbie Burkhardt
Fairbanks, AK
www.tundracomics.com

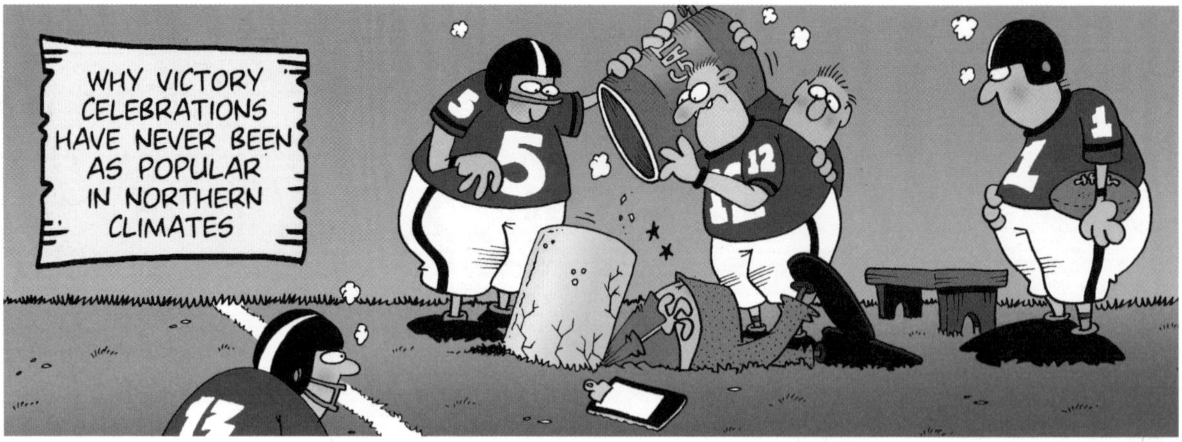
WHY VICTORY CELEBRATIONS HAVE NEVER BEEN AS POPULAR IN NORTHERN CLIMATES

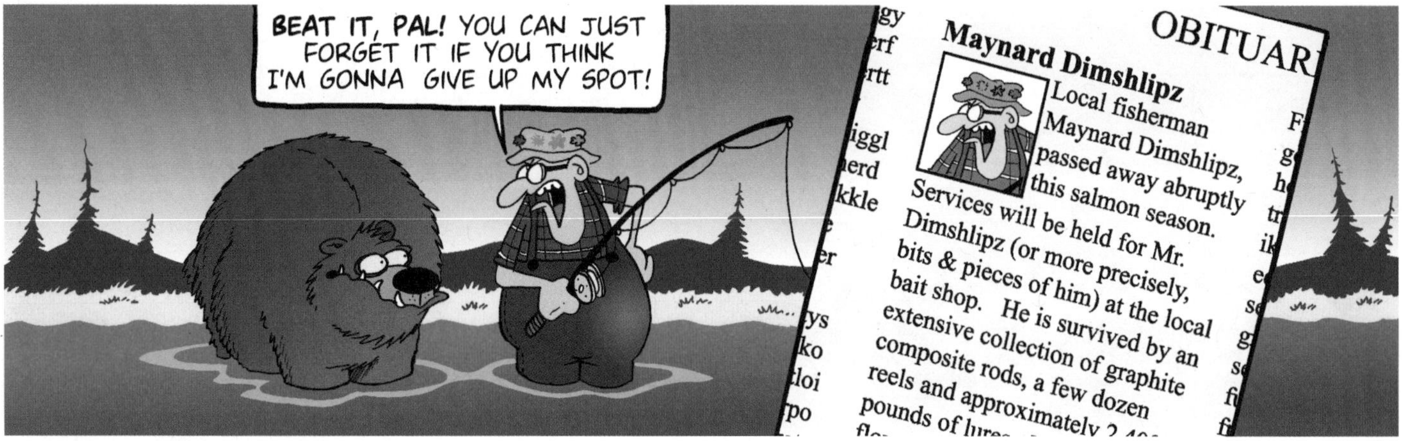
BEAT IT, PAL! YOU CAN JUST FORGET IT IF YOU THINK I'M GONNA GIVE UP MY SPOT!
OBITUAR
Maynard Dimshlipz
Local fisherman Maynard Dimshlipz, passed away abruptly this salmon season. Services will be held for Mr. Dimshlipz (or more precisely, bits & pieces of him) at the local bait shop. He is survived by an extensive collection of graphite composite rods, a few dozen reels and approximately

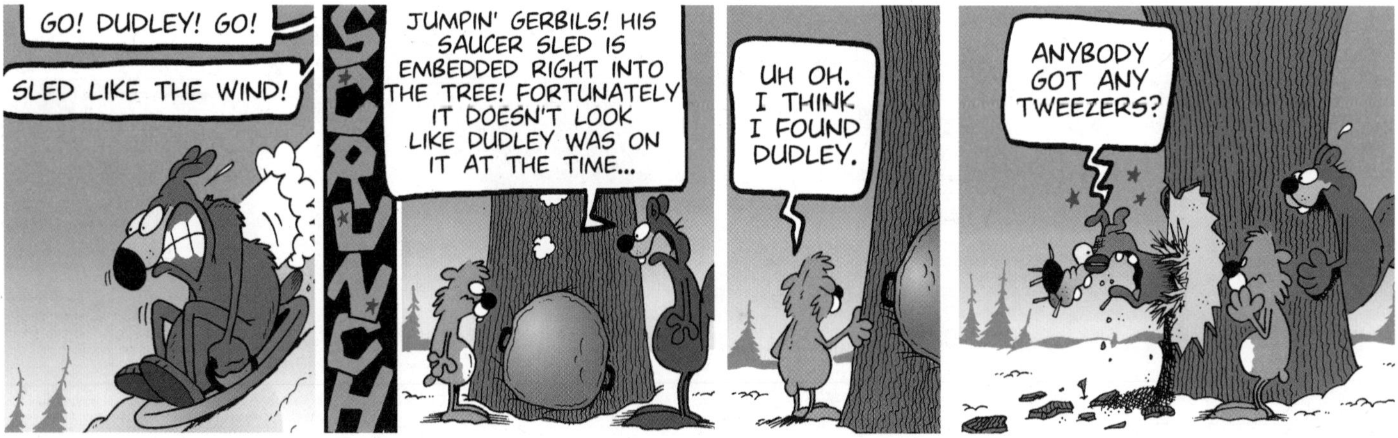
GO! DUDLEY! GO!
SLED LIKE THE WIND!
SCRUNCH
JUMPIN' GERBILS! HIS SAUCER SLED IS EMBEDDED RIGHT INTO THE TREE! FORTUNATELY IT DOESN'T LOOK LIKE DUDLEY WAS ON IT AT THE TIME...
UH OH. I THINK I FOUND DUDLEY.
ANYBODY GOT ANY TWEEZERS?

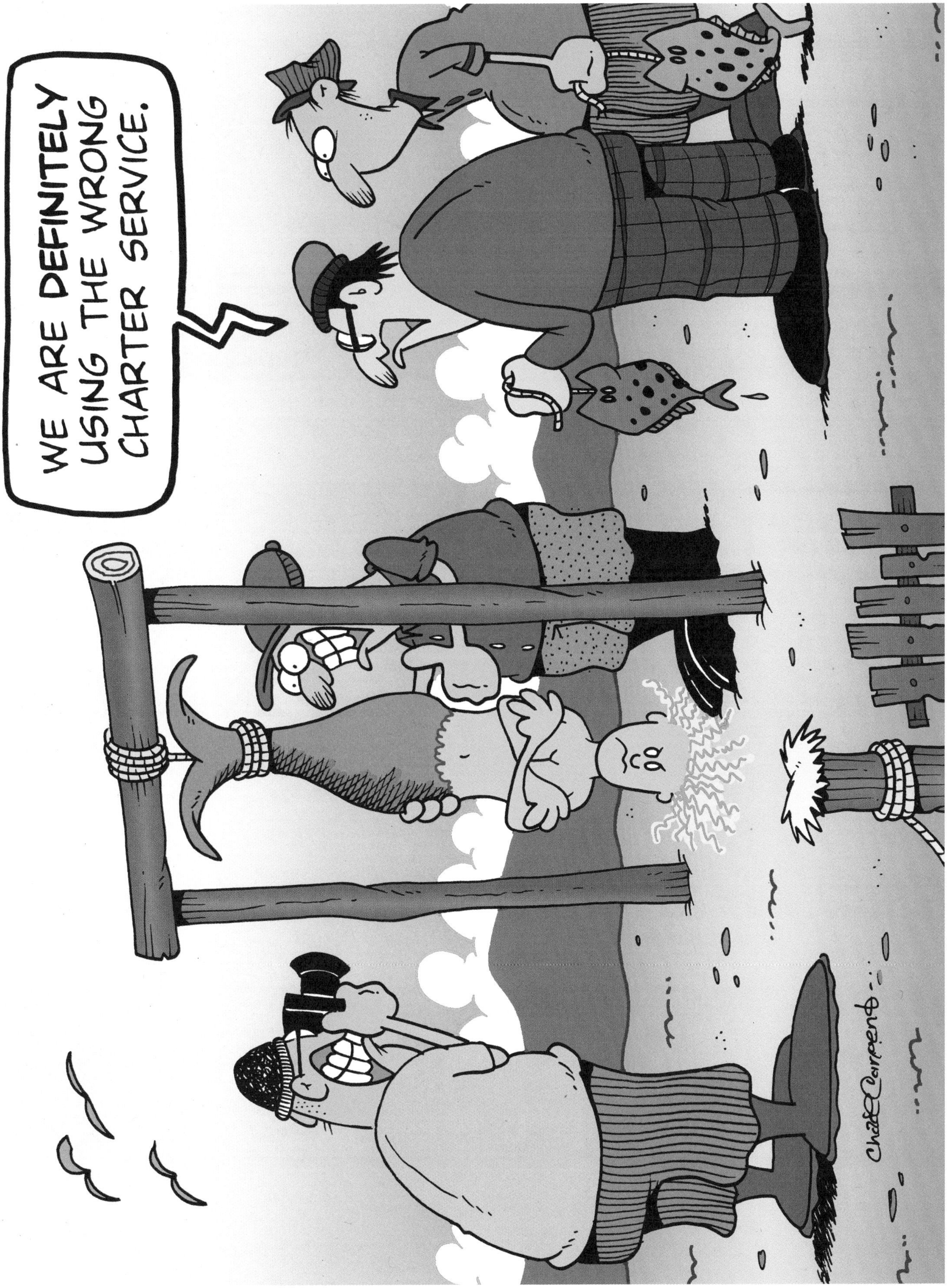
WE ARE **DEFINITELY** USING THE WRONG CHARTER SERVICE.

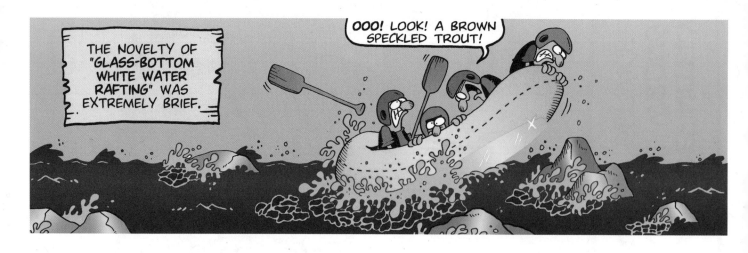

THE NOVELTY OF "GLASS-BOTTOM WHITE WATER RAFTING" WAS EXTREMELY BRIEF.
OOO! LOOK! A BROWN SPECKLED TROUT!

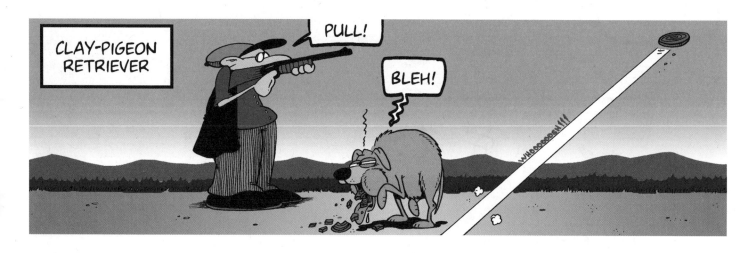

CLAY-PIGEON RETRIEVER
PULL!
BLEH!

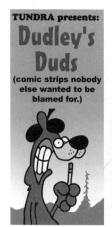

TUNDRA presents:
Dudley's Duds
(comic strips nobody else wanted to be blamed for.)
JIMMY CRACKED CORN: FINALLY, SOMEBODY CARED.
LINE - DO NOT CROSS - POLICE LINE - DO NOT CROSS - POLICE LI

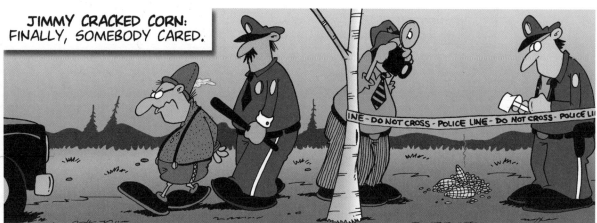

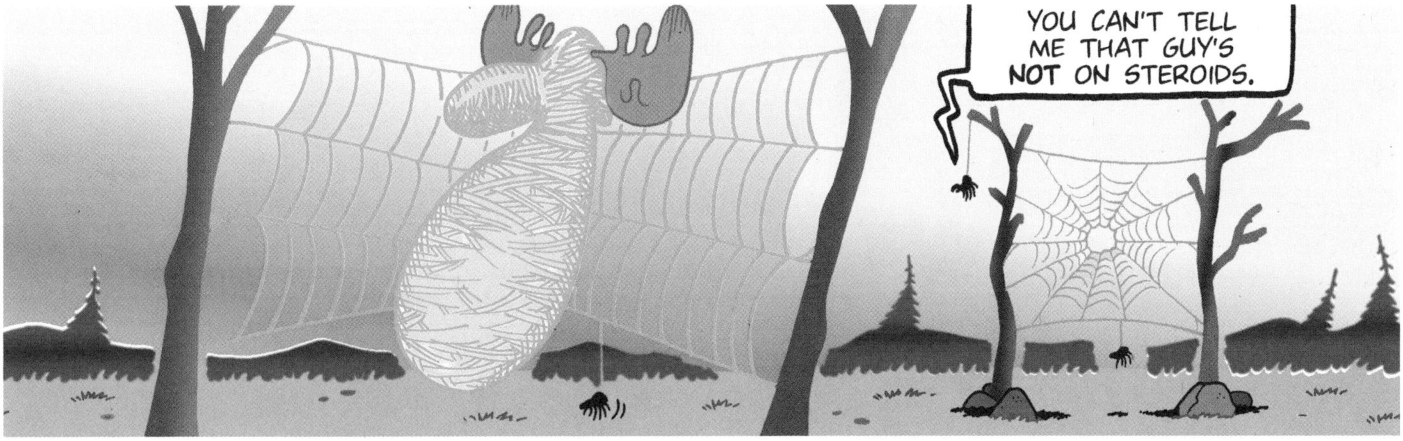
YOU CAN'T TELL ME THAT GUY'S NOT ON STEROIDS.

This comic strip is based on an idea from:

Dan G. Graham

Fairbanks, AK

www.tundracomics.com

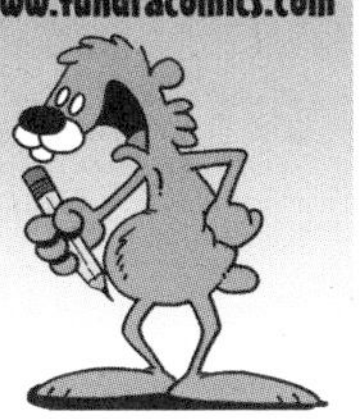

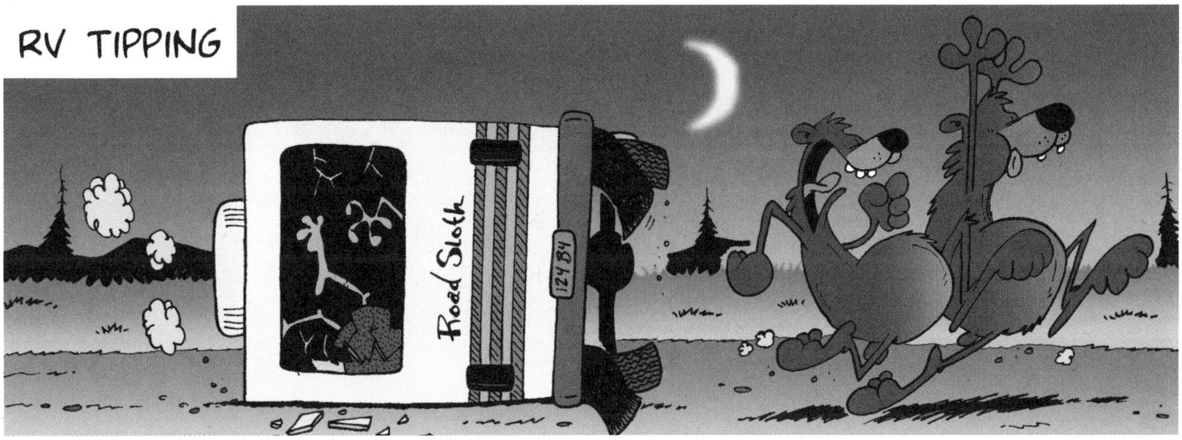
RV TIPPING
Road Sloth

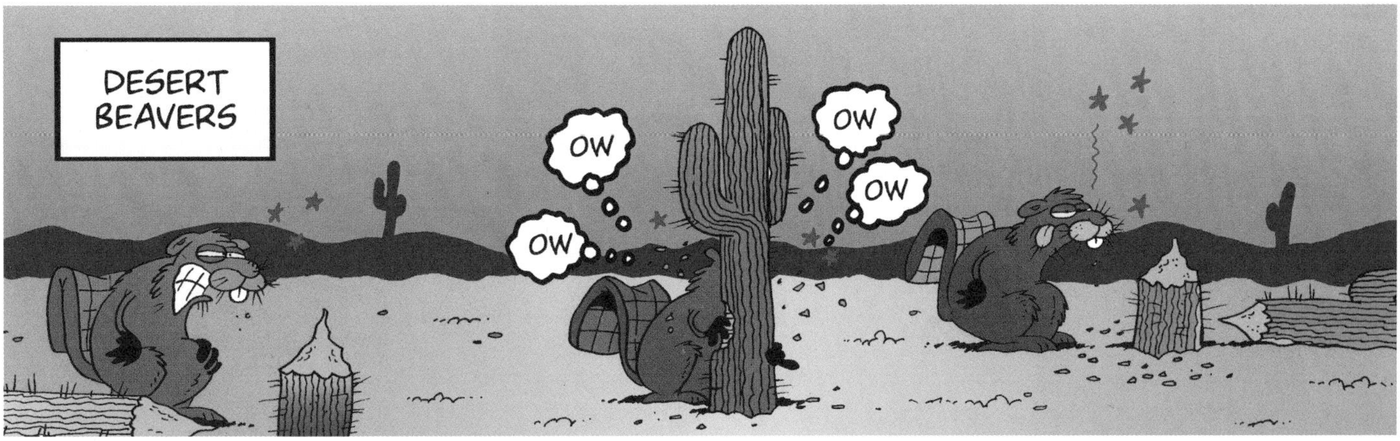
DESERT BEAVERS
OW
OW
OW
OW

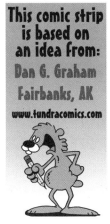

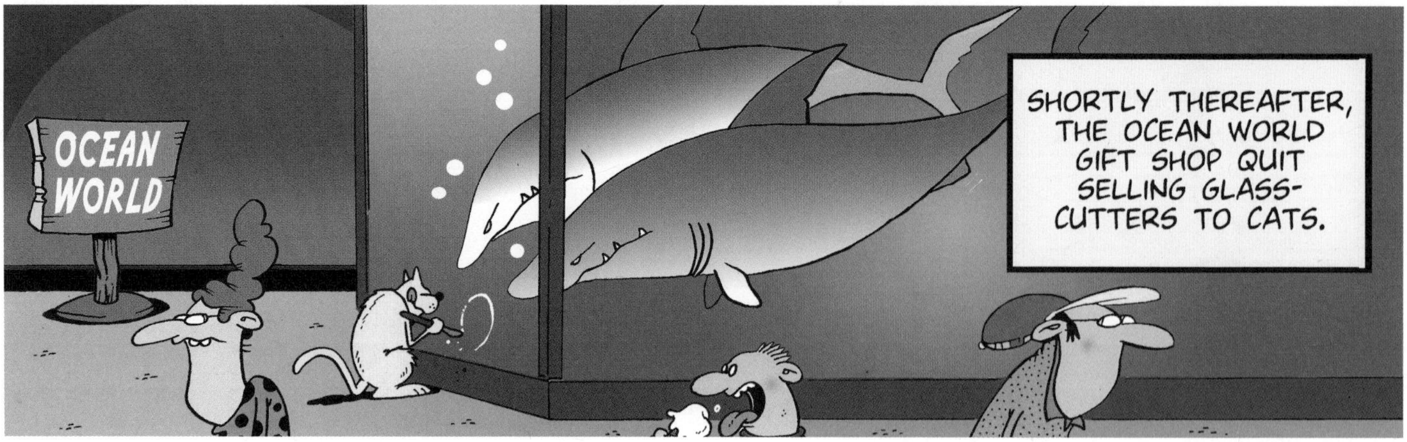
OCEAN WORLD
SHORTLY THEREAFTER, THE OCEAN WORLD GIFT SHOP QUIT SELLING GLASS-CUTTERS TO CATS.

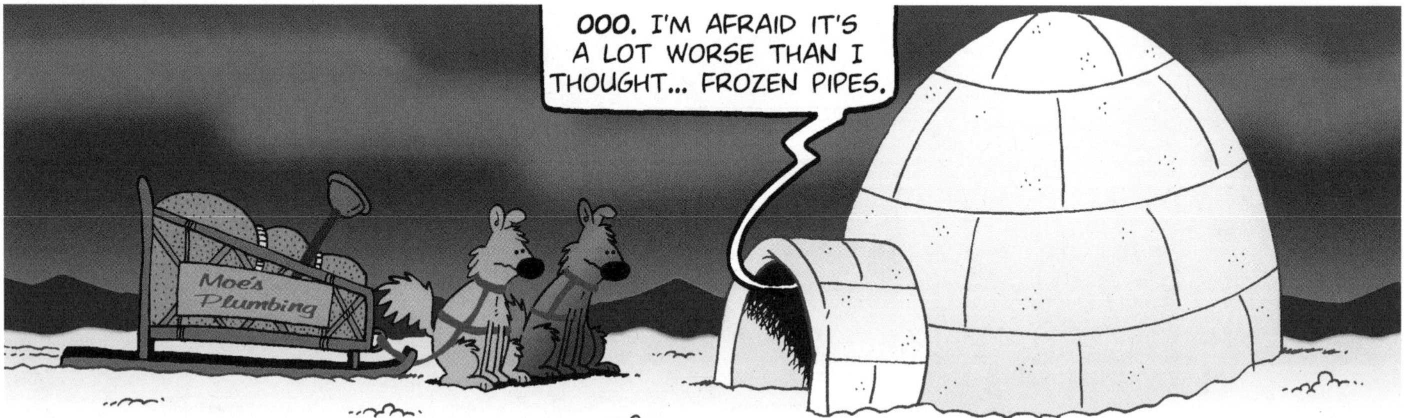
OOO. I'M AFRAID IT'S A LOT WORSE THAN I THOUGHT... FROZEN PIPES.
Moe's Plumbing

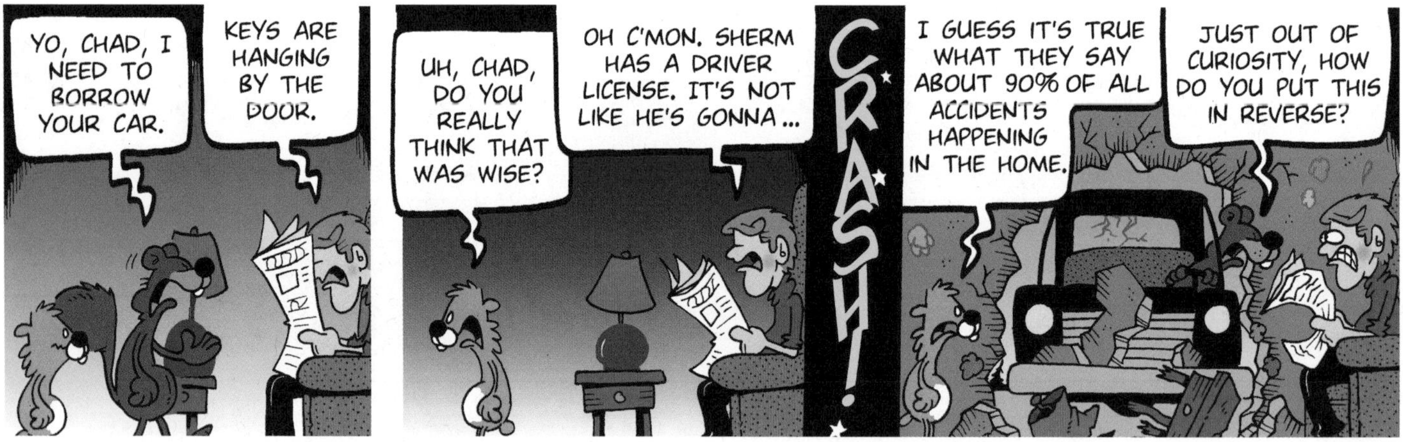
YO, CHAD, I NEED TO BORROW YOUR CAR.
KEYS ARE HANGING BY THE DOOR.
UH, CHAD, DO YOU REALLY THINK THAT WAS WISE?
OH C'MON. SHERM HAS A DRIVER LICENSE. IT'S NOT LIKE HE'S GONNA...
CRASH!
I GUESS IT'S TRUE WHAT THEY SAY ABOUT 90% OF ALL ACCIDENTS HAPPENING IN THE HOME.
JUST OUT OF CURIOSITY, HOW DO YOU PUT THIS IN REVERSE?

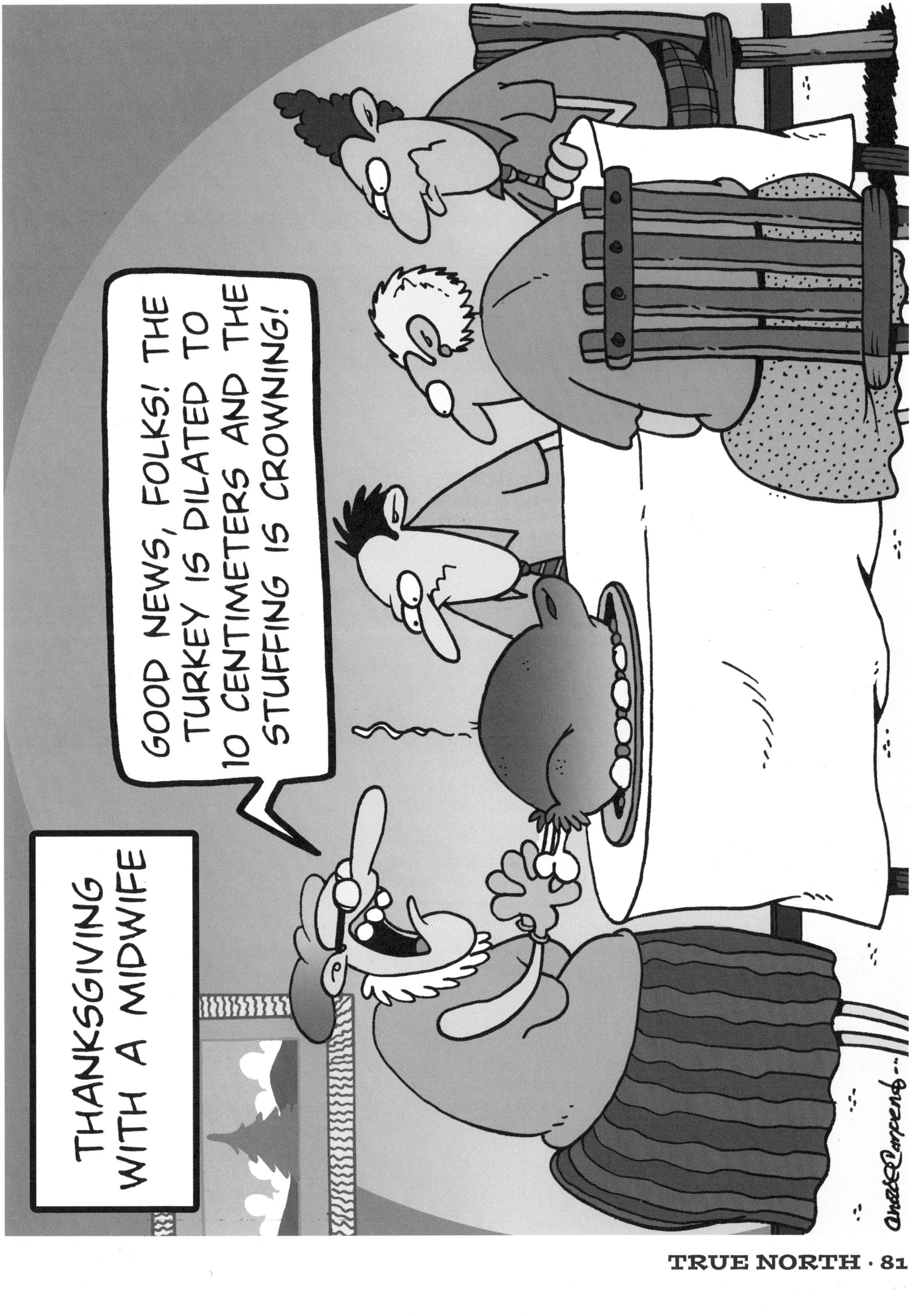
THANKSGIVING WITH A MIDWIFE
GOOD NEWS, FOLKS! THE TURKEY IS DILATED TO 10 CENTIMETERS AND THE STUFFING IS CROWNING!

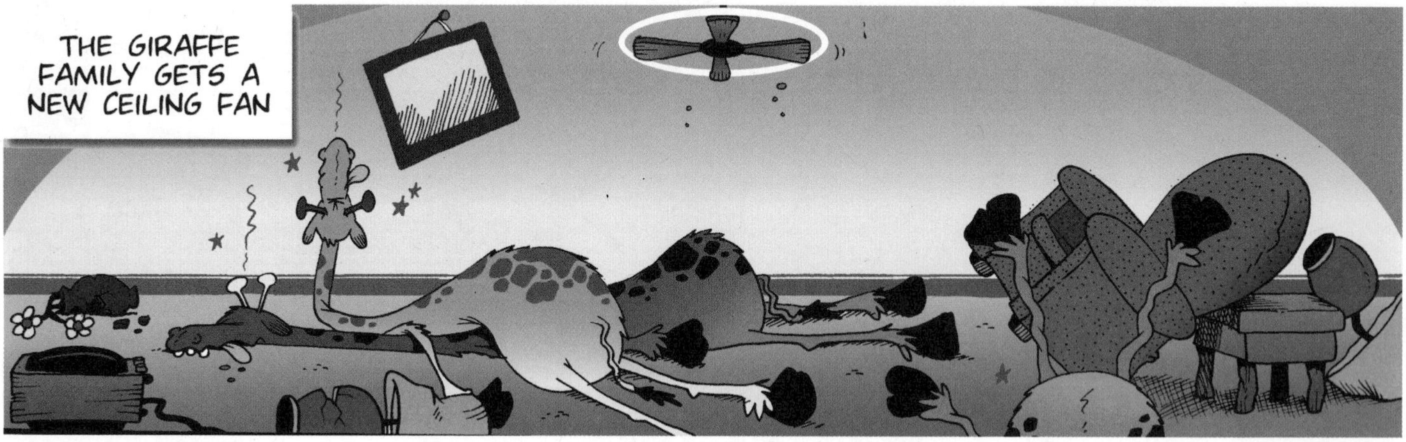
THE GIRAFFE FAMILY GETS A NEW CEILING FAN

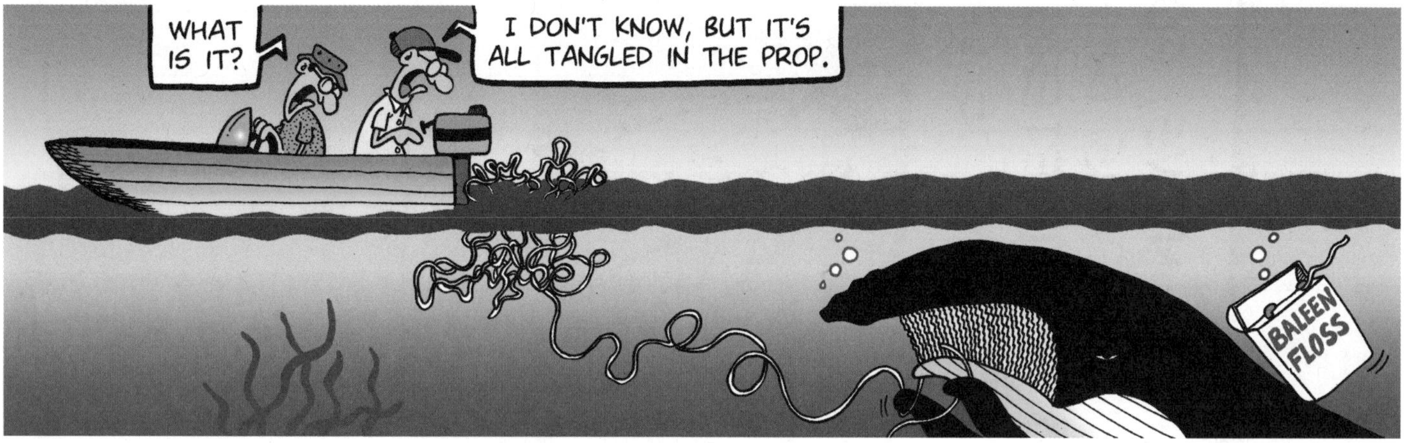
WHAT IS IT?
I DON'T KNOW, BUT IT'S ALL TANGLED IN THE PROP.
BALEEN FLOSS

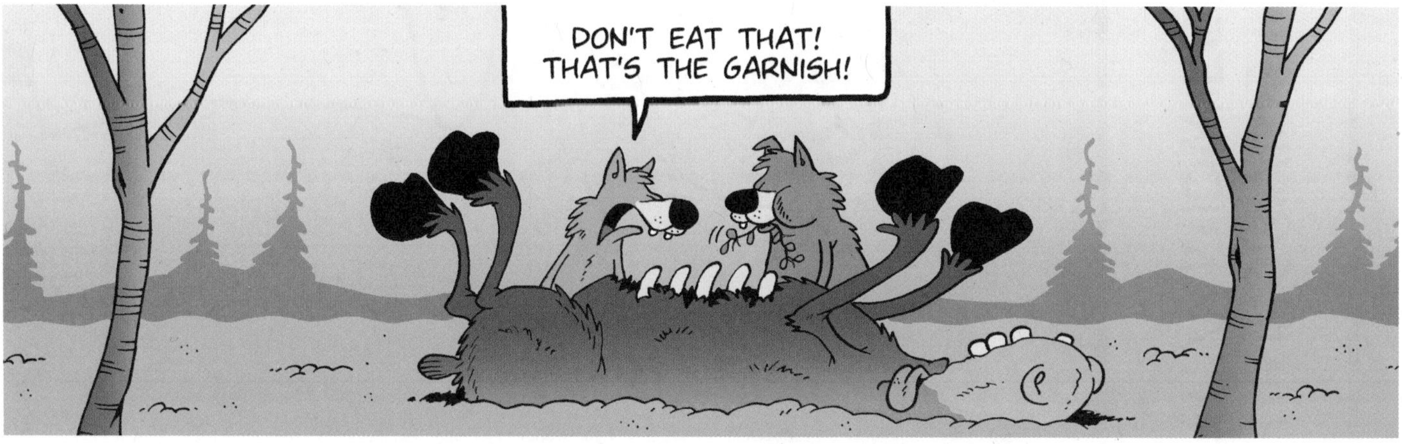
DON'T EAT THAT! THAT'S THE GARNISH!

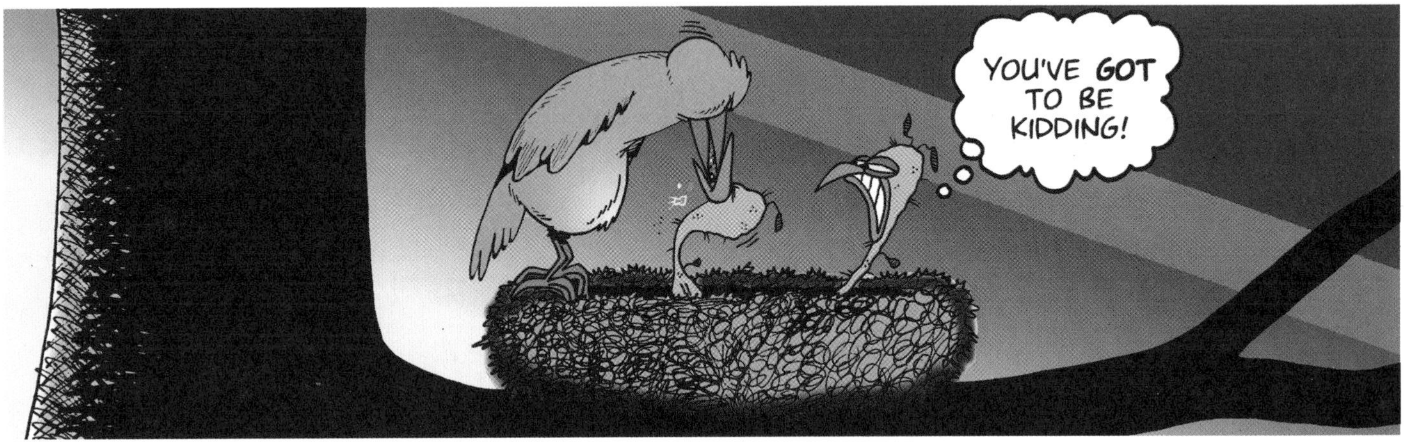
YOU'VE **GOT** TO BE KIDDING!

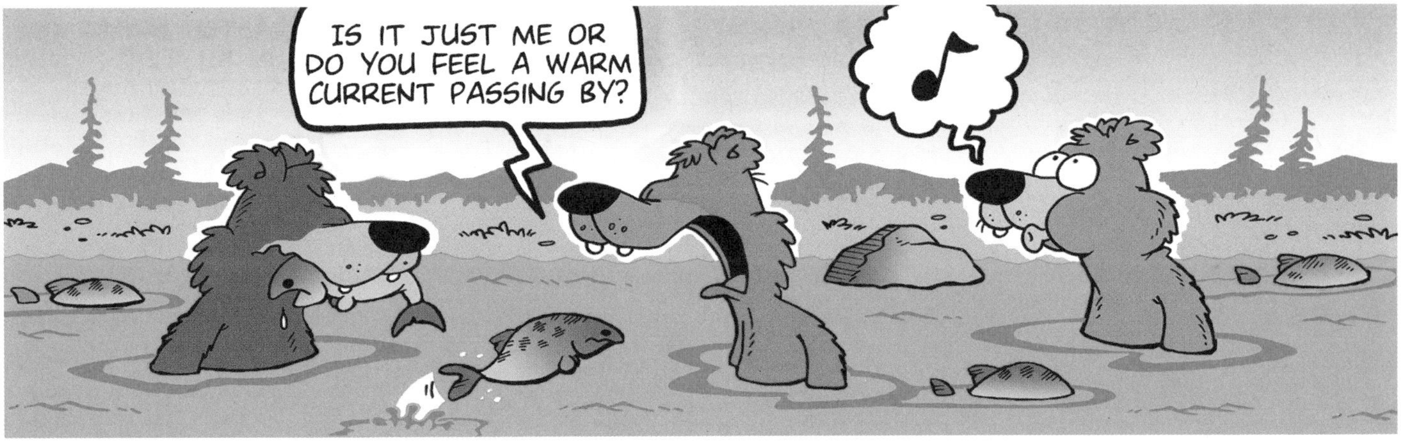
IS IT JUST ME OR DO YOU FEEL A WARM CURRENT PASSING BY?

This comic strip is based on an idea from:

Ken Miller

Fairbanks, AK

www.tundracomics.com

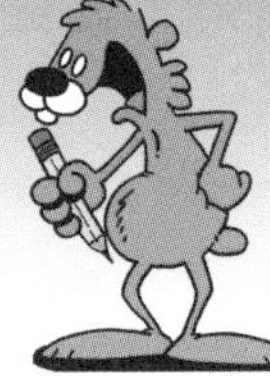

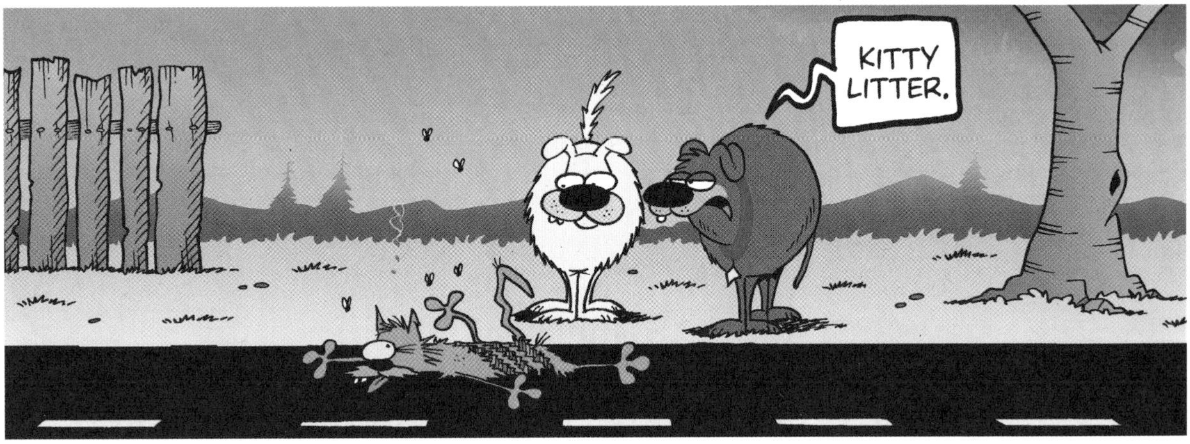
KITTY LITTER.

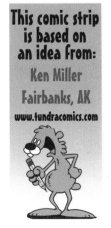

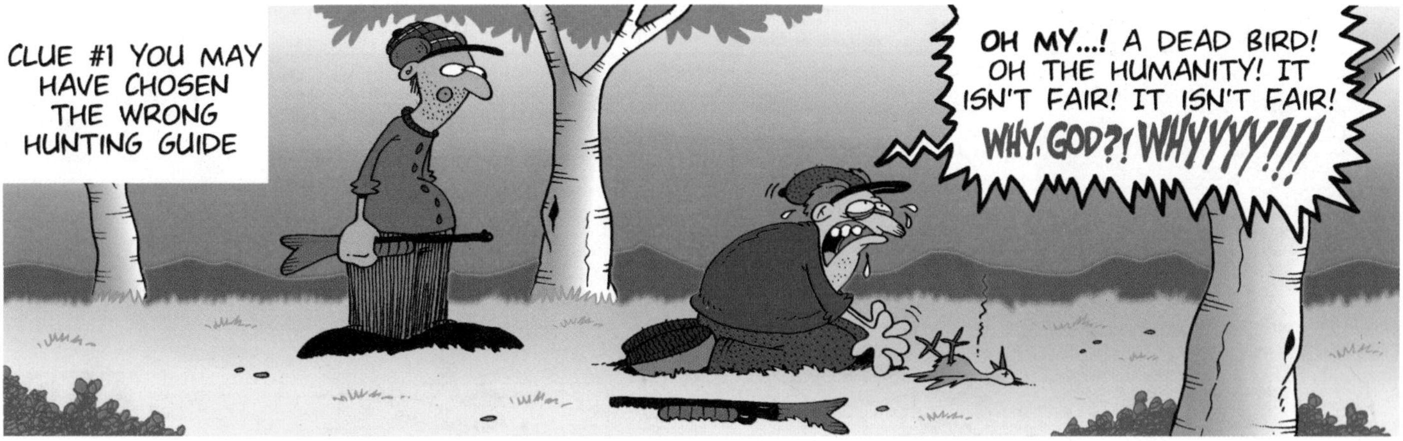

CLUE #1 YOU MAY HAVE CHOSEN THE WRONG HUNTING GUIDE
OH MY...! A DEAD BIRD! OH THE HUMANITY! IT ISN'T FAIR! IT ISN'T FAIR! WHY, GOD?! WHYYYY!!!

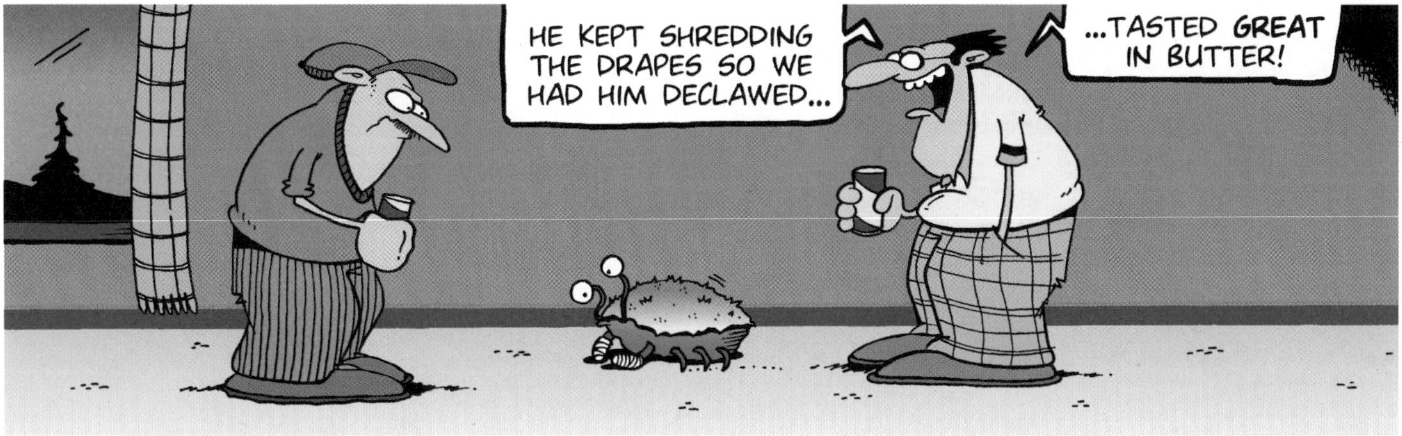

HE KEPT SHREDDING THE DRAPES SO WE HAD HIM DECLAWED...
...TASTED GREAT IN BUTTER!

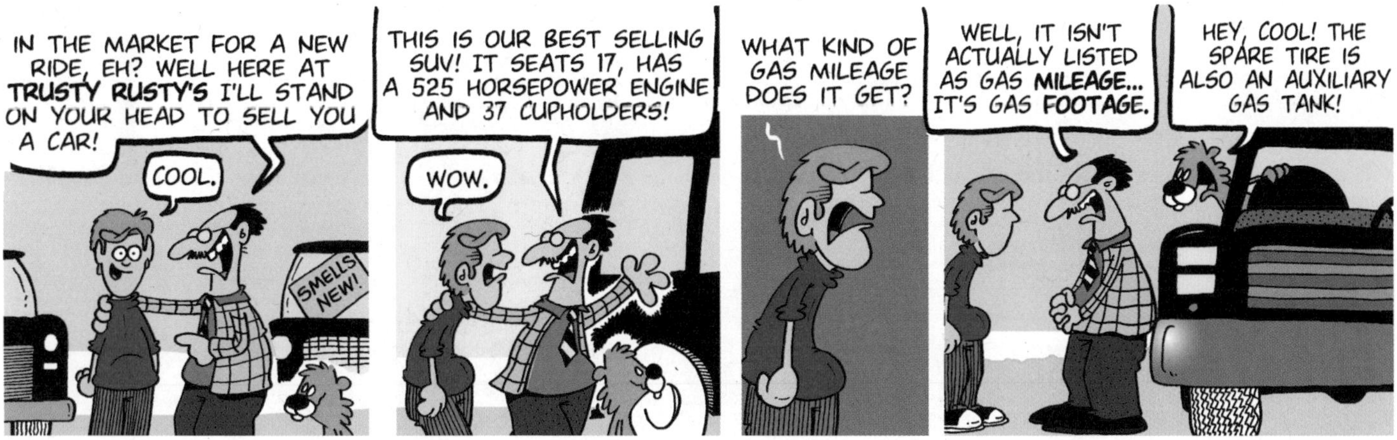

IN THE MARKET FOR A NEW RIDE, EH? WELL HERE AT TRUSTY RUSTY'S I'LL STAND ON YOUR HEAD TO SELL YOU A CAR!
COOL.
SMELLS NEW!
THIS IS OUR BEST SELLING SUV! IT SEATS 17, HAS A 525 HORSEPOWER ENGINE AND 37 CUPHOLDERS!
WOW.
WHAT KIND OF GAS MILEAGE DOES IT GET?
WELL, IT ISN'T ACTUALLY LISTED AS GAS MILEAGE... IT'S GAS FOOTAGE.
HEY, COOL! THE SPARE TIRE IS ALSO AN AUXILIARY GAS TANK!

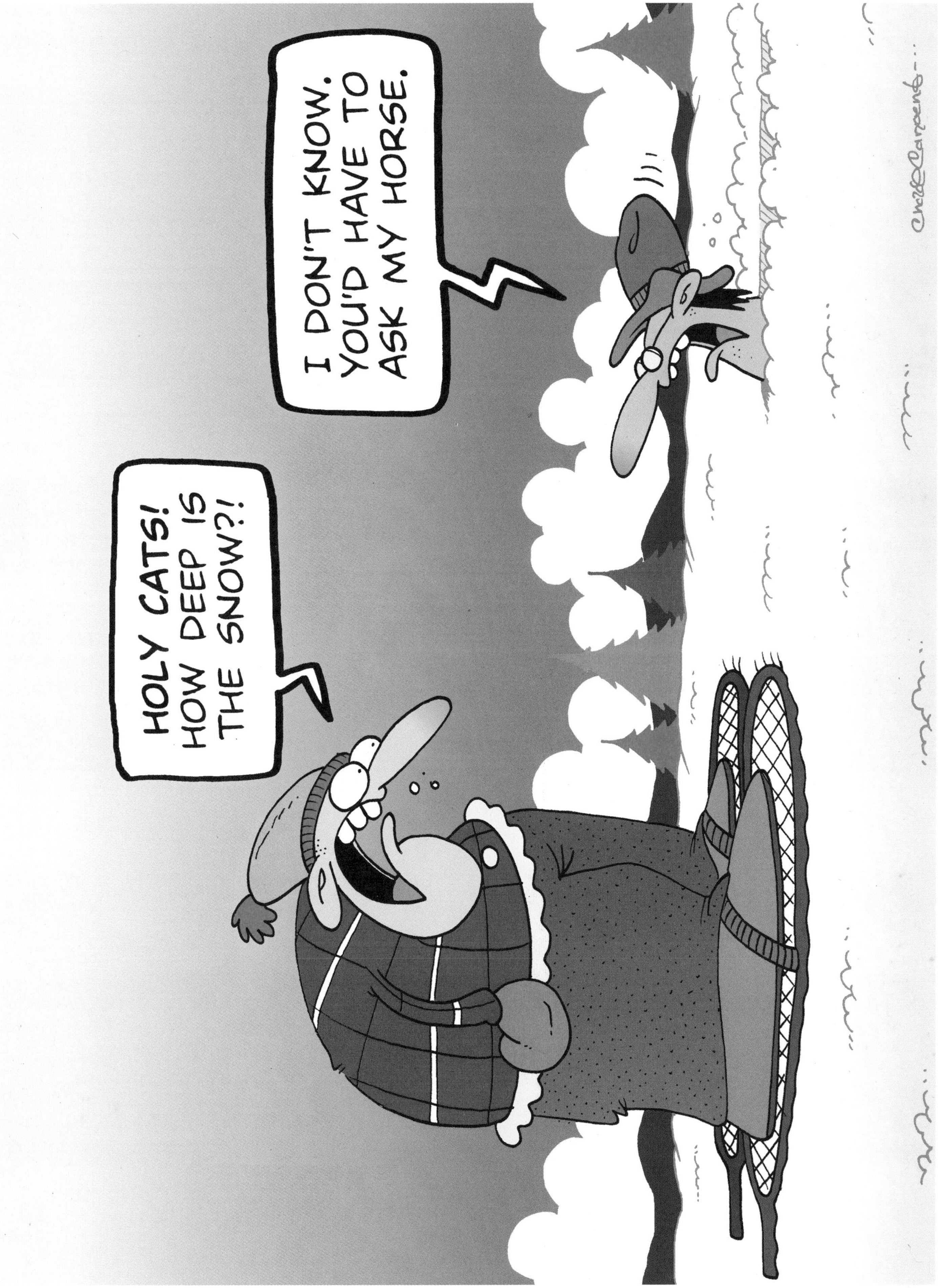
HOLY CATS! HOW DEEP IS THE SNOW?!
I DON'T KNOW. YOU'D HAVE TO ASK MY HORSE.

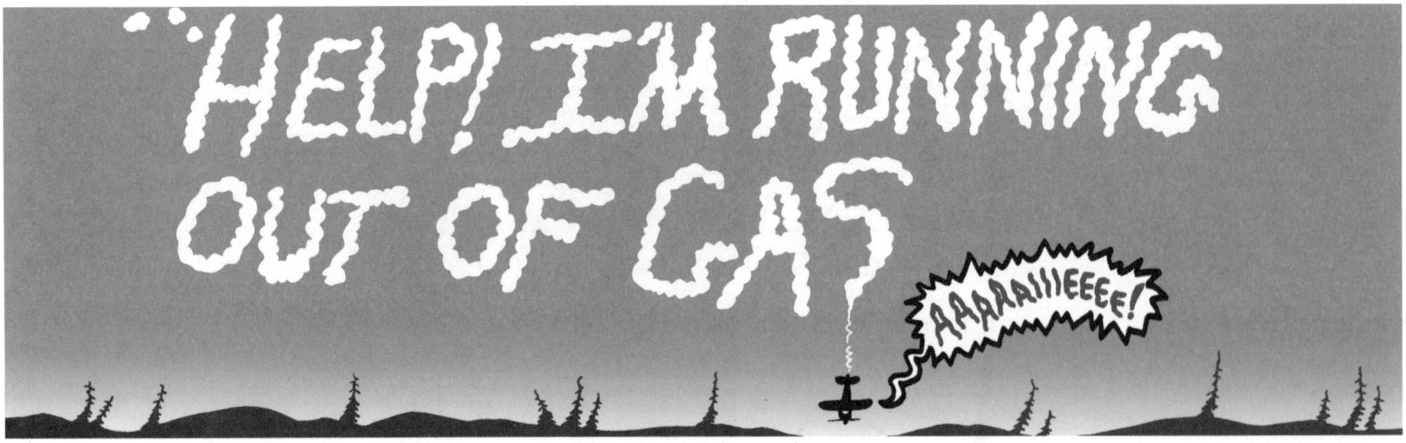
HELP! I'M RUNNING OUT OF GAS
AAAAAIIIIEEEE!

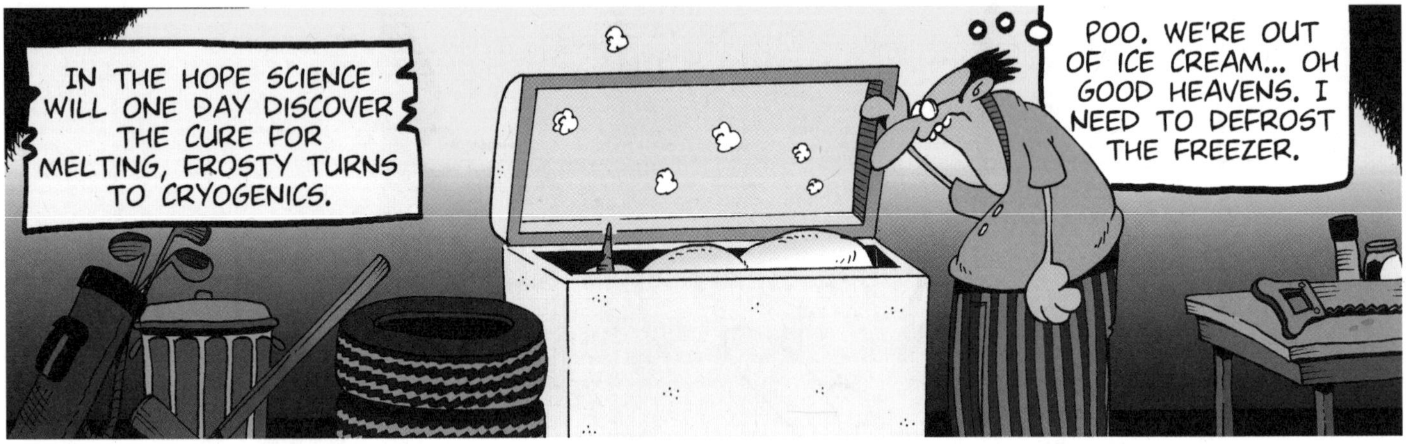
IN THE HOPE SCIENCE WILL ONE DAY DISCOVER THE CURE FOR MELTING, FROSTY TURNS TO CRYOGENICS.
POO. WE'RE OUT OF ICE CREAM... OH GOOD HEAVENS. I NEED TO DEFROST THE FREEZER.

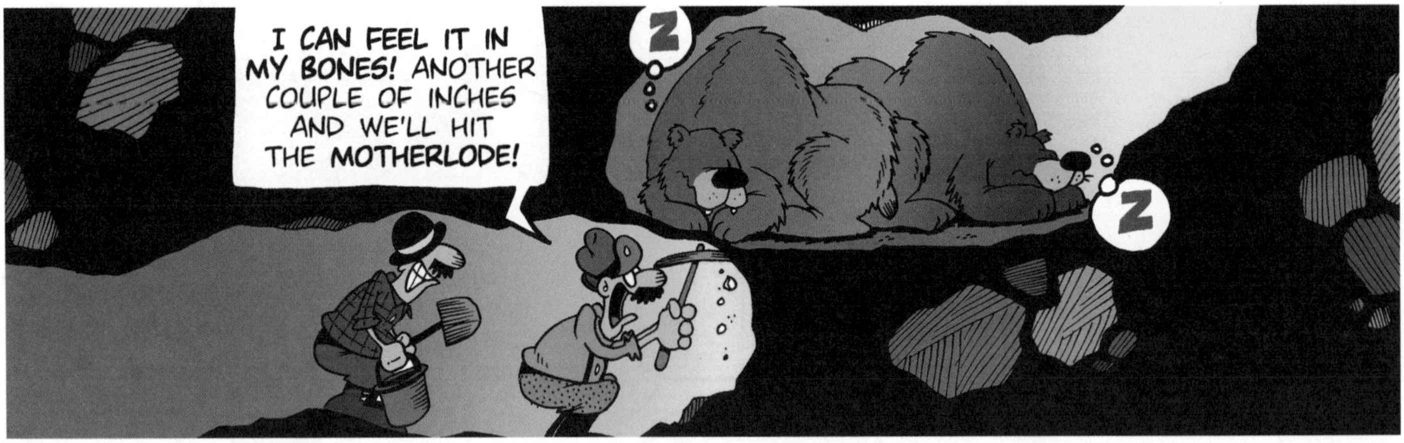
Z
I CAN FEEL IT IN MY BONES! ANOTHER COUPLE OF INCHES AND WE'LL HIT THE MOTHERLODE!
Z

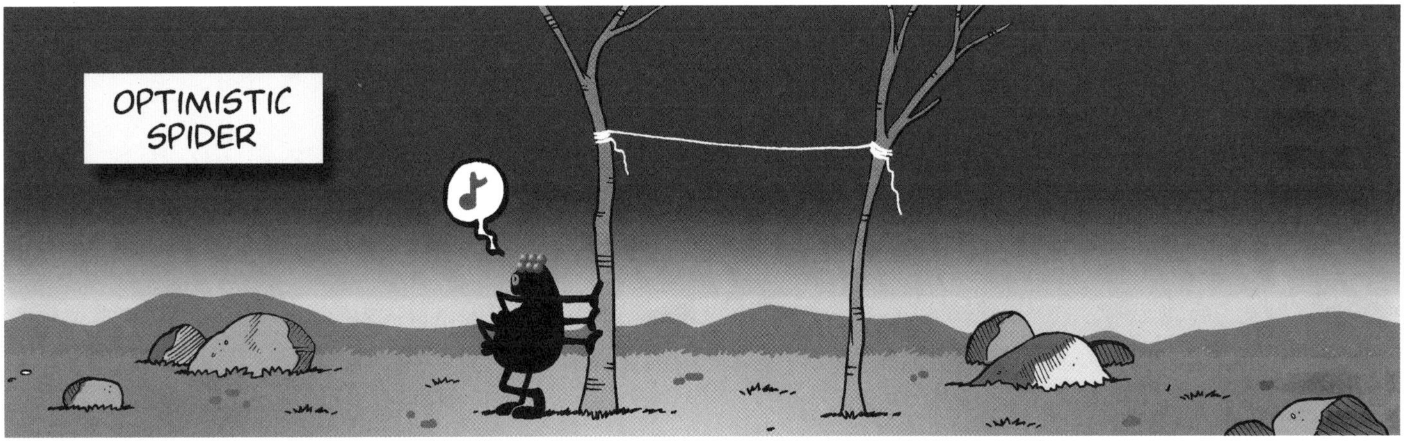
OPTIMISTIC
SPIDER

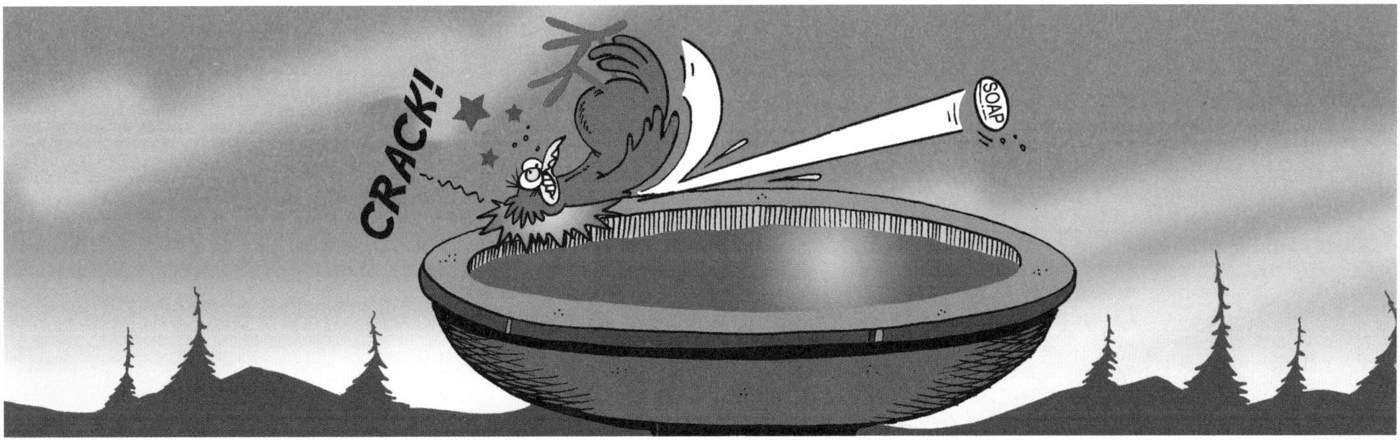
CRACK!
SOAP

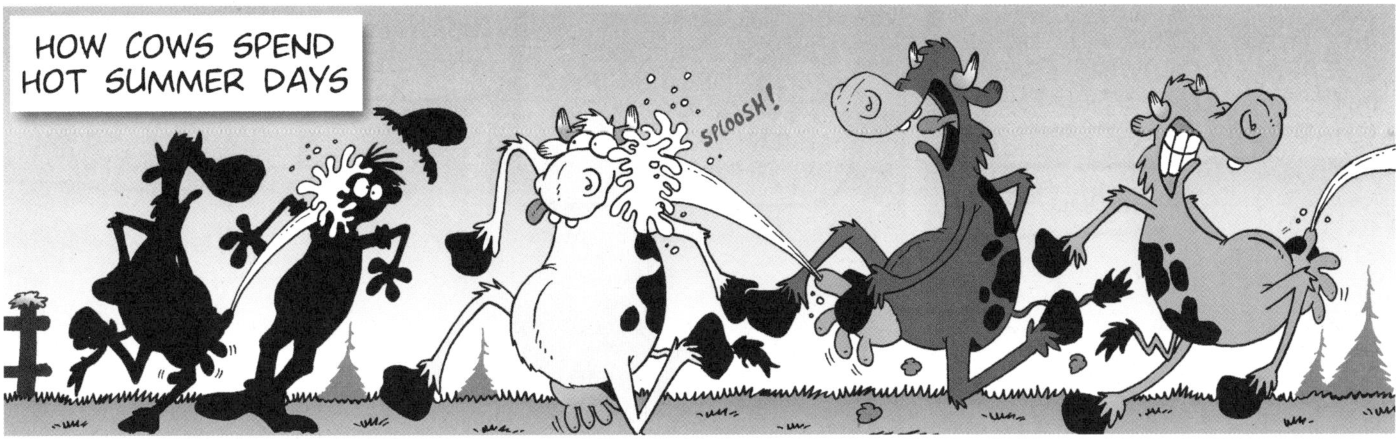
HOW COWS SPEND
HOT SUMMER DAYS
SPLOOSH!

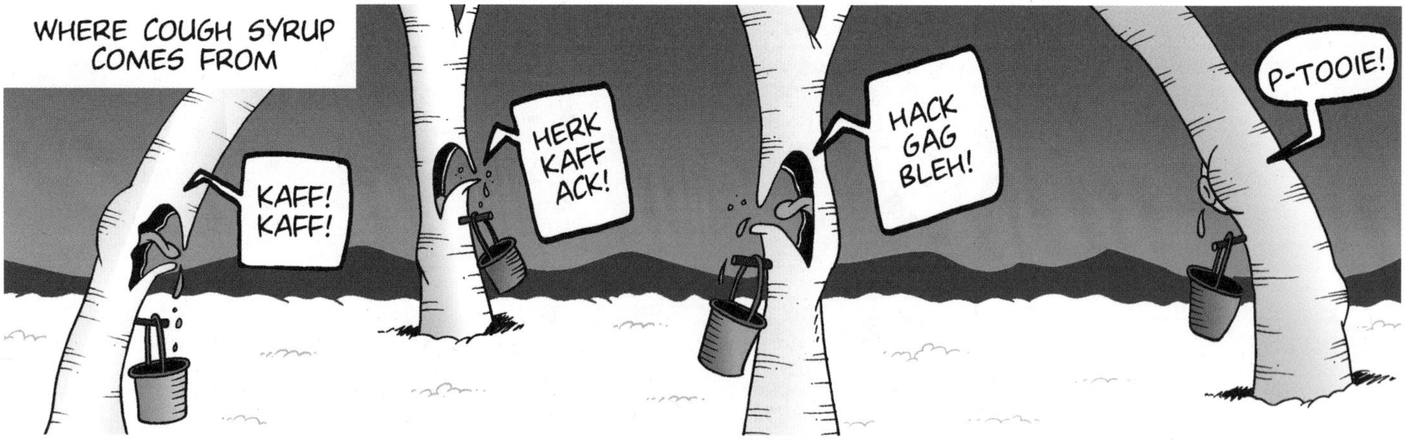
WHERE COUGH SYRUP COMES FROM
KAFF! KAFF!
HERK KAFF ACK!
HACK GAG BLEH!
P-TOOIE!

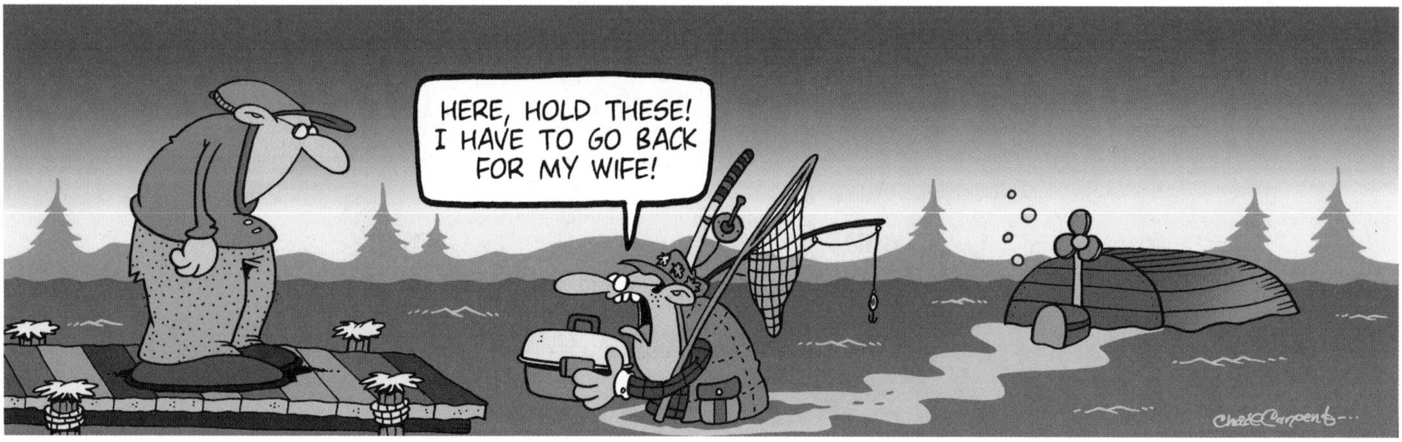
HERE, HOLD THESE! I HAVE TO GO BACK FOR MY WIFE!

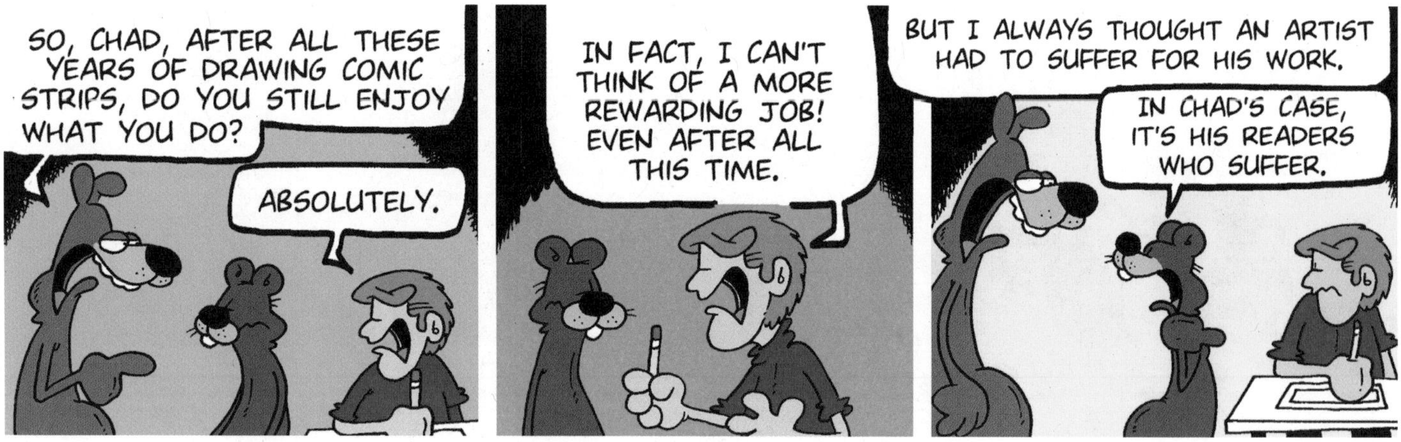
SO, CHAD, AFTER ALL THESE YEARS OF DRAWING COMIC STRIPS, DO YOU STILL ENJOY WHAT YOU DO?
ABSOLUTELY.
IN FACT, I CAN'T THINK OF A MORE REWARDING JOB! EVEN AFTER ALL THIS TIME.
BUT I ALWAYS THOUGHT AN ARTIST HAD TO SUFFER FOR HIS WORK.
IN CHAD'S CASE, IT'S HIS READERS WHO SUFFER.

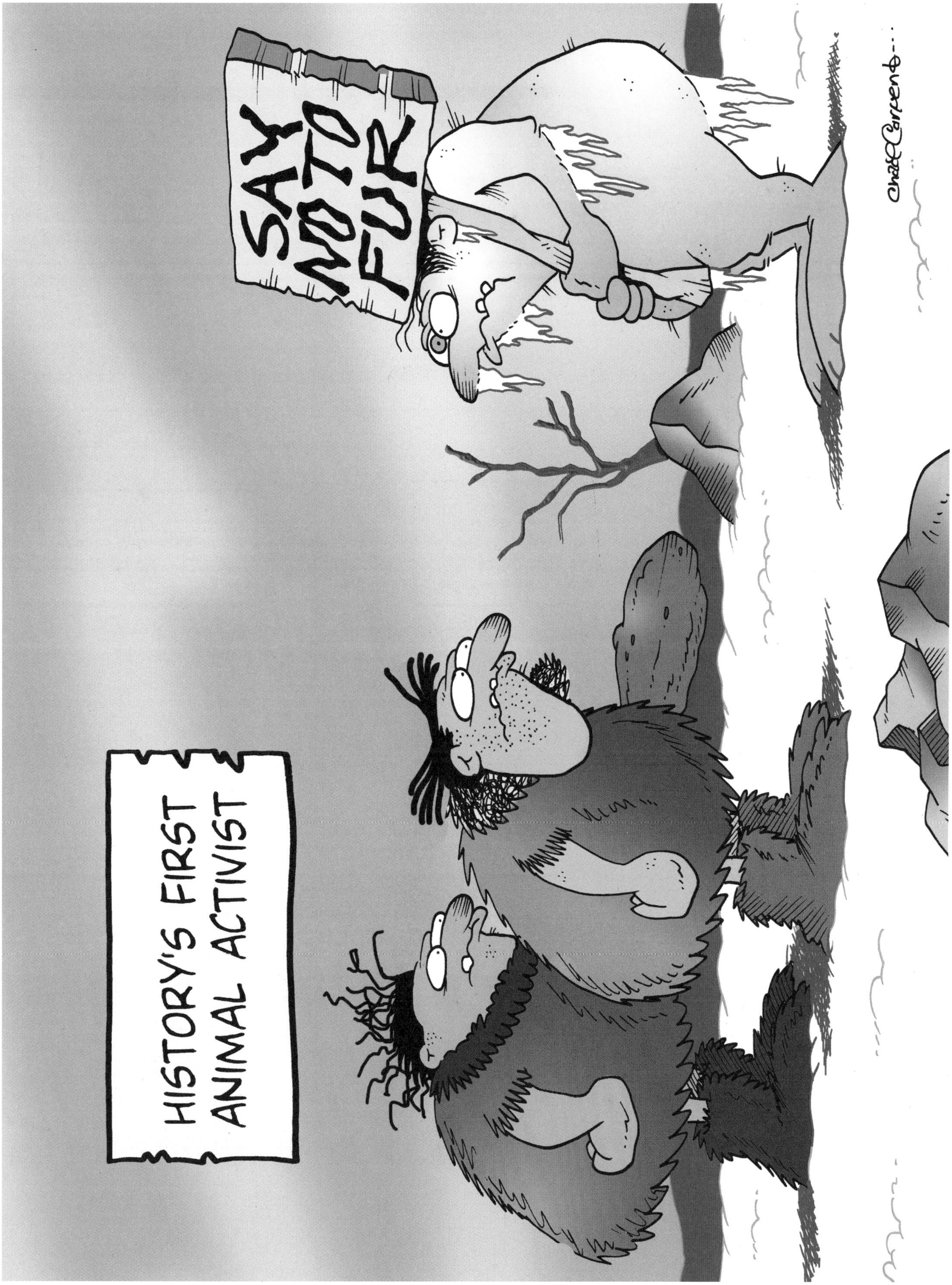
HISTORY'S FIRST ANIMAL ACTIVIST
SAY NO TO FUR

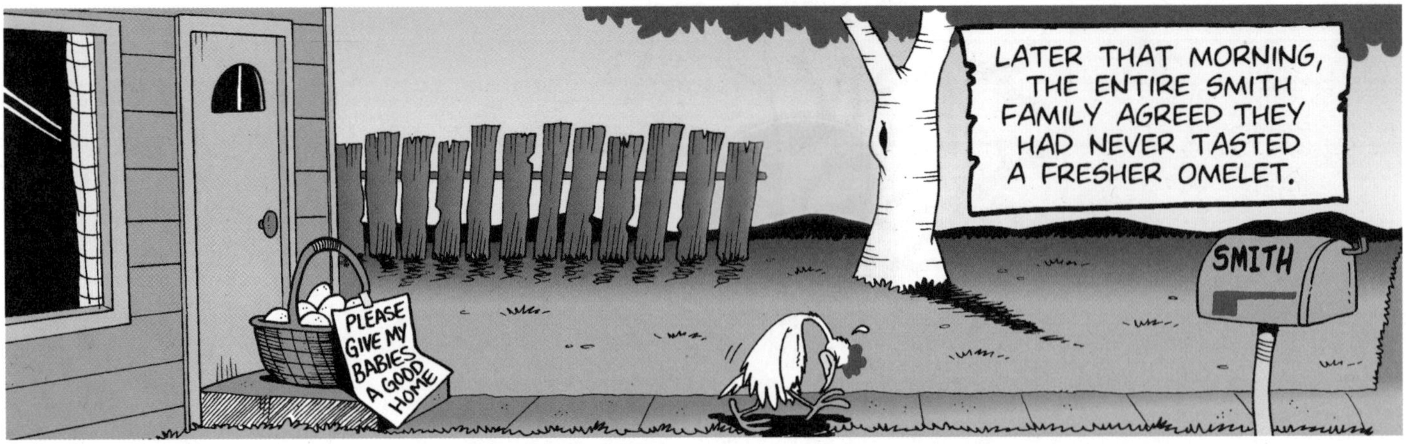
LATER THAT MORNING, THE ENTIRE SMITH FAMILY AGREED THEY HAD NEVER TASTED A FRESHER OMELET.
SMITH
PLEASE GIVE MY BABIES A GOOD HOME

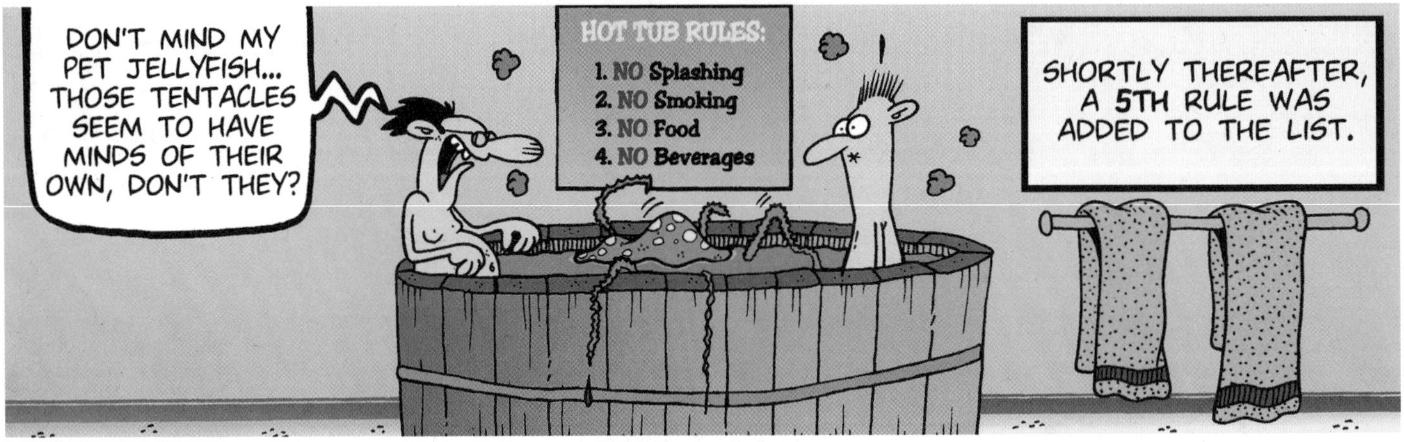
DON'T MIND MY PET JELLYFISH... THOSE TENTACLES SEEM TO HAVE MINDS OF THEIR OWN, DON'T THEY?
HOT TUB RULES:
1. NO Splashing
2. NO Smoking
3. NO Food
4. NO Beverages
SHORTLY THEREAFTER, A 5TH RULE WAS ADDED TO THE LIST.

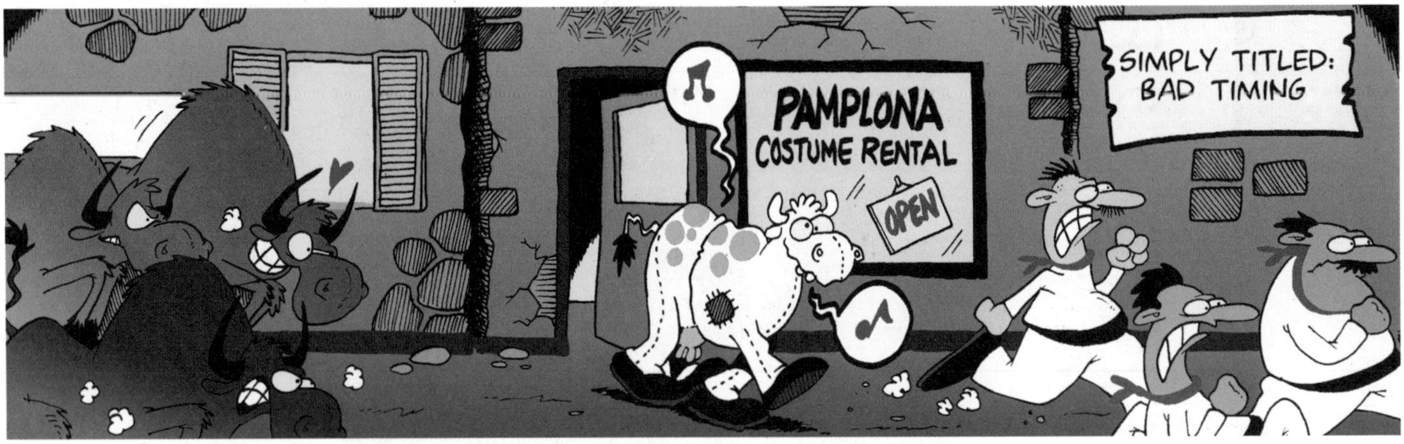
SIMPLY TITLED: BAD TIMING
PAMPLONA
COSTUME RENTAL
OPEN

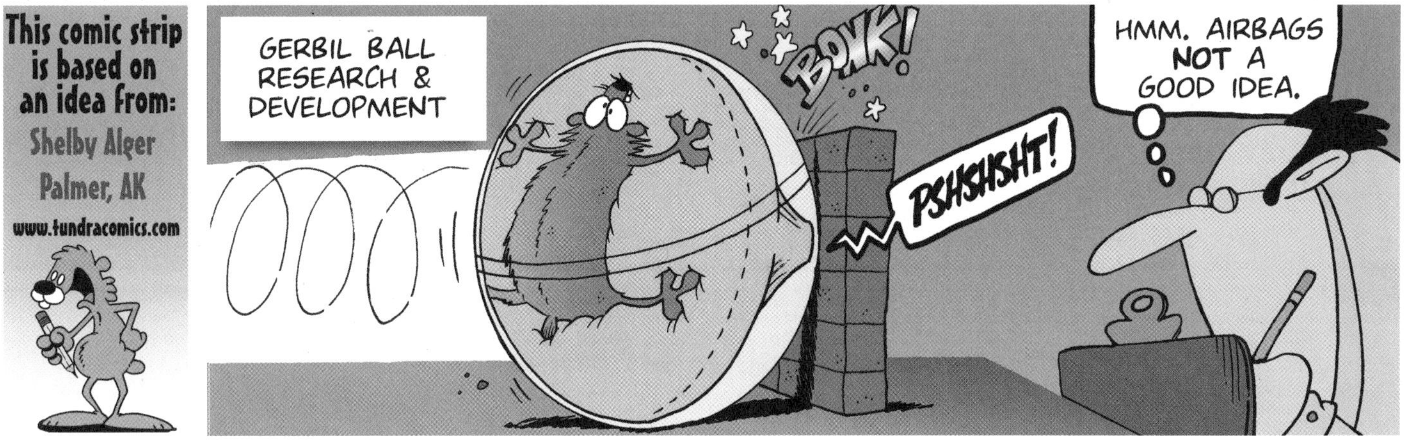
This comic strip is based on an idea from:
Shelby Alger
Palmer, AK
www.tundracomics.com
GERBIL BALL RESEARCH & DEVELOPMENT
BONK!
PSHSHSHT!
HMM. AIRBAGS NOT A GOOD IDEA.

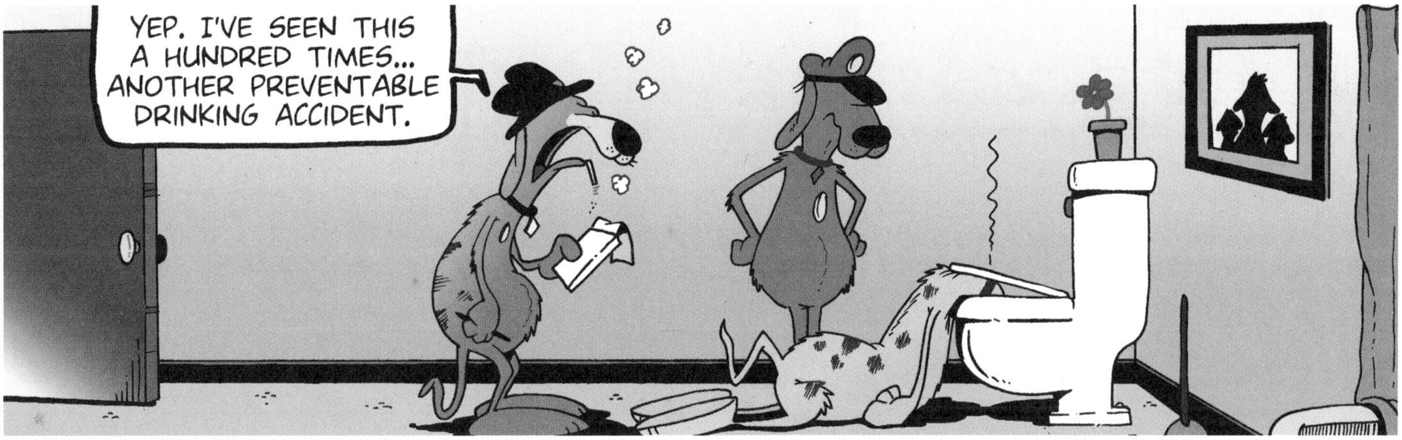
YEP. I'VE SEEN THIS A HUNDRED TIMES... ANOTHER PREVENTABLE DRINKING ACCIDENT.

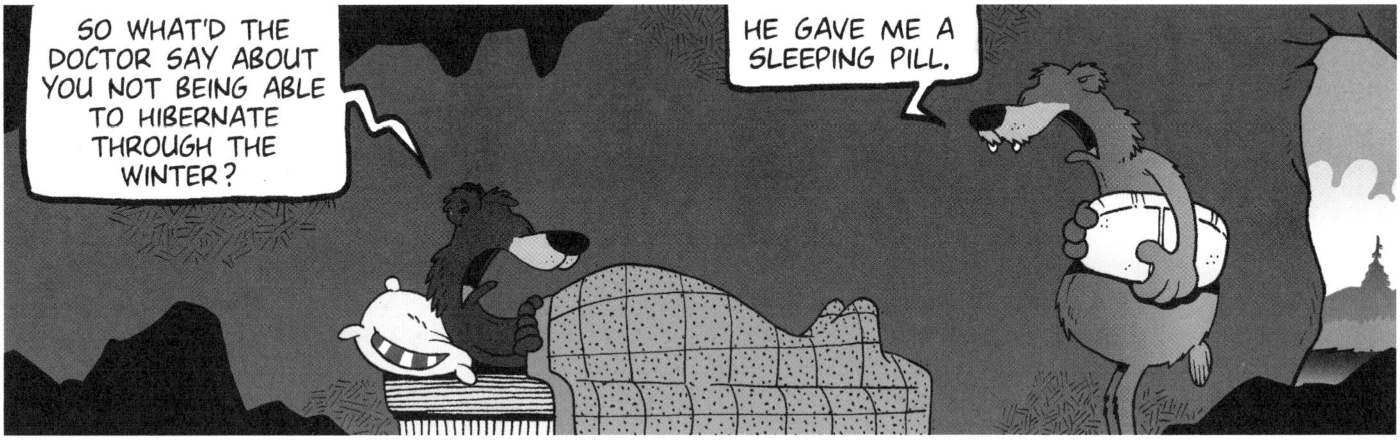
SO WHAT'D THE DOCTOR SAY ABOUT YOU NOT BEING ABLE TO HIBERNATE THROUGH THE WINTER?
HE GAVE ME A SLEEPING PILL.

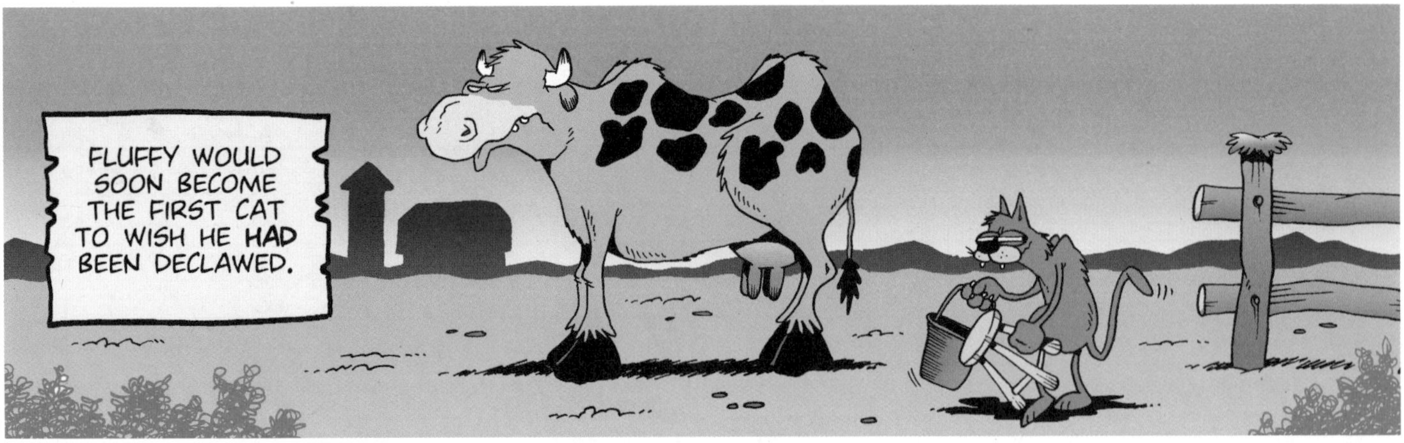
FLUFFY WOULD SOON BECOME THE FIRST CAT TO WISH HE HAD BEEN DECLAWED.

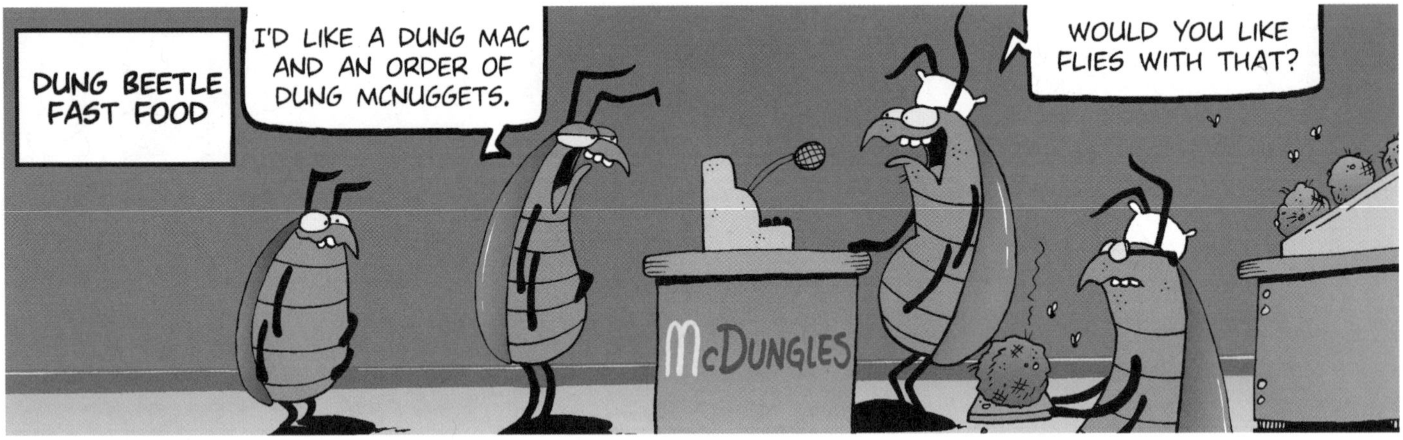
DUNG BEETLE FAST FOOD
I'D LIKE A DUNG MAC AND AN ORDER OF DUNG MCNUGGETS.
WOULD YOU LIKE FLIES WITH THAT?
McDUNGLES

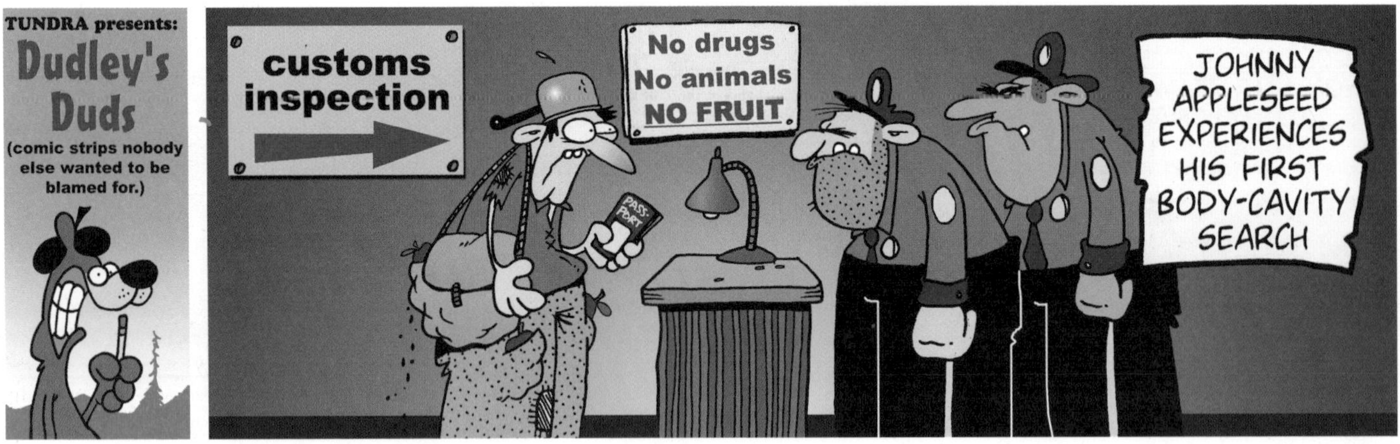
TUNDRA presents:
Dudley's Duds
(comic strips nobody else wanted to be blamed for.)
customs inspection
No drugs
No animals
NO FRUIT
PASS-PORT
JOHNNY APPLESEED EXPERIENCES HIS FIRST BODY-CAVITY SEARCH

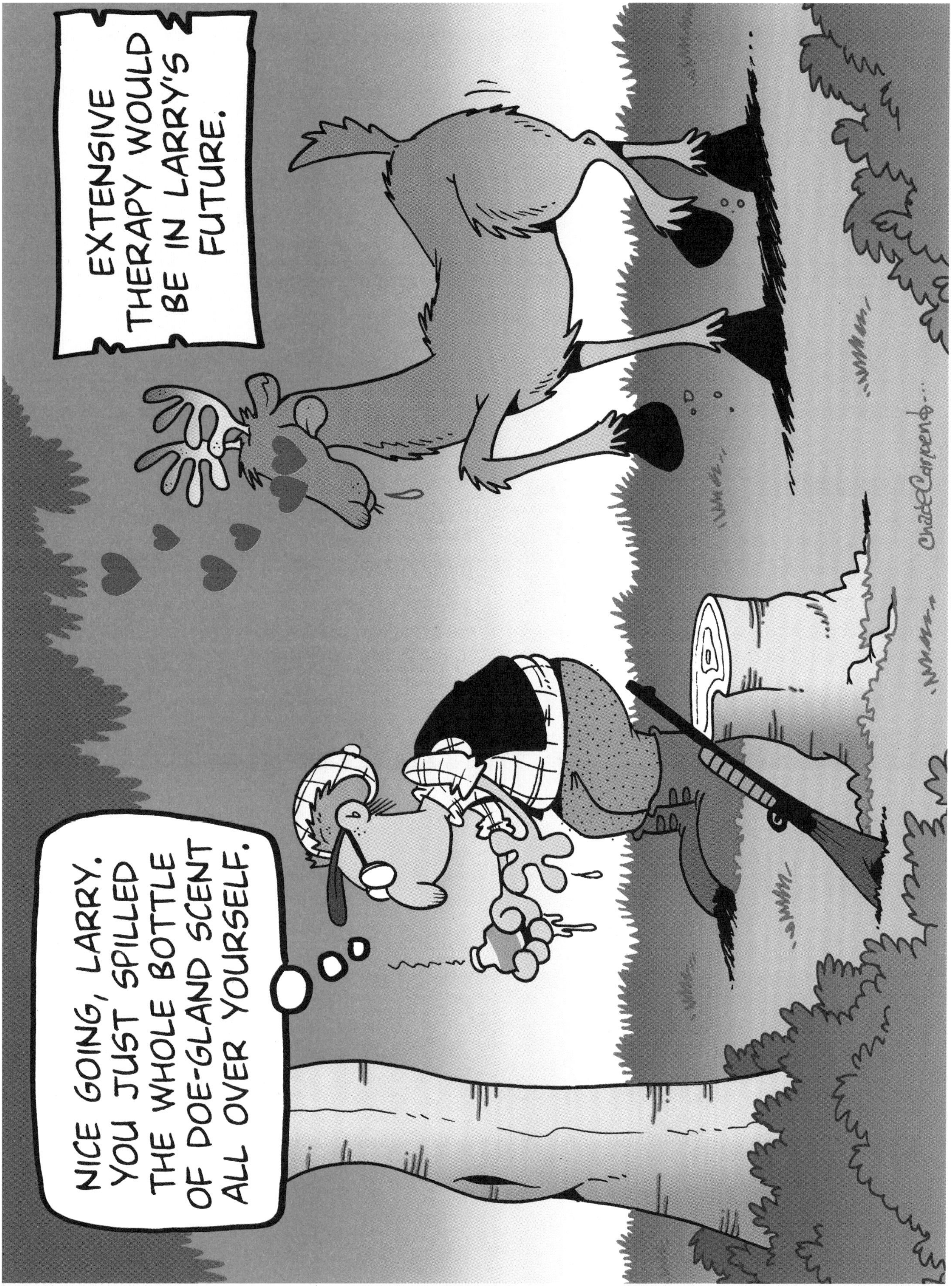
NICE GOING, LARRY. YOU JUST SPILLED THE WHOLE BOTTLE OF DOE-GLAND SCENT ALL OVER YOURSELF.
EXTENSIVE THERAPY WOULD BE IN LARRY'S FUTURE.

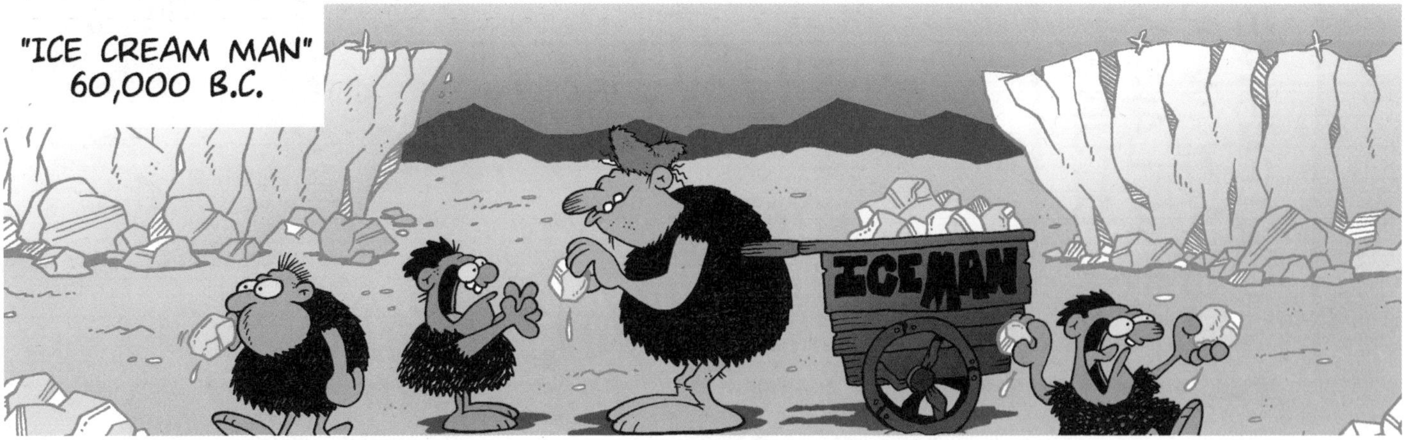
"ICE CREAM MAN"
60,000 B.C.
ICEMAN

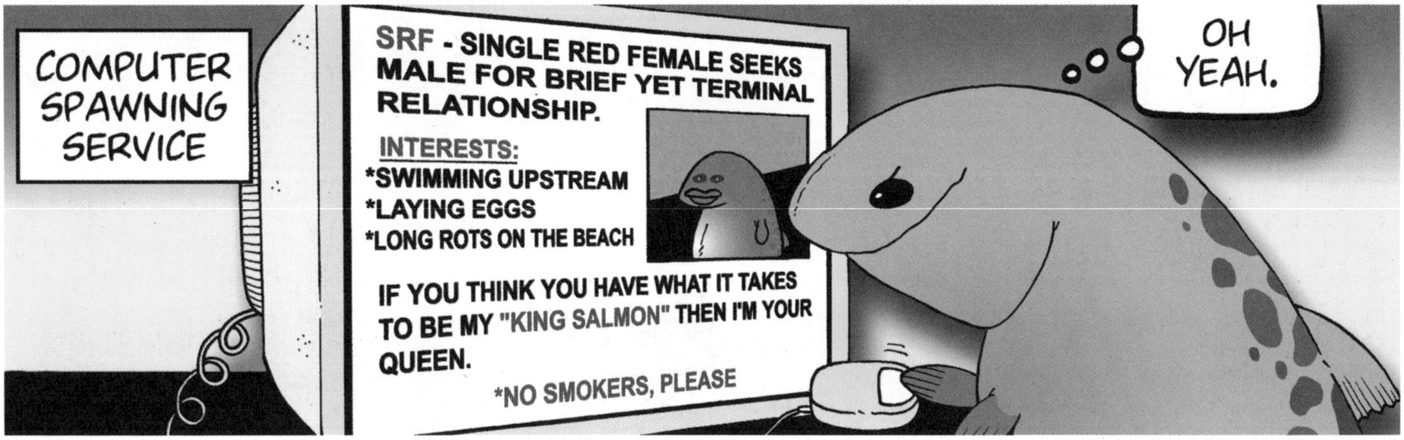
COMPUTER SPAWNING SERVICE
SRF - SINGLE RED FEMALE SEEKS MALE FOR BRIEF YET TERMINAL RELATIONSHIP.
INTERESTS:
*SWIMMING UPSTREAM
*LAYING EGGS
*LONG ROTS ON THE BEACH
IF YOU THINK YOU HAVE WHAT IT TAKES TO BE MY "KING SALMON" THEN I'M YOUR QUEEN.
*NO SMOKERS, PLEASE
OH YEAH.

This comic strip is based on an idea from:

Tim O'Connor

Enid, OK

www.tundracomics.com

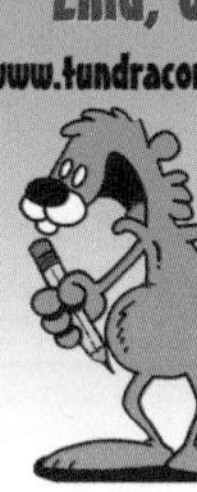

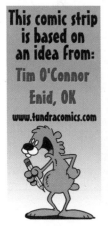

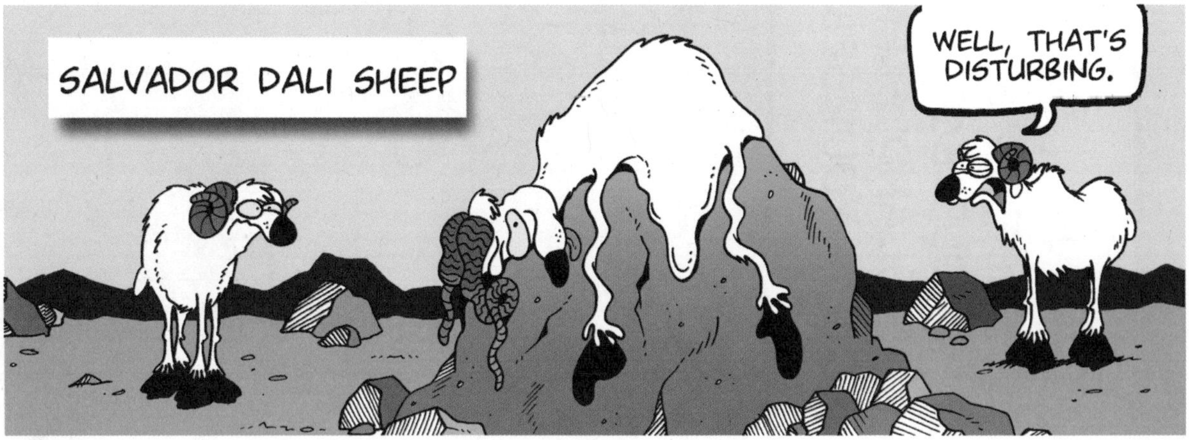
SALVADOR DALI SHEEP
WELL, THAT'S DISTURBING.

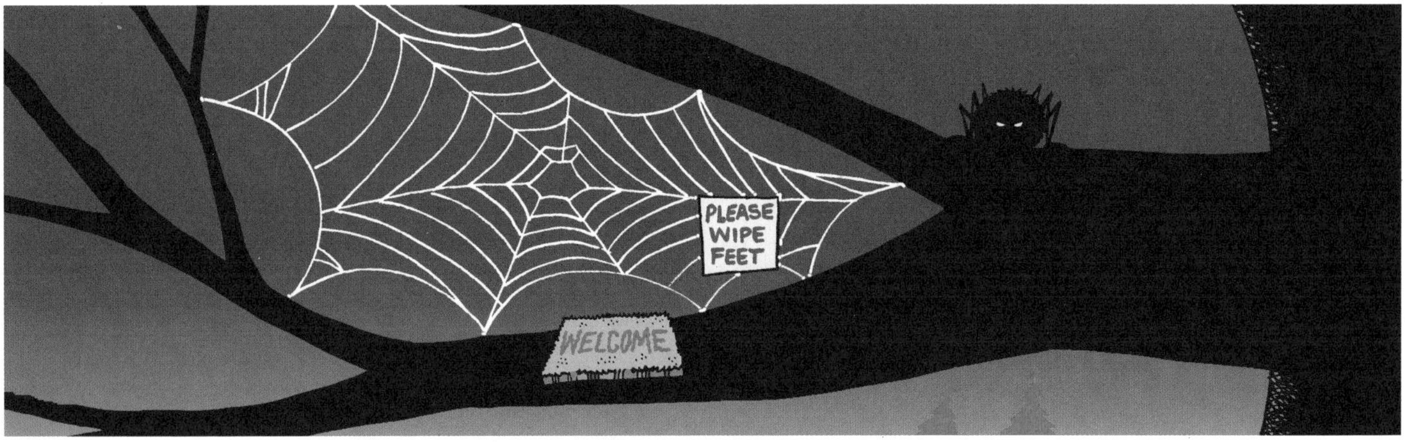
PLEASE
WIPE
FEET
WELCOME

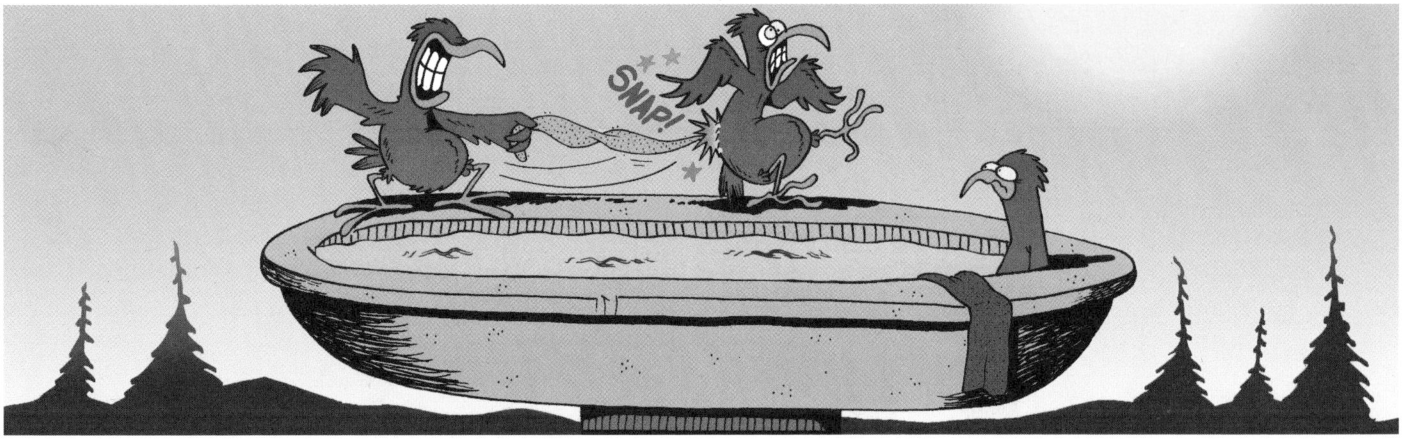
SNAP!

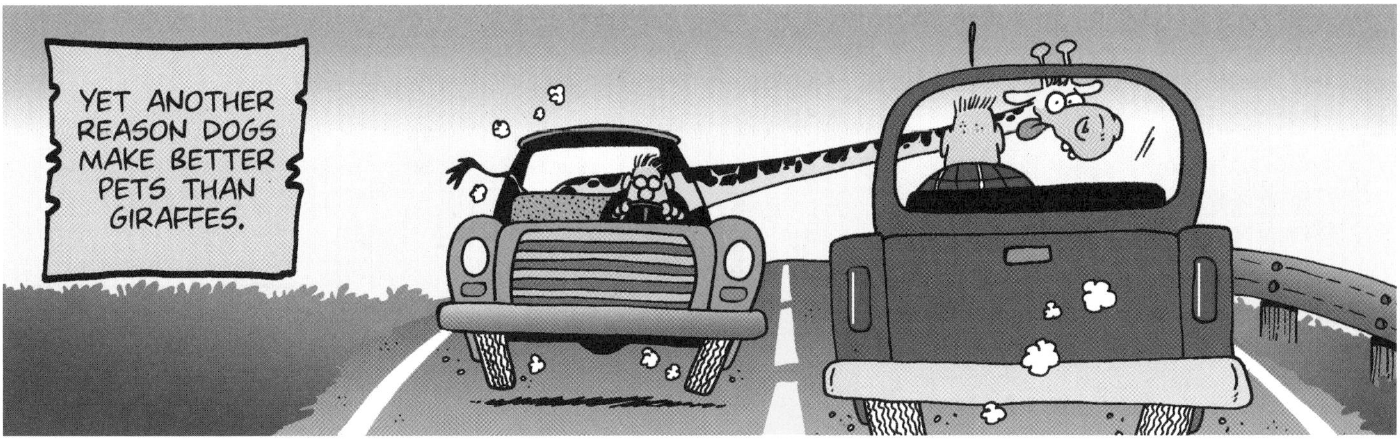
YET ANOTHER REASON DOGS MAKE BETTER PETS THAN GIRAFFES.

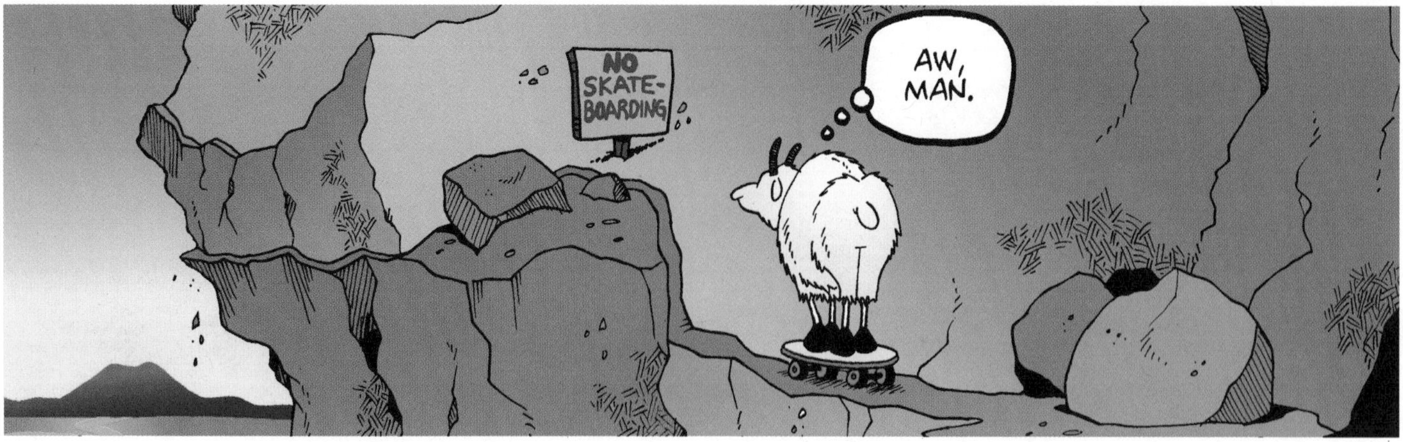
NO SKATE-BOARDING
AW, MAN.

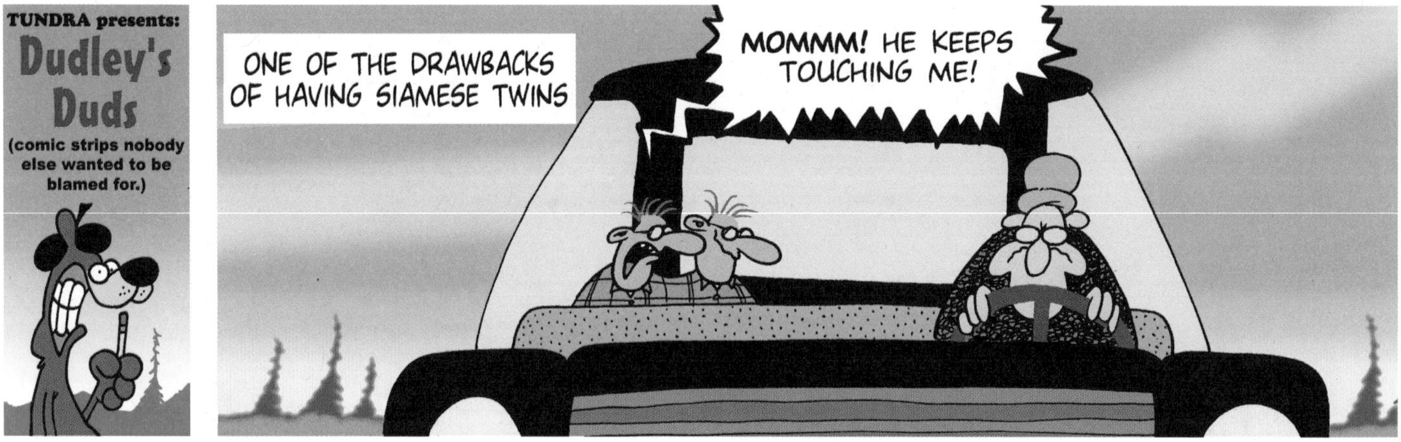
TUNDRA presents:
Dudley's Duds
(comic strips nobody else wanted to be blamed for.)
ONE OF THE DRAWBACKS OF HAVING SIAMESE TWINS
MOMMM! HE KEEPS TOUCHING ME!

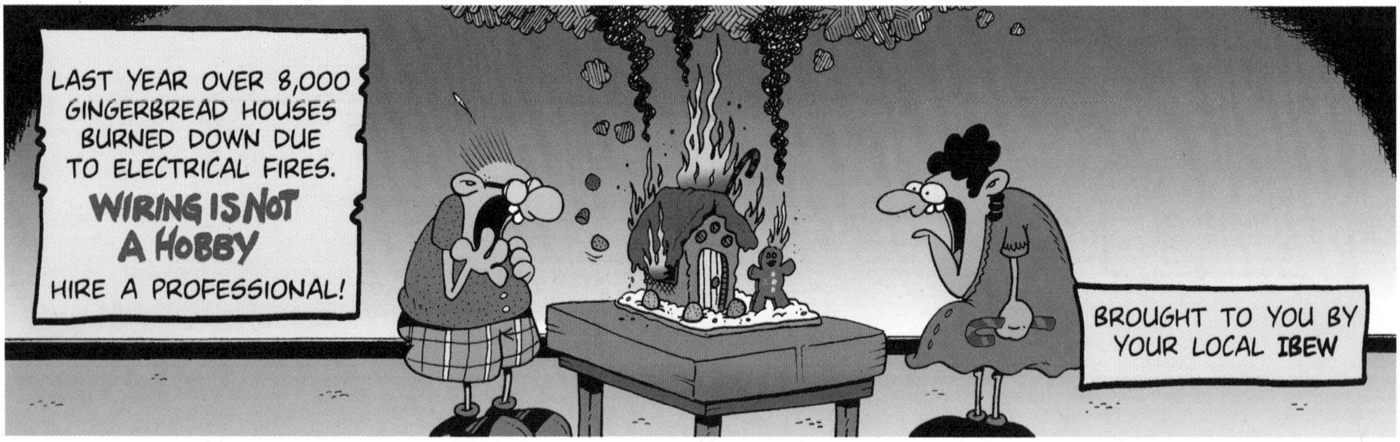
LAST YEAR OVER 8,000 GINGERBREAD HOUSES BURNED DOWN DUE TO ELECTRICAL FIRES.
WIRING IS NOT A HOBBY
HIRE A PROFESSIONAL!
BROUGHT TO YOU BY YOUR LOCAL IBEW

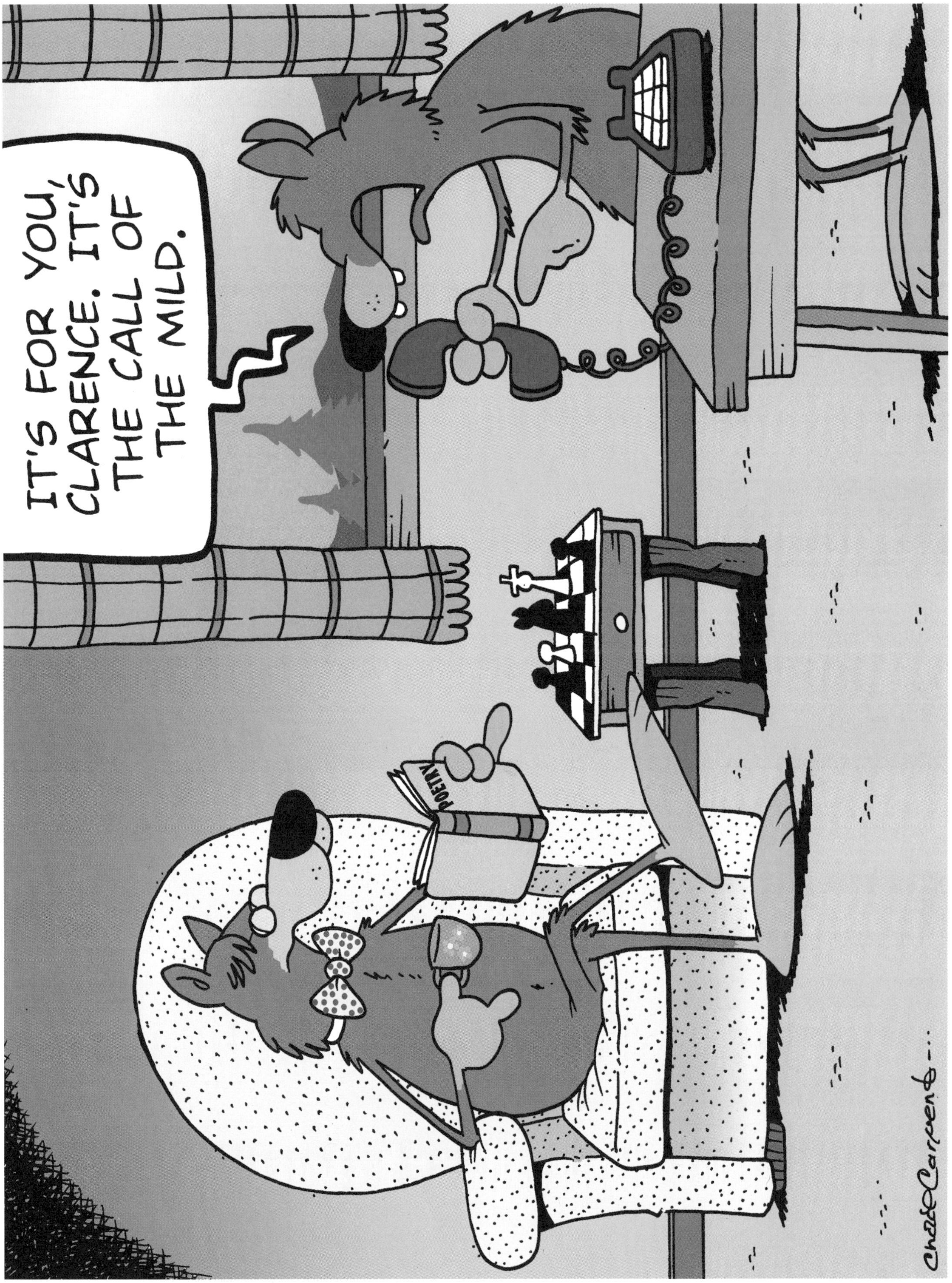
IT'S FOR YOU, CLARENCE. IT'S THE CALL OF THE MILD.
POETRY

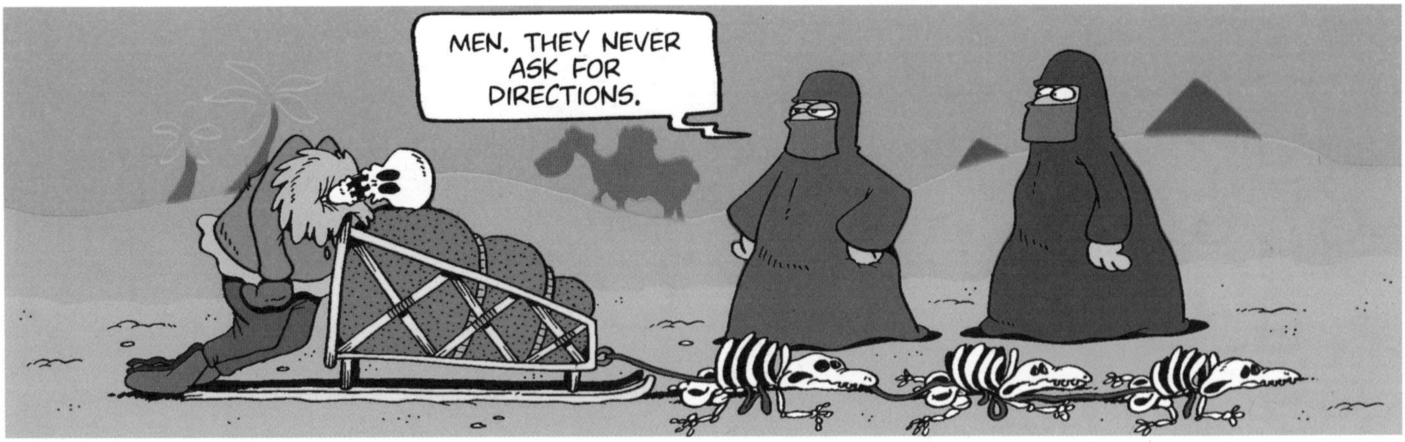
MEN. THEY NEVER ASK FOR DIRECTIONS.

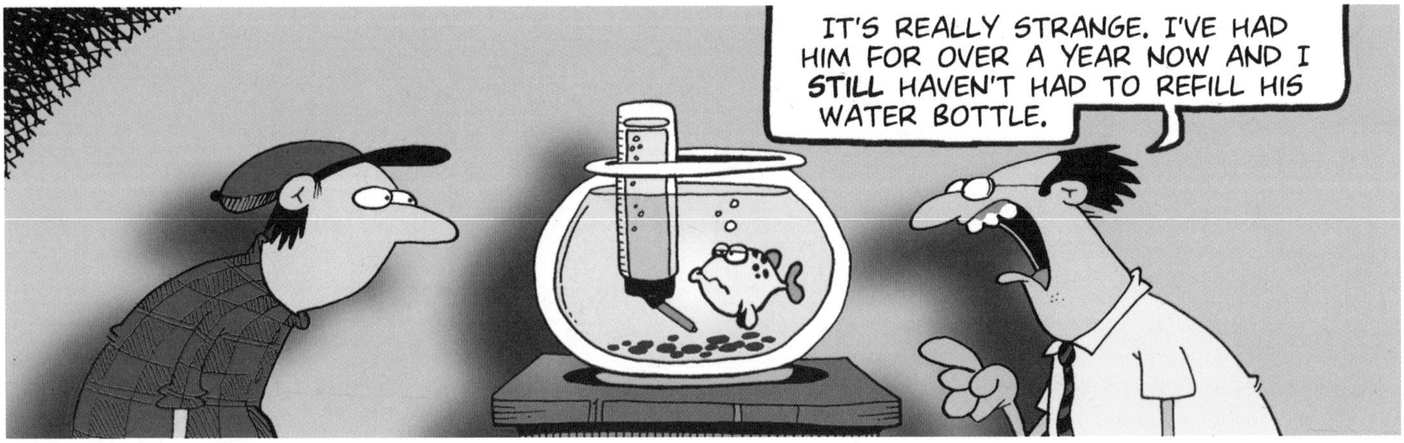
IT'S REALLY STRANGE. I'VE HAD HIM FOR OVER A YEAR NOW AND I STILL HAVEN'T HAD TO REFILL HIS WATER BOTTLE.

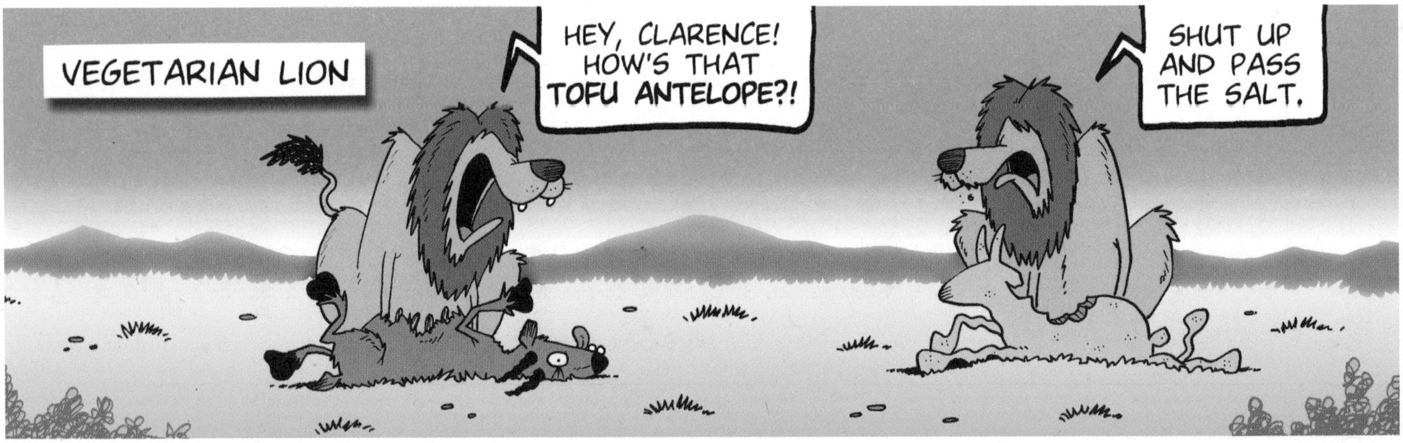
VEGETARIAN LION
HEY, CLARENCE! HOW'S THAT TOFU ANTELOPE?!
SHUT UP AND PASS THE SALT.

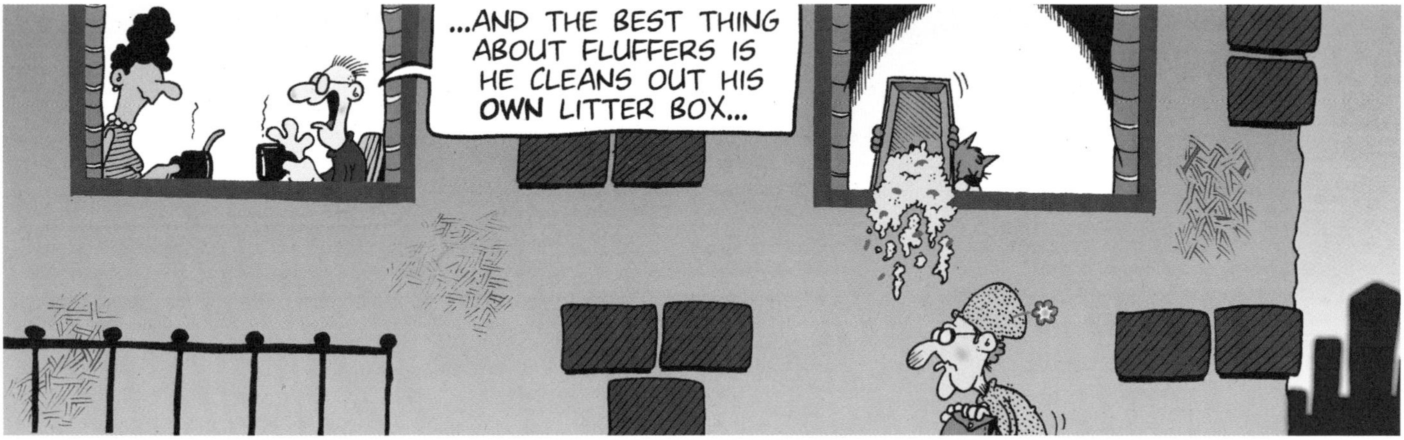
...AND THE BEST THING ABOUT FLUFFERS IS HE CLEANS OUT HIS **OWN** LITTER BOX...

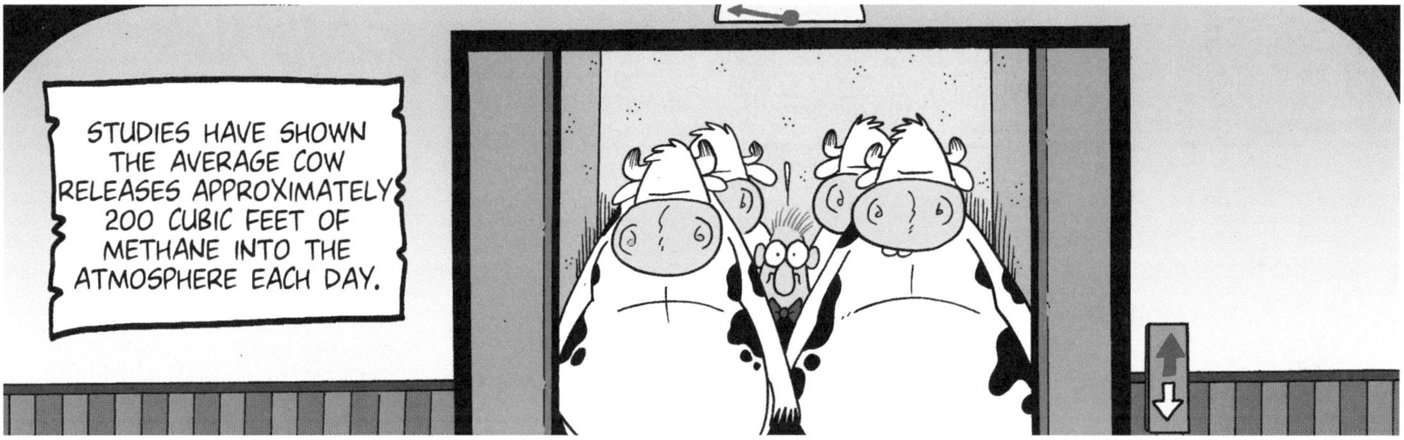
STUDIES HAVE SHOWN THE AVERAGE COW RELEASES APPROXIMATELY 200 CUBIC FEET OF METHANE INTO THE ATMOSPHERE EACH DAY.

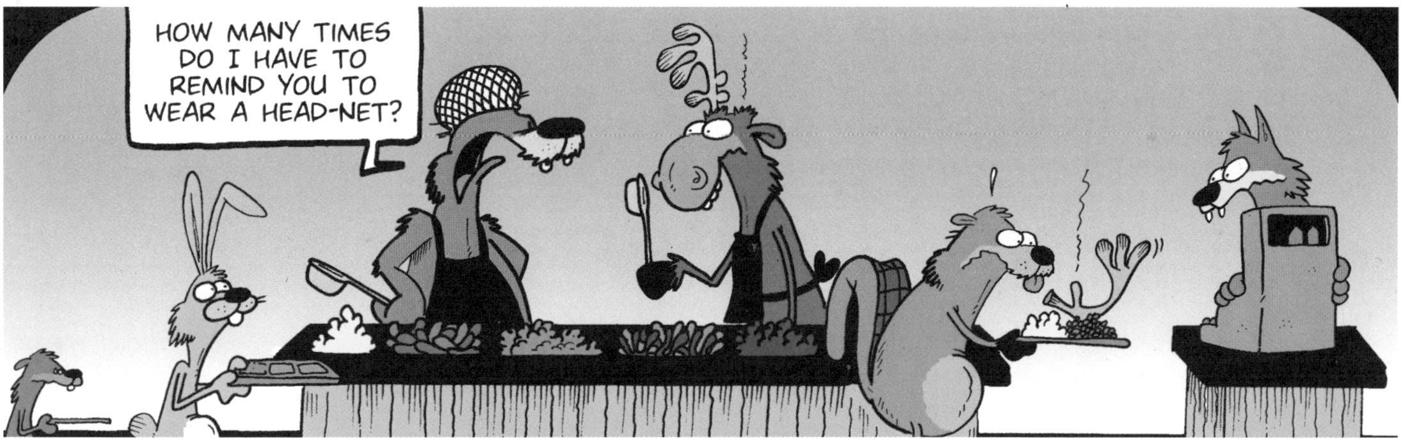
HOW MANY TIMES DO I HAVE TO REMIND YOU TO WEAR A HEAD-NET?

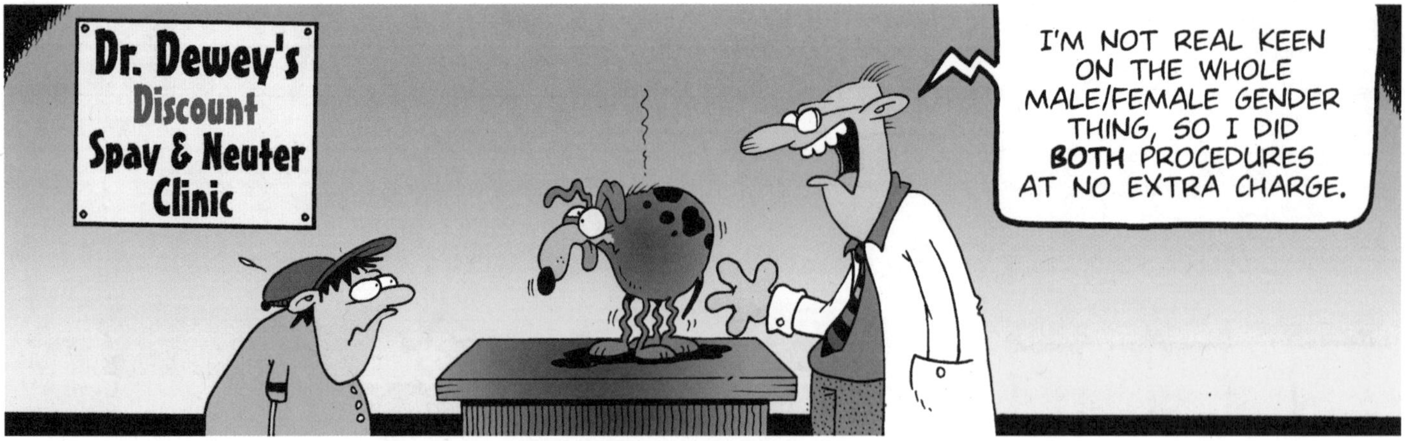
Dr. Dewey's
Discount
Spay & Neuter
Clinic
I'M NOT REAL KEEN ON THE WHOLE MALE/FEMALE GENDER THING, SO I DID BOTH PROCEDURES AT NO EXTRA CHARGE.

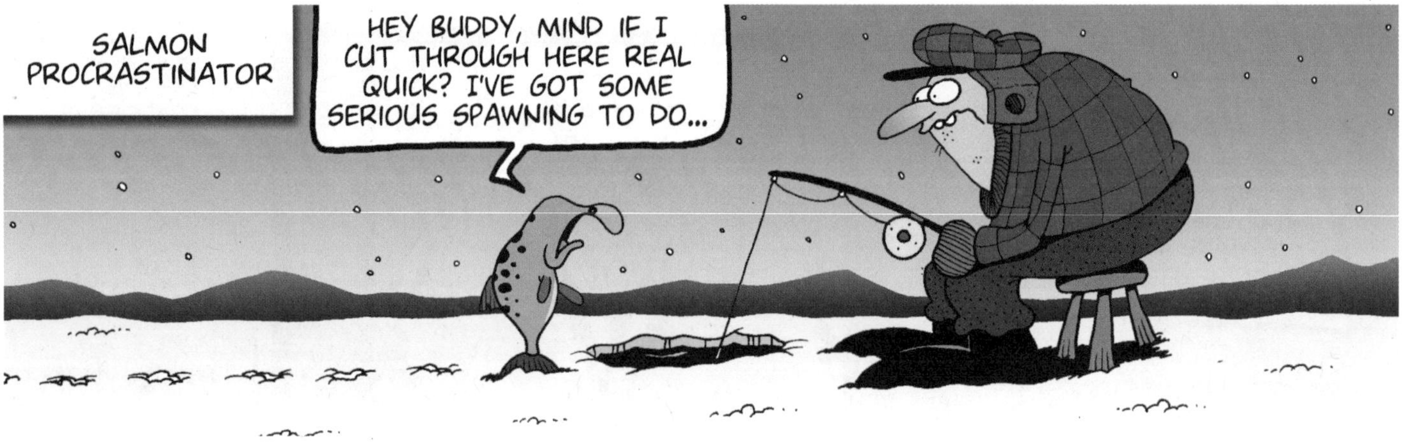
SALMON PROCRASTINATOR
HEY BUDDY, MIND IF I CUT THROUGH HERE REAL QUICK? I'VE GOT SOME SERIOUS SPAWNING TO DO...

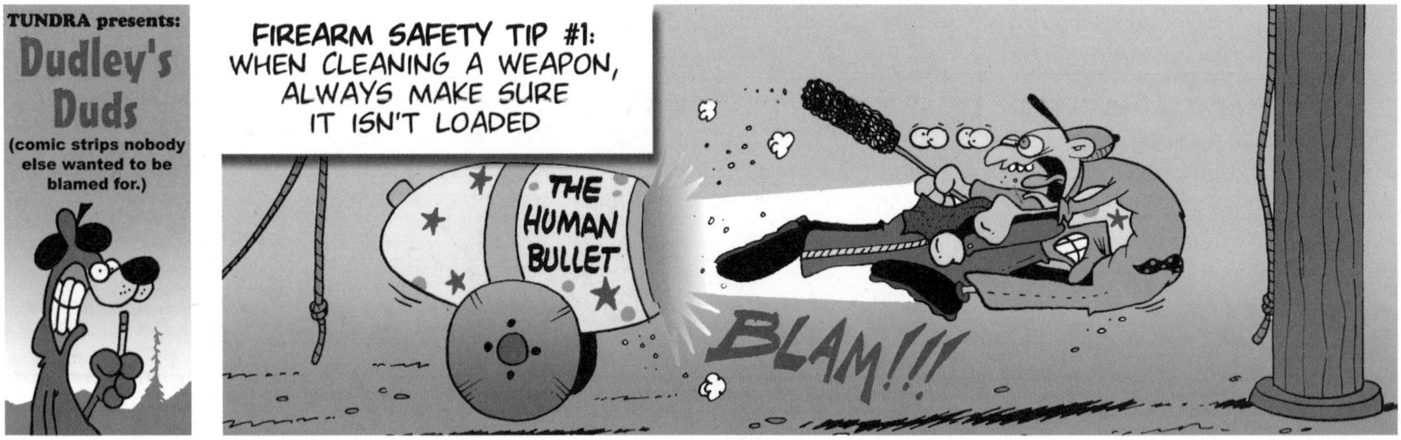
TUNDRA presents:
Dudley's
Duds
(comic strips nobody else wanted to be blamed for.)
FIREARM SAFETY TIP #1: WHEN CLEANING A WEAPON, ALWAYS MAKE SURE IT ISN'T LOADED
THE HUMAN BULLET
BLAM!!!

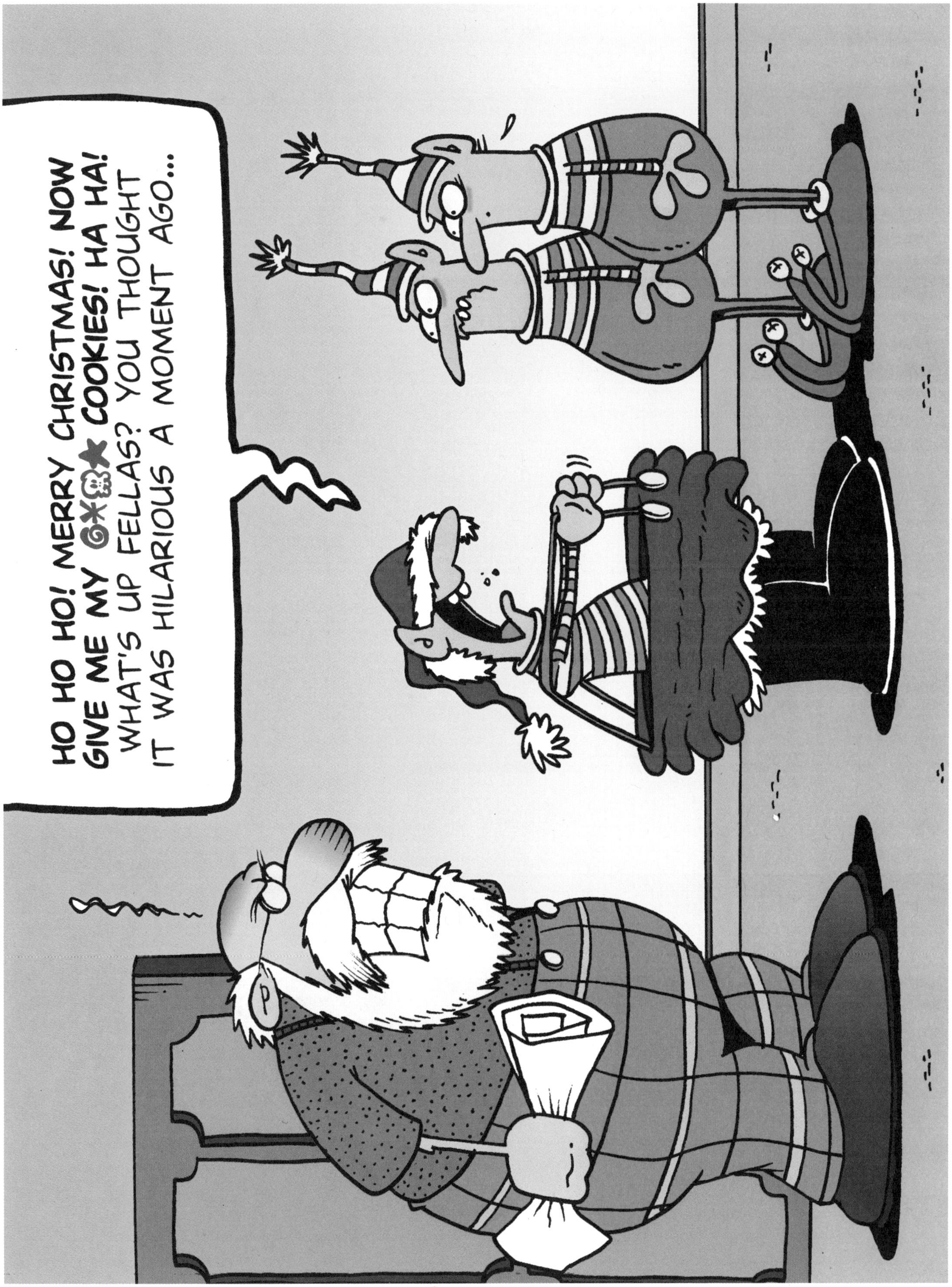
HO HO HO! MERRY CHRISTMAS! NOW GIVE ME MY @*☠★ COOKIES! HA HA! WHAT'S UP FELLAS? YOU THOUGHT IT WAS HILARIOUS A MOMENT AGO...

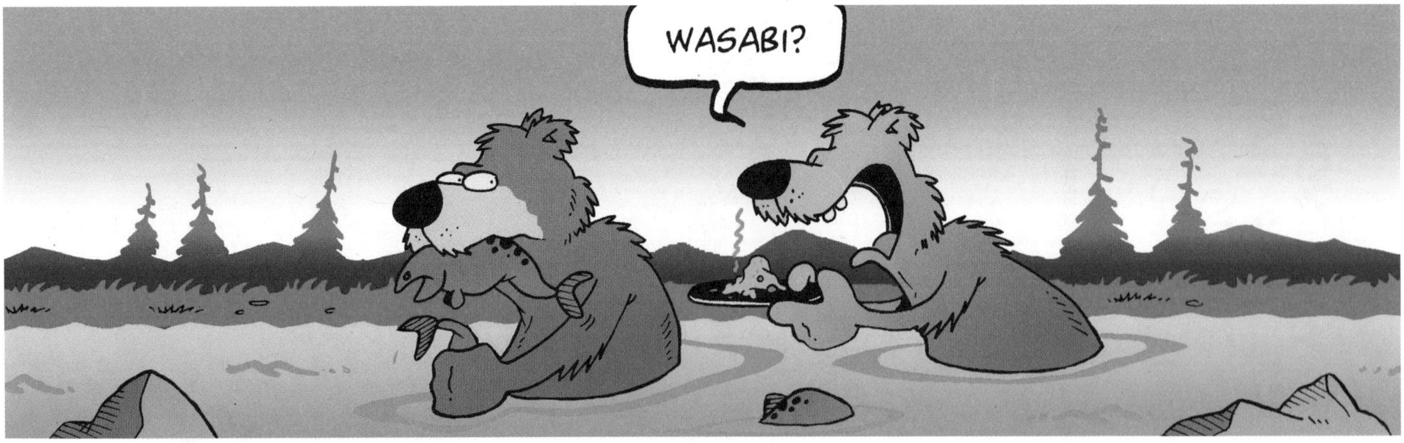
WASABI?

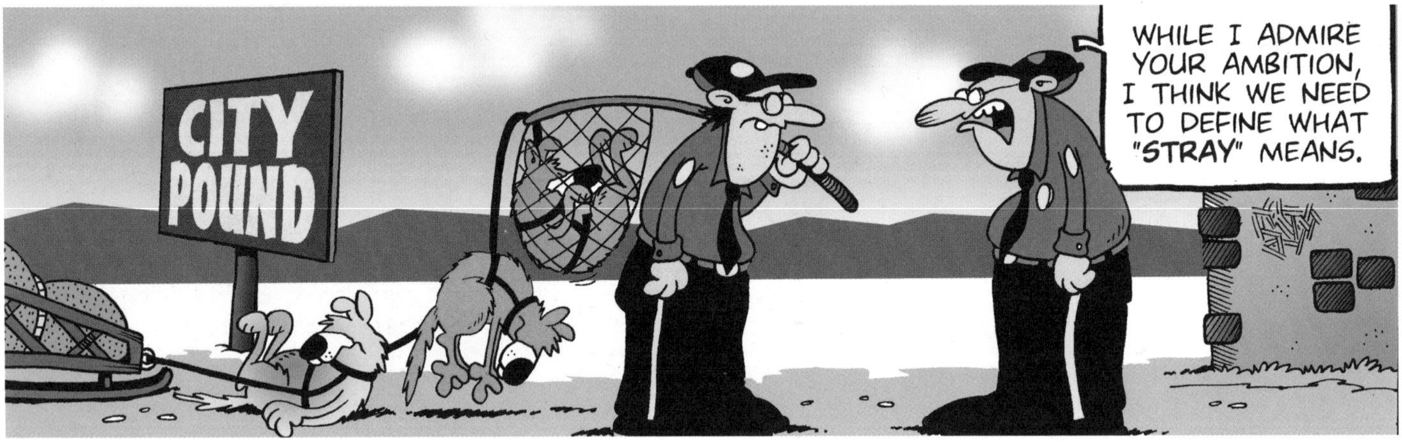
CITY POUND
WHILE I ADMIRE YOUR AMBITION, I THINK WE NEED TO DEFINE WHAT "STRAY" MEANS.

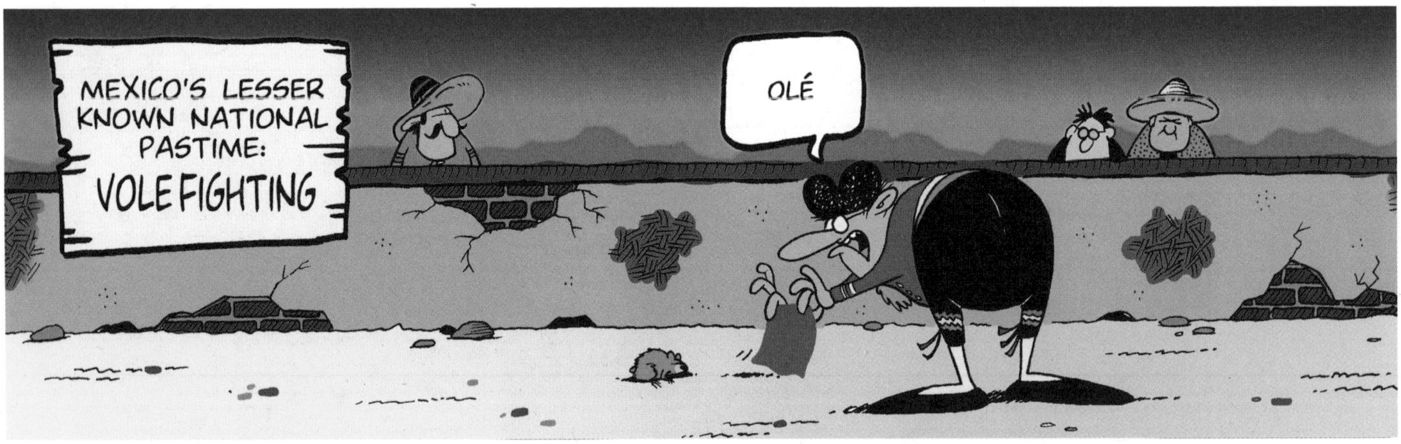
MEXICO'S LESSER KNOWN NATIONAL PASTIME:
VOLE FIGHTING
OLÉ

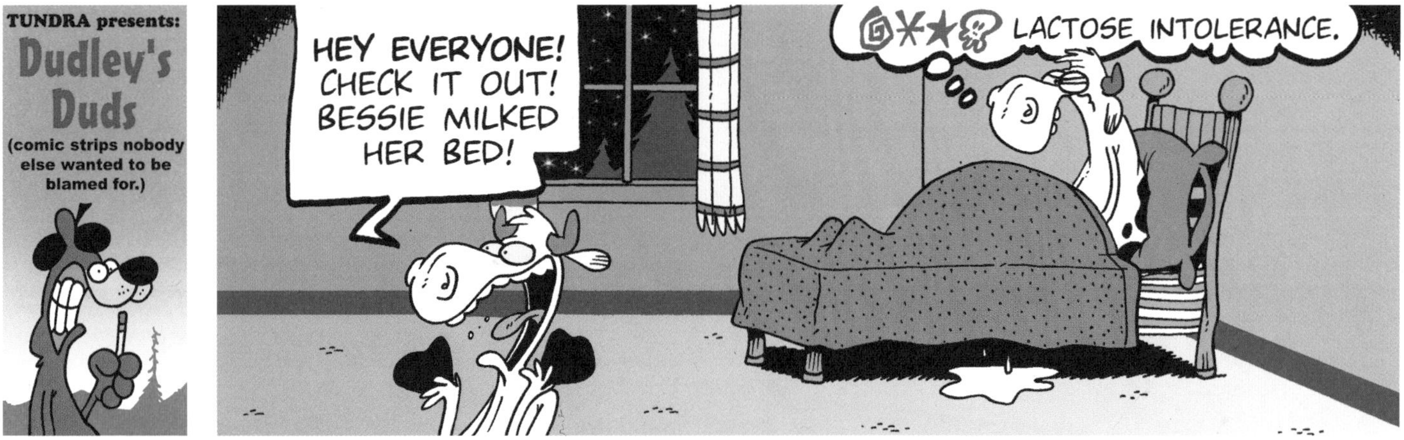
TUNDRA presents:
Dudley's Duds
(comic strips nobody else wanted to be blamed for.)
HEY EVERYONE! CHECK IT OUT! BESSIE MILKED HER BED!
LACTOSE INTOLERANCE.

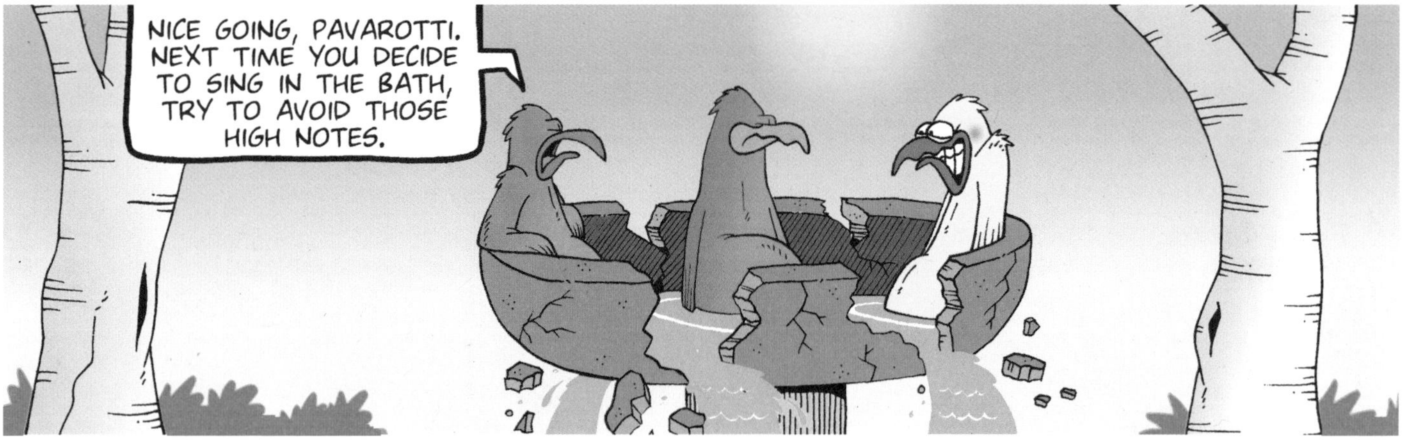
NICE GOING, PAVAROTTI. NEXT TIME YOU DECIDE TO SING IN THE BATH, TRY TO AVOID THOSE HIGH NOTES.

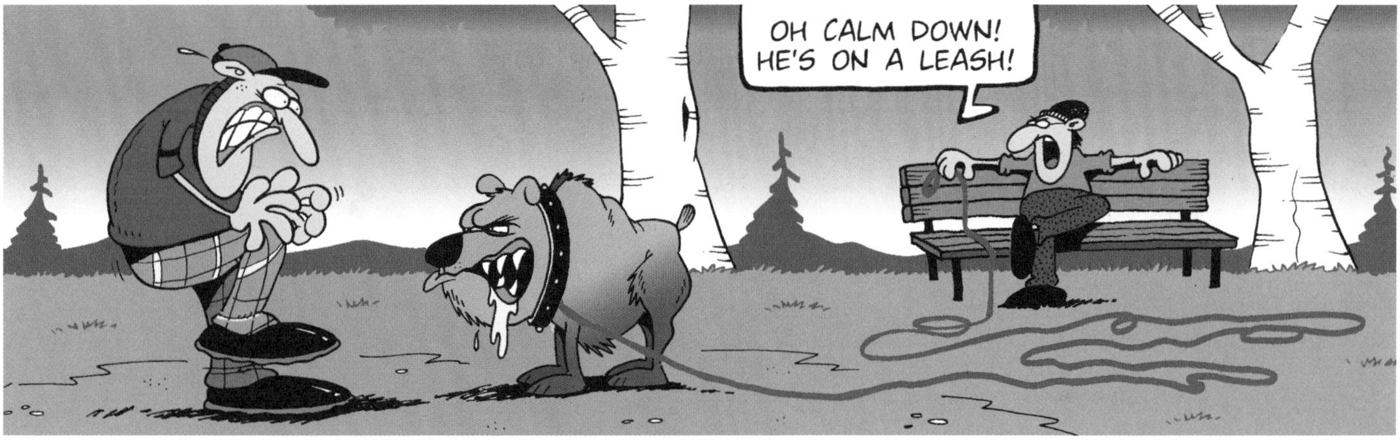
OH CALM DOWN! HE'S ON A LEASH!

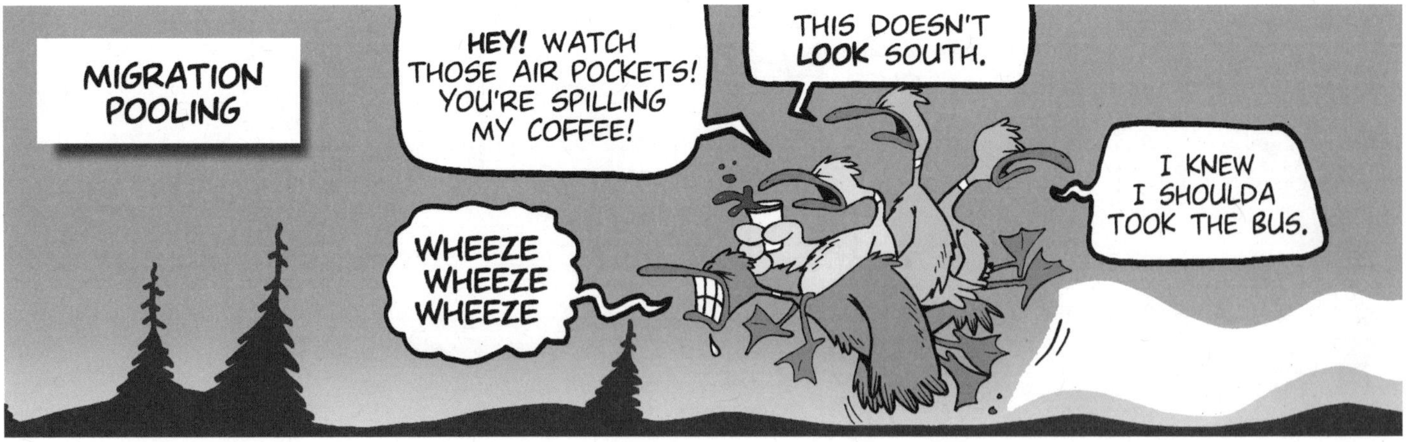
MIGRATION POOLING
HEY! WATCH THOSE AIR POCKETS! YOU'RE SPILLING MY COFFEE!
THIS DOESN'T LOOK SOUTH.
WHEEZE WHEEZE WHEEZE
I KNEW I SHOULDA TOOK THE BUS.

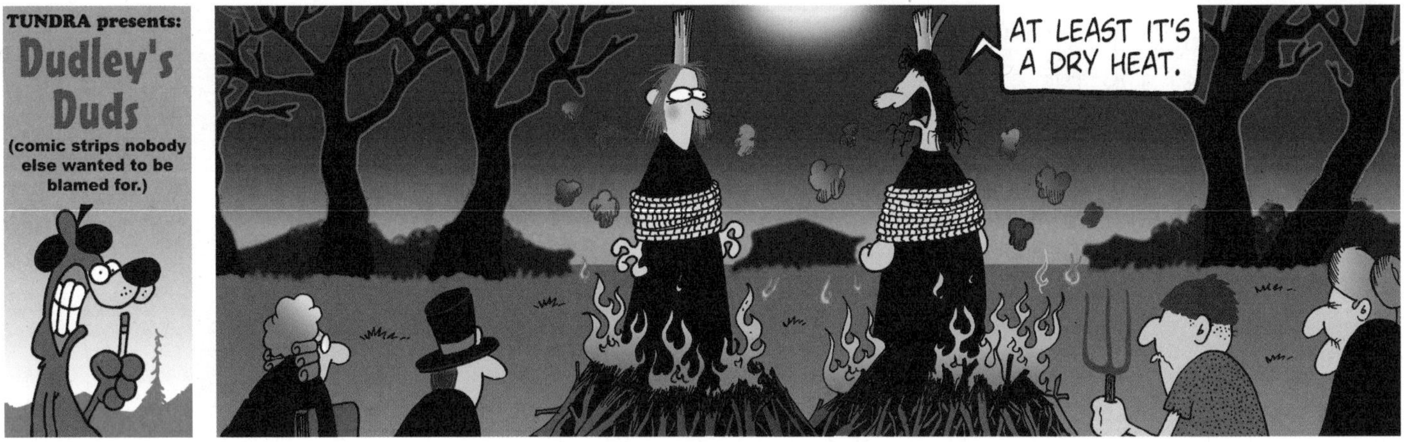
TUNDRA presents:
Dudley's Duds
(comic strips nobody else wanted to be blamed for.)
AT LEAST IT'S A DRY HEAT.

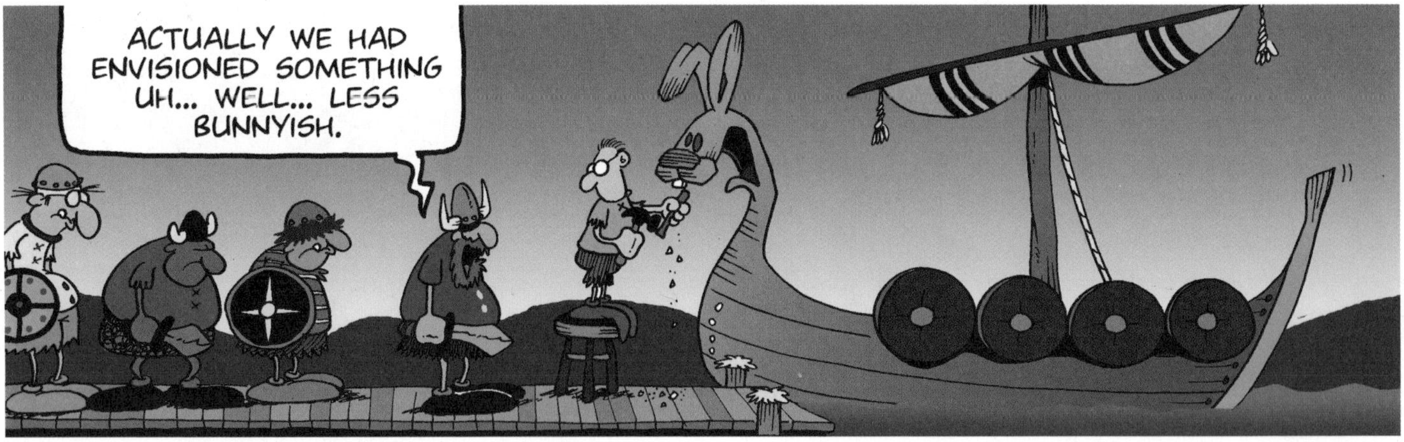
ACTUALLY WE HAD ENVISIONED SOMETHING UH... WELL... LESS BUNNYISH.

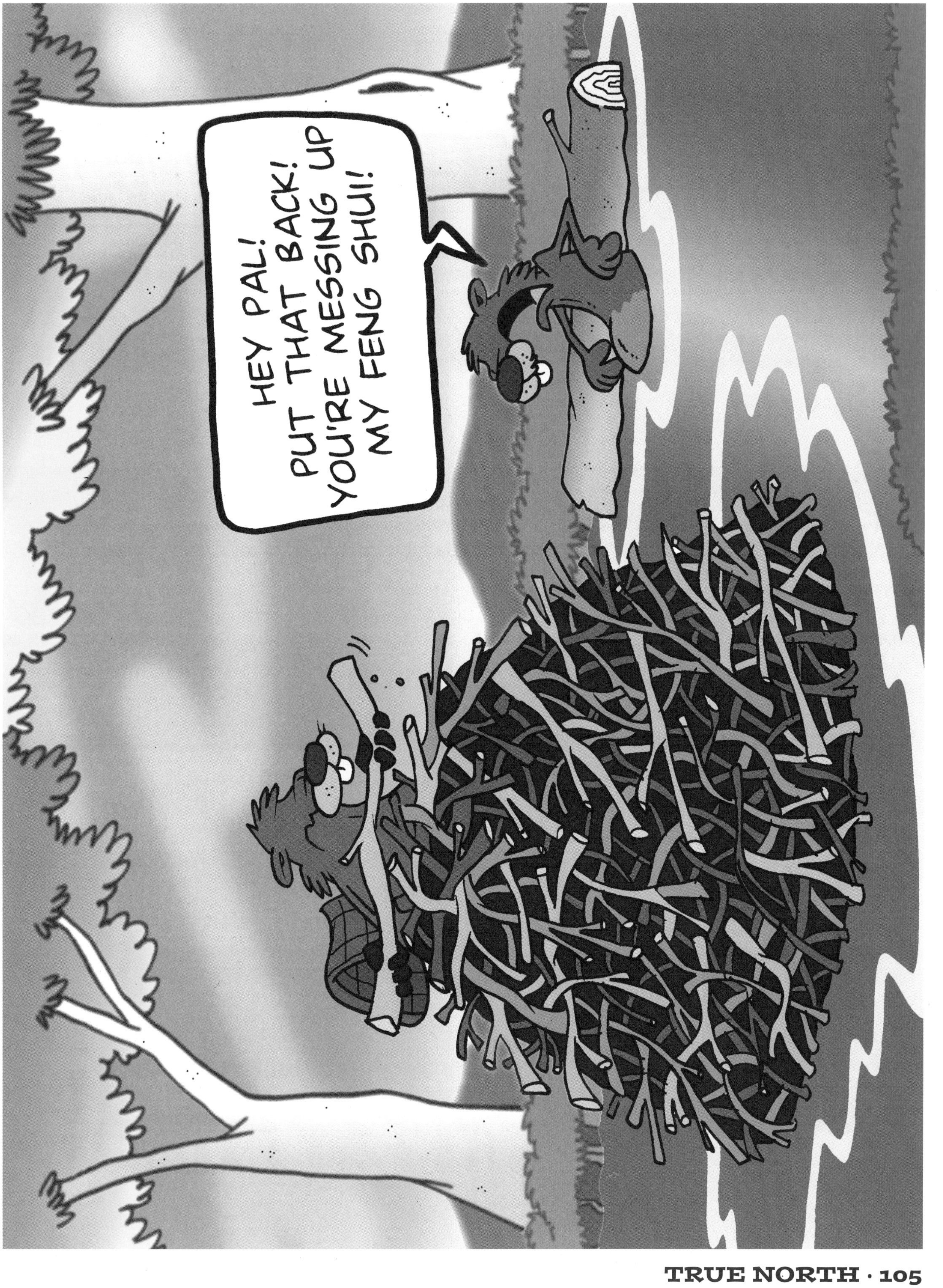
HEY PAL!
PUT THAT BACK!
YOU'RE MESSING UP
MY FENG SHUI!!

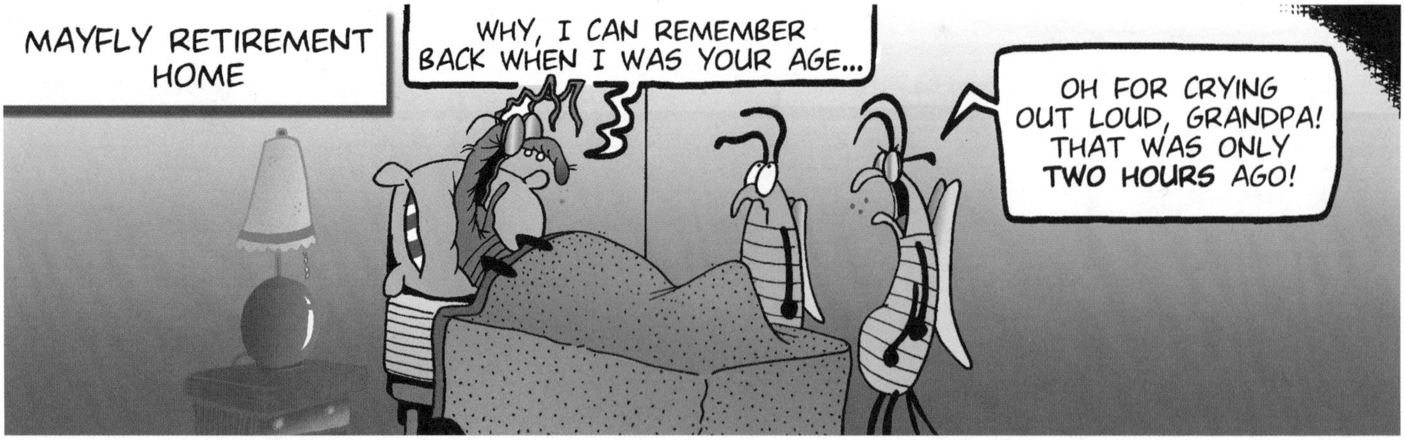
MAYFLY RETIREMENT HOME
WHY, I CAN REMEMBER BACK WHEN I WAS YOUR AGE...
OH FOR CRYING OUT LOUD, GRANDPA! THAT WAS ONLY TWO HOURS AGO!

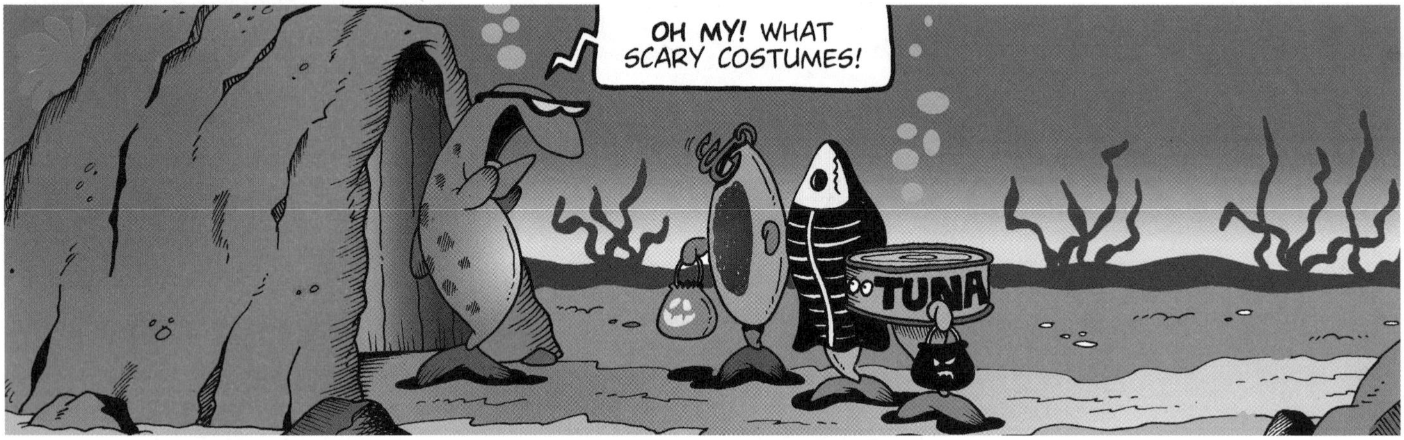
OH MY! WHAT SCARY COSTUMES!
TUNA

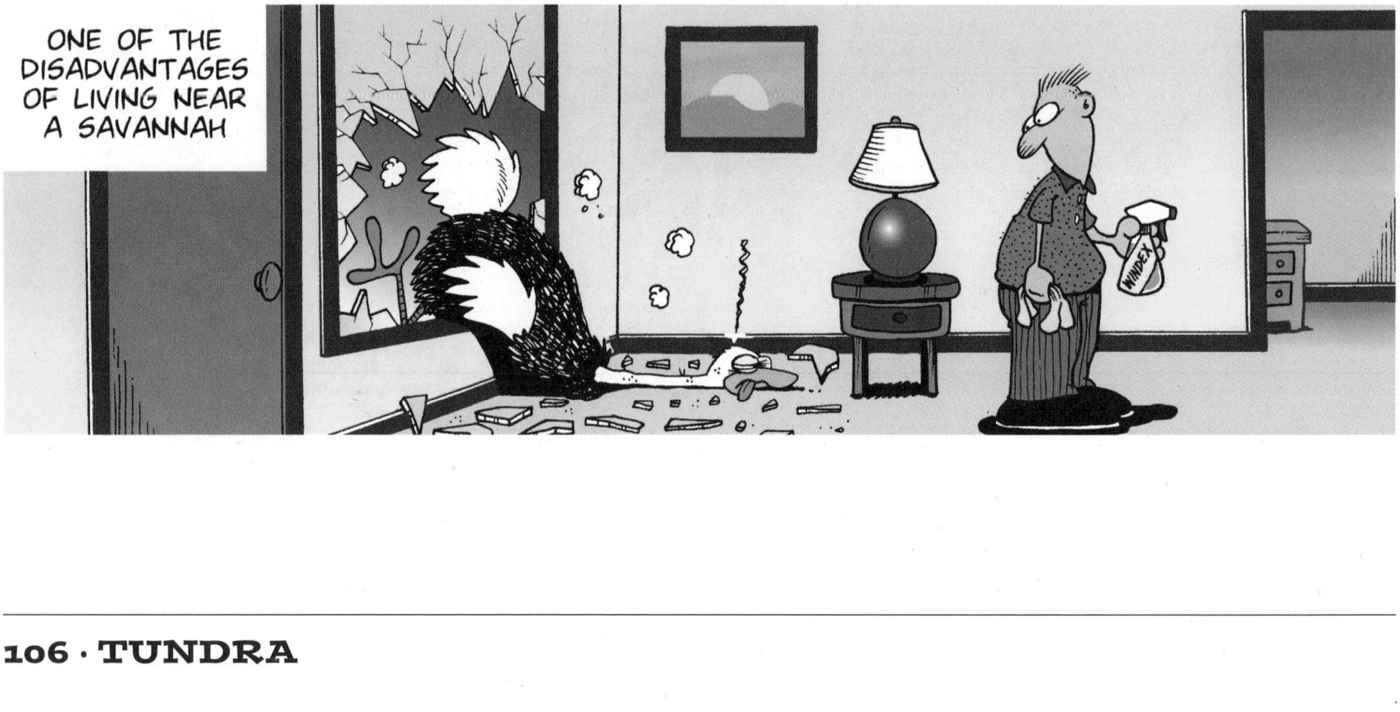
ONE OF THE DISADVANTAGES OF LIVING NEAR A SAVANNAH
WINDEX

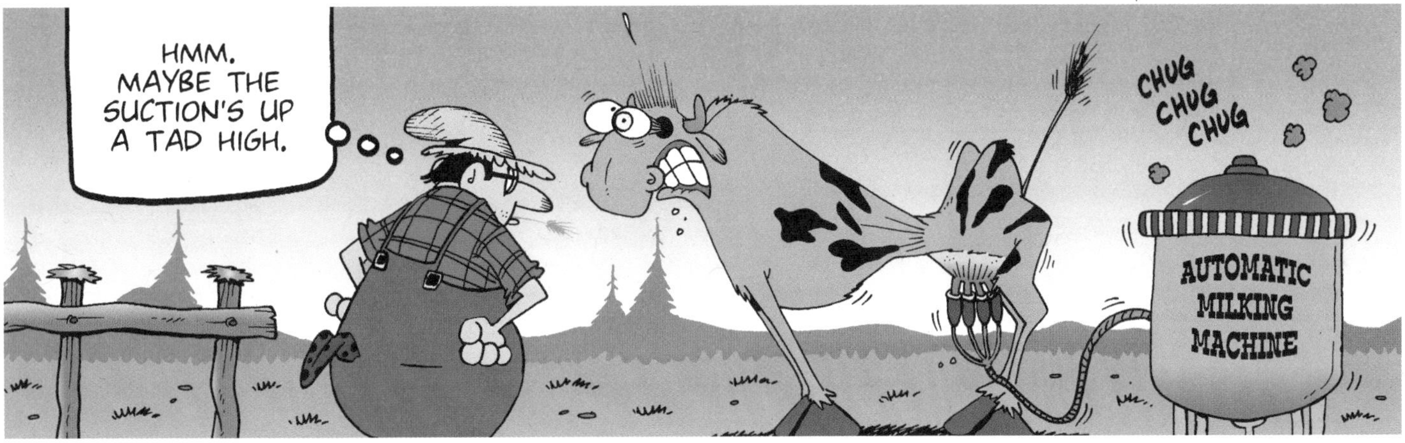
HMM. MAYBE THE SUCTION'S UP A TAD HIGH.
CHUG CHUG CHUG
AUTOMATIC MILKING MACHINE

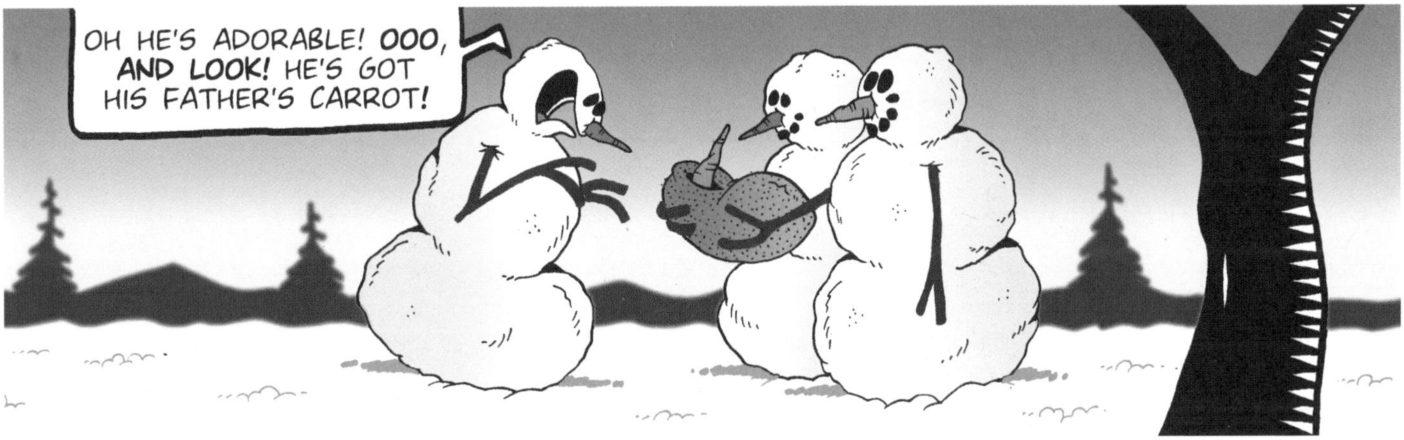
OH HE'S ADORABLE! OOO, AND LOOK! HE'S GOT HIS FATHER'S CARROT!

This comic strip is based on an idea from:
Kim Kellogg
Anchorage, AK
www.tundracomics.com

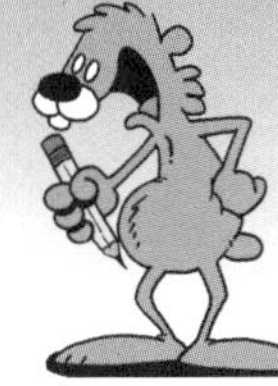

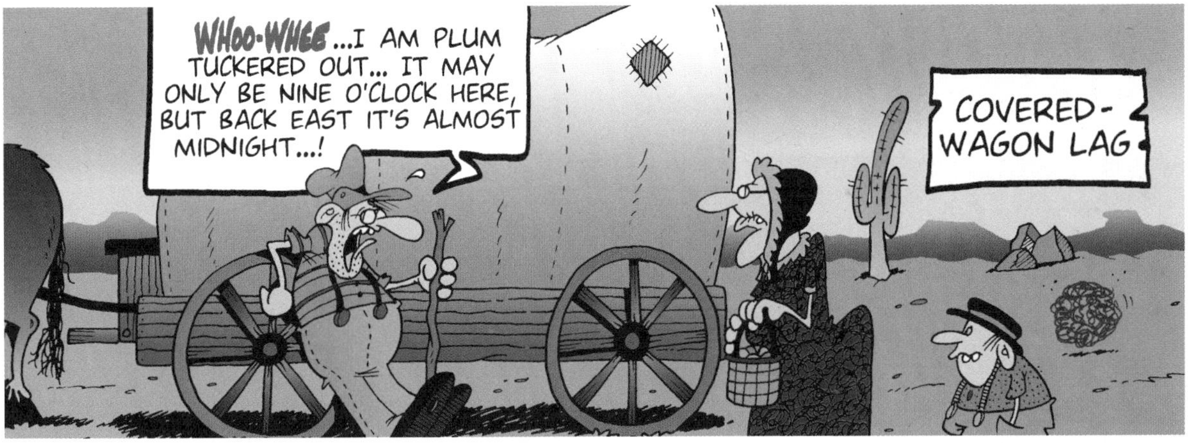
WHOO-WHEE ...I AM PLUM TUCKERED OUT... IT MAY ONLY BE NINE O'CLOCK HERE, BUT BACK EAST IT'S ALMOST MIDNIGHT...!
COVERED-WAGON LAG

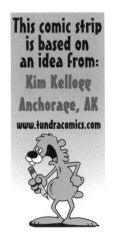

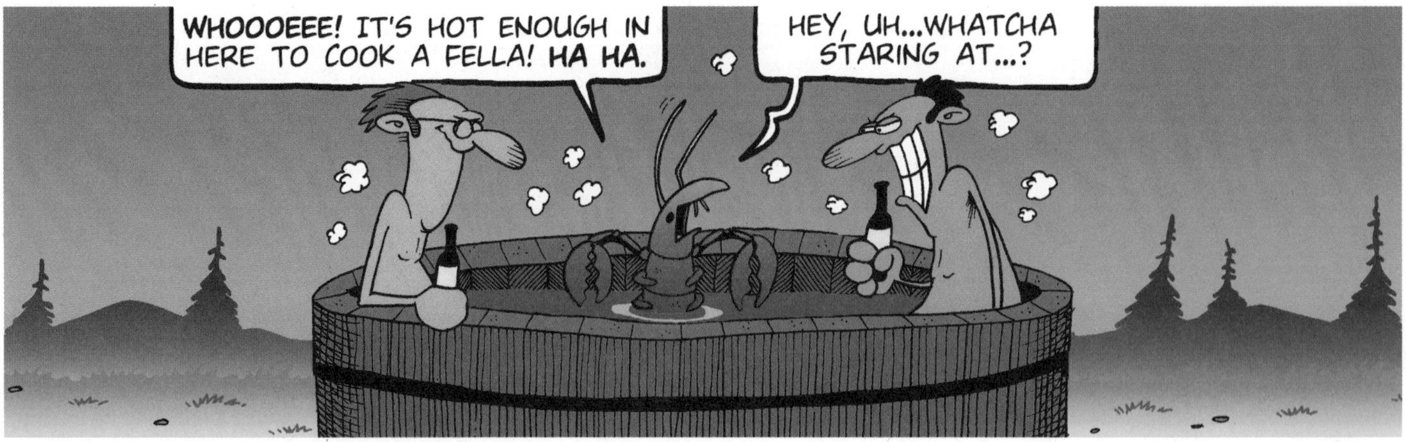
WHOOOEEE! IT'S HOT ENOUGH IN HERE TO COOK A FELLA! HA HA.
HEY, UH...WHATCHA STARING AT...?

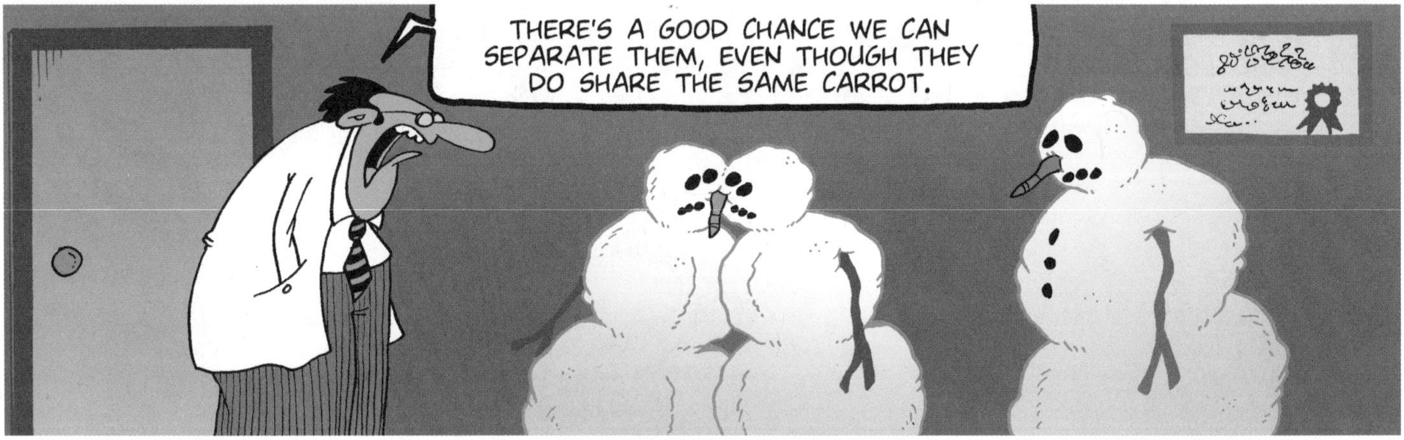
THERE'S A GOOD CHANCE WE CAN SEPARATE THEM, EVEN THOUGH THEY DO SHARE THE SAME CARROT.

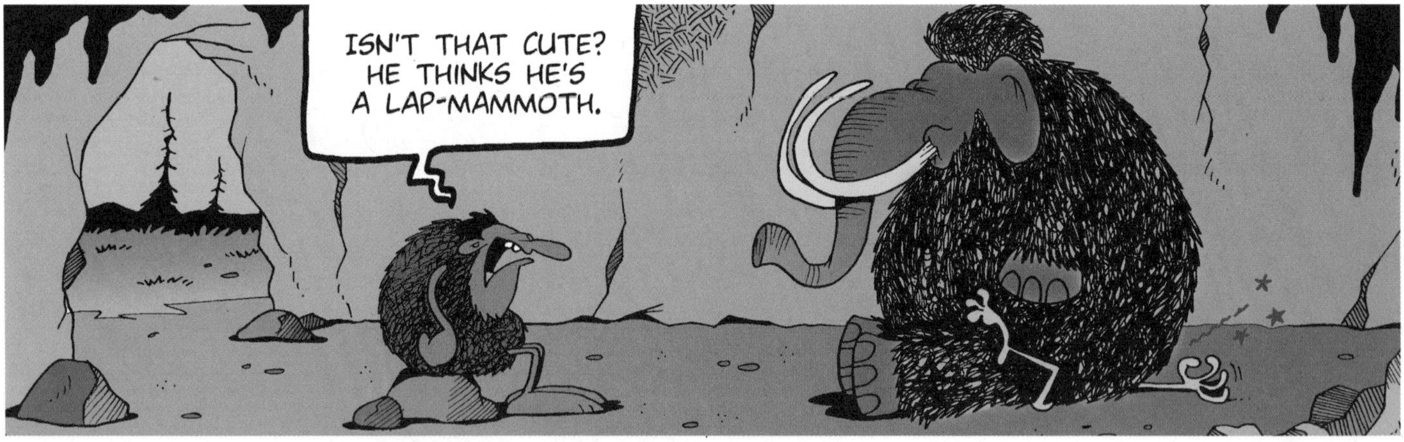
ISN'T THAT CUTE? HE THINKS HE'S A LAP-MAMMOTH.

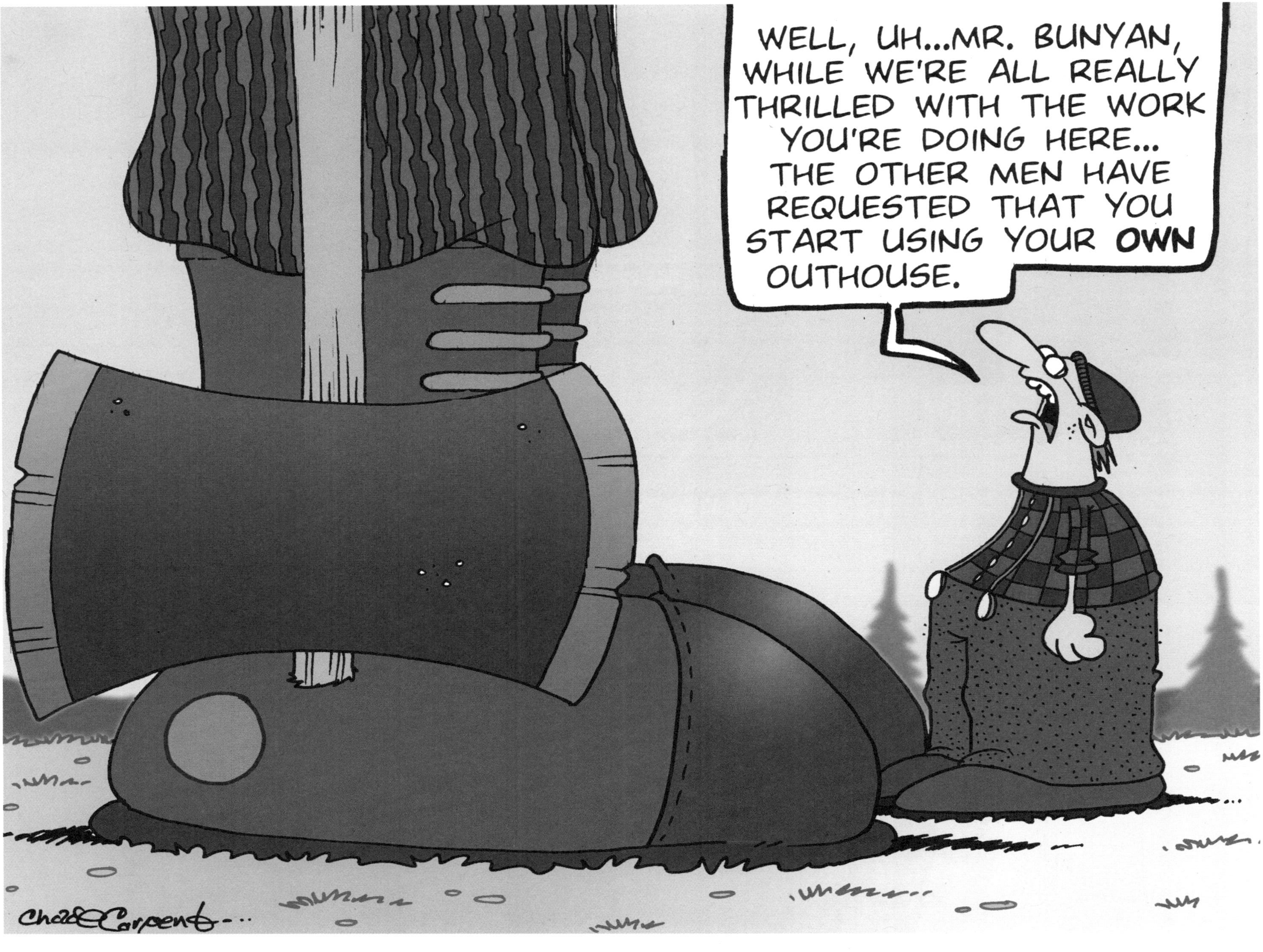
WELL, UH...MR. BUNYAN, WHILE WE'RE ALL REALLY THRILLED WITH THE WORK YOU'RE DOING HERE... THE OTHER MEN HAVE REQUESTED THAT YOU START USING YOUR **OWN** OUTHOUSE.
Chad Carpenter...

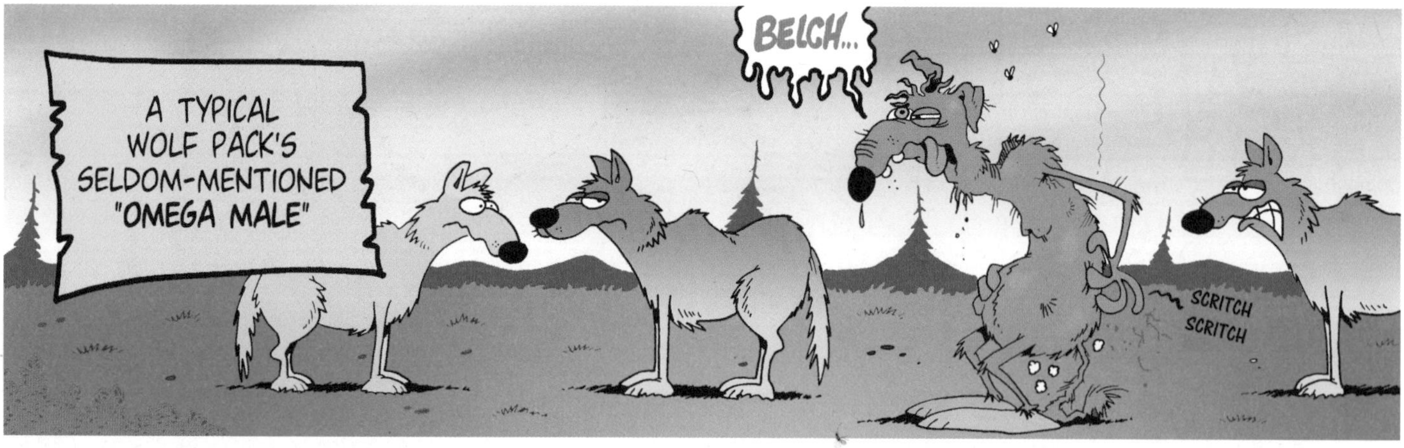
A TYPICAL WOLF PACK'S SELDOM-MENTIONED "OMEGA MALE"
BELCH...
SCRITCH SCRITCH

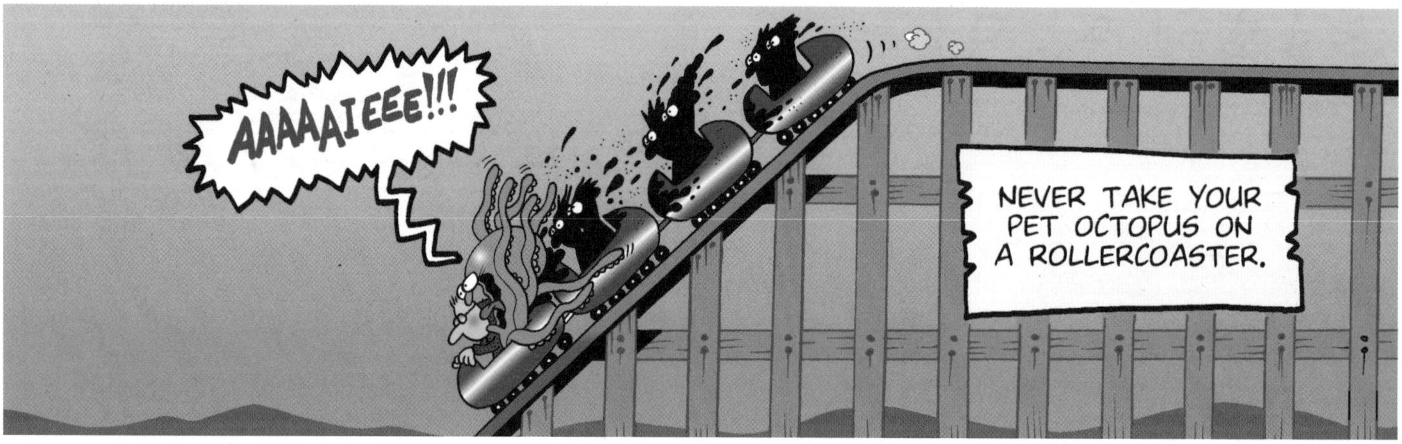
AAAAAIEEE!!!
NEVER TAKE YOUR PET OCTOPUS ON A ROLLERCOASTER.

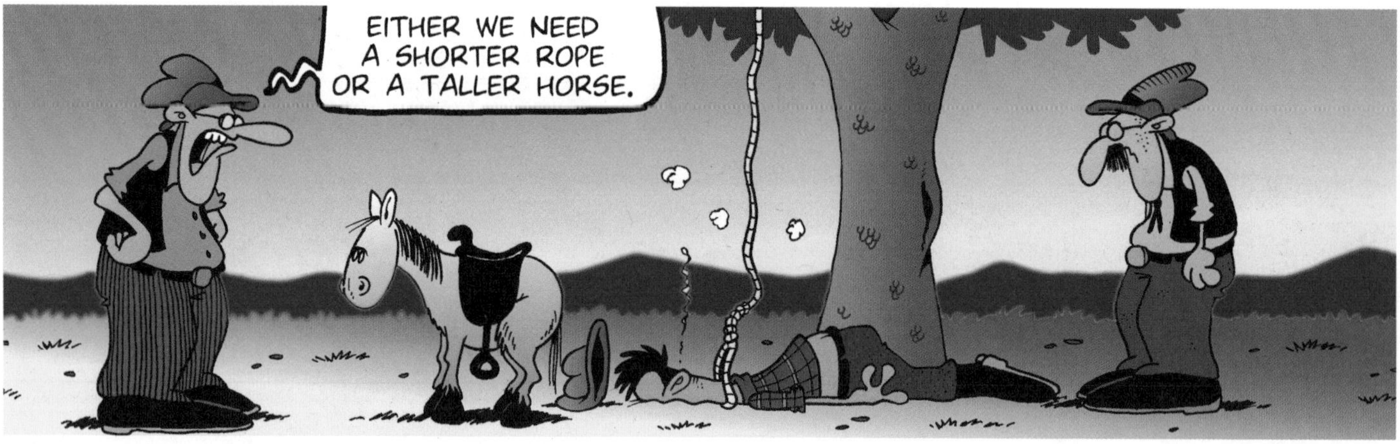
EITHER WE NEED A SHORTER ROPE OR A TALLER HORSE.

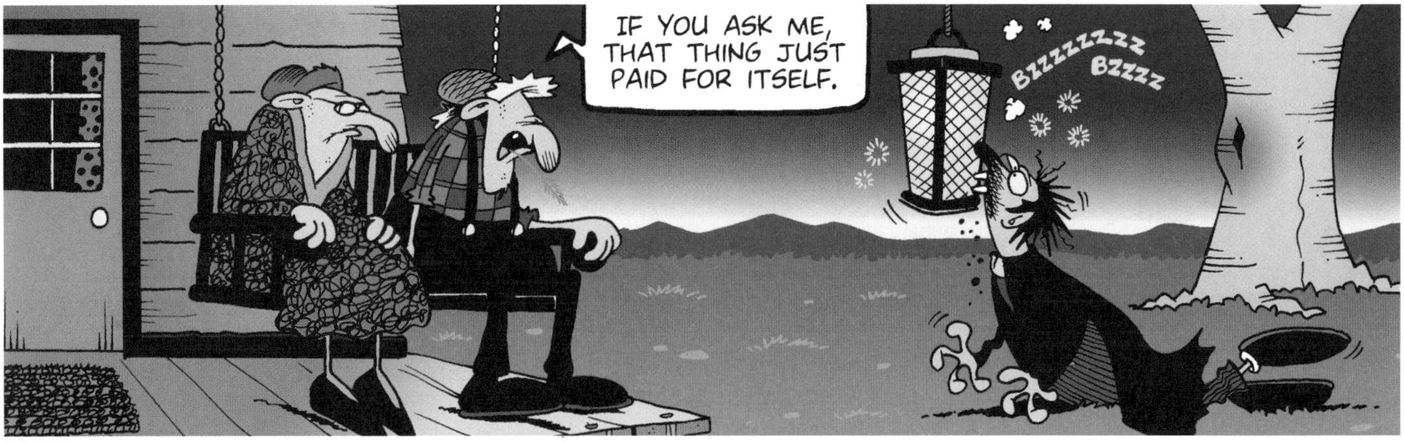
IF YOU ASK ME, THAT THING JUST PAID FOR ITSELF.
BZZZZZZZZ BZZZZ

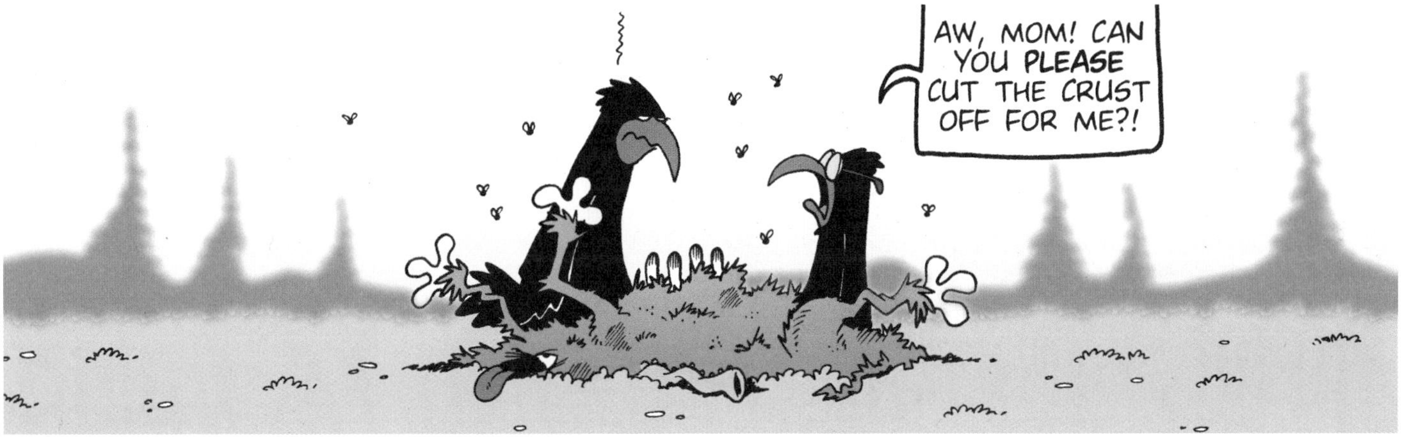
AW, MOM! CAN YOU **PLEASE** CUT THE CRUST OFF FOR ME?!

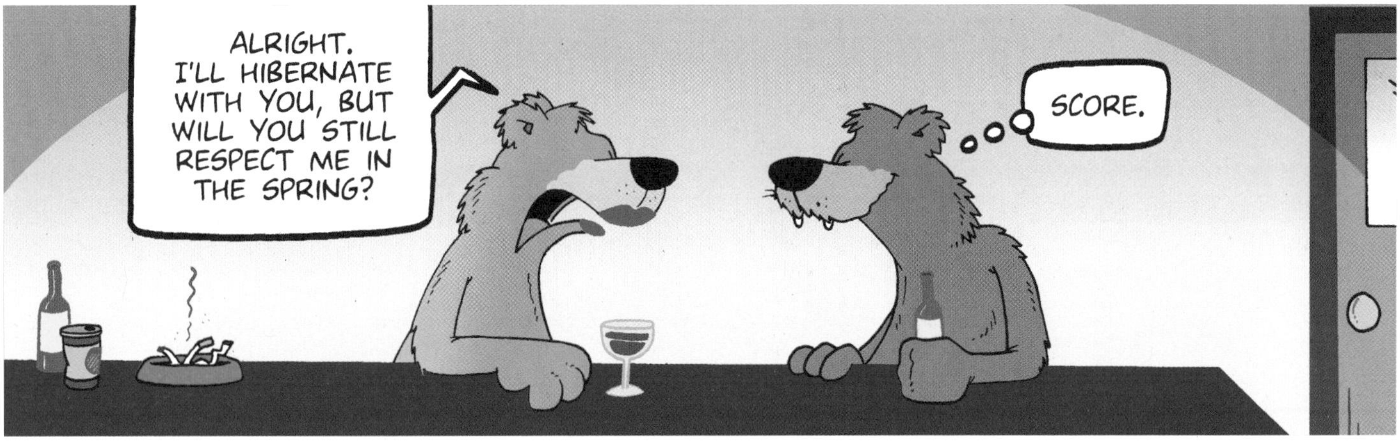
ALRIGHT. I'LL HIBERNATE WITH YOU, BUT WILL YOU STILL RESPECT ME IN THE SPRING?
SCORE.

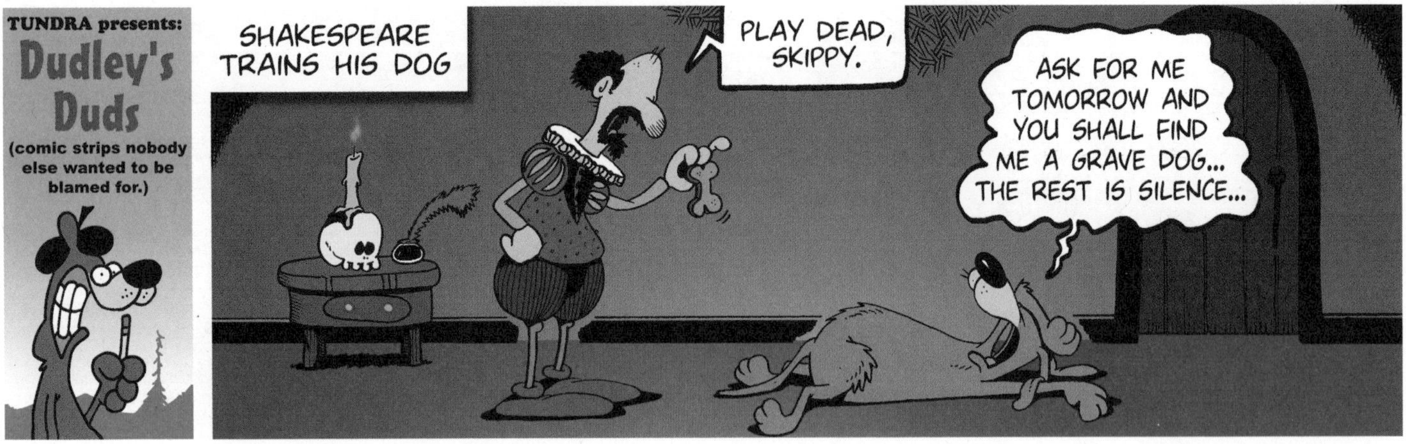
TUNDRA presents:
Dudley's Duds
(comic strips nobody else wanted to be blamed for.)
SHAKESPEARE TRAINS HIS DOG
PLAY DEAD, SKIPPY.
ASK FOR ME TOMORROW AND YOU SHALL FIND ME A GRAVE DOG... THE REST IS SILENCE...

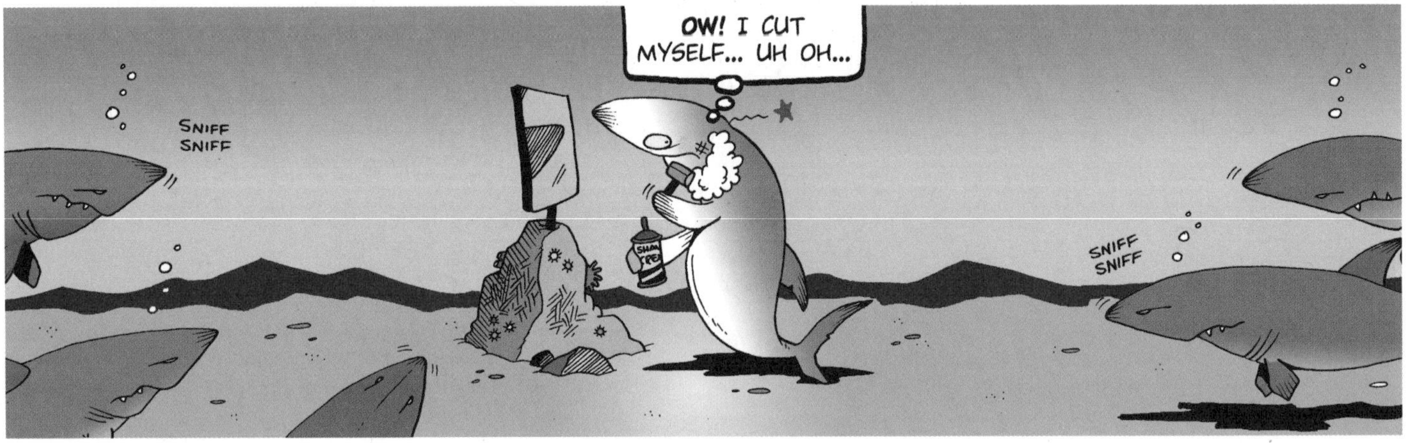
OW! I CUT MYSELF... UH OH...
SNIFF SNIFF
SNIFF SNIFF

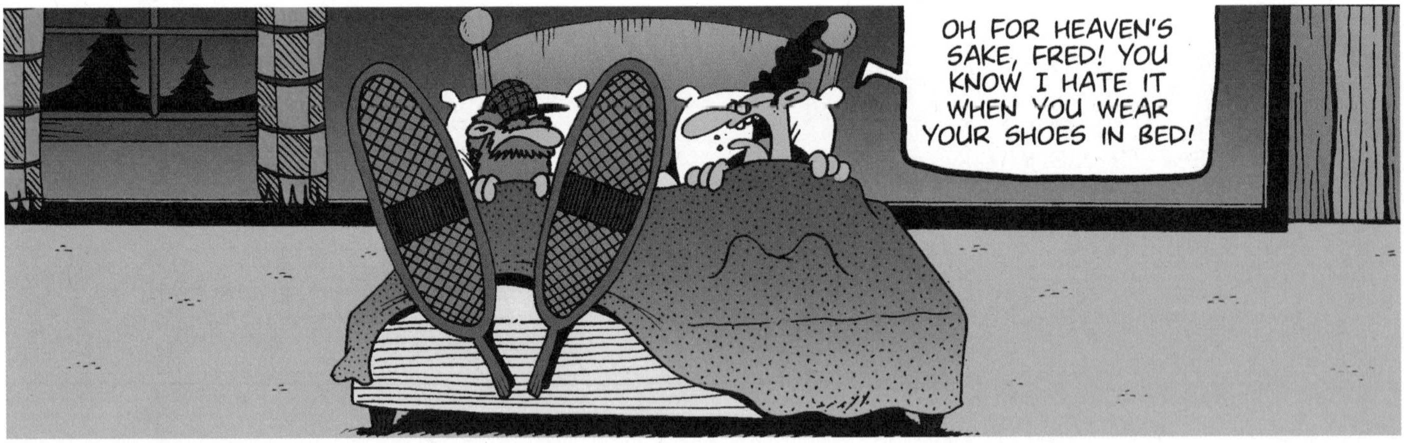
OH FOR HEAVEN'S SAKE, FRED! YOU KNOW I HATE IT WHEN YOU WEAR YOUR SHOES IN BED!

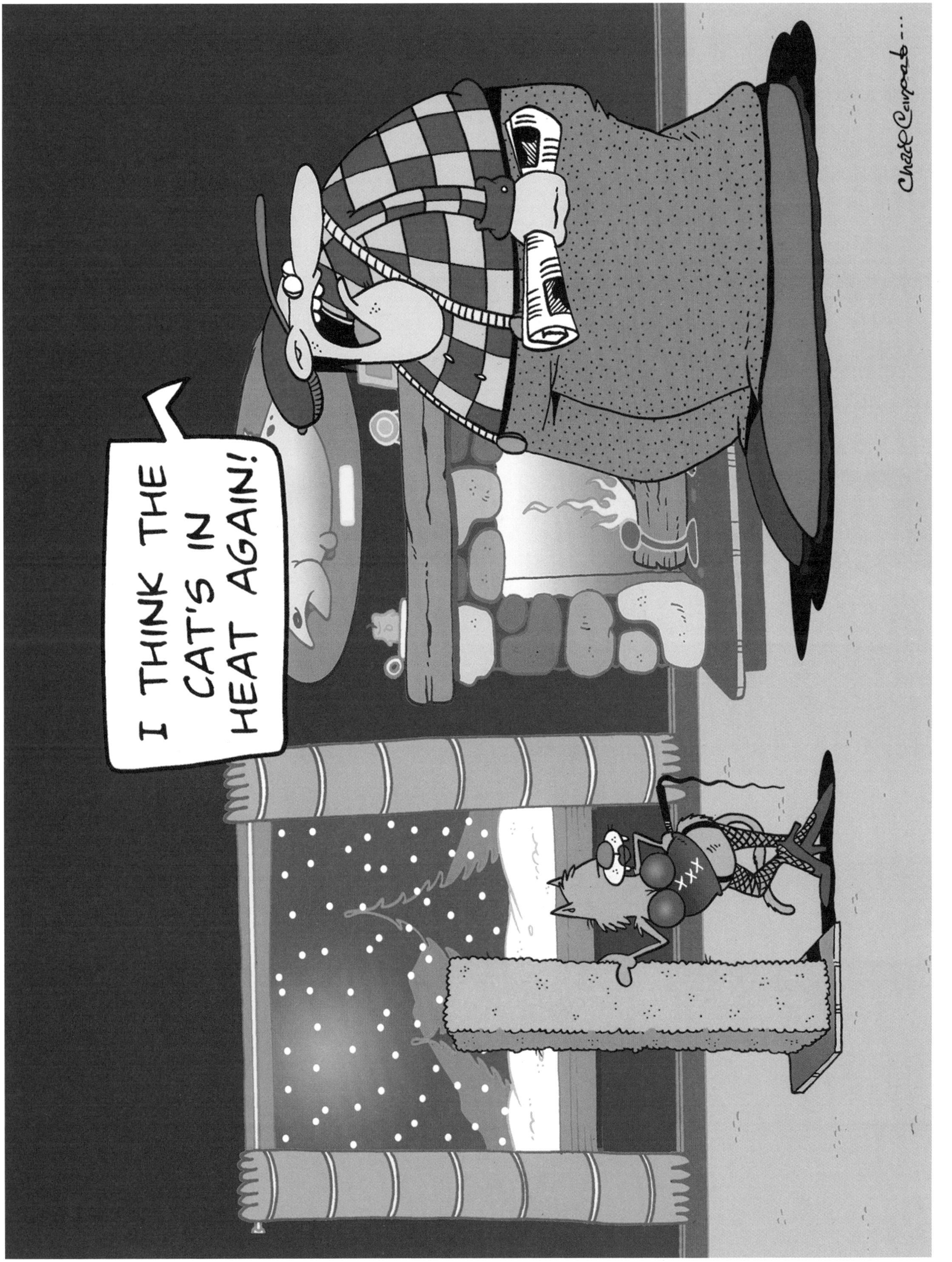
I THINK THE CAT'S IN HEAT AGAIN!
Chase Campbell...

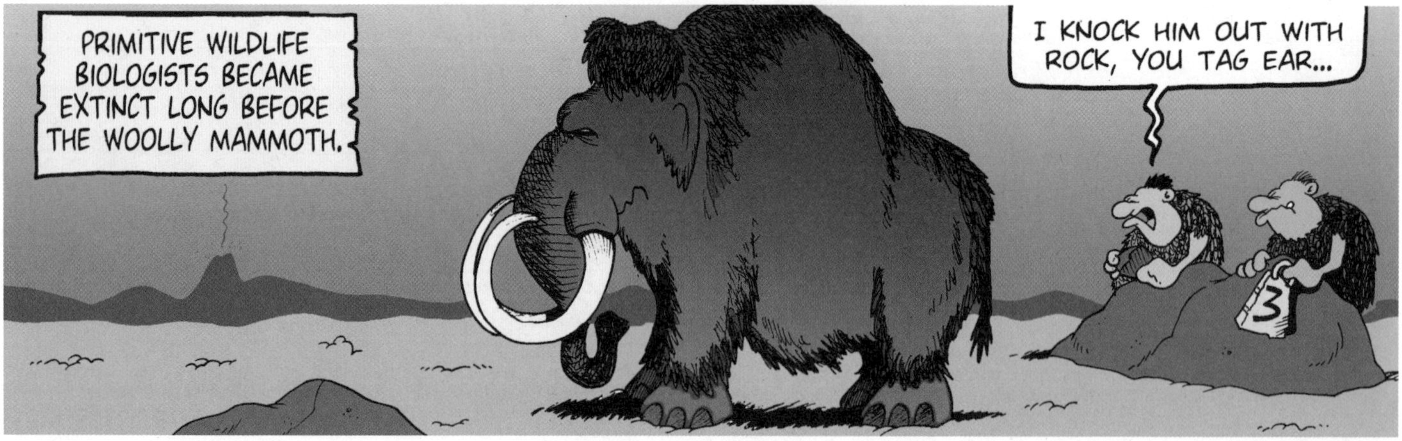
PRIMITIVE WILDLIFE BIOLOGISTS BECAME EXTINCT LONG BEFORE THE WOOLLY MAMMOTH.
I KNOCK HIM OUT WITH ROCK, YOU TAG EAR...
3

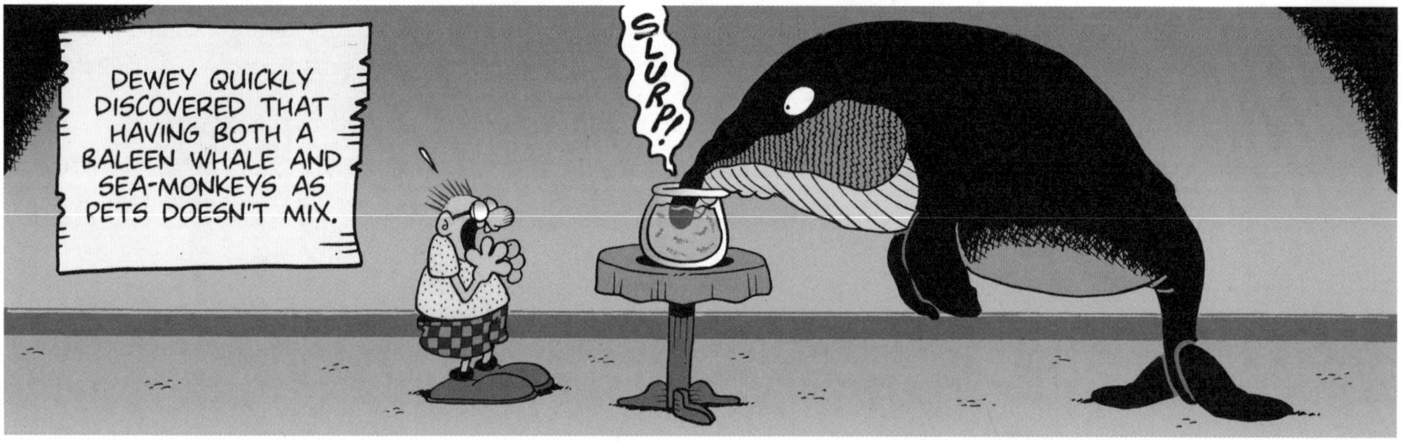
DEWEY QUICKLY DISCOVERED THAT HAVING BOTH A BALEEN WHALE AND SEA-MONKEYS AS PETS DOESN'T MIX.
SLURP!

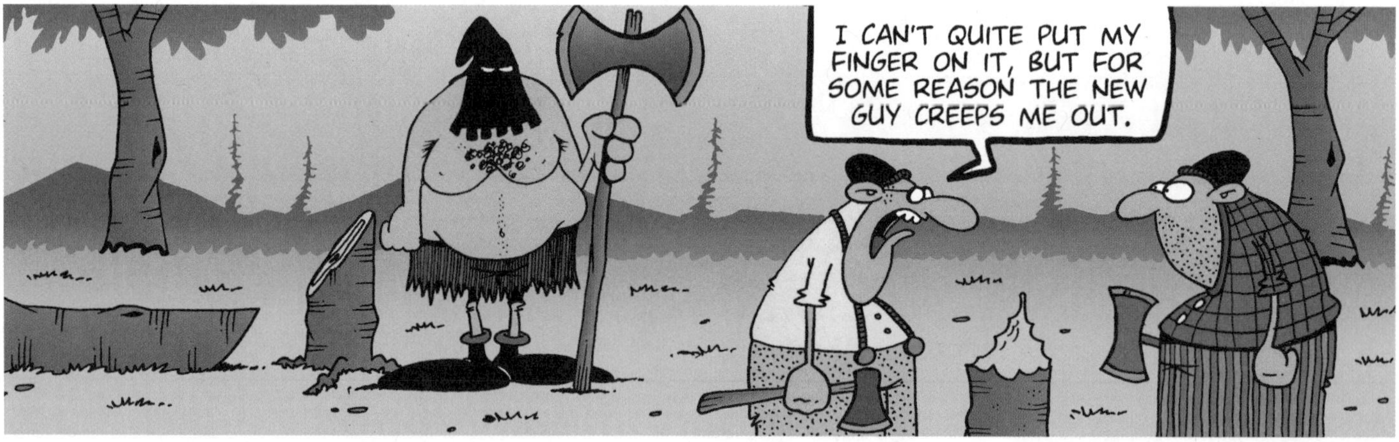
I CAN'T QUITE PUT MY FINGER ON IT, BUT FOR SOME REASON THE NEW GUY CREEPS ME OUT.

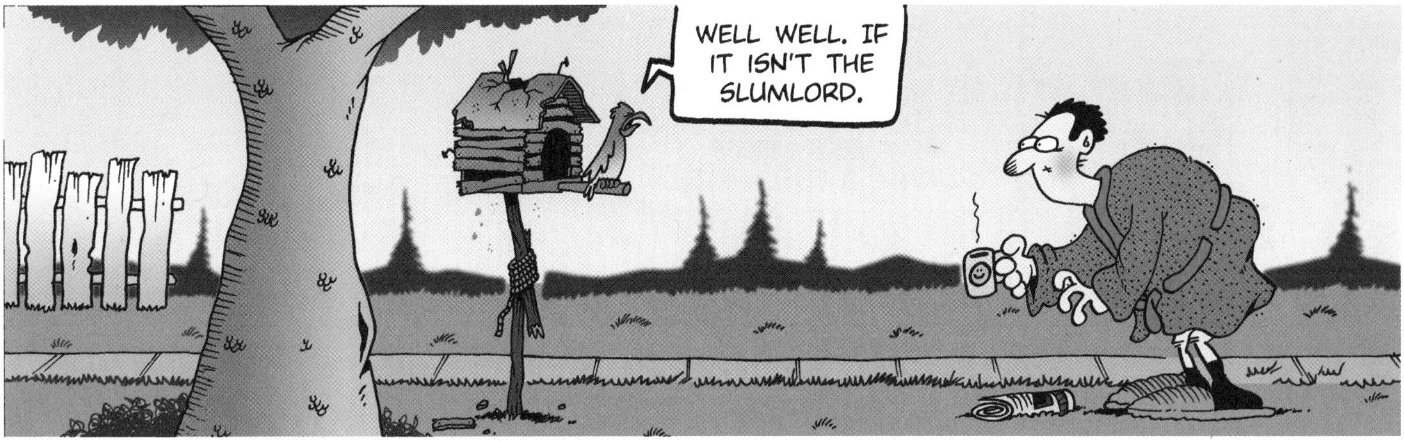
WELL WELL. IF IT ISN'T THE SLUMLORD.

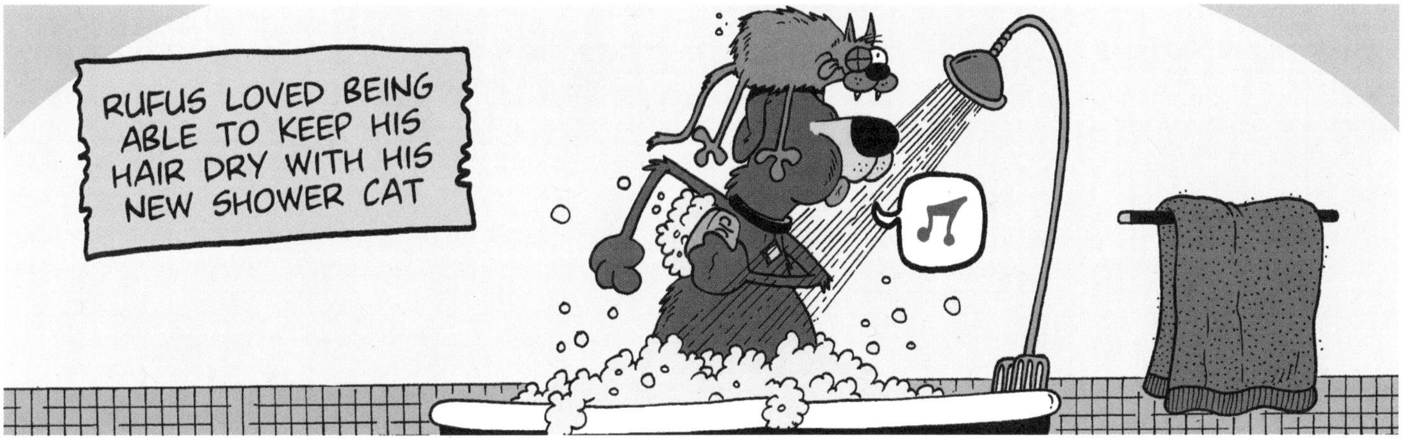
RUFUS LOVED BEING ABLE TO KEEP HIS HAIR DRY WITH HIS NEW SHOWER CAT

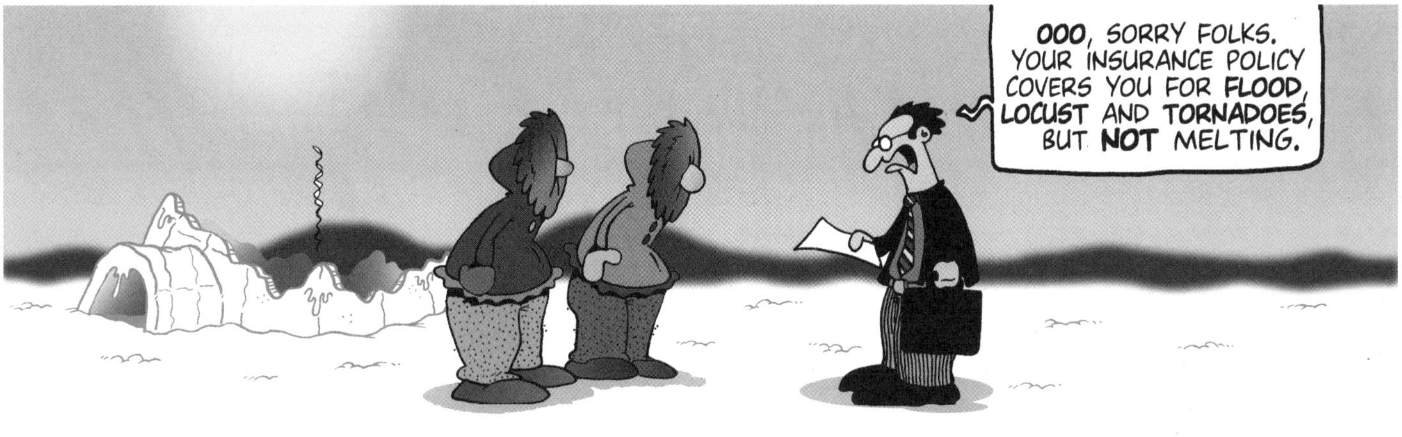
OOO, SORRY FOLKS. YOUR INSURANCE POLICY COVERS YOU FOR FLOOD, LOCUST AND TORNADOES, BUT NOT MELTING.

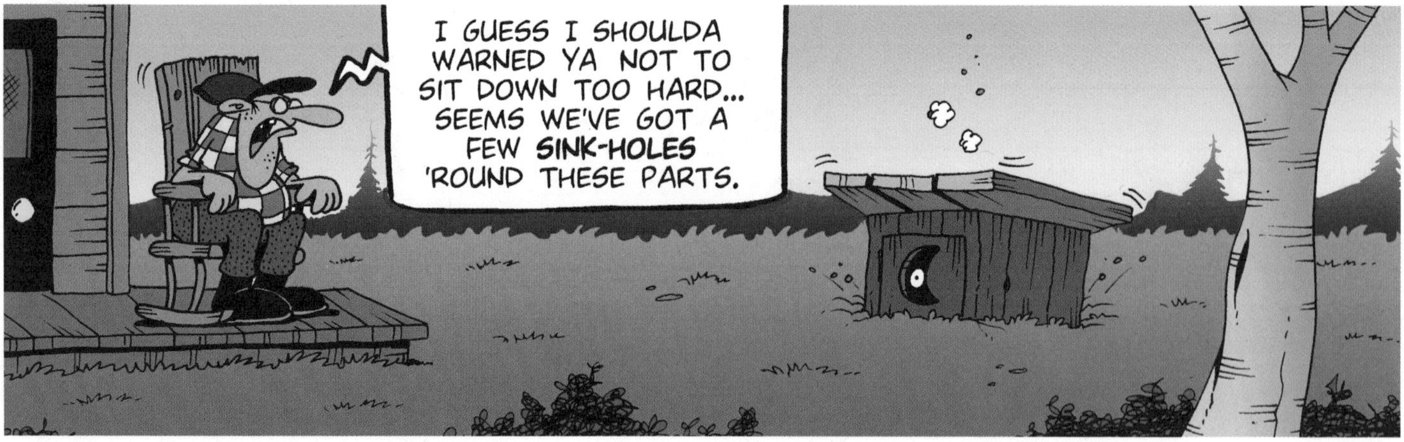
I GUESS I SHOULDA WARNED YA NOT TO SIT DOWN TOO HARD... SEEMS WE'VE GOT A FEW **SINK-HOLES** 'ROUND THESE PARTS.

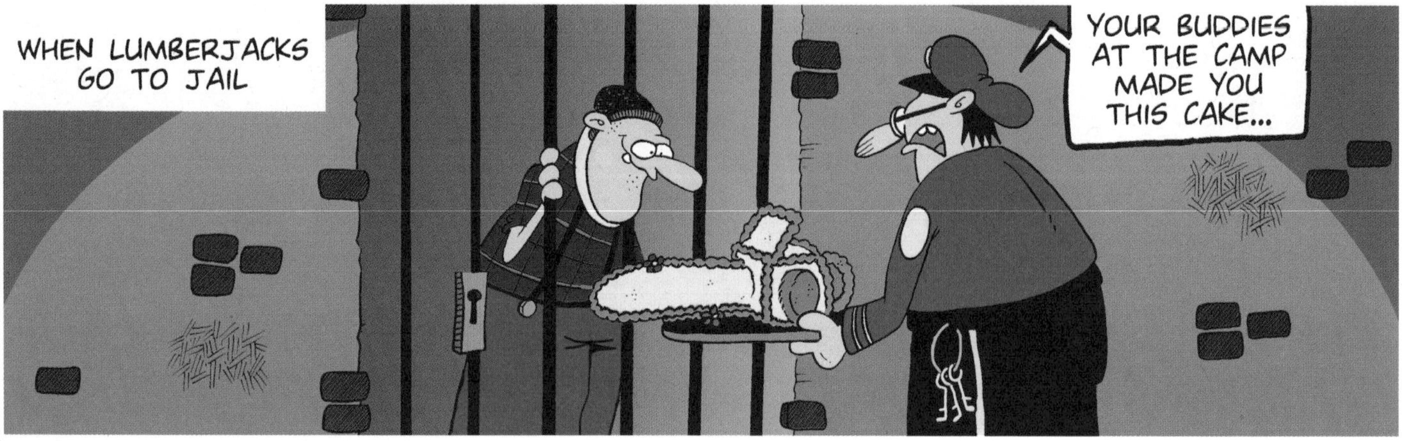
WHEN LUMBERJACKS GO TO JAIL
YOUR BUDDIES AT THE CAMP MADE YOU THIS CAKE...

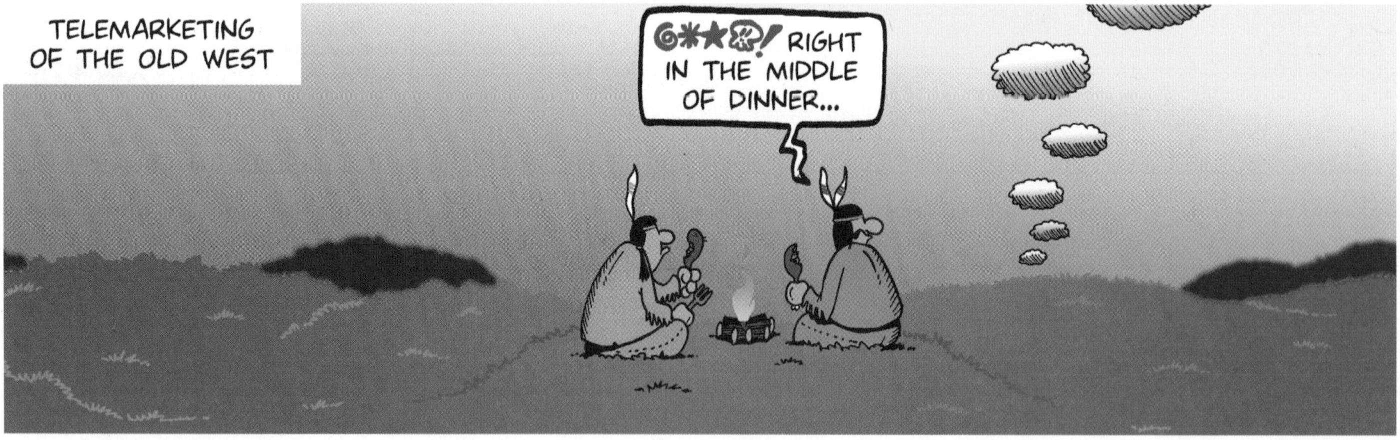
TELEMARKETING OF THE OLD WEST
@*★%! RIGHT IN THE MIDDLE OF DINNER...

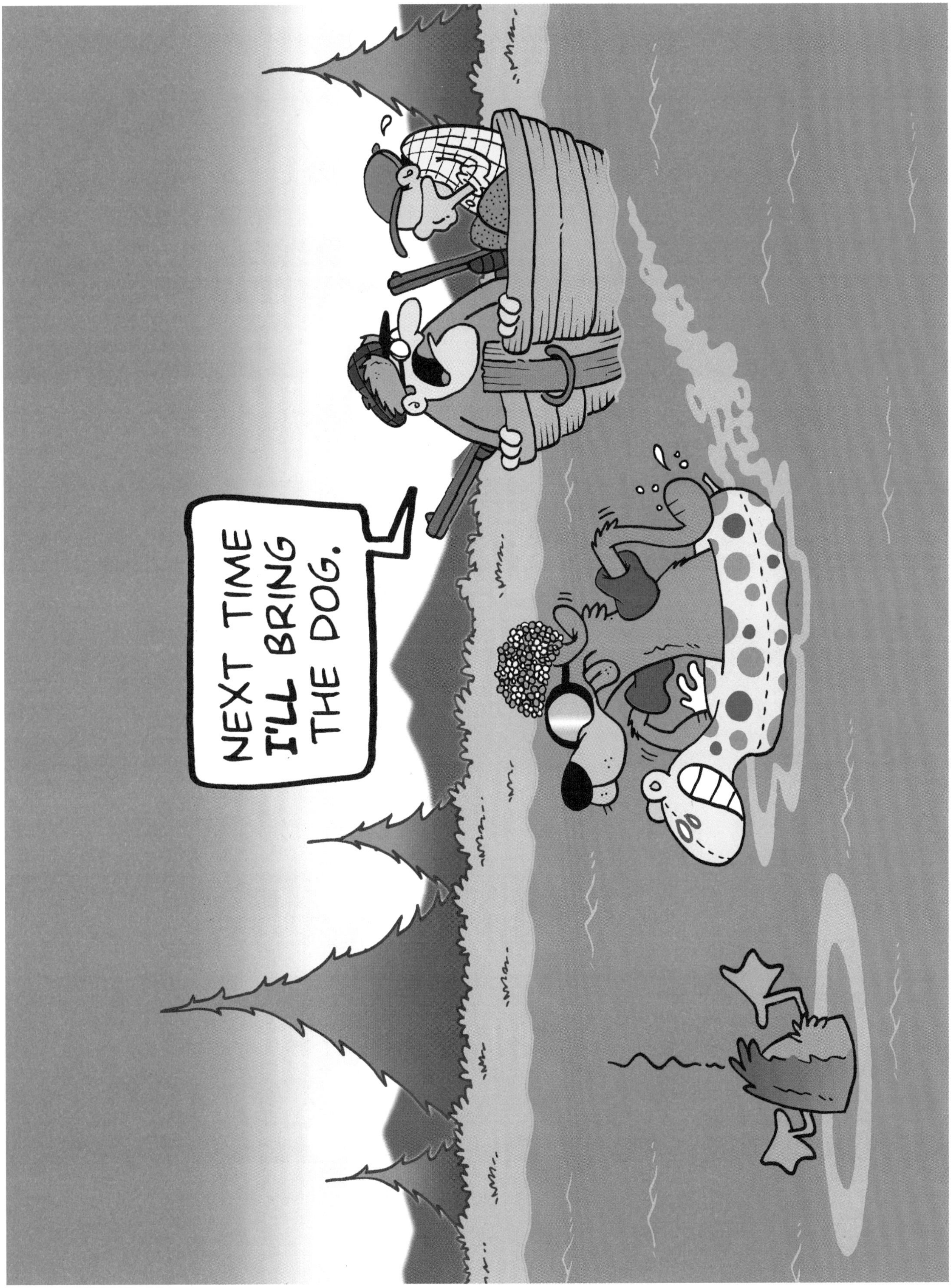
NEXT TIME I'LL BRING THE DOG.

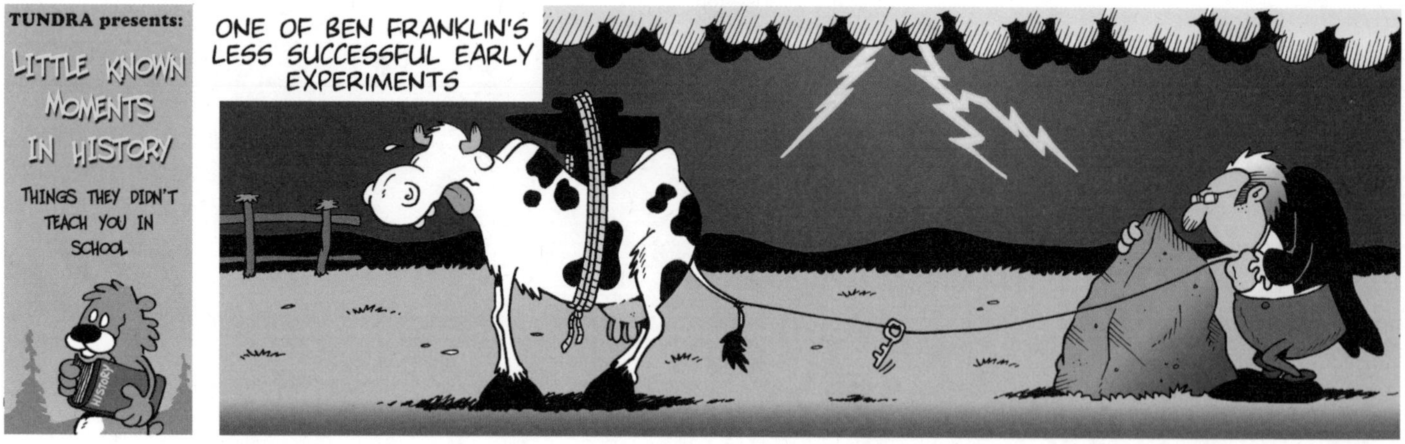
TUNDRA presents:
LITTLE KNOWN MOMENTS IN HISTORY
THINGS THEY DIDN'T TEACH YOU IN SCHOOL
HISTORY
ONE OF BEN FRANKLIN'S LESS SUCCESSFUL EARLY EXPERIMENTS

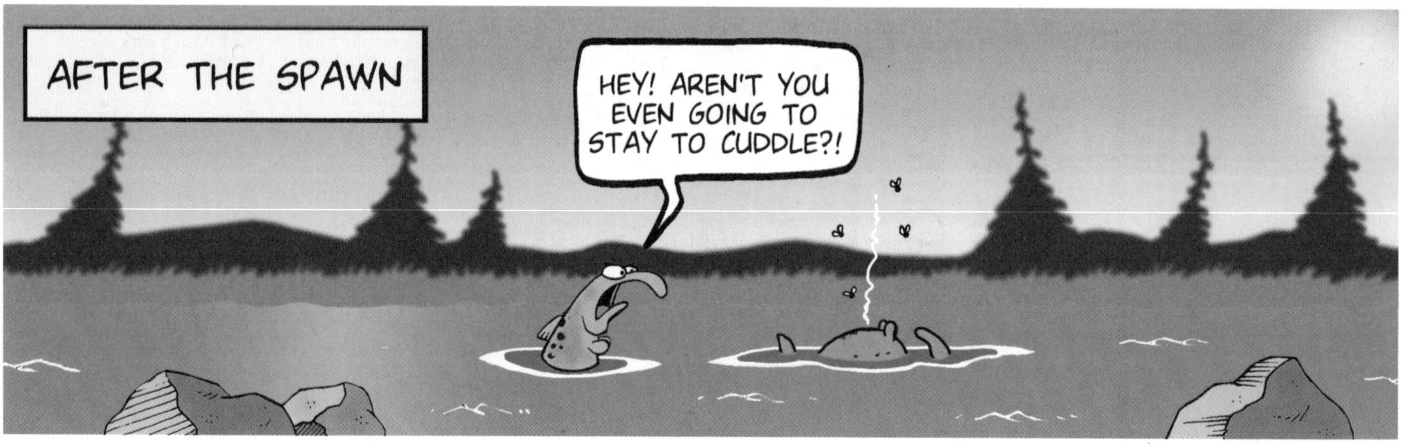
AFTER THE SPAWN
HEY! AREN'T YOU EVEN GOING TO STAY TO CUDDLE?!

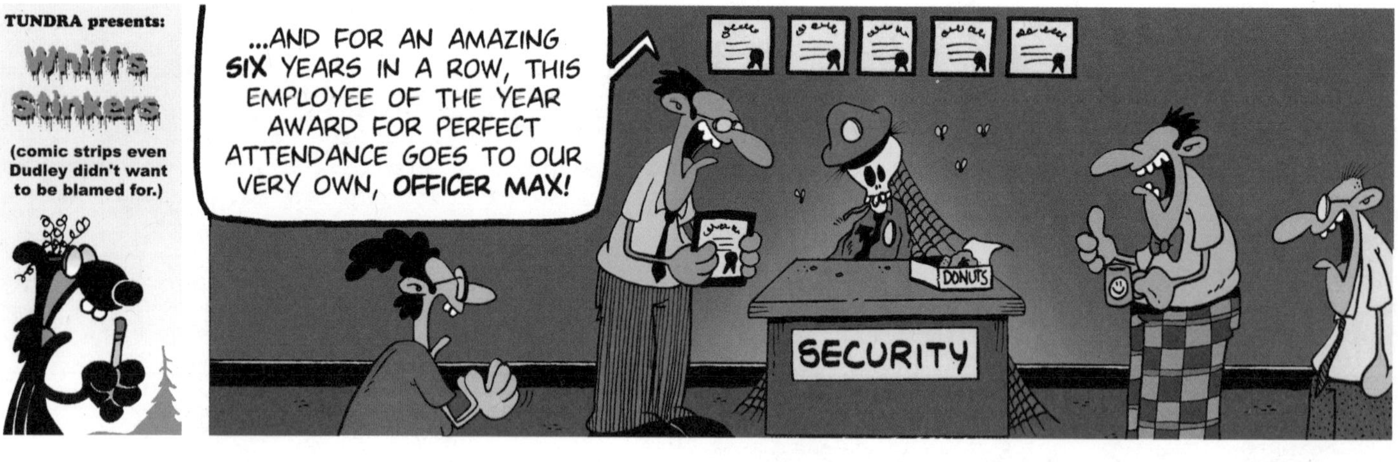
TUNDRA presents:
Whiff's Stinkers
(comic strips even Dudley didn't want to be blamed for.)
...AND FOR AN AMAZING **SIX** YEARS IN A ROW, THIS EMPLOYEE OF THE YEAR AWARD FOR PERFECT ATTENDANCE GOES TO OUR VERY OWN, **OFFICER MAX!**
DONUTS
SECURITY

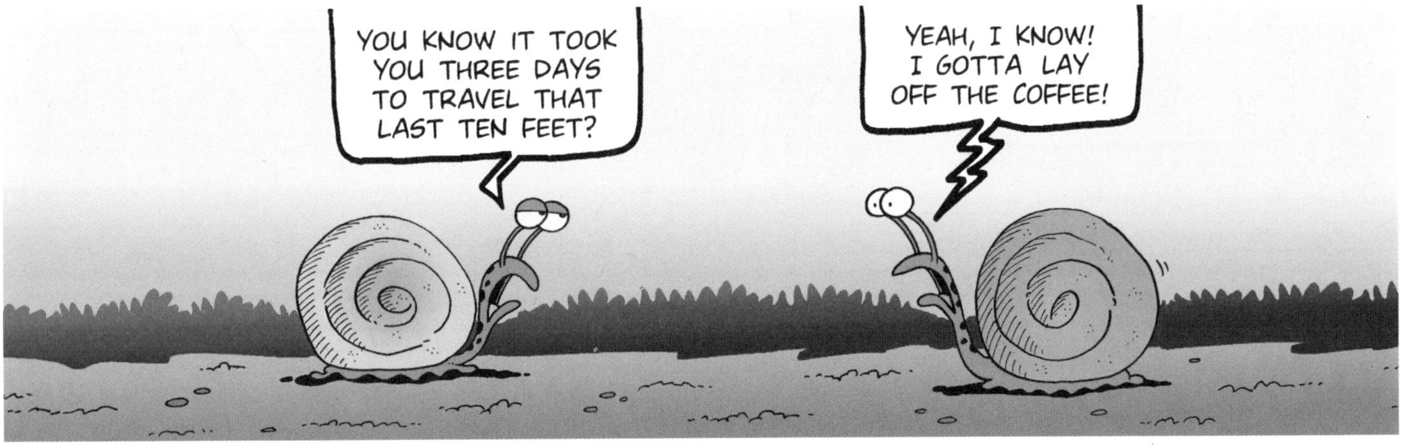
YOU KNOW IT TOOK YOU THREE DAYS TO TRAVEL THAT LAST TEN FEET?
YEAH, I KNOW! I GOTTA LAY OFF THE COFFEE!

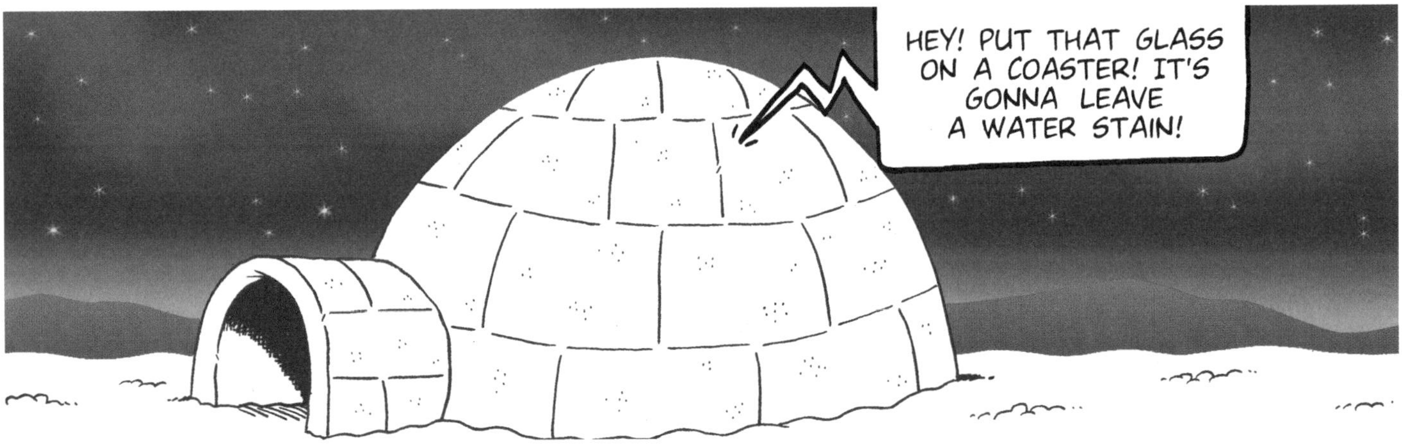
HEY! PUT THAT GLASS ON A COASTER! IT'S GONNA LEAVE A WATER STAIN!

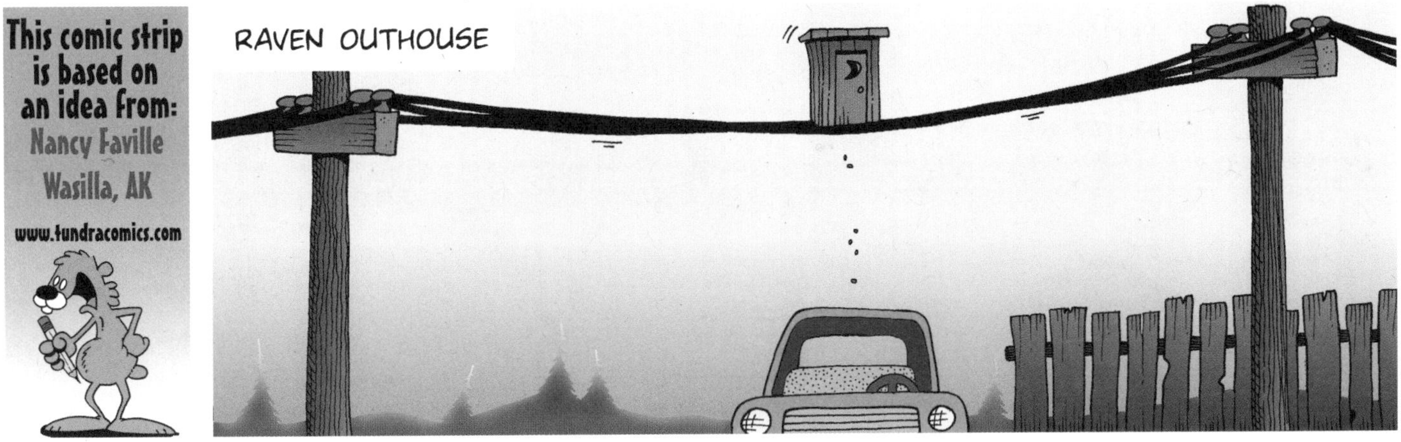
This comic strip is based on an idea from:
Nancy Faville
Wasilla, AK
www.tundracomics.com
RAVEN OUTHOUSE

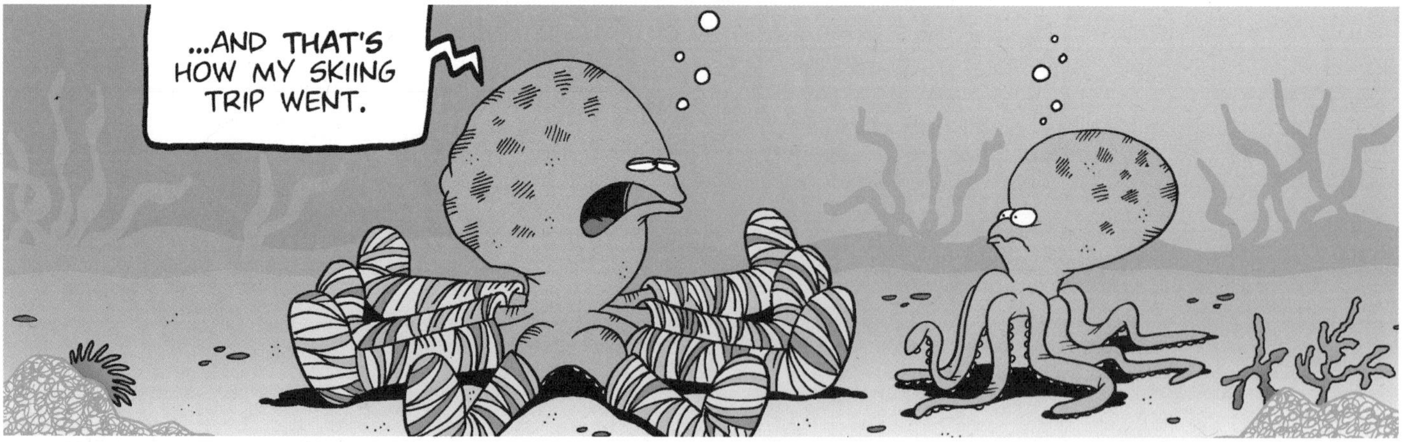
...AND THAT'S HOW MY SKIING TRIP WENT.

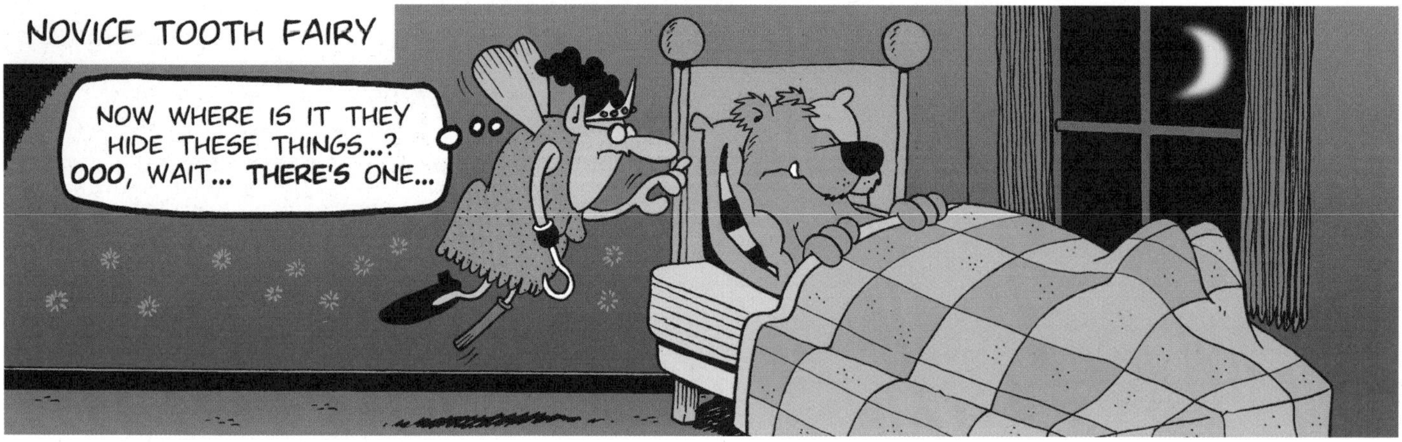
NOVICE TOOTH FAIRY
NOW WHERE IS IT THEY HIDE THESE THINGS...? OOO, WAIT... THERE'S ONE...

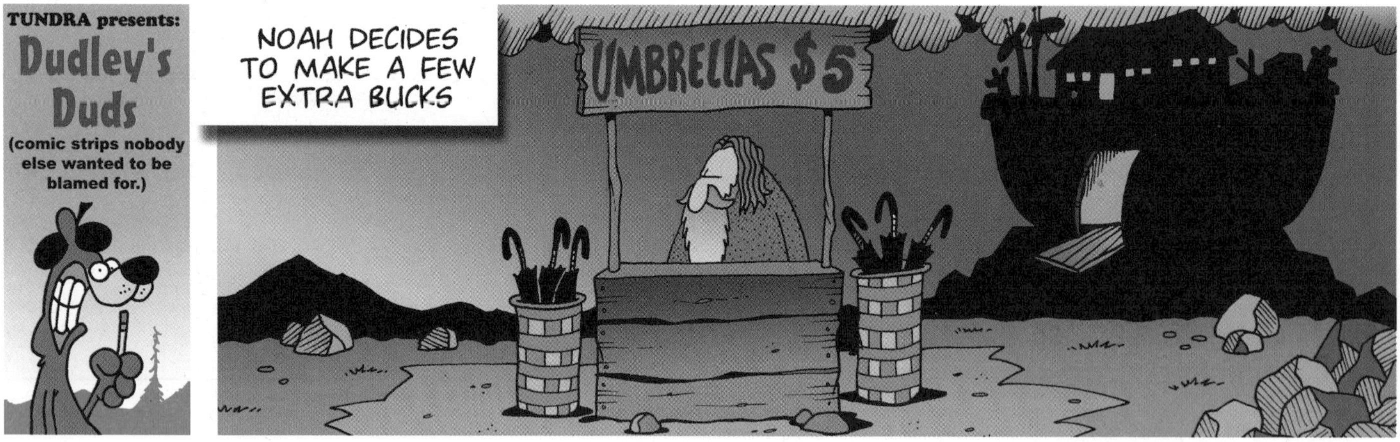
TUNDRA presents:
Dudley's Duds
(comic strips nobody else wanted to be blamed for.)
NOAH DECIDES TO MAKE A FEW EXTRA BUCKS
UMBRELLAS $5

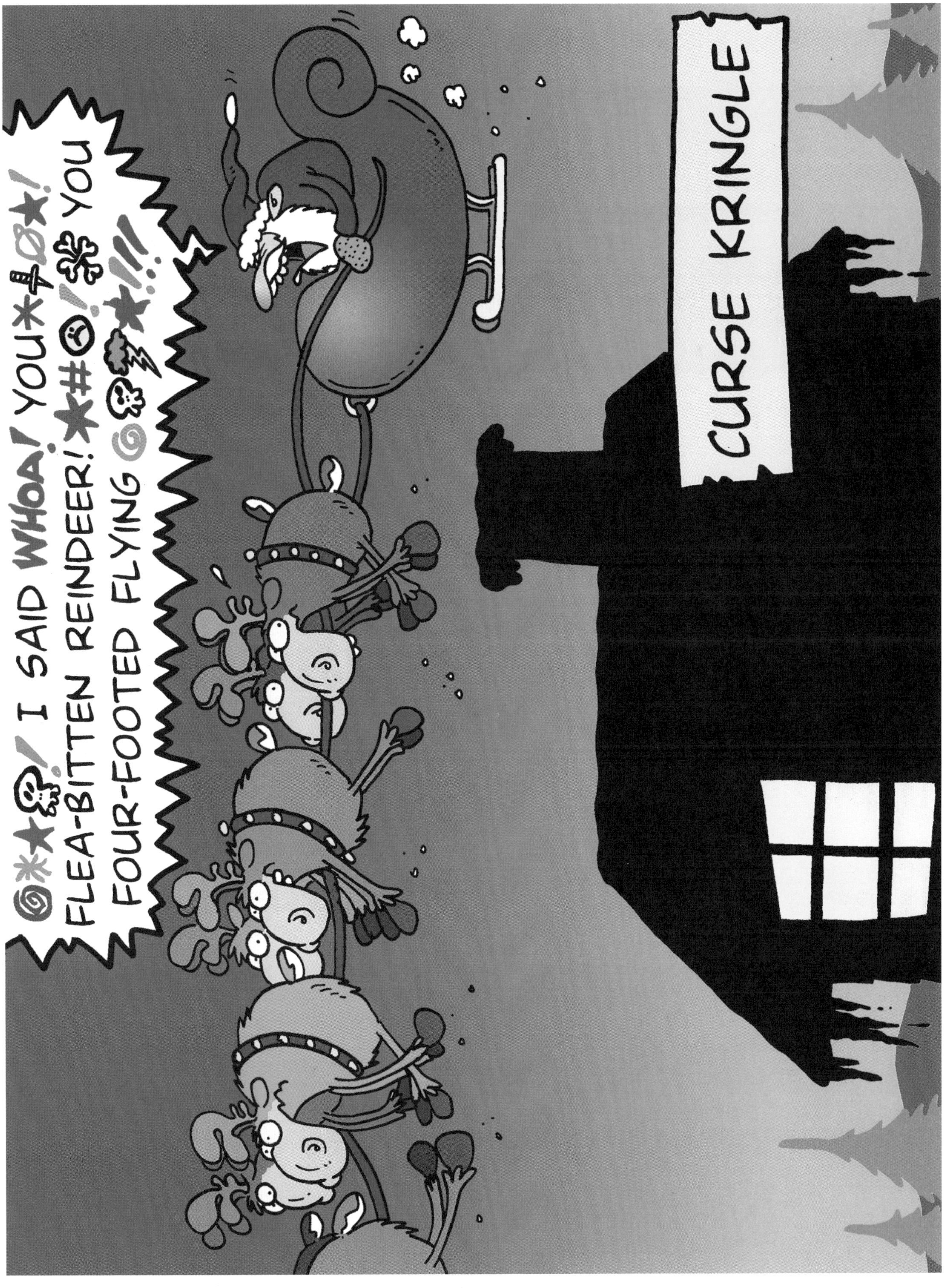

I SAID WHOA! YOU
FLEA-BITTEN REINDEER! YOU
FOUR-FOOTED FLYING
CURSE KRINGLE

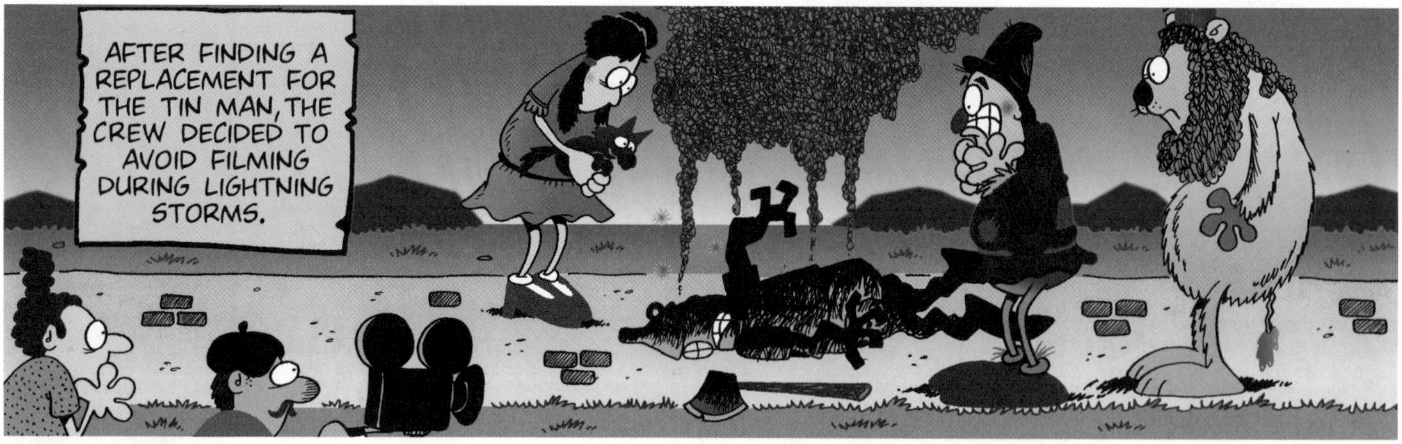
AFTER FINDING A REPLACEMENT FOR THE TIN MAN, THE CREW DECIDED TO AVOID FILMING DURING LIGHTNING STORMS.

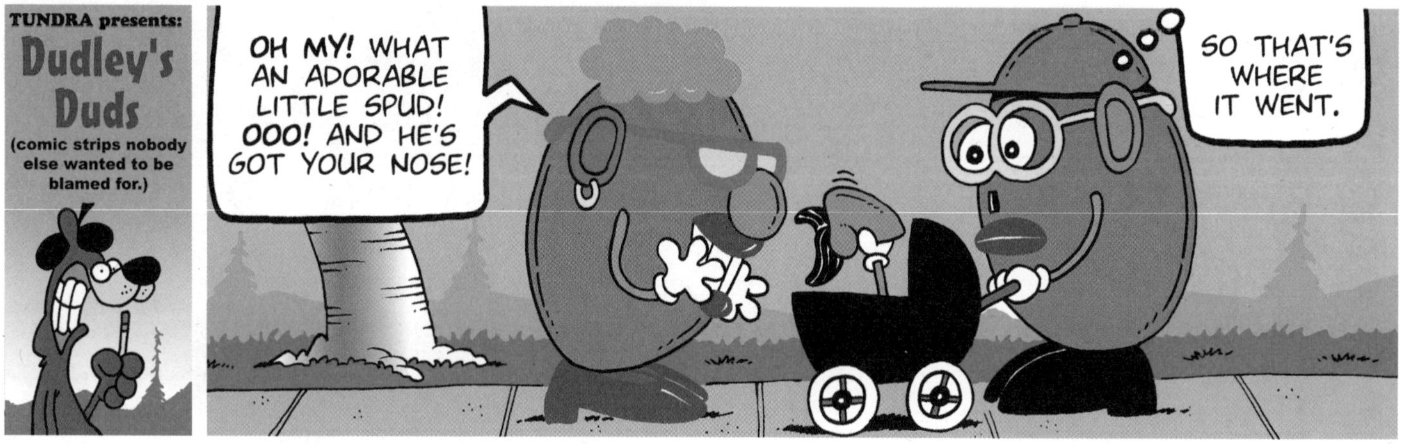
TUNDRA presents:
Dudley's Duds
(comic strips nobody else wanted to be blamed for.)
OH MY! WHAT AN ADORABLE LITTLE SPUD! OOO! AND HE'S GOT YOUR NOSE!
SO THAT'S WHERE IT WENT.

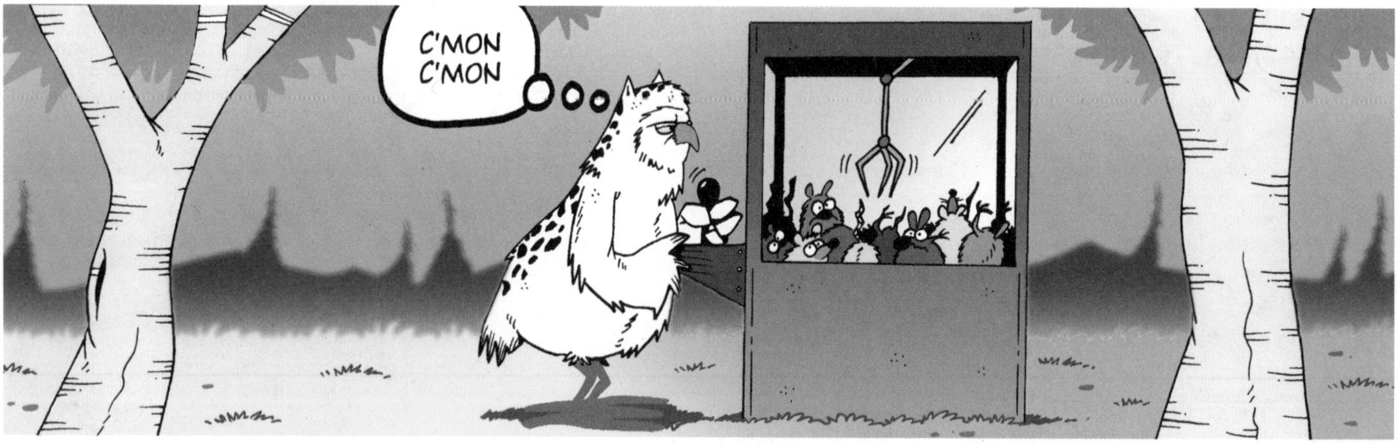
C'MON C'MON

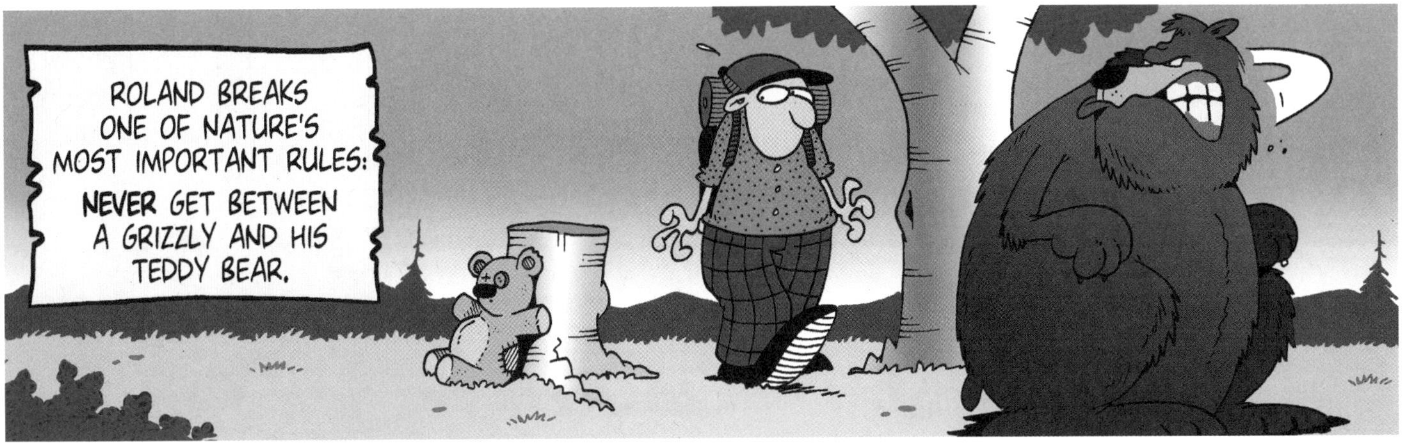
ROLAND BREAKS ONE OF NATURE'S MOST IMPORTANT RULES:
NEVER GET BETWEEN A GRIZZLY AND HIS TEDDY BEAR.

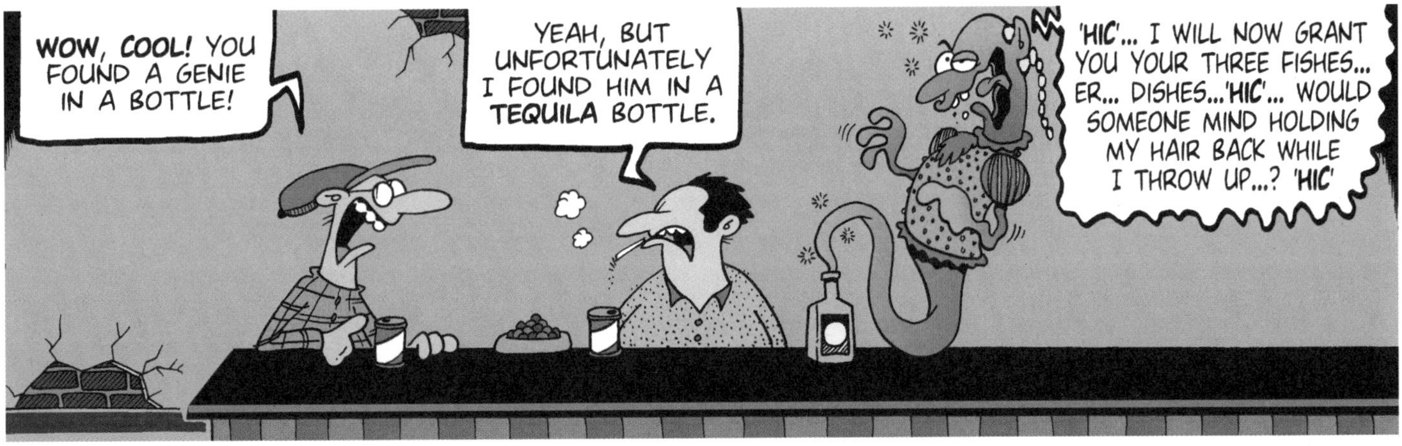
WOW, COOL! YOU FOUND A GENIE IN A BOTTLE!
YEAH, BUT UNFORTUNATELY I FOUND HIM IN A **TEQUILA** BOTTLE.
'**HIC**'... I WILL NOW GRANT YOU YOUR THREE FISHES... ER... DISHES...'**HIC**'... WOULD SOMEONE MIND HOLDING MY HAIR BACK WHILE I THROW UP...? '**HIC**'

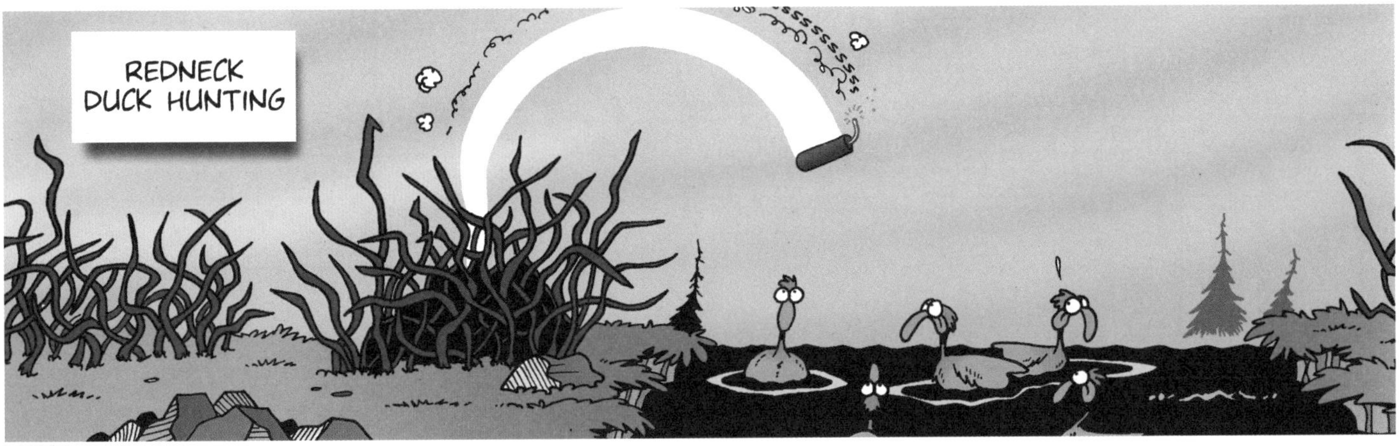
REDNECK DUCK HUNTING

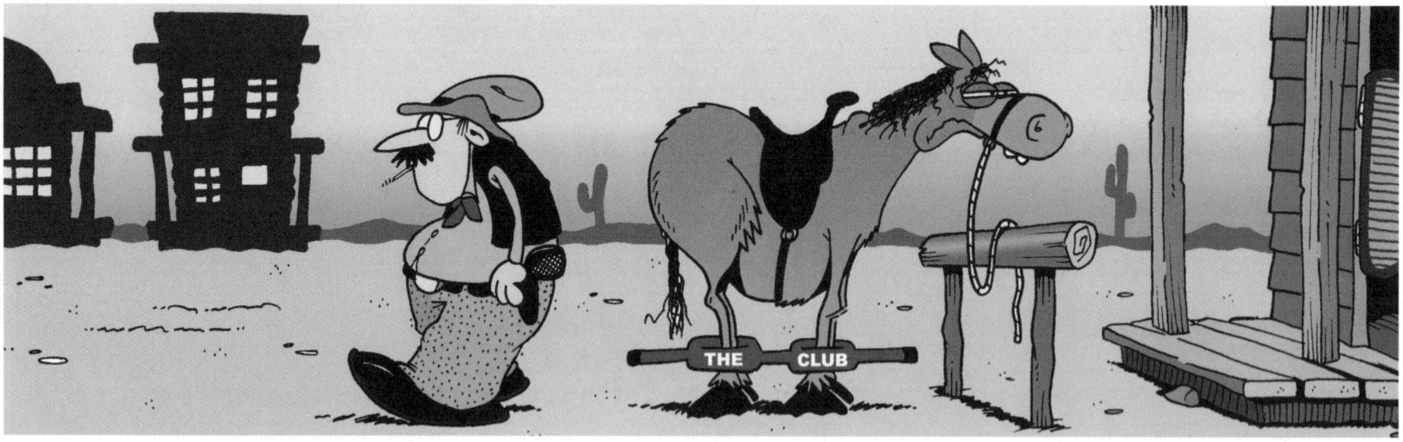
THE
CLUB

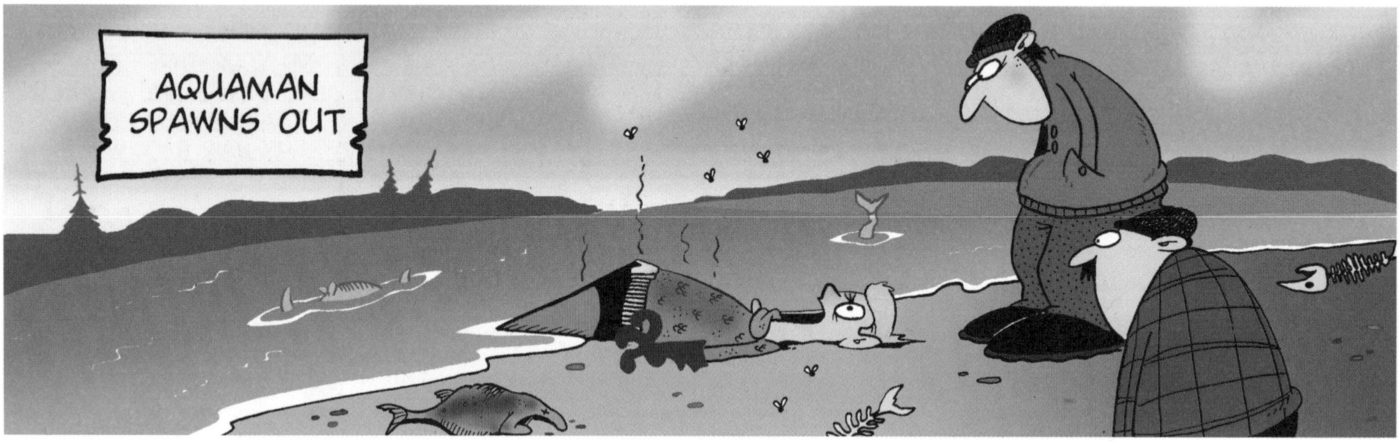
AQUAMAN SPAWNS OUT

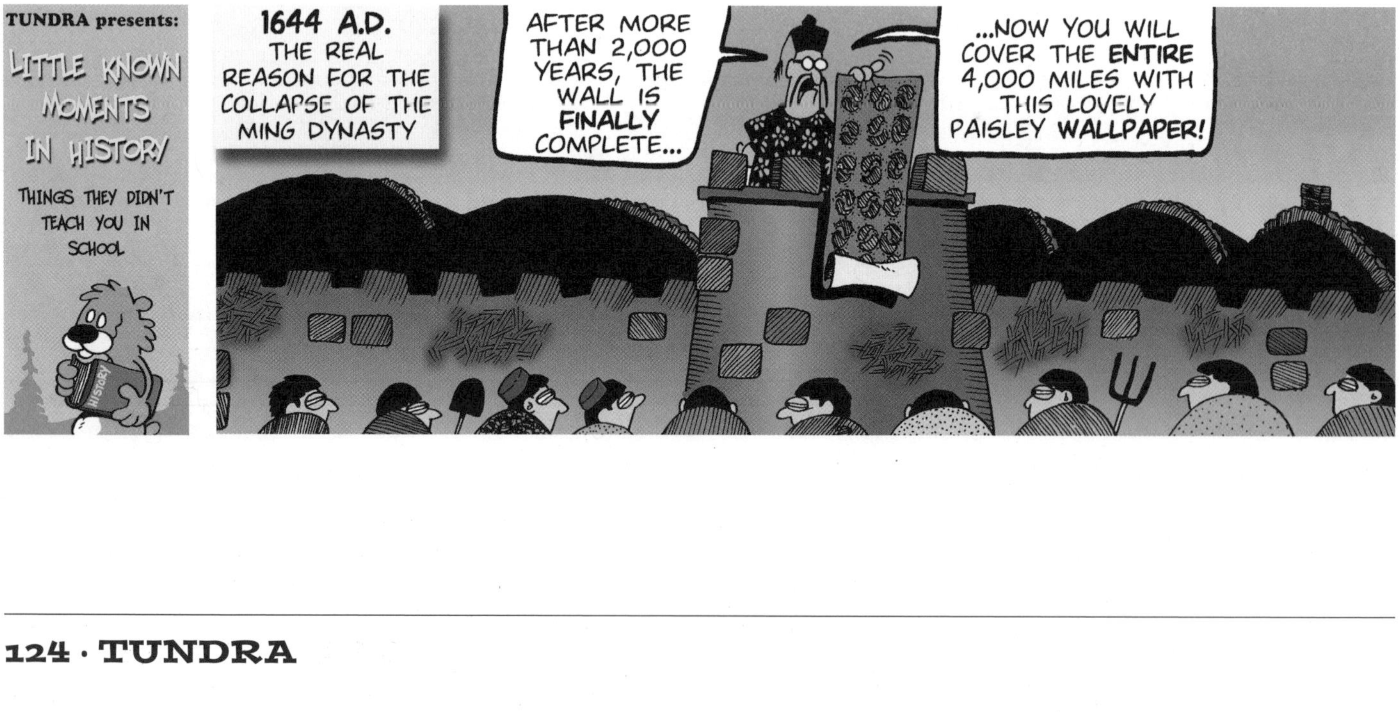
TUNDRA presents:
LITTLE KNOWN MOMENTS IN HISTORY
THINGS THEY DIDN'T TEACH YOU IN SCHOOL
HISTORY
1644 A.D. THE REAL REASON FOR THE COLLAPSE OF THE MING DYNASTY
AFTER MORE THAN 2,000 YEARS, THE WALL IS FINALLY COMPLETE...
...NOW YOU WILL COVER THE ENTIRE 4,000 MILES WITH THIS LOVELY PAISLEY WALLPAPER!

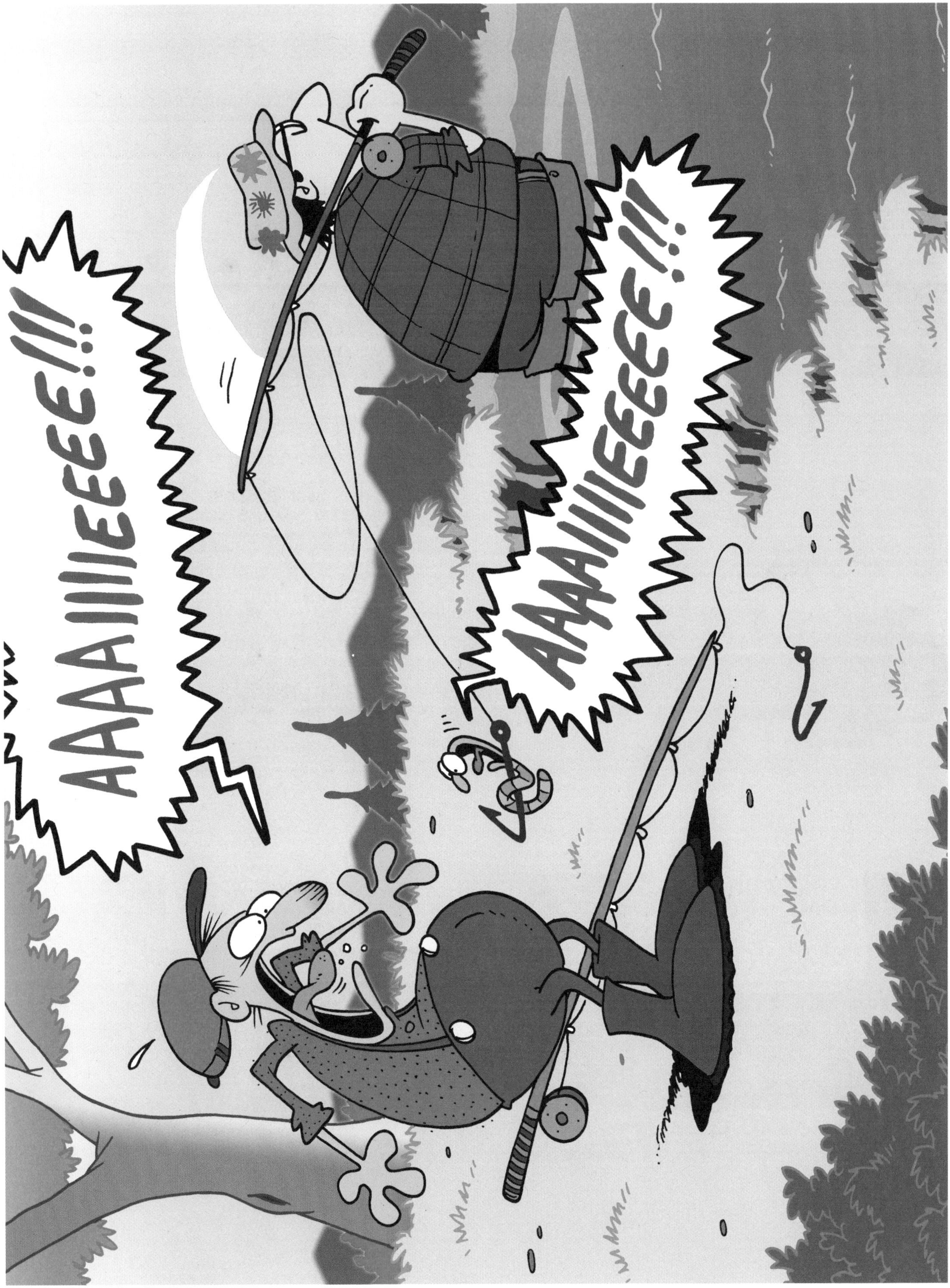
AAAAIIIIIEEEE!!!
AAAAIIIIIEEEEEE!!!

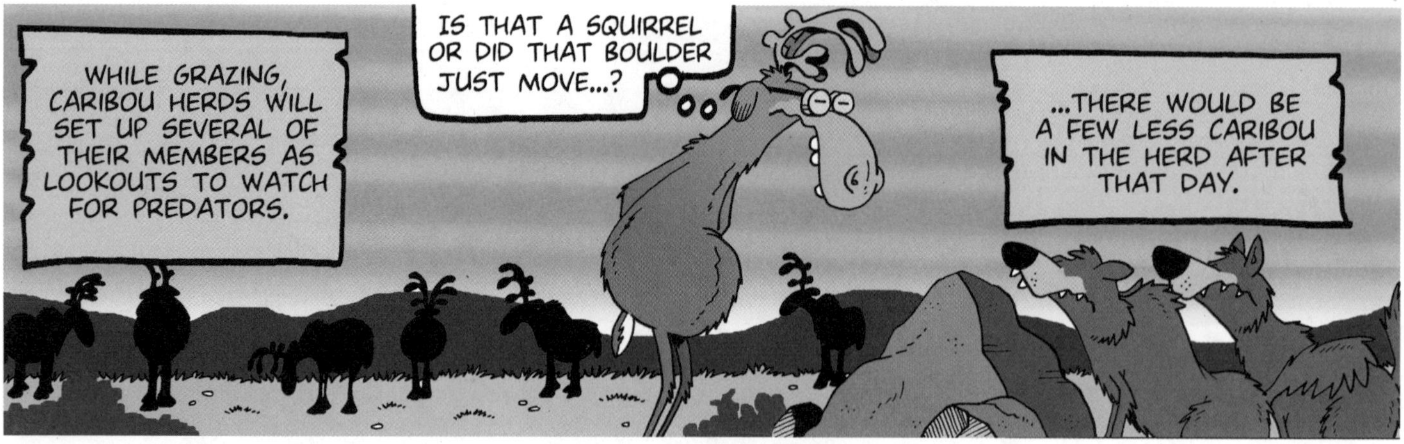
WHILE GRAZING, CARIBOU HERDS WILL SET UP SEVERAL OF THEIR MEMBERS AS LOOKOUTS TO WATCH FOR PREDATORS.
IS THAT A SQUIRREL OR DID THAT BOULDER JUST MOVE...?
...THERE WOULD BE A FEW LESS CARIBOU IN THE HERD AFTER THAT DAY.

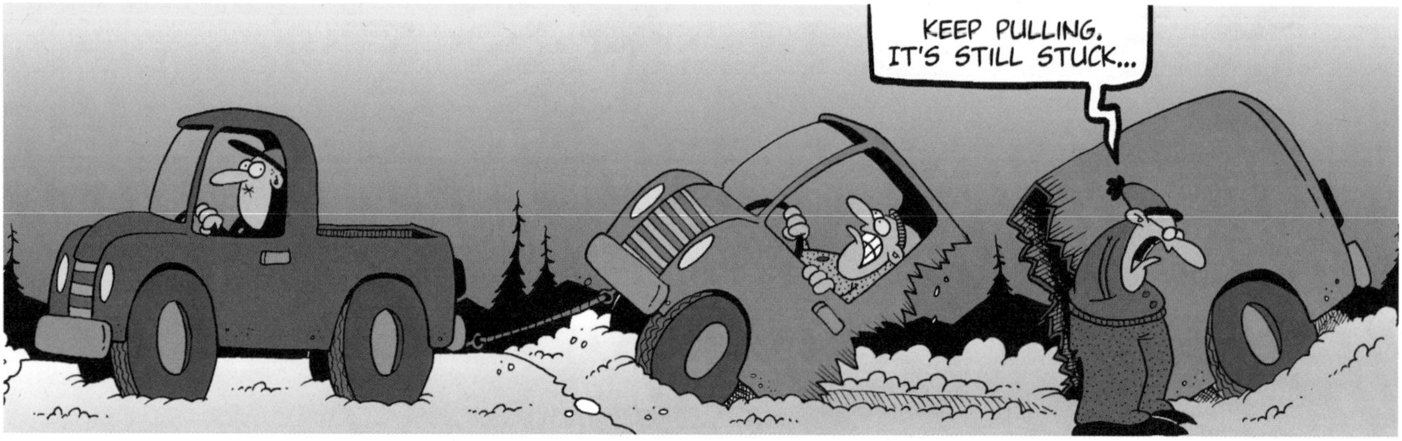
KEEP PULLING. IT'S STILL STUCK...

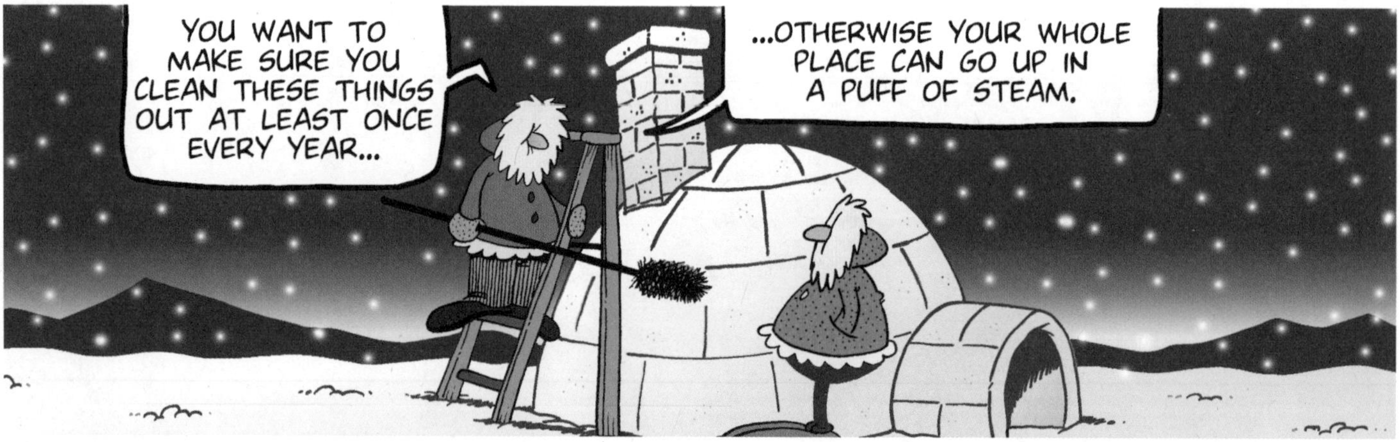
YOU WANT TO MAKE SURE YOU CLEAN THESE THINGS OUT AT LEAST ONCE EVERY YEAR...
...OTHERWISE YOUR WHOLE PLACE CAN GO UP IN A PUFF OF STEAM.

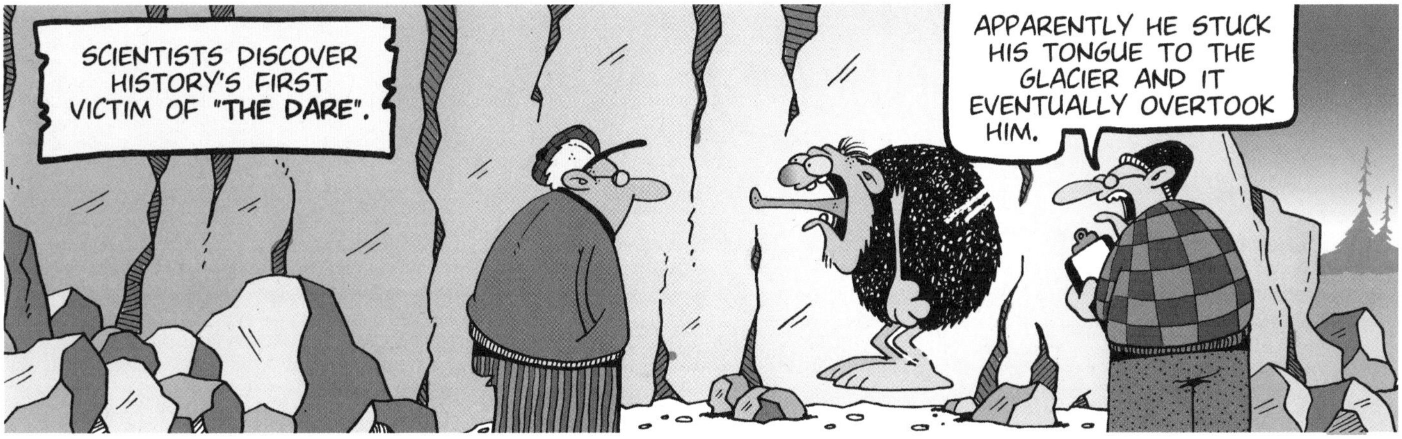
SCIENTISTS DISCOVER HISTORY'S FIRST VICTIM OF "THE DARE".
APPARENTLY HE STUCK HIS TONGUE TO THE GLACIER AND IT EVENTUALLY OVERTOOK HIM.

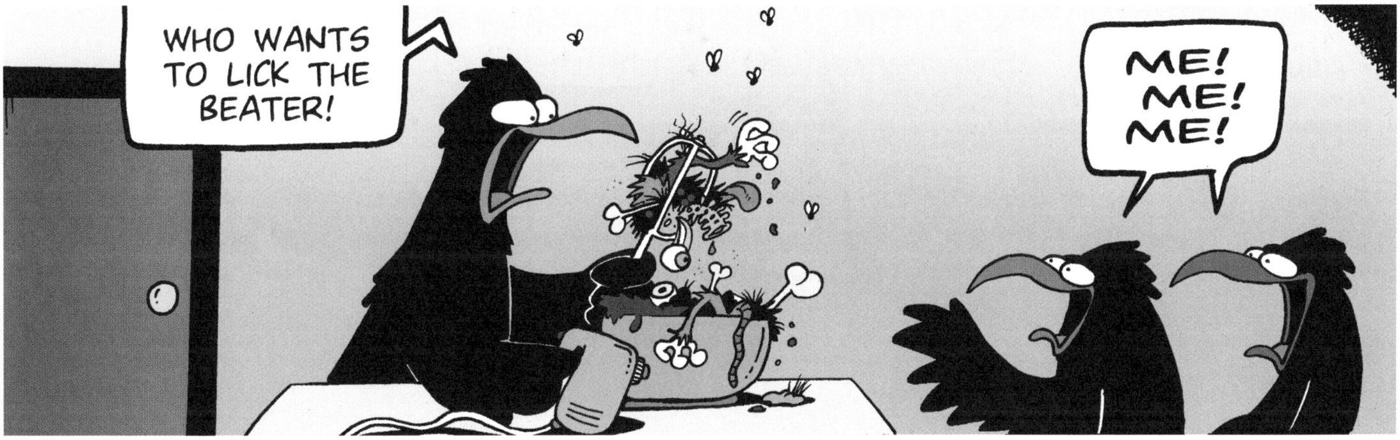
WHO WANTS TO LICK THE BEATER!
ME! ME! ME!

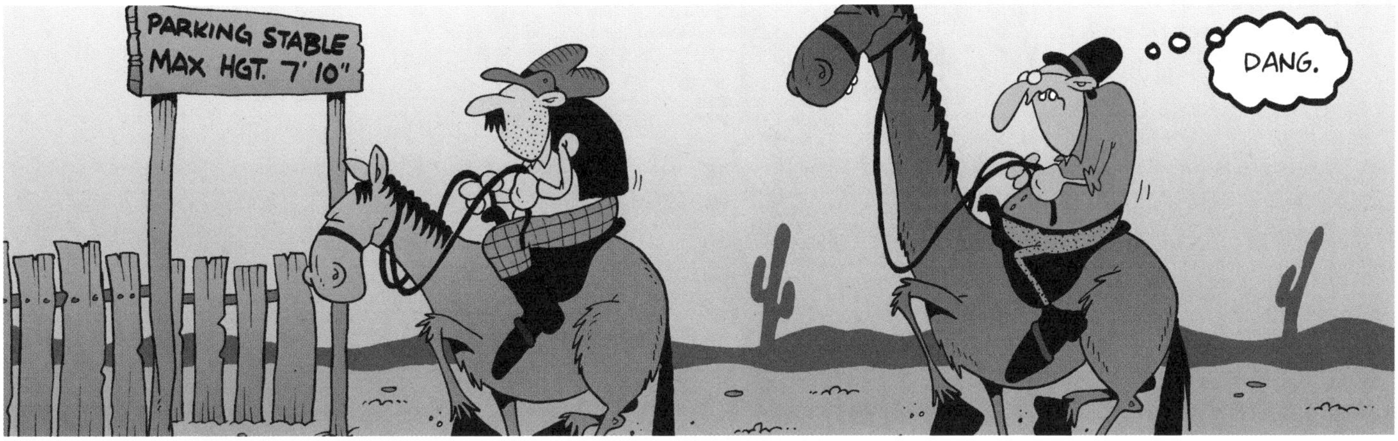
PARKING STABLE MAX HGT. 7' 10"
DANG.

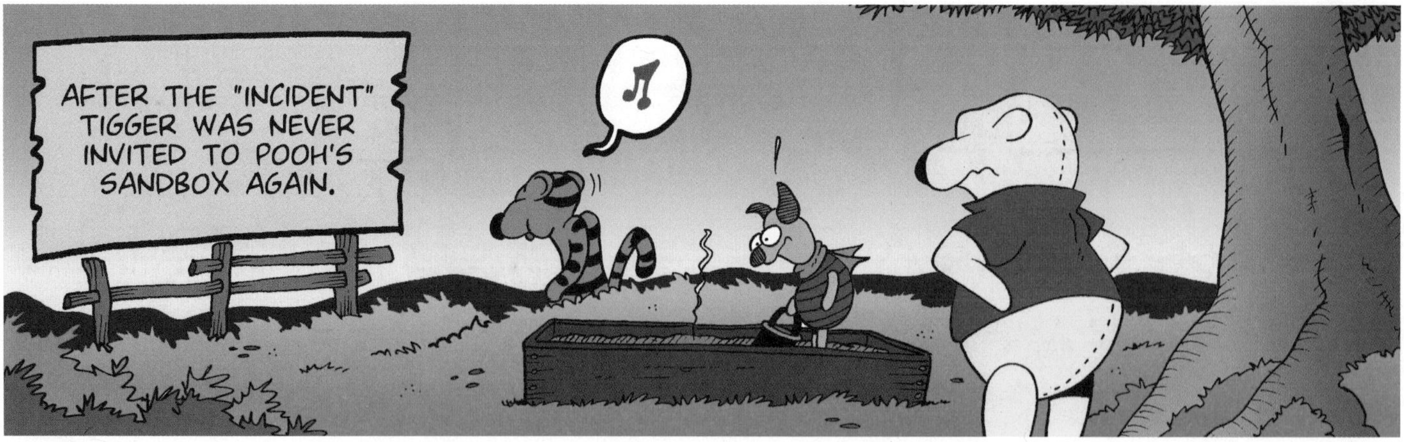
AFTER THE "INCIDENT" TIGGER WAS NEVER INVITED TO POOH'S SANDBOX AGAIN.

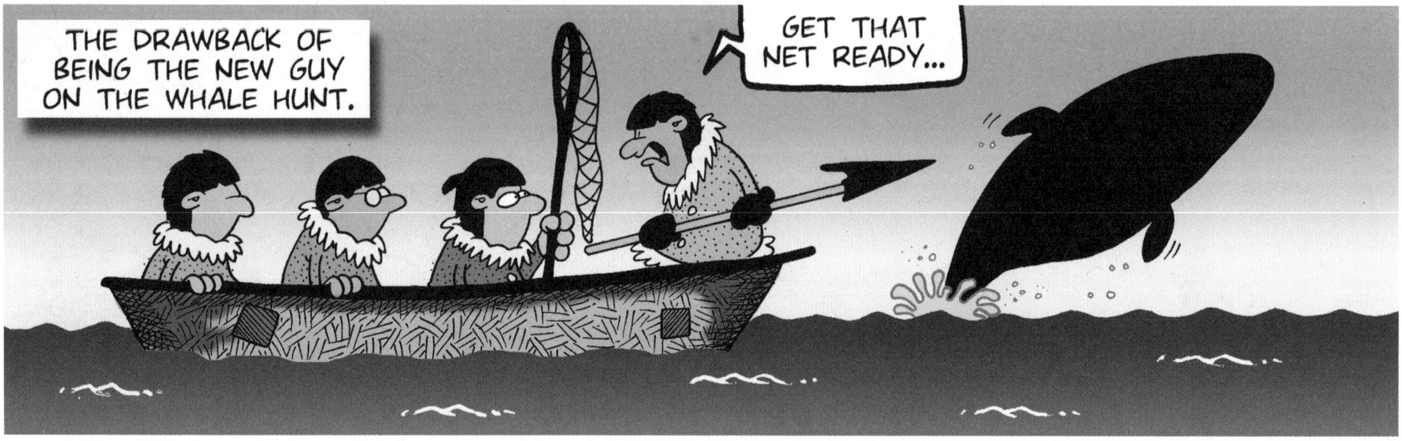
THE DRAWBACK OF BEING THE NEW GUY ON THE WHALE HUNT.
GET THAT NET READY...

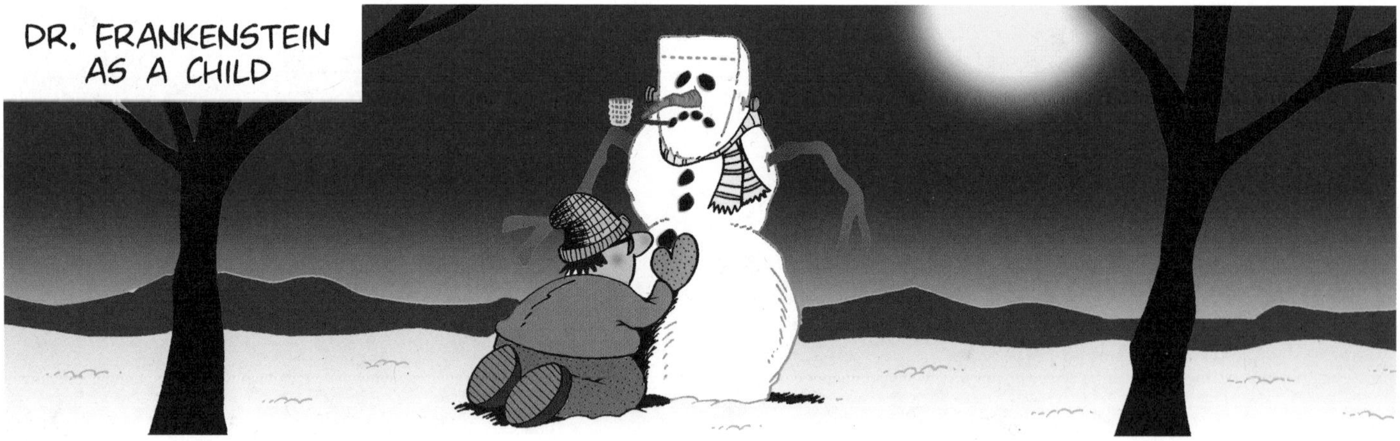
DR. FRANKENSTEIN AS A CHILD

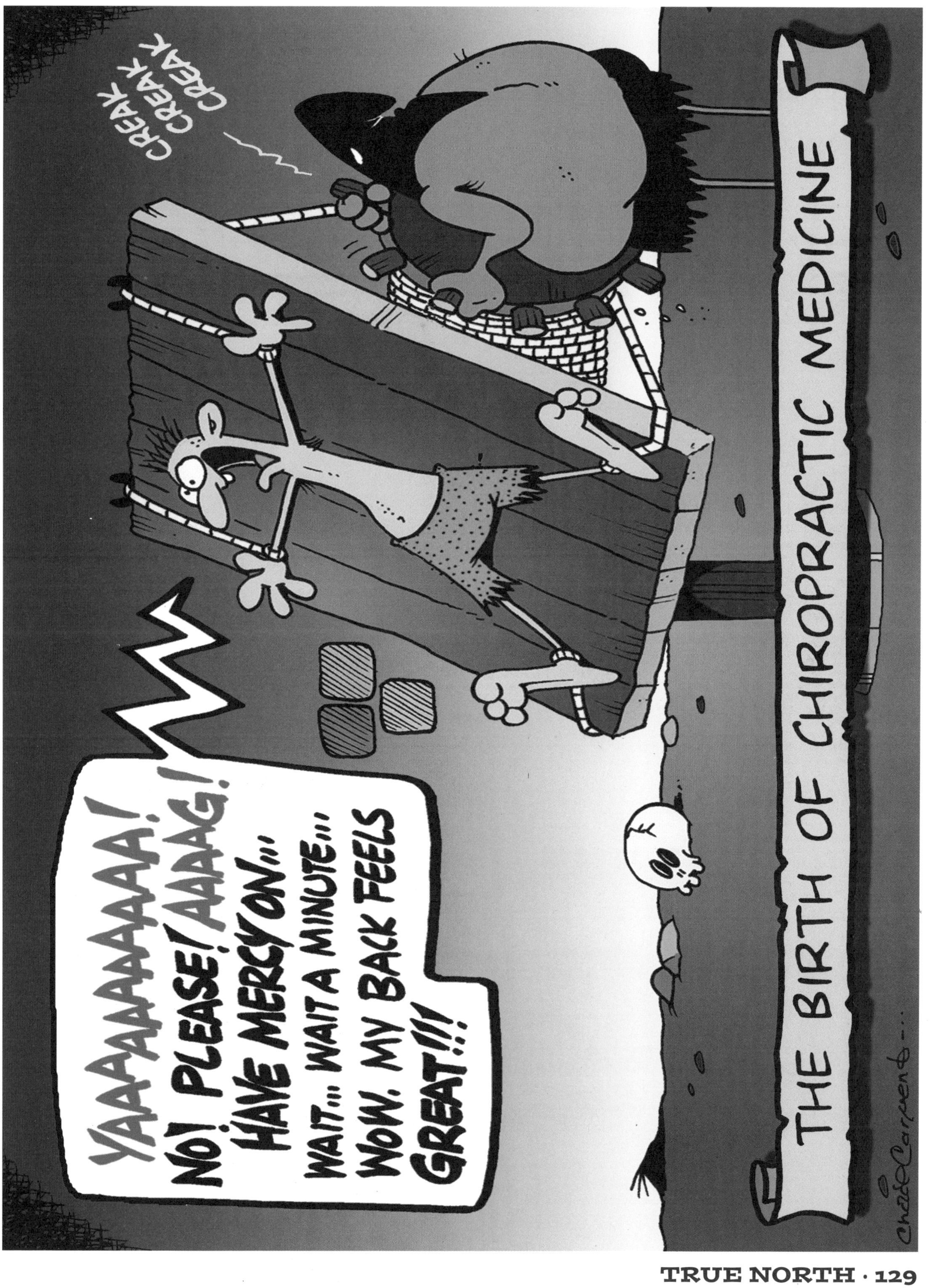
YAAAAAAAAAAA! NO! PLEASE! AAAAG! HAVE MERCY ON... WAIT... WAIT A MINUTE... WOW. MY BACK FEELS GREAT!!!
CREAK CREAK
THE BIRTH OF CHIROPRACTIC MEDICINE

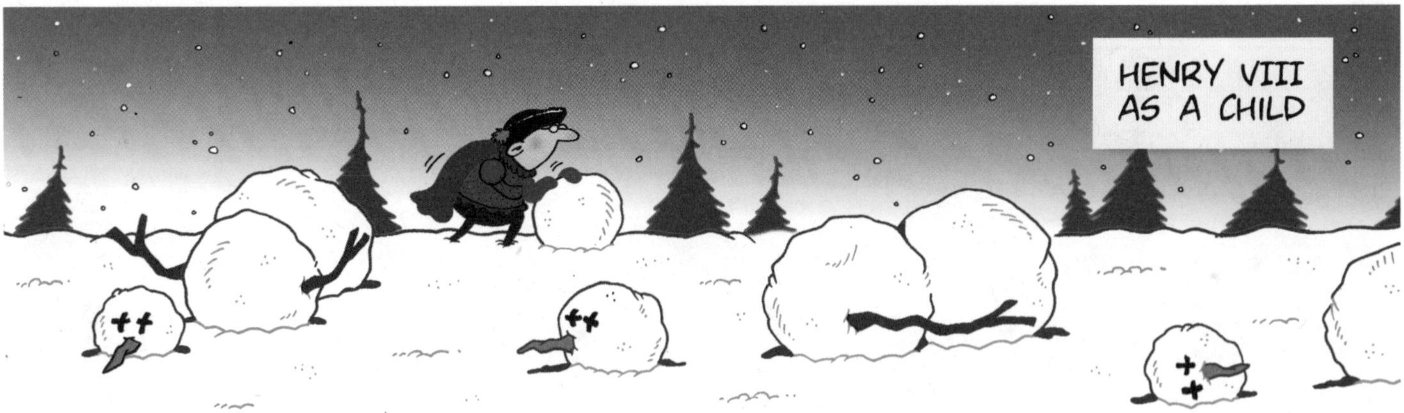
HENRY VIII
AS A CHILD

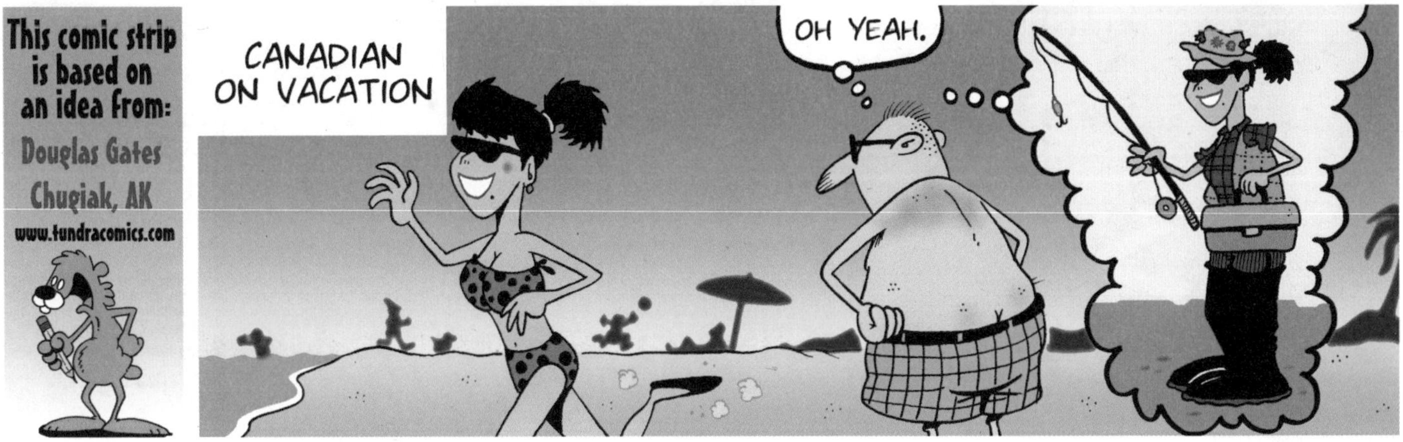
This comic strip is based on an idea from:
Douglas Gates
Chugiak, AK
www.tundracomics.com
CANADIAN ON VACATION
OH YEAH.

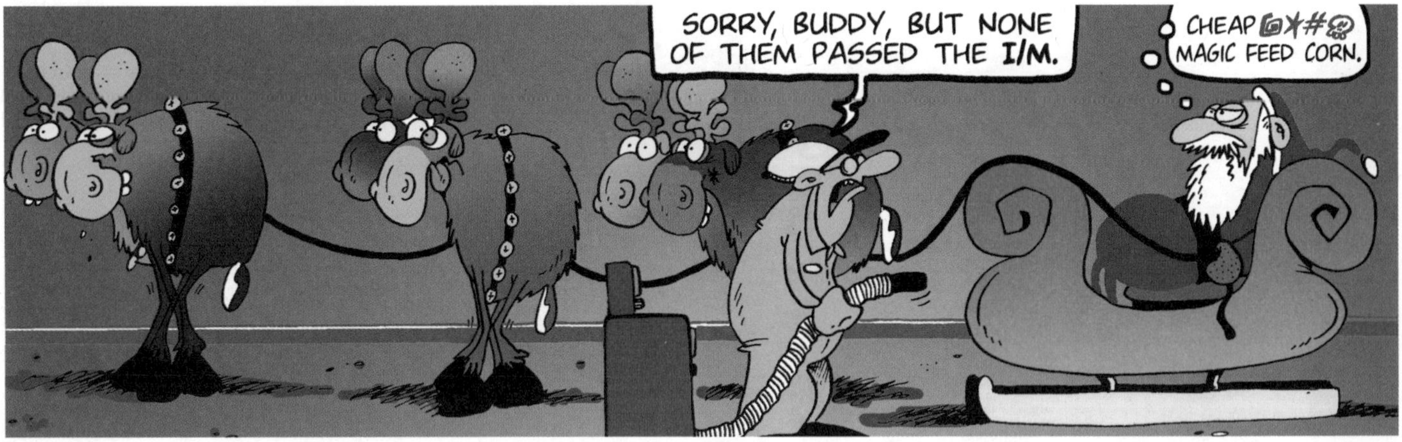
SORRY, BUDDY, BUT NONE OF THEM PASSED THE I/M.
CHEAP
MAGIC FEED CORN.

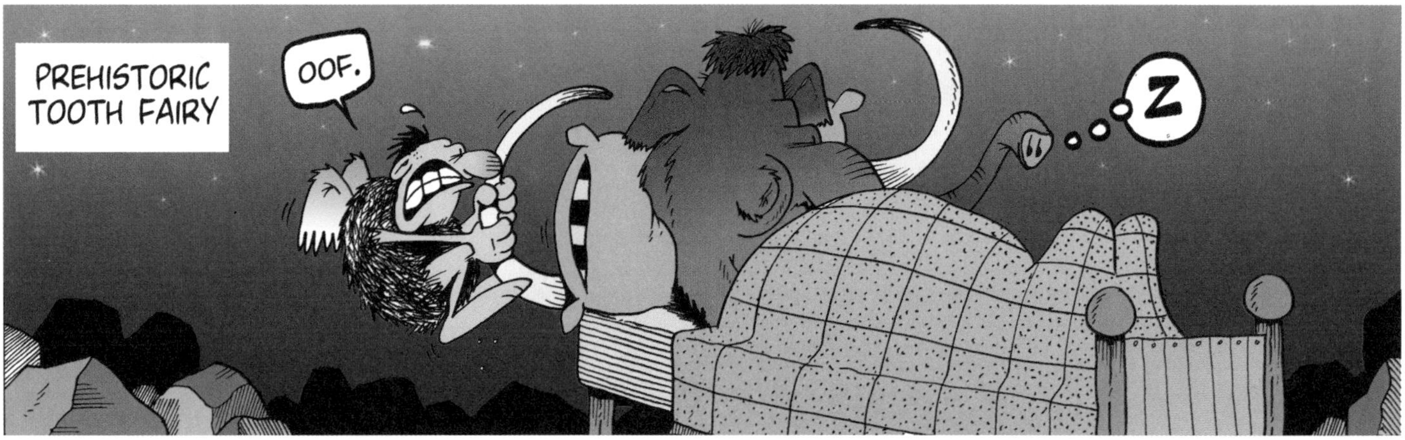
PREHISTORIC TOOTH FAIRY
OOF.
Z

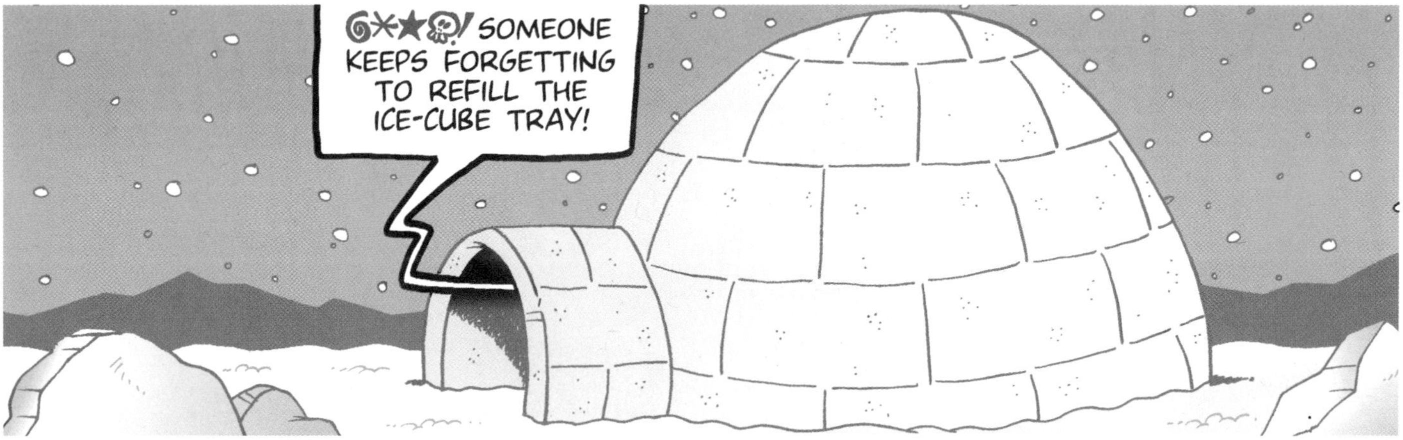
@*★☠! SOMEONE KEEPS FORGETTING TO REFILL THE ICE-CUBE TRAY!

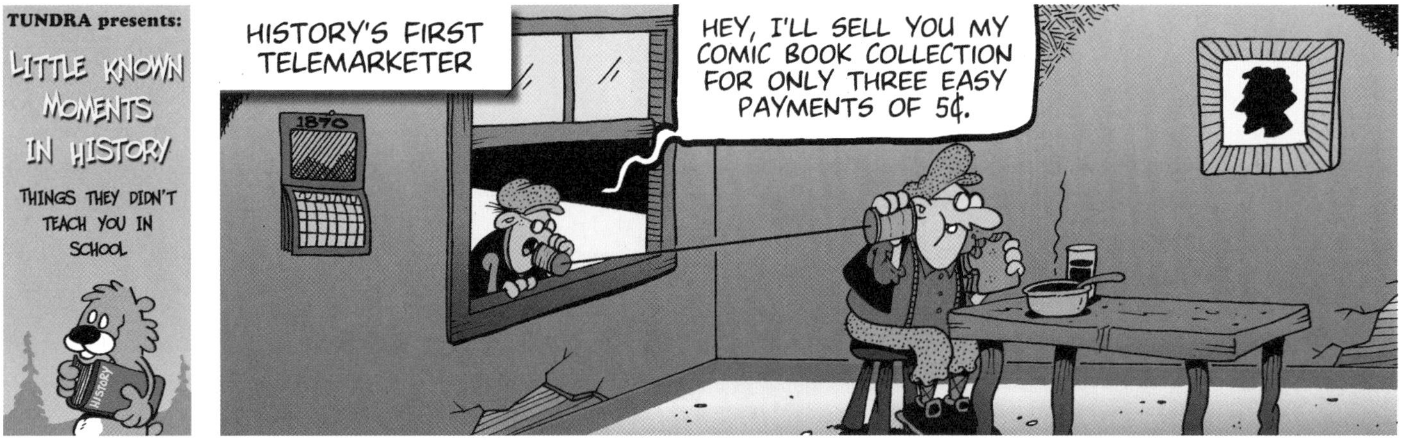
TUNDRA presents:
LITTLE KNOWN MOMENTS IN HISTORY
THINGS THEY DIDN'T TEACH YOU IN SCHOOL
HISTORY
HISTORY'S FIRST TELEMARKETER
1870
HEY, I'LL SELL YOU MY COMIC BOOK COLLECTION FOR ONLY THREE EASY PAYMENTS OF 5¢.

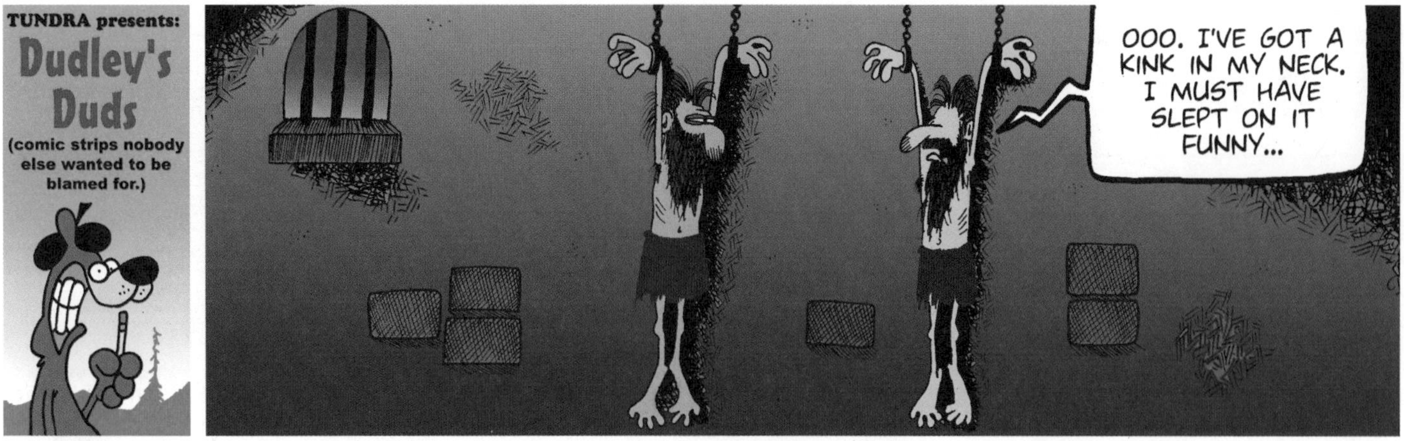
TUNDRA presents:
Dudley's Duds
(comic strips nobody else wanted to be blamed for.)
OOO. I'VE GOT A KINK IN MY NECK. I MUST HAVE SLEPT ON IT FUNNY...

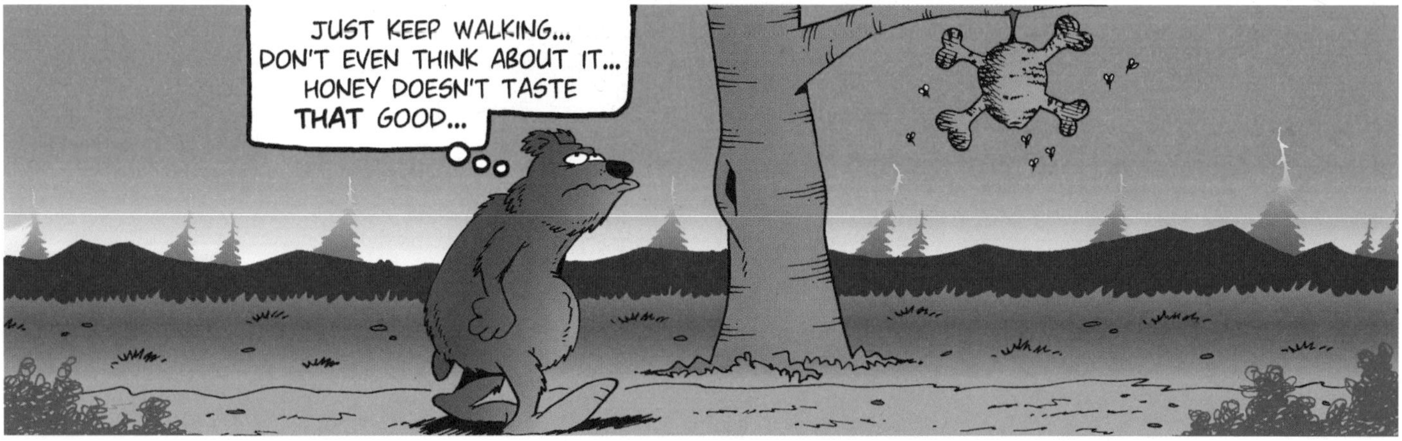
JUST KEEP WALKING... DON'T EVEN THINK ABOUT IT... HONEY DOESN'T TASTE THAT GOOD...

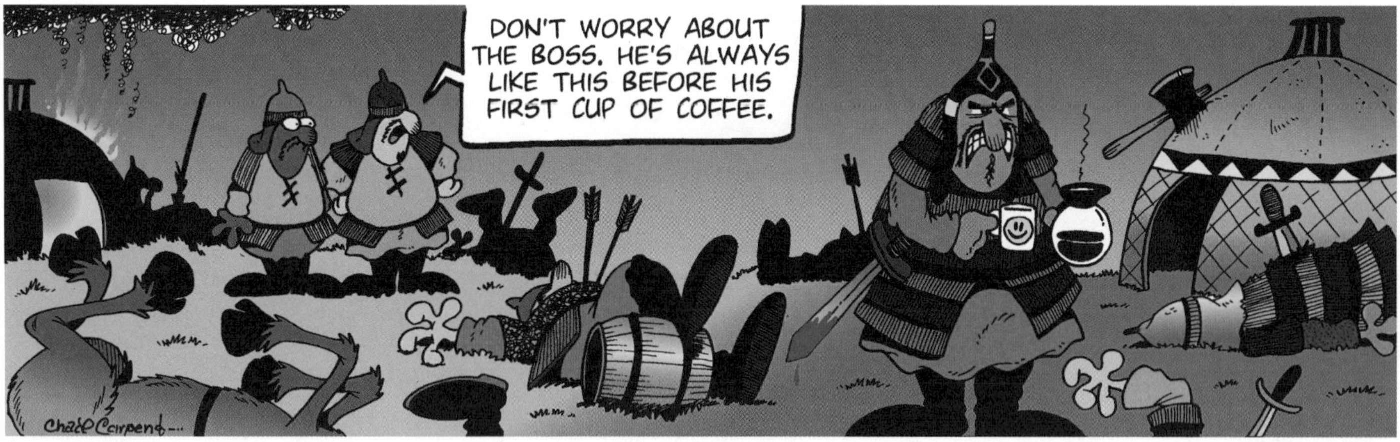
DON'T WORRY ABOUT THE BOSS. HE'S ALWAYS LIKE THIS BEFORE HIS FIRST CUP OF COFFEE.

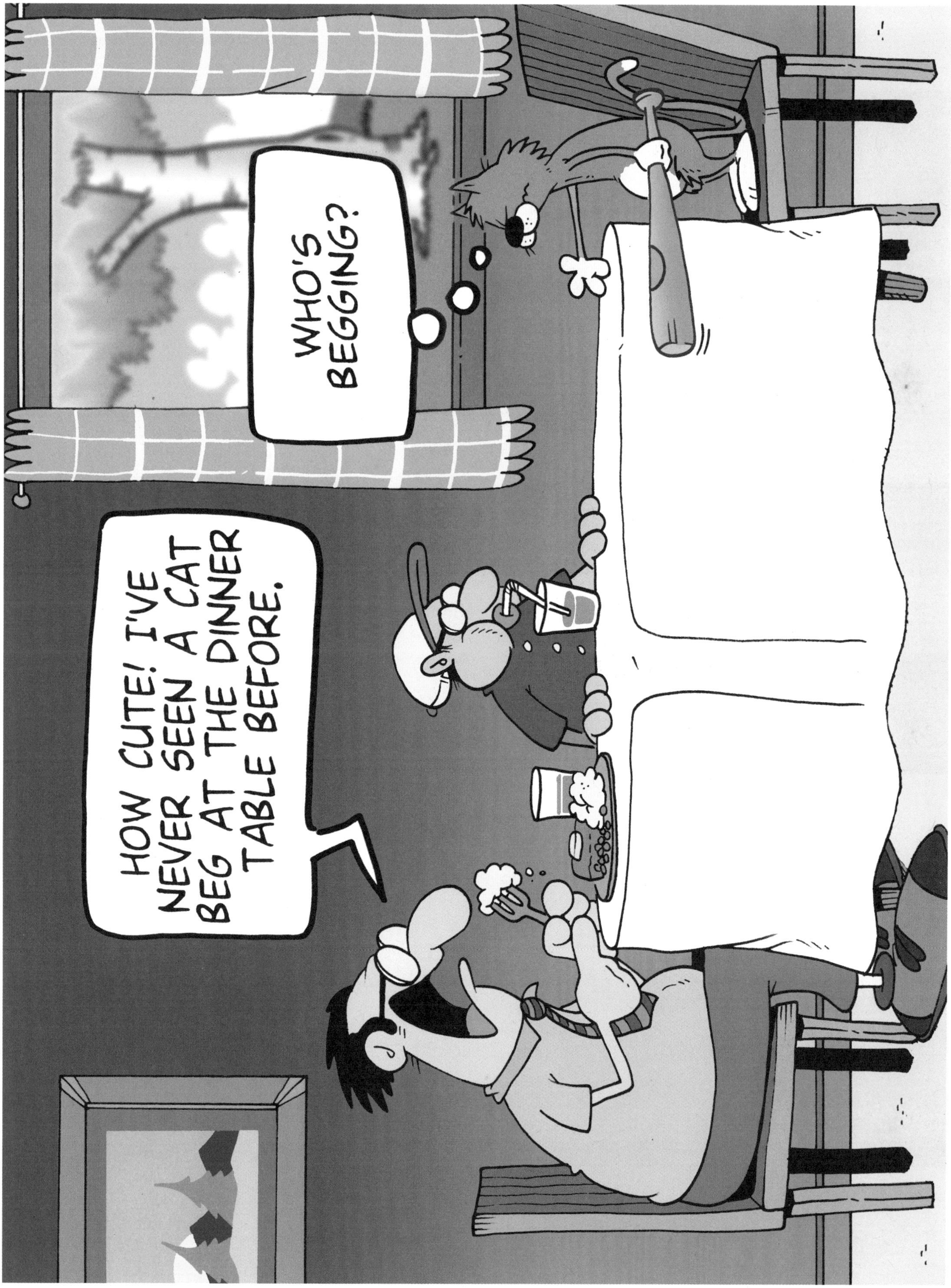
HOW CUTE! I'VE NEVER SEEN A CAT BEG AT THE DINNER TABLE BEFORE.
WHO'S BEGGING?

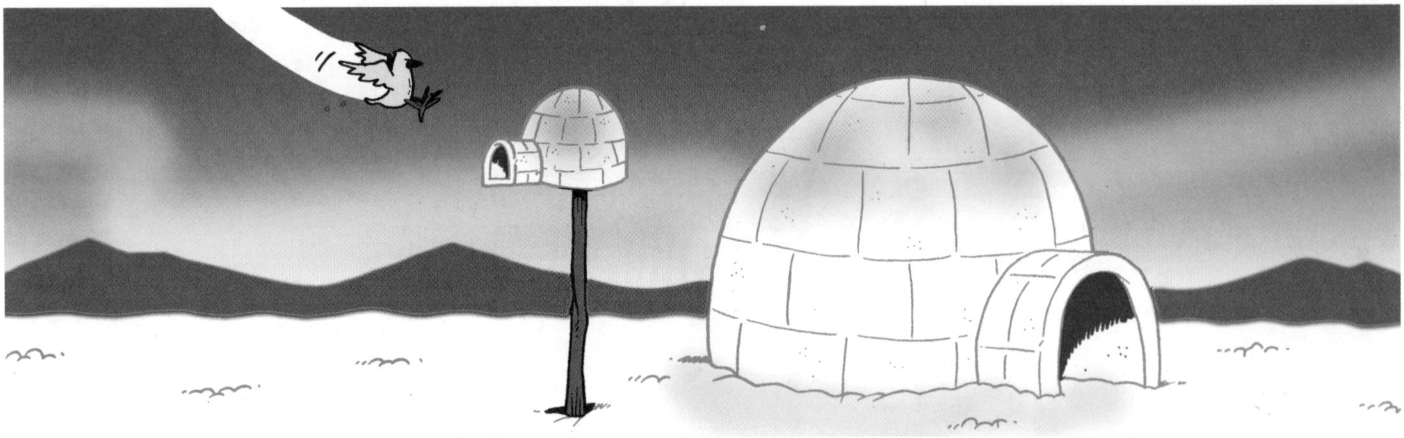

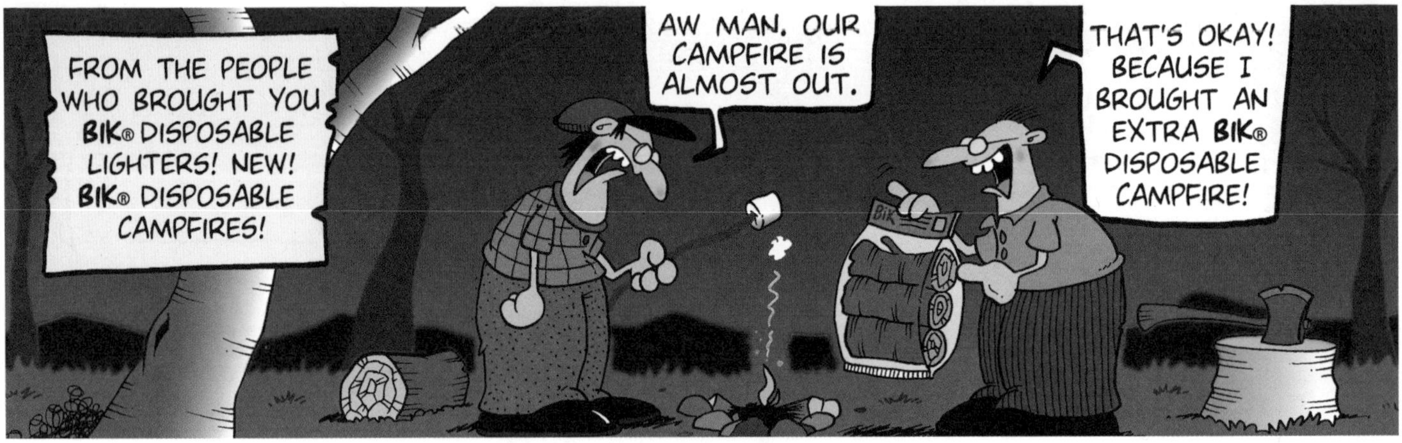
FROM THE PEOPLE WHO BROUGHT YOU BIK® DISPOSABLE LIGHTERS! NEW! BIK® DISPOSABLE CAMPFIRES!
AW MAN. OUR CAMPFIRE IS ALMOST OUT.
THAT'S OKAY! BECAUSE I BROUGHT AN EXTRA BIK® DISPOSABLE CAMPFIRE!
BIK

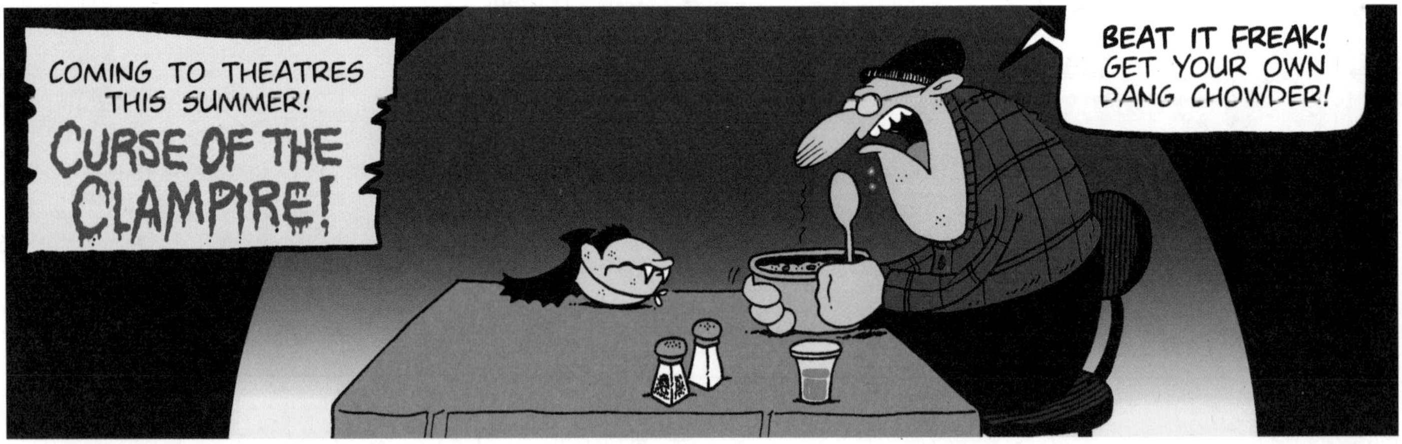
COMING TO THEATRES THIS SUMMER!
CURSE OF THE CLAMPIRE!
BEAT IT FREAK! GET YOUR OWN DANG CHOWDER!

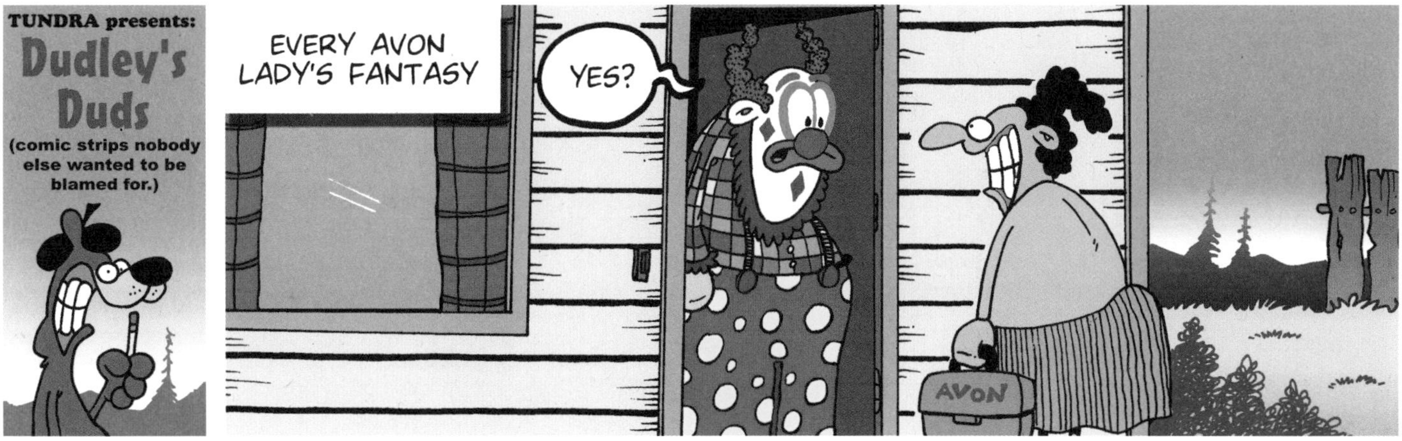
TUNDRA presents:
Dudley's Duds
(comic strips nobody else wanted to be blamed for.)
EVERY AVON LADY'S FANTASY
YES?
AVON

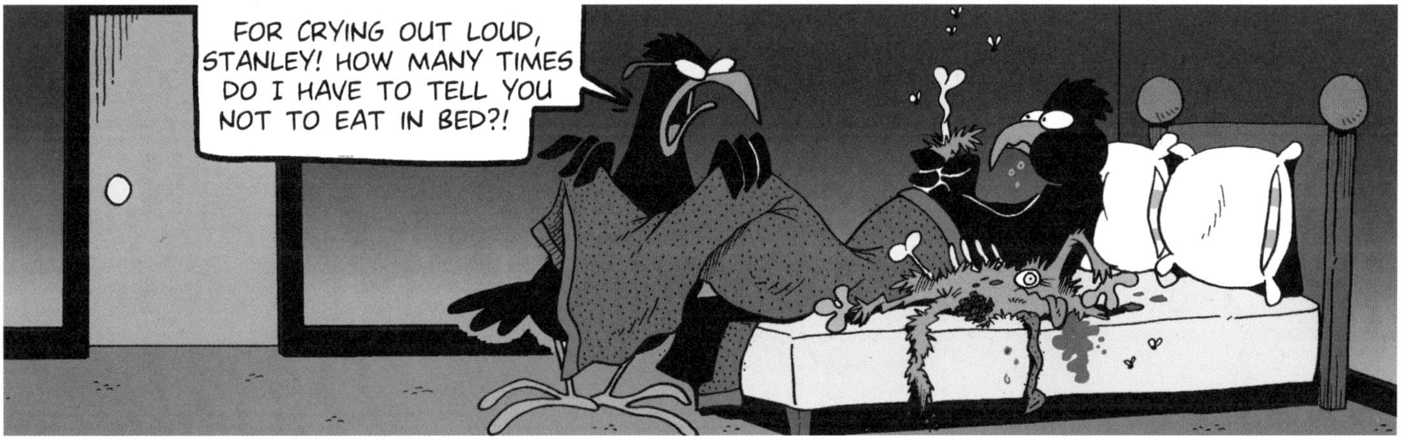
FOR CRYING OUT LOUD, STANLEY! HOW MANY TIMES DO I HAVE TO TELL YOU NOT TO EAT IN BED?!

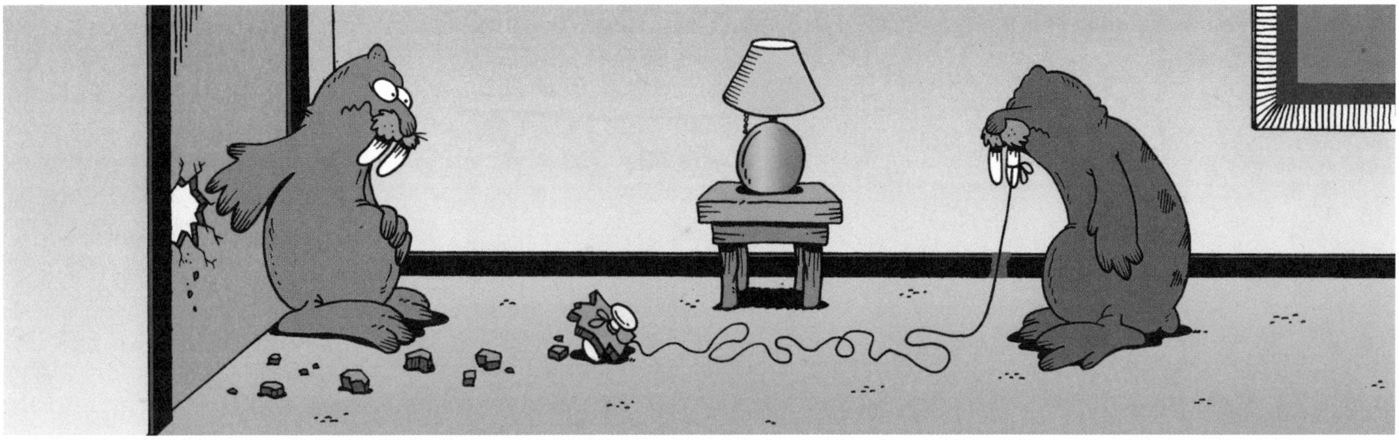

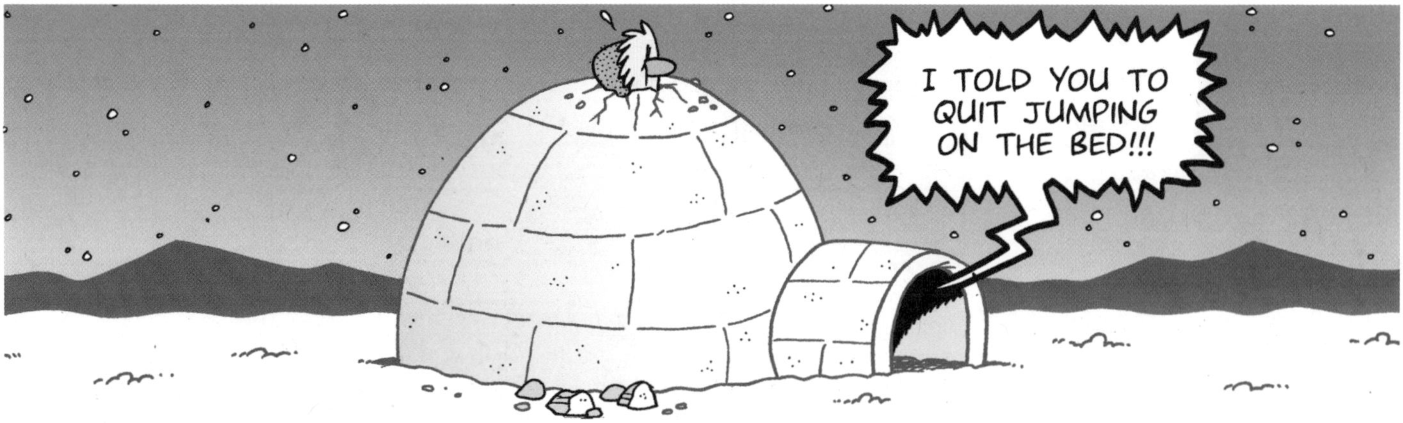
I TOLD YOU TO QUIT JUMPING ON THE BED!!!

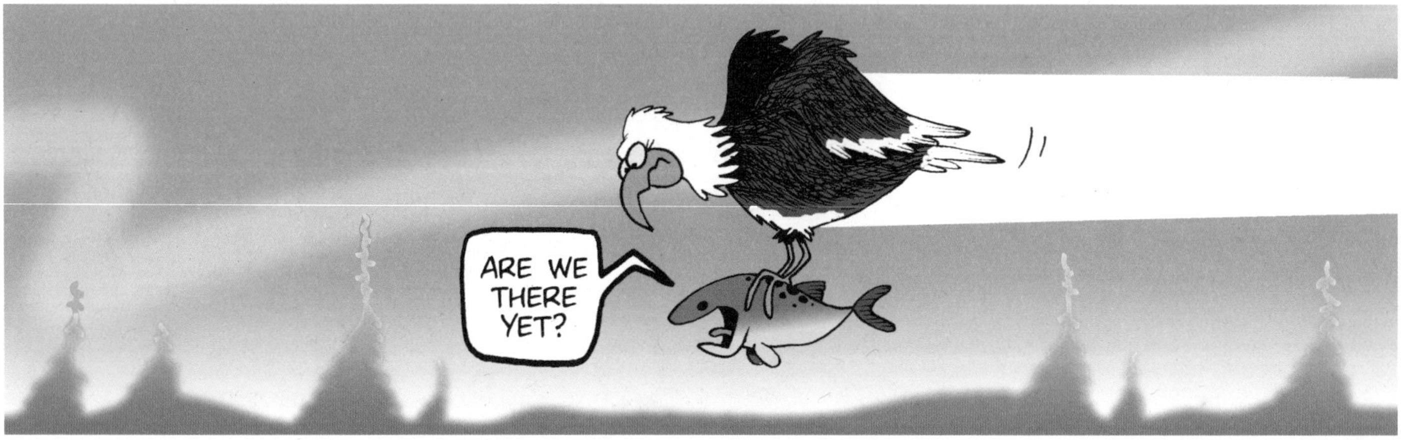
ARE WE THERE YET?

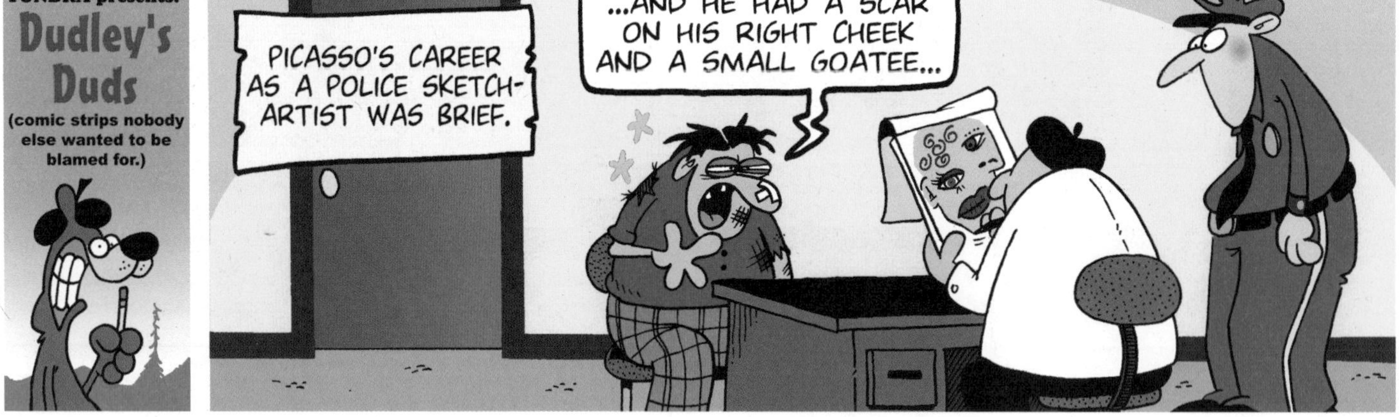
TUNDRA presents:
Dudley's Duds
(comic strips nobody else wanted to be blamed for.)
PICASSO'S CAREER AS A POLICE SKETCH-ARTIST WAS BRIEF.
...AND HE HAD A SCAR ON HIS RIGHT CHEEK AND A SMALL GOATEE...

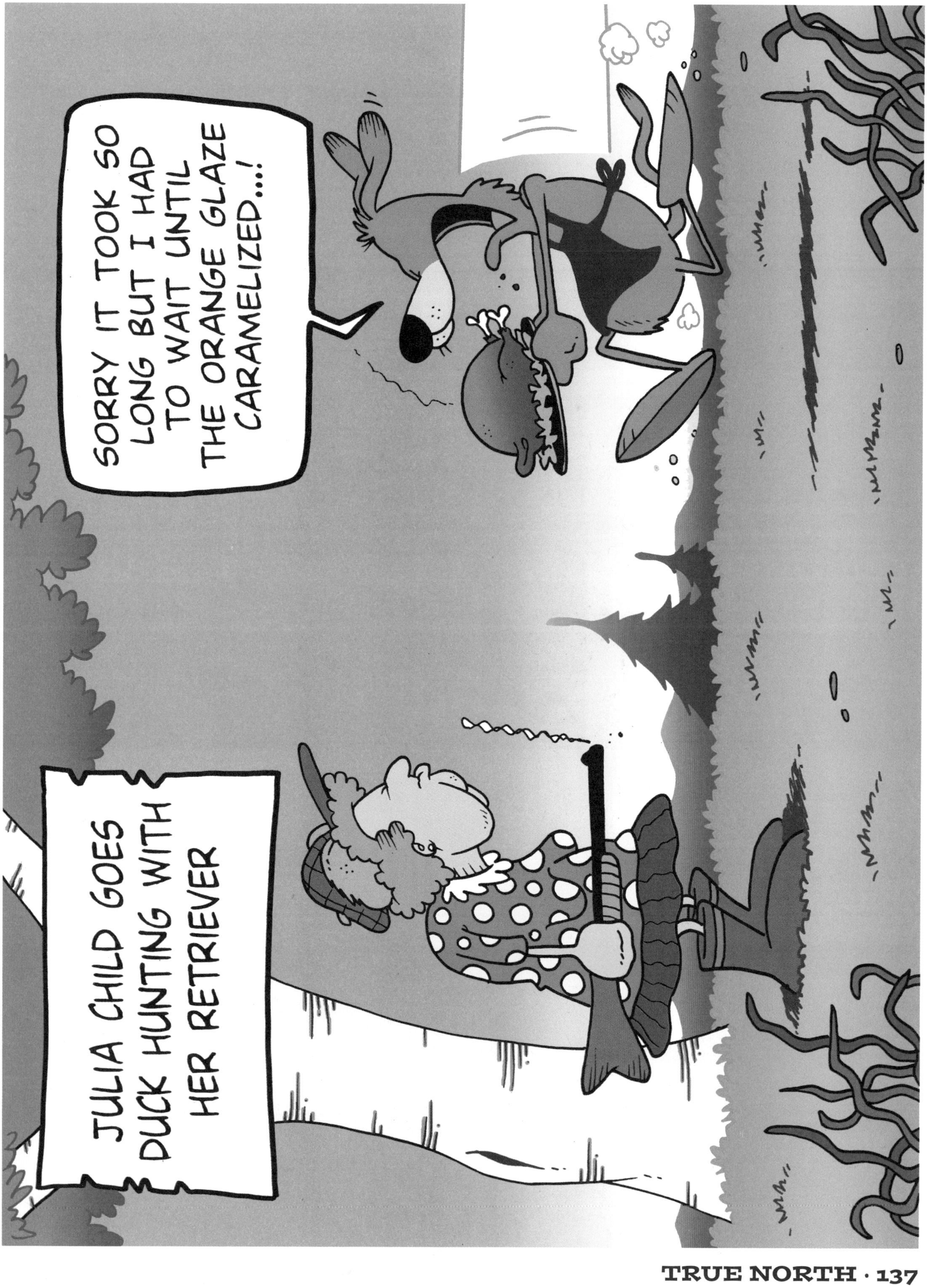
JULIA CHILD GOES DUCK HUNTING WITH HER RETRIEVER
SORRY IT TOOK SO LONG BUT I HAD TO WAIT UNTIL THE ORANGE GLAZE CARAMELIZED...!

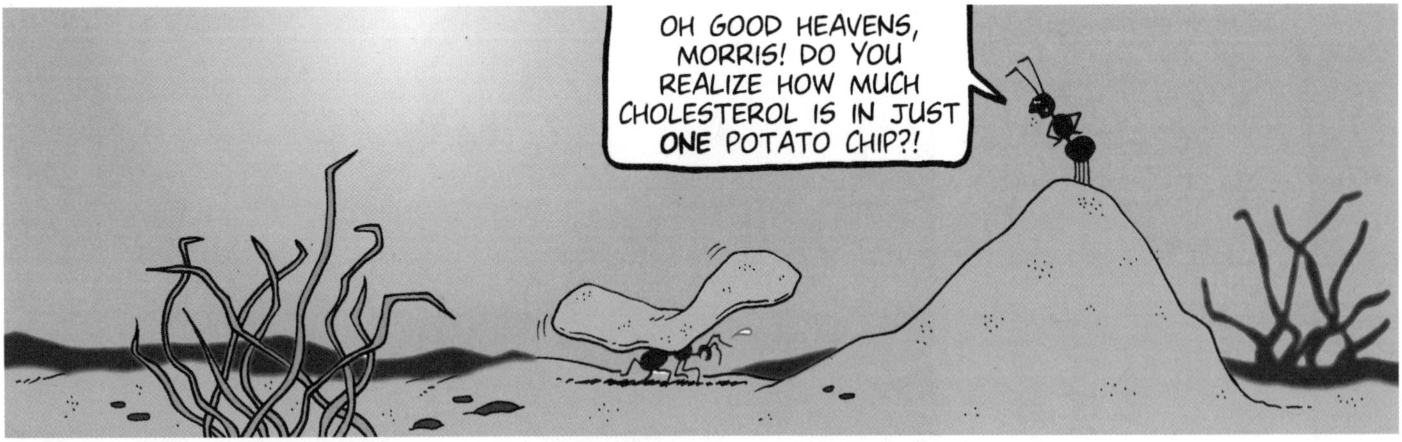
OH GOOD HEAVENS, MORRIS! DO YOU REALIZE HOW MUCH CHOLESTEROL IS IN JUST **ONE** POTATO CHIP?!

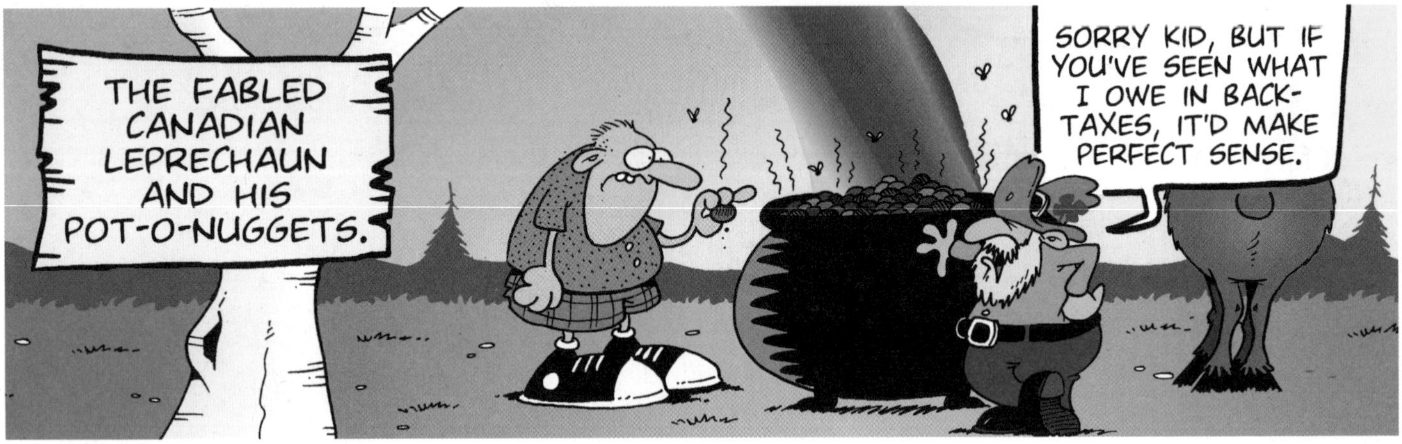
THE FABLED CANADIAN LEPRECHAUN AND HIS POT-O-NUGGETS.
SORRY KID, BUT IF YOU'VE SEEN WHAT I OWE IN BACK-TAXES, IT'D MAKE PERFECT SENSE.

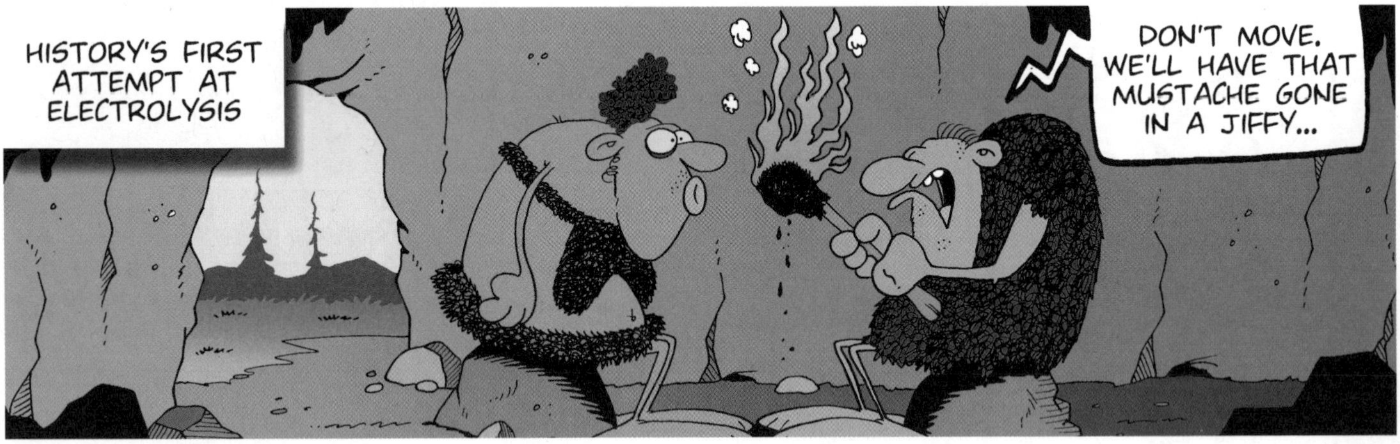
HISTORY'S FIRST ATTEMPT AT ELECTROLYSIS
DON'T MOVE. WE'LL HAVE THAT MUSTACHE GONE IN A JIFFY...

TUNDRA presents:

Whiff's Stinkers

(comic strips even Dudley didn't want to be blamed for.)

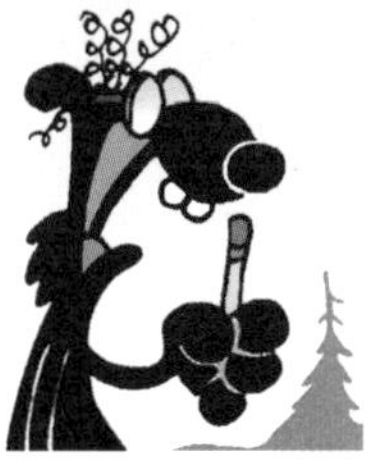

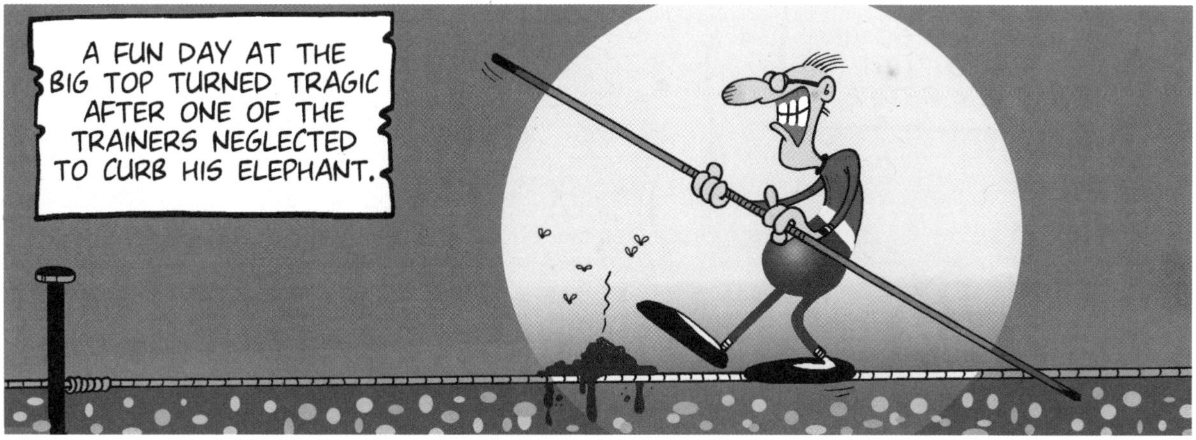
A FUN DAY AT THE BIG TOP TURNED TRAGIC AFTER ONE OF THE TRAINERS NEGLECTED TO CURB HIS ELEPHANT.

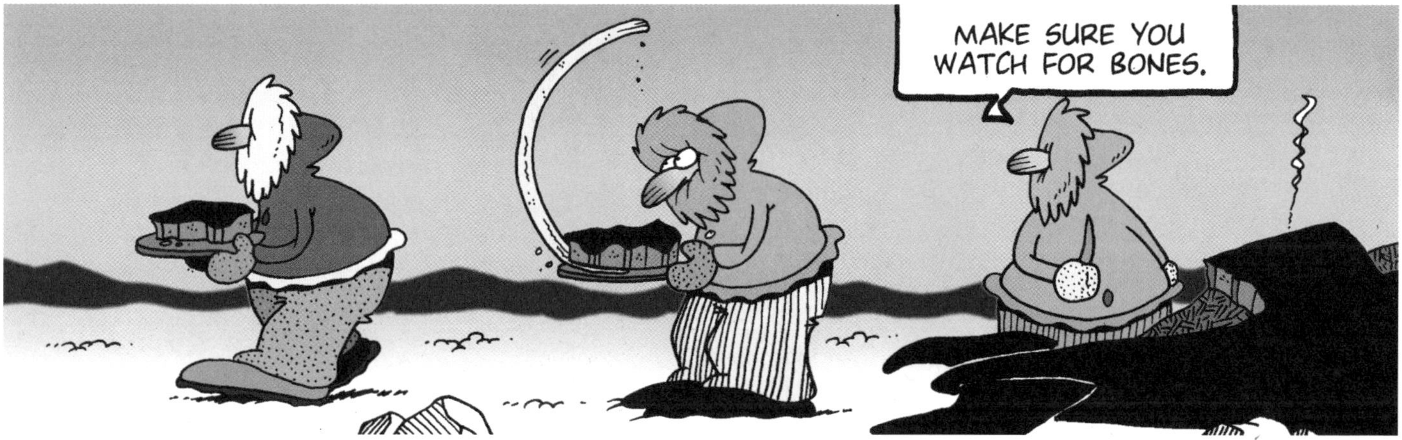
MAKE SURE YOU WATCH FOR BONES.

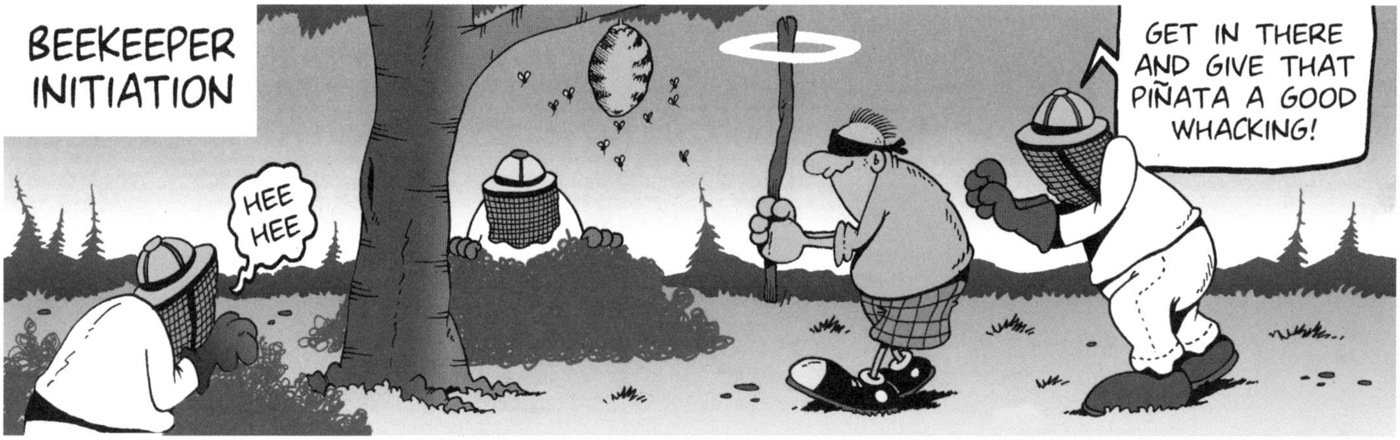
BEEKEEPER INITIATION
HEE HEE
GET IN THERE AND GIVE THAT PIÑATA A GOOD WHACKING!

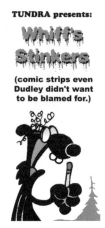

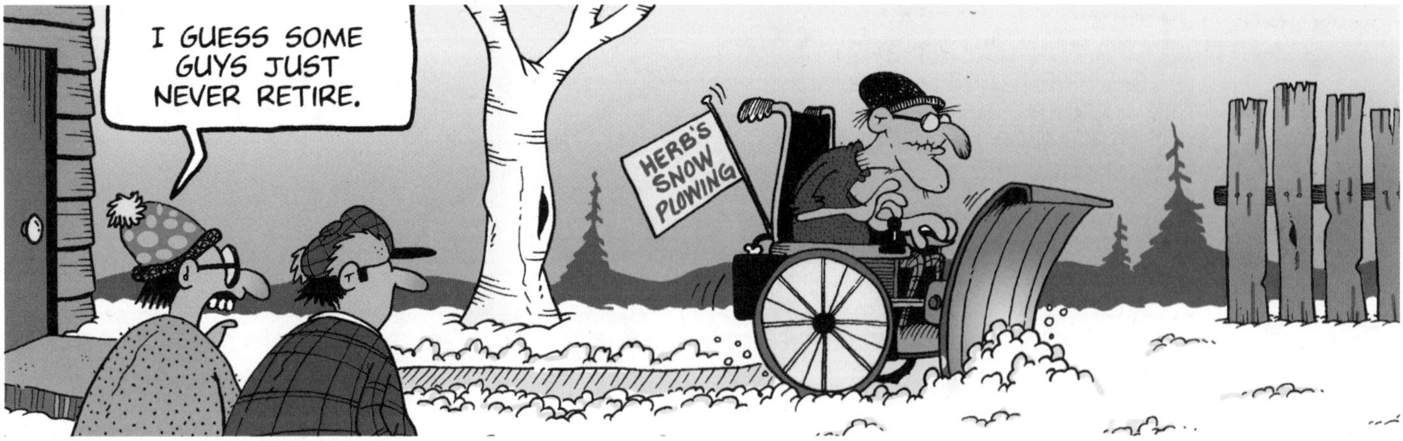
I GUESS SOME GUYS JUST NEVER RETIRE.
HERB'S SNOW PLOWING

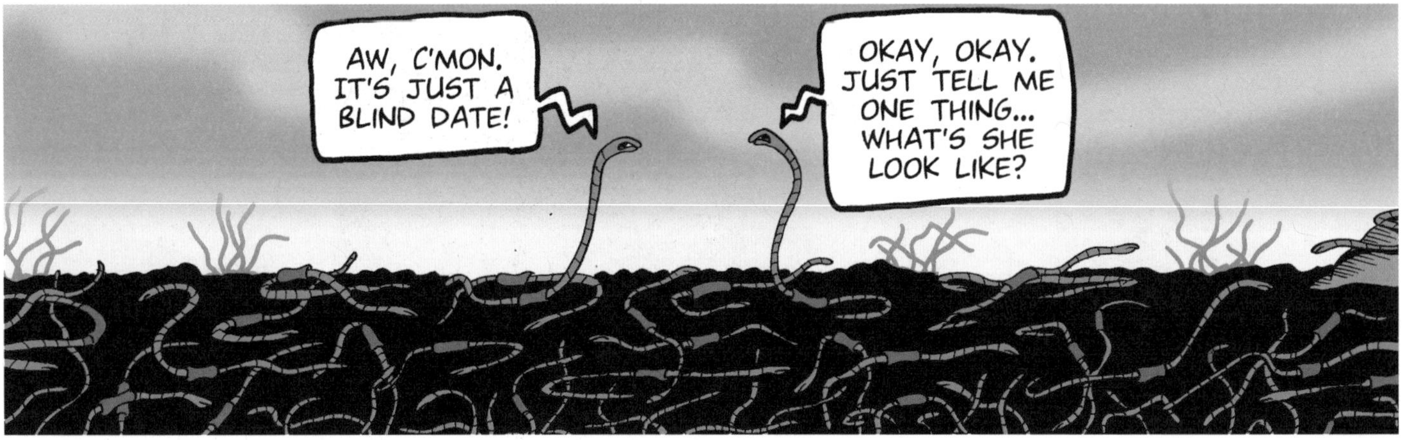
AW, C'MON. IT'S JUST A BLIND DATE!
OKAY, OKAY. JUST TELL ME ONE THING... WHAT'S SHE LOOK LIKE?

This comic strip is based on an idea from:

Nick Foley

Wasilla, AK

www.tundracomics.com

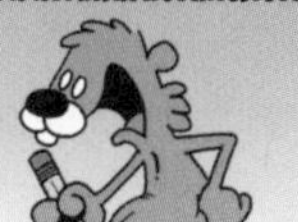

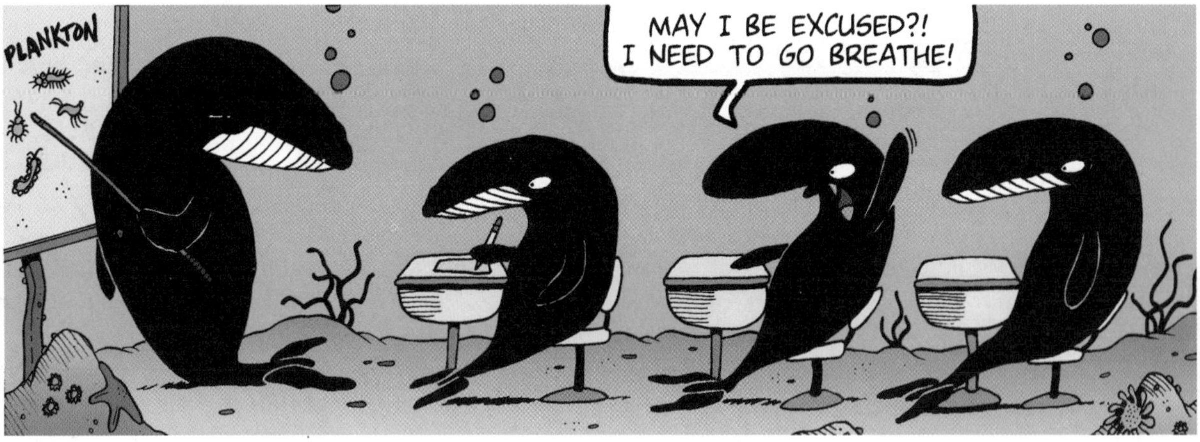
PLANKTON
MAY I BE EXCUSED?! I NEED TO GO BREATHE!

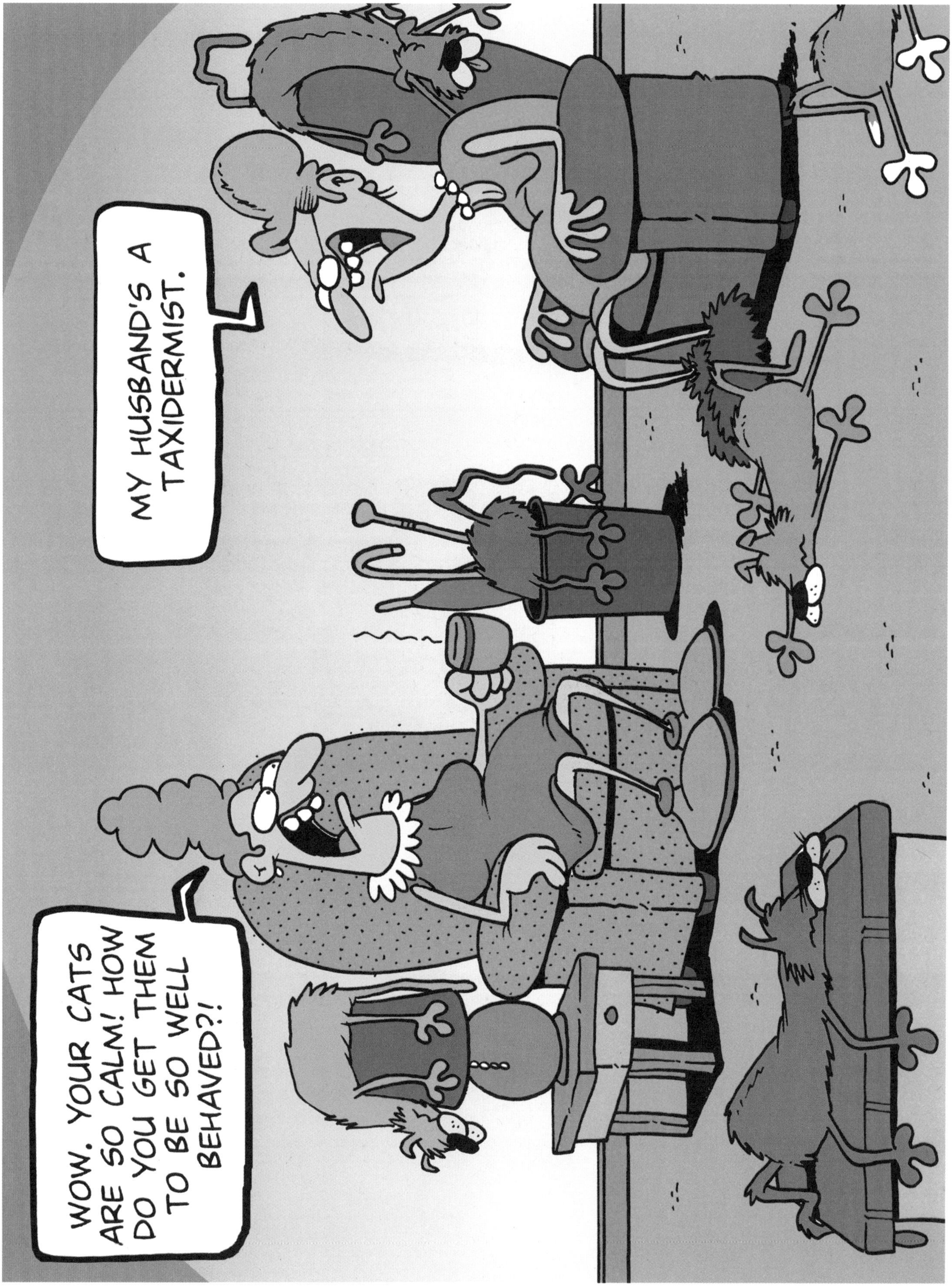
WOW. YOUR CATS ARE SO CALM! HOW DO YOU GET THEM TO BE SO WELL BEHAVED?!
MY HUSBAND'S A TAXIDERMIST.

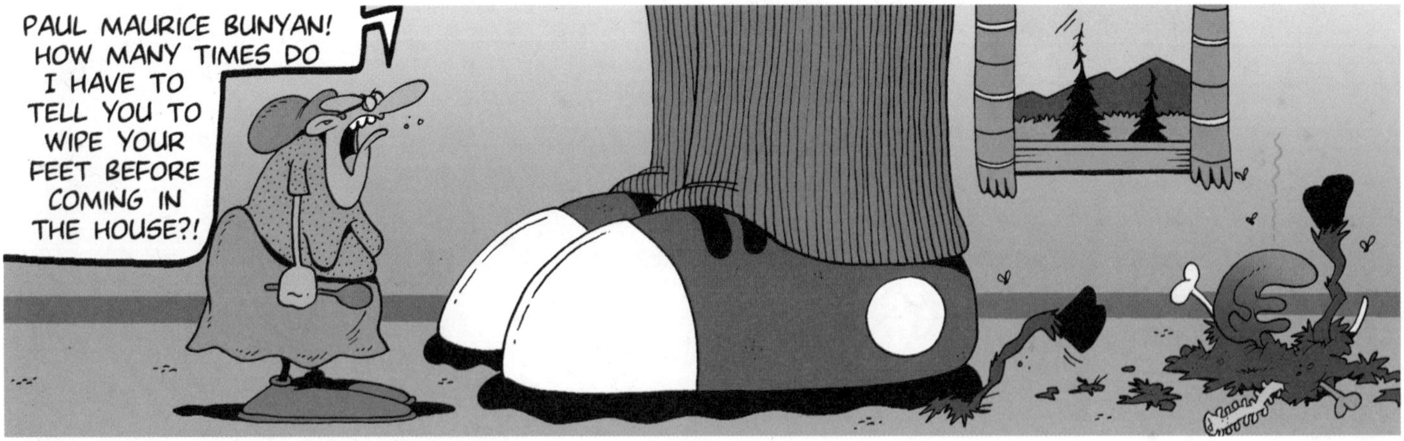
PAUL MAURICE BUNYAN! HOW MANY TIMES DO I HAVE TO TELL YOU TO WIPE YOUR FEET BEFORE COMING IN THE HOUSE?!

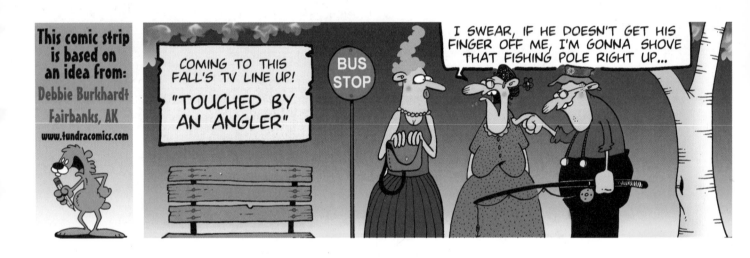

This comic strip is based on an idea from:
Debbie Burkhardt
Fairbanks, AK
www.tundracomics.com

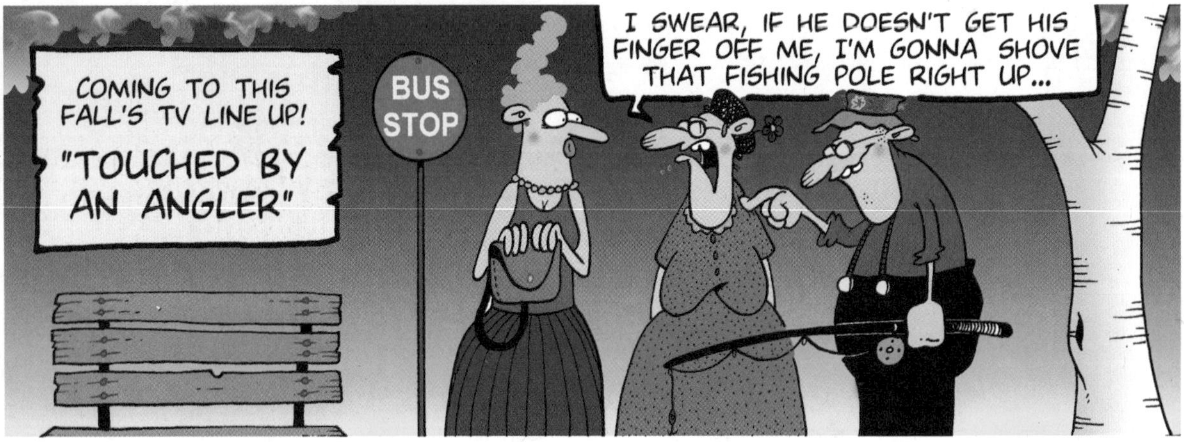
COMING TO THIS FALL'S TV LINE UP!
"TOUCHED BY AN ANGLER"
BUS STOP
I SWEAR, IF HE DOESN'T GET HIS FINGER OFF ME, I'M GONNA SHOVE THAT FISHING POLE RIGHT UP...

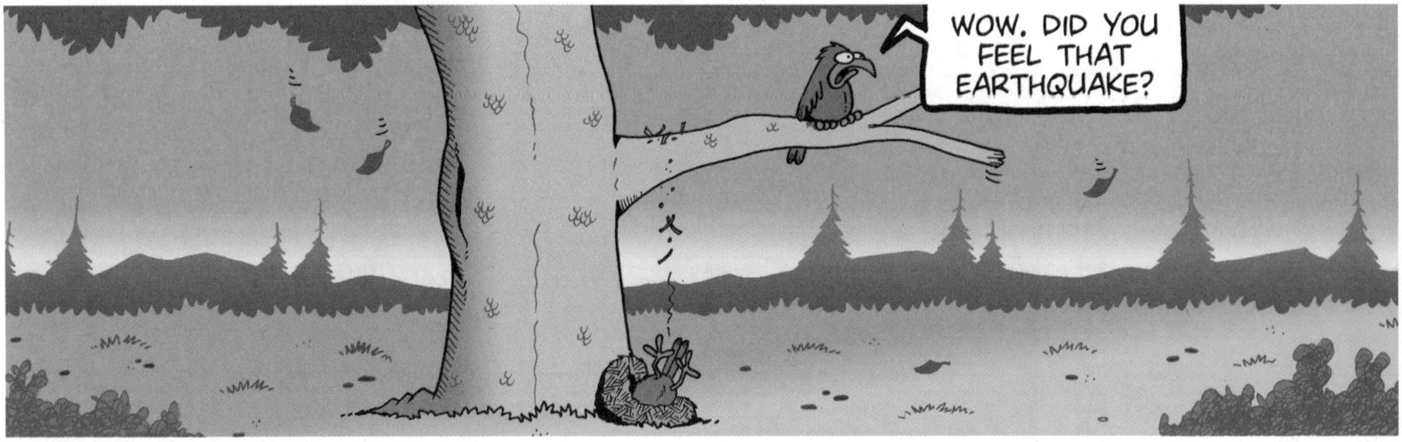
WOW. DID YOU FEEL THAT EARTHQUAKE?

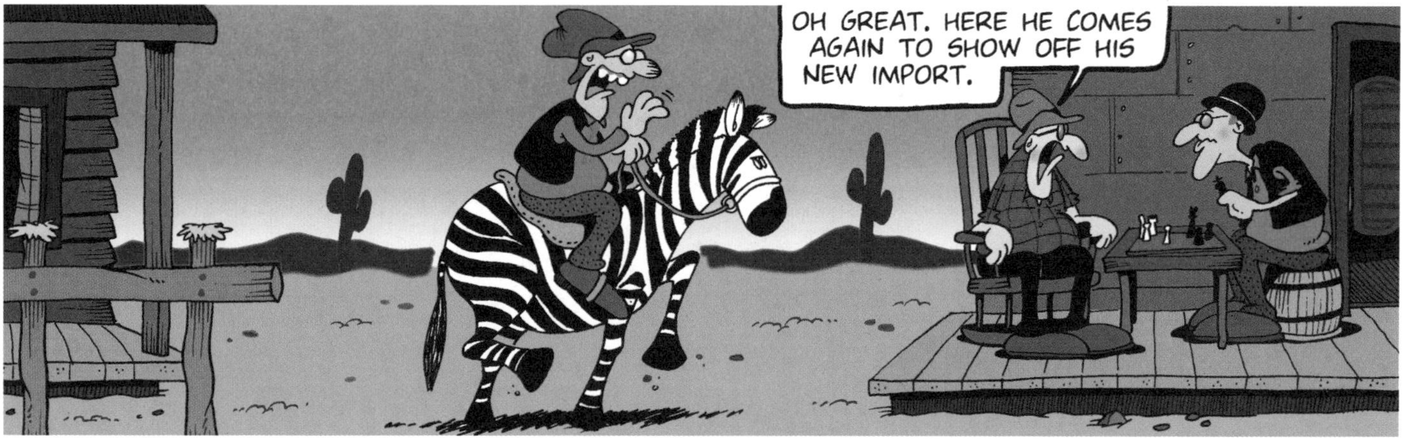
OH GREAT. HERE HE COMES AGAIN TO SHOW OFF HIS NEW IMPORT.

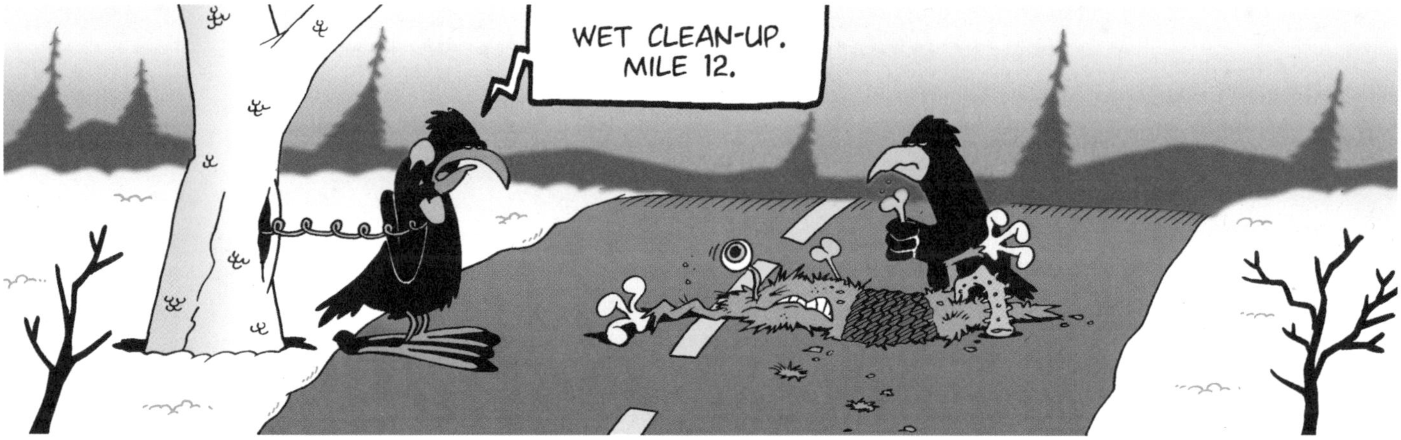
WET CLEAN-UP. MILE 12.

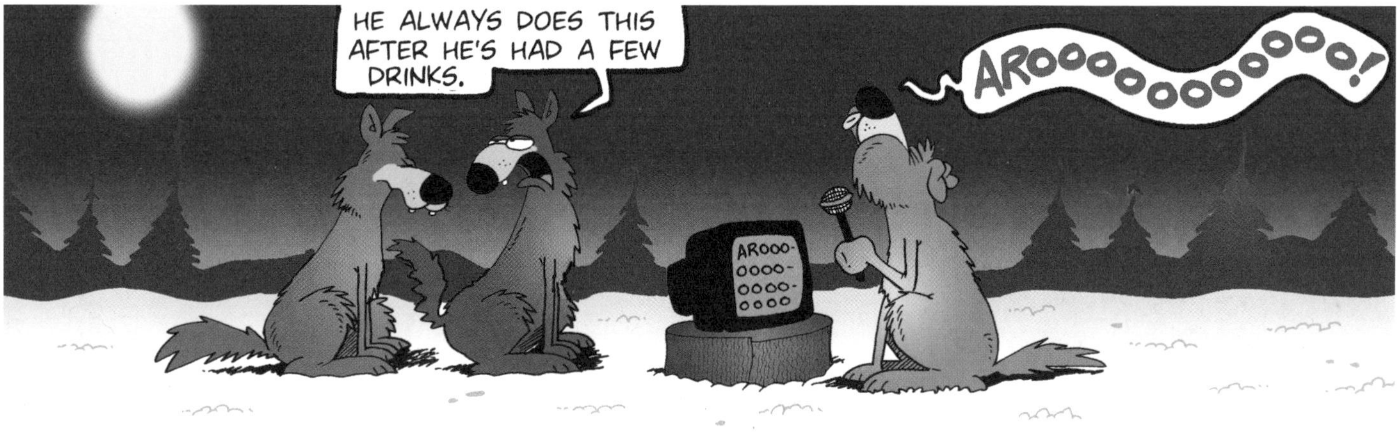
HE ALWAYS DOES THIS AFTER HE'S HAD A FEW DRINKS.
AROOOOOOOOOOOO!
AROOO-OOOO-OOOOO-OOOO

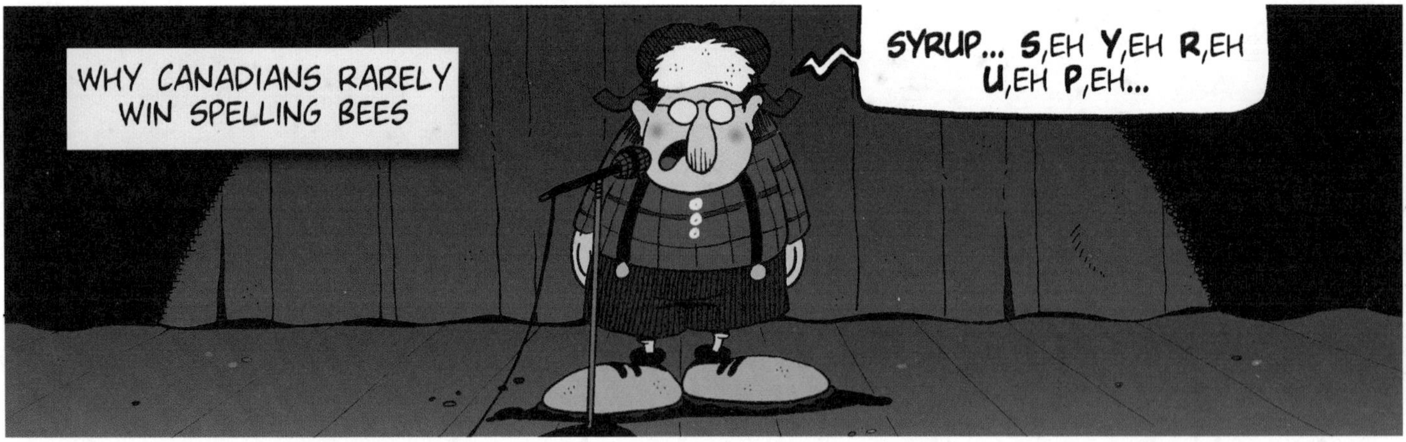
WHY CANADIANS RARELY WIN SPELLING BEES
SYRUP... S,EH Y,EH R,EH U,EH P,EH...

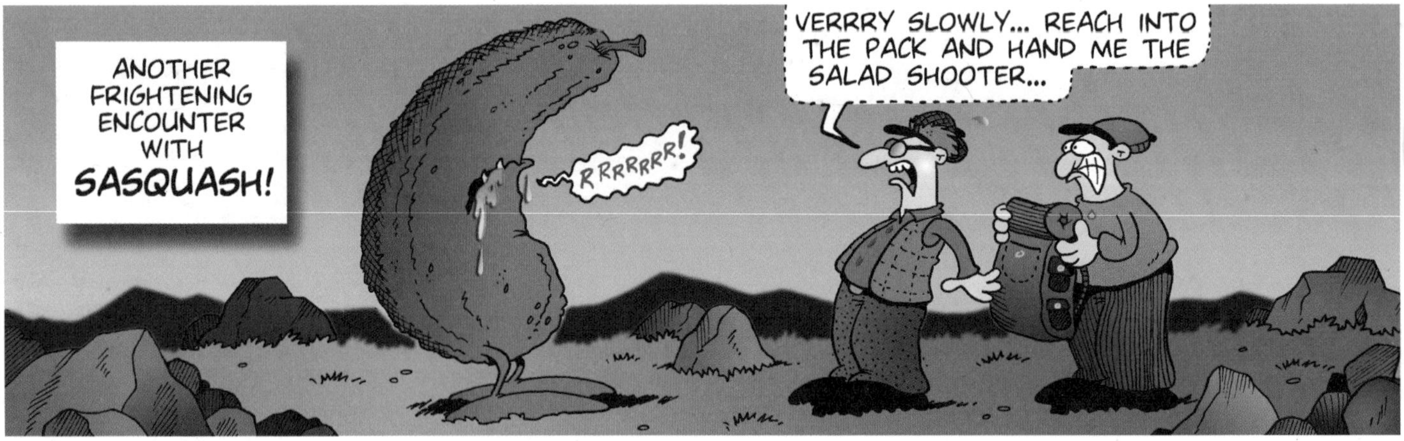
ANOTHER FRIGHTENING ENCOUNTER WITH SASQUASH!
RRRRRRR!
VERRRY SLOWLY... REACH INTO THE PACK AND HAND ME THE SALAD SHOOTER...

Chad Carpenter's Tundra comic strips appear in newspapers throughout Canada and Alaska, as well as in newspapers throughout the lower 48 states. It has been called (by those in the know) one of the fastest growing newspaper comic strips in the business today. Chad currently lives with his wife Karen and three kids in the picturesque Matanuska Valley in Alaska. For more information about Tundra, and a few great ways to waste some time, please visit the official Tundra Web site at www.tundracomics.com.